THE PSYCHOLOGY OF LEARNING AND MOTIVATION

Advances in Research and Theory

VOLUME 9

CONTRIBUTORS TO THIS VOLUME

Richard C. Anderson

W. Barry Biddle

Allan Collins

Lawrence T. Frase

M. F. Garrett

Eliot Hearst

Douglas L. Medin

Allan Paivio

Joseph J. Passafiume

Eleanor H. Warnock

THE PSYCHOLOGY
OF LEARNING AND MOTIVATION

Advances in Research and Theory

EDITED BY GORDON H. BOWER

STANFORD UNIVERSITY, STANFORD, CALIFORNIA

Volume 9

1975

ACADEMIC PRESS New York • San Francisco • London
A SUBSIDIARY OF HARCOURT BRACE JOVANOVICH, PUBLISHERS

ACADEMIC PRESS, INC.
111 Fifth Avenue, New York, New York 10003

United Kingdom Edition published by
ACADEMIC PRESS, INC. (LONDON) LTD.
24/28 Oval Road, London NW1

LIBRARY OF CONGRESS CATALOG CARD NUMBER: 66–30104

ISBN 0–12–543309–3

PRINTED IN THE UNITED STATES OF AMERICA

CONTENTS

List of Contributors ix

Contents of Previous Volumes xi

PROSE PROCESSING

Lawrence T. Frase

   I. Introduction 1
  II. The Processing Model 4
 III. Sources of Encoding Efficiency and Inefficiency 12
 IV. Conclusion 42
     References 45

ANALYSIS AND SYNTHESIS OF TUTORIAL DIALOGUES

Allan Collins, Eleanor H. Warnock, and Joseph J. Passafiume

   I. Introduction 49
  II. A Brief Description of SCHOLAR 50
 III. Analysis of Tutorial Dialogues 54
 IV. Synthesis of Tutorial Dialogues 74
  V. Discussion 84
 VI. Summary 86
     References 87

ON ASKING PEOPLE QUESTIONS
ABOUT WHAT THEY ARE READING

Richard C. Anderson and W. Barry Biddle

   I. Introduction 90
  II. Direct and Indirect Consequences of Questions 91

III. Conditions under Which Adjunct Questions Are Facilitative 93
IV. Explanations for the Indirect Effects of Adjunct Questions 103
V. Toward an Account of the Direct Effects of Questions 109
VI. General Discussion 126
VII. Practical Education Implications of Questioning Techniques 127
References 129

THE ANALYSIS OF SENTENCE PRODUCTION

M. F. Garrett

I. Introduction 133
II. Speech Errors: The Corpus 137
III. Speech Errors: The Analysis 140
IV. Sound Exchange Errors 143
V. Word and Morpheme Exchanges 148
VI. Stranded Morphemes, Shifts, and Exchanges 154
VII. Fusions and Substitutions: Semantic Errors 172
VIII. Summary 175
References 177

CODING DISTINCTIONS AND REPETITION EFFECTS IN MEMORY

Allan Paivio

I. Introduction 179
II. General Evidence on Memory-Code Distinctions 185
III. Repetition Effects and Memory-Code Independence 186
IV. Concluding Remarks 208
References 211

PAVLOVIAN CONDITIONING AND DIRECTED MOVEMENTS

Eliot Hearst

I. Introduction 216
II. Pavlovian Conditioning, Auto-Shaping, and Sign-Tracking 217

III. Empirical Manipulations and Their Effects 222
IV. Conjunctions, Contingencies, and Cognitions: Stimulus–Stimulus
    versus Response–Stimulus Relations 244
V. Concluding Comments 258
   References 260

A THEORY OF CONTEXT IN DISCRIMINATION LEARNING

Douglas L. Medin

I. Introduction 263
II. Units of Analysis in Discrimination Learning 264
III. Basic Notions of the Context Theory 269
IV. Extensions of the Context Model to Selective Learning 295
V. Discussion and Summary 303
   References 304
   Appendix 310

Subject Index 315

LIST OF CONTRIBUTORS

Numbers in parentheses indicate the pages on which the authors' contributions begin.

Richard C. Anderson, University of Illinois at Urbana-Champaign, Champaign, Illinois (89)

W. Barry Biddle, Department of Educational Psychology, University of Illinois at Urbana-Champaign, Urbana, Illinois (89)

Allan Collins, Bolt Beranek and Newman Inc., Cambridge, Massachusetts (49)

Lawrence T. Frase, Bell Laboratories, Murray Hill, New Jersey (1)

M. F. Garrett, Massachusetts Institute of Technology, Cambridge, Massachusetts (133)

Eliot Hearst, Indiana University, Bloomington, Indiana (215)

Douglas L. Medin, The Rockefeller University, New York, New York (263)

Allan Paivio, University of Western Ontario, London, Ontario, Canada (179)

Joseph J. Passafiume, Bolt Beranek and Newman Inc., Cambridge, Massachusetts (49)

Eleanor H. Warnock,[1] Bolt Beranek and Newman Inc., Cambridge, Massachusetts (49)

[1] Present address: Center for Human Information Processing, University of California, San Diego, La Jolla, California.

CONTENTS OF PREVIOUS VOLUMES

Volume 1

Partial Reinforcement Effects on Vigor and Persistence
  Abram Amsel

A Sequential Hypothesis of Instrumental Learning
  E. J. Capaldi

Satiation and Curiosity
  Harry Fowler

A Multicomponent Theory of the Memory Trace
  Gordon Bower

Organization and Memory
  George Mandler

Author Index—Subject Index

Volume 2

Incentive Theory and Changes in Reward
  Frank A. Logan

Shift in Activity and the Concept of Persisting Tendency
  David Birch

Human Memory: A Proposed System and Its Control Processes
  R. C. Atkinson and R. M. Shiffrin

Mediation and Conceptual Behavior
  Howard K. Kendler and Tracy S. Kendler

Author Index—Subject Index

Volume 3

Stimulus Selection and a "Modified Continuity Theory"
  Allan R. Wagner

Abstraction and the Process of Recognition
  Michael I. Posner

Neo-Noncontinuity Theory
  Marvin Levine

Computer Simulation of Short-Term Memory: A Component-Decay Model
  Kenneth R. Laughery

Replication Processes in Human Memory and Learning
  Harley A. Bernbach

Experimental Analysis of Learning to Learn
  Leo Postman

Short-Term Memory in Binary Prediction by Children: Some Stochastic Information Processing Models
  Richard S. Bogartz

Author Index—Subject Index

Volume 4

Learned Associations over Long Delays
  Sam Revusky and John Garcia

On the Theory of Interresponse-Time Reinforcement
  G. S. Reynolds and Alastair McLeod

Sequential Choice Behavior
  Jerome L. Meyers

The Role of Chunking and Organization in the Process of Recall
Neal F. Johnson

Organization of Serial Pattern Learning
Frank Restle and Eric Brown

Author Index—Subject Index

Volume 5

Conditioning and a Decision Theory of Response Evocation
G. Robert Grice

Short-Term Memory
Bennet B. Murdock, Jr.

Storage Mechanisms in Recall
Murray Glanzer

By-Products of Discrimination Learning
H. S. Terrace

Serial Learning and Dimensional Organization
Sheldon M. Ebenholtz

FRAN: A Simulation Model of Free Recall
John Robert Anderson

Author Index—Subject Index

Volume 6

Informational Variables in Pavlovian Conditioning
Robert A. Rescorla

The Operant Conditioning of Central Nervous System Electrical Activity
A. H. Black

The Avoidance Learning Problem
Robert C. Bolles

Mechanisms of Directed Forgetting
William Epstein

Toward a Theory of Redintegrative Memory: Adjective-Noun Phrases
Leonard M. Horowitz and Leon Manelis

Elaborative Strategies in Verbal Learning and Memory
William E. Montague

Author Index—Subject Index

Volume 7

Grammatical Word Classes: A Learning Process and Its Simulation
George R. Kiss

Reaction Time Measurements in the Study of Memory Processes: Theory and Data
John Theios

Individual Differences in Cognition: A New Approach to Intelligence
Earl Hunt, Nancy Frost, and Clifford Lunneborg

Stimulus Encoding Processes in Human Learning and Memory
Henry C. Ellis

Subproblem Analysis of Discrimination Learning
Thomas Tighe

Delayed Matching and Short-Term Memory in Monkeys
M. R. D'Amato

Percentile Reinforcement: Paradigms for Experimental Analysis of Response Shaping
John R. Platt

Prolonged Rewarding Brain Stimulation
J. A. Deutsch

Patterned Reinforcement
Stewart H. Hulse

Author Index—Subject Index

Volume 8

Semantic Memory and Psychological Semantics
Edward E. Smith, Lance J. Rips, and Edward J. Shoben

Working Memory
  Alan D. Baddeley and Graham Hitch

The Role of Adaptation-Level in Stimulus
  Generalization
  David R. Thomas

Recent Developments in Choice
  Edmund Fantino and Douglas Navarick

Reinforcing Properties of Escape from
  Frustration Aroused in Various Learning
  Situations
  Helen B. Daly

Conceptual and Neurobiological Issues in
  Studies of Treatments Affecting Memory
  Storage
  James L. McGaugh and Paul E. Gold

The Logic of Memory Representations
  Endel Tulving and Gordon H. Bower

Subject Index

PROSE PROCESSING

Lawrence T. Frase

BELL LABORATORIES, MURRAY HILL, NEW JERSEY

I.	Introduction	1
II.	The Processing Model	4
	A. Level I—Content and Performance Sets	8
	B. Level II—Encoding	8
	C. Level III—Rehearsal and Integration	9
	D. Level IV—Retrieval and Relation	11
	E. Summary	11
III.	Sources of Encoding Efficiency and Inefficiency	12
	A. Words as a Unit of Processing Control	13
	B. Topics as a Unit of Processing Control	17
	C. Intersentence Relations as a Unit of Processing Control	24
	D. Questioning as Self-Control	36
IV.	Conclusion	42
	A. Attention as a Multidimensional Concept	42
	B. Reading Goals	43
	C. Prose Processing—A Negative or Positive View?	43
	D. Comments on Research Focus	44
	References	45

I. Introduction

This chapter is written from the standpoint of its relevance to instructional processes. Although the orientation is toward practice, a conceptual model of prose processing may be useful at this time, and so a tentative model will be elaborated that builds on earlier instructionally oriented research and that is consistent with what is known about human information processing in general. Any modeling, given the present state of knowledge, is a treacherous endeavor, especially when it comes to the complex area of learning from written materials. On the other hand, the exercise can be useful in summarizing research and in suggesting further work. The present model therefore represents a general scheme that incorporates proc-

1

essing activities which loom important in the everyday activities of reading.

The importance of reading, as a topic of experimental study, needs little justification. Chapanis (1971) estimates that an engineering psychologist would have to read 30–40 written documents per day to keep up with the relevant literature. Most educational activities involve written materials in one way or another. For members of our society, then, difficulties or deficiencies in reading impose a limit upon the individual's ability to function on the job and in general to participate in our common social heritage.

The research literature on prose learning, within the past ten years, has shown an encouraging growth. For the first time, a section in the *Annual Review of Psychology* has been devoted to prose learning (Glaser & Resnick, 1972). The presentation of prose related research papers at annual meetings of educational and psychological associations continues to grow at an accelerating rate. Yet much remains to be done to specify the processes entailed in skilled reading performance.

The analysis of reading processes was undertaken many years ago by Huey (1908). He gave examples of specific process analysis at the level of word perception, the effects of typographical forms on performance, and so on. Yet his work had only a limited impact on subsequent generations of researchers.

In contrast, Ausubel's text (1963), on meaningful verbal learning, contained useful and stimulating theoretical speculations, but these speculations were put forth without a coordinate development of experimental methods that allowed empirical tests of those conjectures. For instance, tests of the notion that learning higher level concepts can affect the acquisition of lower-level concepts had to await more objective ways of defining the hierarchical structure of semantic content (see Meyer & McConkie, 1973). Methodologies for studying complex verbal knowledge are just now being worked out in some detail (Crothers, 1972; Frederiksen, 1972). An inhibiting factor to research on prose learning thus has been the complexity of the stimulus environment that prose represents.

A second inhibiting factor is that the complexity of prose environments elicits complex chains of performance. It is these ever-changing adaptive modifications in human reading performance that pose a special challenge to researchers. Carroll's paper (1968) usefully brought into focus relations between prose learning and psycholinguistic research in which there was a more direct emphasis on complex transformational processes. Carroll's later review (1971) of the literature on learning from verbal discourse also set the stage for a better understanding of process. In addition, the recent book by Carroll and Freedle (1972) contains articles that sketch, in outline, the broad range of problems involved in understanding language comprehension.

The focus on instructionally relevant processes in prose learning was given impetus by Rothkopf's work (1963, 1965) on what he has called "mathemagenic behaviors," behaviors that support learning. Rothkopf has emphasized the study of the stimulus controls for these behaviors, rather than attempting to characterize those behaviors in detail, although a preliminary sketch of mathemagenic behaviors was given in his 1965 and 1970 papers (Rothkopf, 1965, 1970).

Much of the work reported in this paper has been conducted with a focus on the stimulus controls for effective prose processing. The tentative characterization of reading performance that is offered as a model in this paper extends earlier conceptions of prose learning activities. A good deal of the research conducted within this framework has had to do with the effects of questions on learning. Involved are the effects of different spacing of questions (Frase, 1967), the shaping of learning activities over time (Morasky & Willcox, 1970; Rothkopf & Bisbicos, 1967), and the different processes that are elicited as a function of the position of questions (before or after text-relevant material; e.g., Rothkopf, 1965). Anderson and Biddle (this volume) have reviewed much of the research on questions; hence, I will not belabor the data by repeating their summary. The Anderson and Biddle paper focuses upon the review effects of questions, that is, the effects which certain stimulus events have upon information already stored in memory. The present paper issues from a rather different orientation, namely, that important learning behaviors occur at the time of reading. These include encoding processes which are under the control of the reader's goal-directed activities and which arise as a consequence of his interaction with the text.

Many of the studies to be cited and described later involve an incidental learning paradigm. Subjects are given a covering task (learning or search directions) and then they are tested over both the material that is relevant to and the material that is incidental to the covering instructions. The effect of different processing activities on the recall of both types of information is then inferred from the nature of the learning directions and other task characteristics that constrain the reader's performance. Such studies suggest conjectures about that performance. These conjectures are included in the model in this chapter. First, I will describe the model, which in many ways goes beyond the data that I shall report. Then, I will discuss research studies which focus upon the learning outcomes that result from different activities that occur during reading. A major theme running throughout this chapter is that learning from prose is a matter of context, in the sense that learning outcomes are the result of an interaction between what the reader attempts to do and the constraints that the stimulus materials place on those adaptive activities.

II. The Processing Model

The intention of the present model is to capture some of the complexity of the behaviors that occur during reading and to communicate this complexity as broad categories of activities that occur, sometimes in optional sequences, in response to the reader's goal orientation.

In the interest of maintaining a practical frame of reference for the activities involved in skilled reading, I will briefly consider the behaviors that reading teachers encourage in order to improve reading, and then I will summarize these performances in the proposed model.

The SQ3R method (Robinson, 1961), or its recent elaboration, the PQ4R method (Thomas & Robinson, 1972) is representative. What does this method entail? The PQ4R method involves the following activities in which a reader is encouraged to engage: (a) preview, (b) make up salient questions, (c) read the text, (d) reflect upon it, (e) recite it, and (f) review it. In previewing, the reader is encouraged to survey the text quickly, that is, to determine the general characteristics of the semantic terrain within which he must operate. In short, the reader should first analyze a text for the features which can be used to control subsequent processing. Previewing entails search activities, presumably a relatively low level of semantic processing. It has the potential effect of clarifying the limits of the stimulus environment within which the reader will operate and, for instance, of allowing him to focus on related information dispersed throughout the text. With preview activities, the text is represented superficially and only briefly in memory. Studies that I will report later show that simple search activities have consequences for memory and that memory after brief searches of a text varies with the semantic context that the reader brings to bear on the reading materials. Since this context changes as a reader progresses in a text, his criterion for determining relations among sentences may change in the course of reading.

The construction of questions, the second activity in PQ4R, focuses on transforming the information in the text into new representations. These new representations might be modest changes in syntactic form of the text information (for instance, converting a sentence into a *Wh-* question) (see Bormuth, 1970, for a review of transformations). A question might go beyond the text, relating what is in the text to previously learned knowledge about the content. Studies, to be reported later, show that subjects' self-generated questions rarely go beyond the text information. Making-up questions involves rehearsal of information in the sense that it must be maintained in memory for longer periods of time than it would under preview.

Reading, the third activity, presumably involves encoding of the information in a more complete form. Reading further entails additional rehearsal in the sense that the subject is re-exposed to content previously seen.

Reflection, the fourth activity, requires determining relations between what is in the text and what is already known, that is, the retrieval of items from memory and comparison of those items with the information from the text. Reflection also entails relating information that was presented in disparate parts of the text.

Recitation, the fifth activity, involves phonetic production, more rehearsal, and perhaps retrieval of the text information from memory. It also imposes an overt response requirement that may better allow the reader to monitor his own recall performance.

Finally, review entails more encoding and rehearsal of sentence information.

I have summarized the essence of these activities in the model shown in Fig. 1. The model is divided into three general areas; the stimulus environment (the prose passage), what the reader does (his performance), and what classes of memory events are entailed by those performances. As Scandura (1973) has indicated, each of these areas may entail a theory in itself. Thus, to specify a prose learning episode involves a theory of the content of the text, a theory of the reader's performances, and a theory of how content and performance relate to memory. A theory of test performance, or of the processes required to produce an answer to a problem encountered after reading, might also be included for completeness. Since it would entail activities included under "performance" in Fig. 1, this aspect of the

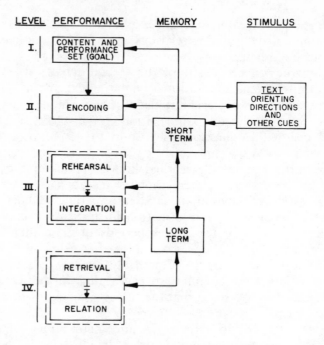

Fig. 1. A conceptual model of reading.

model also applies to test performance. The arrows in Fig. 1 reflect constraint in the system. For example, what is represented in short-term memory constrains the reader's goals, goals constrain encoding, encoding constrains the effective nature of the stimulus, and so on.

The unit of content analysis might focus on words, phrases, individual propositions, logical implications, superordinate semantic structures, and so on. In our research, the unit of analysis has varied, but it has focused mainly on individual propositions.

An important component of the stimulus situation—orienting directions—has been included in the stimulus portion of Fig. 1. Orienting directions include a variety of stimuli, such as specific directions to a reader about what to learn or questions interspersed in the passage, that are related to components of the text. Figure 1 indicates that orienting directions, provided that they are represented in memory, can influence the reader's goal orientation (or performance set—see Gagné's [1973] usage of this term) and consequently subsequent activities. For instance, the effect of interspersing questions in text depends upon how close the questions are to the relevant text content (Frase, Patrick, & Schumer, 1970) and whether the reader engages in activities, such as writing the questions, which are likely to improve their stability in memory (Patrick, 1968). The inclusion of orienting directions in the model is intended to emphasize the importance of the reader's purpose to the explanation of what is learned (see Hochberg & Brooks, 1970). One implication is that only a portion of the stimulus material may be represented in memory as a consequence of the constraints that the reader's goals place on encoding and subsequent activities.

I have indicated two memories; a short-term (or working) memory and a long-term memory (see Atkinson & Shiffrin, 1971). It is clear that readers can perform operations on text contents that allow them to do various things, for instance, to answer questions, yet the components of the solution to these problems are not necessarily remembered. For example, Frase (1969) found that, although subjects could solve logical problems with the text available for reading, they were not later able to produce the inferences that presumably were involved in the solutions to those problems. Short-term memory involves transitory representation, and it is assumed that longer residence or more frequent occurrence of items in short-term memory may result in stable (long-term) memory representations. Long-term memory is assumed to contain previously learned information.

The performance aspect of the model includes components at four different levels. The levels proceed from those which entail short-term memory, to those which entail either inputs to or outputs from long-term memory. Paying attention to text is a summary term for a segment of behavior which may involve all of these different performances.

I will review what has been said, and then I will briefly state what is entailed in performance at the various levels. The focus of this paper will be on Level I and II processes. The characterization of performances at Levels III and IV has a less definitive experimental base, but I believe that they need to be explicitly recognized to account for skilled reading performance. The present model assumes that the reader's activities are goal directed. These goals may be implicit or explicit. In our research, we have made them explicit (by varying task demands) in order to observe their consequences on learning. The model has two memories that communicate with various performances, and with each other. Short-term memory is assumed to have limited capacity, whereas long-term memory is not limited. The performances are arranged in levels, such that long-term memory is more implicated in performance at the higher levels. Performance of the various activities is assumed to take time. Some of these activities are under the control of the reader, but they can be modified by alterations in the stimulus materials and other task requirements. Although the model is intended as a conceptual aid to thinking about prose processing, there is one constraint in the system which does not seem optional for the reader. That is, Level I and II performances necessarily determine the representation of the stimulus in short-term memory, and hence they determine what higher level processes can be brought to bear on certain content. In short, although Level III and IV activities are relevant to learning, the limit of what is encoded from the text is a prior constraint. To the extent that this assertion receives experimental support, then useful directions for research on prose learning are suggested. One implication is that research may profit from a careful investigation of the memory consequences of relatively specific encoding activities that can be made to occur during reading.

A. LEVEL I—CONTENT AND PERFORMANCE SETS

The setting of goals is a prior condition for other performances. It implies constraints on subsequent encoding, for example, whether letters, words, phrases are encoded, or perhaps which sentences receive the bulk of higher level processing. I have assumed that the reader has the vocabulary to comprehend individual words and phrases and that reading activities are not limited by gross reading disabilities. The model suggests that, unless there are direct inputs from the stimulus situation, the reader's goal is determined by memory. In short, prior experience determines various aspects of performance. There is no assumption that performance sets are conscious processes, although they may be.

B. LEVEL II—ENCODING

Level II involves encoding items according to their goal relevance. There is evidence that text information which is judged to be important is better recalled than unimportant information (Duell, 1974). If this is the result of the execution of additional processing activities that operate on important items, then one would expect reading rate to vary as a function of the reader's goal. McConkie, Rayner, and Wilson (1973) have shown that when subjects anticipate detailed or inferential questions after reading, reading rate is slowed. They also found that changes in rate primarily affect the amount of goal-irrelevant information retained.

What a reader perceives to be relevant to a stimulus-initiated goal varies with the goal specificity. That is, the precision of encoding is modifiable. For instance, if subjects are asked to learn text sentences relevant to a topic, agreement will not be perfect. A specific goal definition (such as a locatable word in the text) may better control processing (see Experiment 3).

Level II activities encompass what Rothkopf (1970) has called translation and segmentation stages of processing. Translation and segmentation activities are relatively high in Rothkopf's model, which is composed of three general classes of activities: (I) orientation, (II) object acquisition, and (III) translation and processing activities. The present model focuses on Rothkopf's Class III activities and it specifies them in some detail.

Data from our laboratory suggest that Level II activities may compose the bulk of subjects' ordinary reading behaviors. For instance, we have had subjects verbalize their reading activities while studying for a later test. With few exceptions, subjects merely "read" the text. Additional processing consisted of beginning again, at sentence one, and rereading. Given a specific goal, for instance, to determine if some inference could be drawn from the passage, verbalizations changed radically revealing many stops and rehearsals and integration of content from relevant portions of the text.

Since the reader's set is constrained by items from memory, information gathered from the text (which is in memory) may alter encoding as reading progresses. Previously read sentences may change the semantic context for subsequent sentences. Some evidence for this assertion is given in Experiment 2. The finding that questions exert a stronger influence over learning if they are contiguous with relevant text information is also consistent with this interpretation.

The present model makes no requirement for an overt response. Research shows that thinking, without responding overtly, is sufficient to alter learning outcomes (Anderson, 1970). The present model assumes that activities at Levels I–IV are internal events, so the weight of learning from text is placed on the internal processing activities of the reader.

C. LEVEL III—REHEARSAL AND INTEGRATION

Levels III and IV concern the fate of items once they have been encoded. Level III activities may have inputs to both short- and long-term memory. One condition which may effect the transfer of items from short- to long-term memory is residence time in short-term memory, although some evidence, concerning spaced repetition of items in a text, suggests that re-encoding an item might have special consequences for memory (Rothkopf, 1965).

Level III performance is relatively stimulus bound, in the sense that activities at this level are assumed to operate primarily on items encoded directly from the text. An assumption is that Level III activities operate on text items as though they are relatively independent, at least initially. Integration is placed lower in the sequence, and is separated from rehearsal by a broken arrow. It may not occur. In short, integration (for instance, bringing together separate propositions from the text) is not necessarily an automatic process. Research by Bransford and Franks (1971) shows that integration of information from separate sentences may occur with semantically related items. On the other hand, Peterson and McIntyre (1973) have shown that this effect does not hold when semantic intersentential relations are not present. Furthermore, certain relations, such as class inclusion relations, appear to present special difficulties for integration (Frase, 1969; Griggs, 1974).

Nothing in the model presumes that processing activities always have positive effects upon memory. Both positive and negative learning outcomes might occur as a consequence of rehearsing a portion of text. One effect of a set to respond to certain content would be to affect the distribution of higher level processing activities among items in the text. For instance, when a reader has been asked a question before he reads relevant portions of a text, it is quite probable that recall for information incidental to the question will be suppressed relative to a control group which reads the text without questions (see Anderson & Biddle, this volume). This fact has some implication for improving the efficiency of learning from text. Learning directions might be used, for instance, to suppress processing of interfering content.

Level III activities can also be supported by text characteristics. Propositions may be repeated in a text, related information can be grouped together, and so on. Judicious use of these strategies might facilitate learning for readers who are deficient in encoding, rehearsal, or integration skills. For instance, Cromer (1970) studied two groups of subjects that scored low on reading comprehension; one group had a vocabulary skill deficit, the other group did not. He hypothesized that if the reading materials were presegmented, in order to facilitate encoding of phrases, the level of comprehension of the group without the vocabulary deficit should increase. A vocabulary deficit would severely restrict comprehension. The materials were subdivided according to phrase groupings, for instance, *The cow jumped—over the moon.* As predicted, results showed that the poor readers were helped by phrase segmentation, provided that they did not have a vocabulary deficit.

D. LEVEL IV—RETRIEVAL AND RELATION

Processes most intimately related to long-term memory include retrieval and generating relations between items in a text and what is already known. Level IV processes, although they are conceived as more related to long-term memory than Level III processes, are not necessarily prior in a sequential sense. It is possible for Level IV processes to occur with sentences as they are encountered individually, and thus they may not involve, for instance, integration of text information. Imaging sentences, which establishes relations between currently encoded propositions and previously learned representations, can occur at any point in reading.

Retrieval and relation are separated by a broken line in Fig. 1 to emphasize that they may occur independently. Relation is conceived as an activity that draws upon the reader's previously learned semantic information. Retrieval may involve separate text items. For instance, it is possible for a reader to retrieve an item of information learned earlier in the text without relating that item to anything he knows. In a sense, retrieval is to relation as rehearsal is to integration. Some authors (e.g., Ausubel, 1968) consider the relatability of new material to previously learned material of paramount importance for learning.

Certain stimulus characteristics are coordinate with Level IV activities, just as repetition and grouping are coordinate with Level III activities. Stimulus factors coordinate with Level IV activities involve, for instance, familiarity and imagery value of text (Montague & Carter, 1973).

E. SUMMARY

In the foregoing pages I have suggested a rather general conceptual model in order to provide a context for subsequent remarks. In the discussion and experiments reported below, I will concentrate on research relating to the learning outcomes encouraged by goal-directed reading activities. Most of these activities are related to Levels I–III of the model, although where relevant, I make reference to other components of the model. Level I–III activities concern behaviors that occur during reading, rather than retrieval phenomena. Thus, the present chapter provides a contrast to Anderson and Biddle (this volume) which concentrates on Level IV activities involving the effects of postquestions upon memory.

The present model encourages a closer experimental exploration of reading performances that contribute to learning. Although we have some knowledge of specific factors that contribute to learning from written materials, our understanding of ongoing changes that occur during extended periods of reading is poor. Although suitably encoding and rehearsing information from a text can be shown to alter learning outcomes, the conditions under which these activities are emitted by a reader are not clearly understood. If the characterization of performance given in the model has validity, then it should be useful to explore the effects of various sequences of these activities in which a reader might engage. For instance, engaging in some general search of a text before attempting to learn the material may allow the reader to modify the items selected for integration and rehearsal in ways that reflect important conceptual relationships. We know very little about the effects of alternative sequences of processing during reading, or about the kinds of learning directions that might be used to control effectively these complex chains of performance. It is possible that telling a reader what to learn might interfere with certain learning activities. Potential sources of interference will be suggested below.

III. Sources of Encoding Efficiency and Inefficiency

There are two major points that I wish to make with the following experiments. First, the activities in which readers engage while reading can strongly determine what is remembered. These activities, properly understood, could be used, in an instructional setting, to control precisely learning from complex verbal materials. Second, controlling these activities can have negative, as well as positive, effects upon learning. The stimulus for these activities (performance sets) may arise from episodic task requirements (for instance, learning directions, or organizational characteristics of the text) or they may be stable, learned patterns of responding (such as a tendency to respond to the specific semantic aspects of the information in a text, or to its more general properties).

A. WORDS AS A UNIT OF PROCESSING CONTROL

When a reader has a specific goal in mind, for instance, to find information in a text that is relevant to some problem, he must establish criteria that will identify relevant sentences in the text and he must encode those stimuli to make decisions about what is and is not relevant to achieving his goal. According to the conceptual model proposed, the goal constrains the encoding of items in the text and hence what is represented in short-term memory. Inputs to memory are then strongly related to goal-relevant stimuli.

In one study (Frase & Silbiger, 1970), college undergraduates were told the attributes of a target concept and they were to determine, as rapidly as possible, what the name of that concept was (if it existed) by reading a text. In fact, none of the concepts described in the text satisfied the criteria given to the subjects. There were no requirements to learn. The text described 15 concepts (planets), each with five attributes. Each sentence in the text contained one planet name and one of its attributes. The sentences in the text were ordered in four different ways, so that a subject would have to search the text for either zero, three, nine or eighteen related sentences. In the zero condition, for instance, each paragraph completely described one planet. The problem could be solved by disregarding the planet names and scanning the attributes. On the other hand, for the other conditions, some attributes of a planet were described in other portions of the text. It was assumed that subjects would enter the planet names briefly into memory in order to locate the other attributes of the planet. The hypothesis was that goal-relevant items would be encoded in accordance with their relevance to the solution of the problem. We were able to distinguish three classes of names in regards to the role that they would play in controlling search. *Criterion* names were those that would have to be entered briefly into memory in order to search out related information in other portions of the text. *Compared* names were those in other sentences that would allow the reader to reject irrelevant sentences (sentences that did not contain information about attributes that the subject was searching for), but which would have to be encoded briefly to make a decision that a sentence was not relevant. Finally, *Irrelevant* names were those which could be disregarded because sentences about the planet were grouped together (only the attributes would need to be scanned).

Free recall and recognition tests (immediately after reading and after a 1-month delay) yielded similar results. Mean-proportion delayed recognition for Criterion names (.68) was higher than recognition for Compared names (.58); $t(36) = 3.57$, $p < .001$. In addition, delayed recognition of the Compared names for each group that had to search was significantly higher than for the group that did not have to search (for which those names were Irrelevant). As opposed to the groups that had to search ($\overline{X} = .58$), recognition for the Irrelevant names was .34 for the group that did not have to search. These results are consistent with the assumption that memory for items is a function of whether they enter into subject's meaningful goal-directed activities. Items that must be entered into working memory in order to achieve some goal are retained better than items against which they are merely compared, and the compared items are retained better than items which are irrelevant to the subject's processing activities. The point is that not only the range of encoding determines what is retained (both Criterion and Compared items were well retained), but the items which had to be represented in memory longer (Criterion items) were best retained.

The experiment reported here did not involve complications that might arise from variations in the readers' semantic criterion for searching a text. That is, decisions about the relatedness of information in a text could be based upon identity matches between the names contained in sentences and the name that a subject was searching for. But the categories that provide a criterion for a subject's search may themselves involve significant differences in encoding that reflect either "deep" or relatively "shallow" semantic processing. The previous study presumably involved relatively shallow semantic processing.

An example of deeper semantic processing is the following. In studies with lists of words (Frase & Kammann, 1974), subjects were asked to determine if each word in a list was a member of a relatively general category (e.g., food) or a specific category (e.g., vegetable). The assumption was that general search categories would result in detecting fewer semantic properties of the words. If the search for specific properties of a word entails a finer elaboration of semantic attributes from long-term memory, then recall should be higher with the specific search than for the general search, even though more of the words might be relevant to the general category search. Three experiments (Frase & Kammann, 1974) confirmed that the specific search led to higher recall. This finding held for list words that were not members of the target category as well as members of the target category. In addition, information about the categorical composition of the list, given immediately before recall (but not during reading) did not improve recall. Thus, the category search effect was not a retrieval phenomenon. In the following study (in conjunction with Persis Sturges of California State College at Chico), we attempted to replicate this result using text material.

Experiment 1

a. Subjects. One hundred and twenty-eight college undergraduates participated.

b. Materials. A 460-word passage was used that consisted of a story describing how 16 animals obtained their proper names. The animals were large or small, dangerous or harmless, land or sea animals (e.g., *lion, mouse, shark, herring*). The story told how the animals were named by a king. The proper names were common words (for instance, the lion's name was *Jelly*). This information was presented in a prosaic manner with a great deal of variability in syntax among sentences

c. Design and Procedure. The design entailed several factors, among which were the following. (1) Search directions told subjects to underline *General* category items (e.g., living creatures) or *Specific* category items (e.g., small land creatures). It should be noted that the general categorical search required underlining more items. (2) Subjects were told to underline either the animal *Types* (e.g., *lion, gorilla*) or to underline the proper *Names* (e.g., *Jelly, Office*). (3) The category members were presented consecutively in the text (*Organized*) or they were random (*Unorganized*). (4) Subjects were informed of the categorical composition of the text before reading (*Preinformed*) or they were *Not Preinformed*. (5) Subjects were informed of the categorical composition of the list immediately before testing (*Postinformed*) or they were *Not Postinformed*. (6) A free recall posttest was given immediately after completing the reading task (Immediate) and seven days later (Delayed).

Dependent measures were free recall for the types of animals and proper names of the animals, as well as time to complete the text search.

Subjects were run in small groups. The subjects first read instructions conveying the search directions and preinformation, if appropriate. Text searching began on a signal from the experimenter and the subjects recorded completion time from a digital clock. Subjects then went on to the postinformation conditions and the immediate

free recall test on names and types of animals. After seven days they
returned for another free recall test.

    d. Results and Discussion. One of the major hypotheses of Exper-
iment 1 was that specific search would result in greater recall than
general search. Mean recall (averaged over names and types of animals) was .29 for the specific search and .24 for the general search; F
$(1,96) = 15.49$, $p < .001$. There were no differences in time taken to
complete the reading task among any of the experimental groups.

    Another hypothesis was that the specific search for proper names
(for instance, the proper names of the large land animals) would
entail encoding of the type names (such as *gorilla*). The only condition which would not entail encoding the type of animals was the
general search for the proper names (in which subjects were to
underline the proper names of all the animals). Type recall for the
general name search averaged .24. All other groups were above .42 on
recall for the types of animals.

    Pre- and postinformation about the categorical composition of the
text did not influence recall overall; however, the availability of
categorical information during reading influenced the effectiveness of
the specific search directions. Specific search groups averaged .32 if
preinformation was available, and .26 if it was not available; the
general search groups averaged .24 with or without preinformation
(interaction F $(1,96) = 5.84$, $p < .025$). Thus categorical information
affected recall only if the subjects were required to respond actively
to the categorical distinctions in the text. The fact that recall was not
improved by giving categorical information just before testing eliminates the possibility that the recall effect of specific word categories
is only a retrieval aid.

    Other findings from Experiment 1 do not bear directly on the
processing hypothesis, so they are not reported.

    The data from Experiment 1 confirm that stable learning outcomes
arise from processing a text for relatively specific semantic information, and that important learning outcomes are not only limited by
the range of items to which a subject is constrained to respond (e.g.,
Frase & Silbiger, 1970), but they vary according to the semantic
criterion by which they are evaluated.

    A question arises as to whether procedures used by classroom
teachers, for instance, directing students to learn content relevant to
certain topical categories, is precise enough to control effectively
their learning behaviors. In the following study an attempt was made
to explore the efficiency of topical learning directions as opposed to
defining the content to be learned by listing specific words from the

text which could provide the occasion for higher level processing behaviors. The assumption was that topical learning directions might result in more complete processing of all text sentences, and that such directions might result in higher level learning than very precise reference to the information to be learned. On the other hand, topical reference to different sentences in a text does not necessarily represent an entrée into the reader's semantic long-term memory, as presumably was observed in Experiment 1.

Before conducting the learning study, however, we wanted to obtain information on the locatability of content, given the topics that were intended to refer to that content. Experiment 2, therefore, was designed to provide that information. Some data gathered during this investigation appear worth reporting on their own. In particular, changes in false detections of sentences as the subjects gathered more experience with the text and the imperfections of topical reference to content appear to be useful findings.

B. TOPICS AS A UNIT OF PROCESSING CONTROL

In conjunction with Valerie Kreitzberg, at City University of New York, and Barry Schwartz of Bell Laboratories, studies were run to determine whether topical reference to sentences that should be learned from a text is sufficient to produce recall improvements over study alone. In Experiment 2 we obtained data on how well subjects discriminate among sentences of a text on the basis of topical reference, and in Experiment 3 we used these topics in learning directions.

1. Experiment 2

a. Subjects. Twenty college undergraduate volunteers were paid for participating.

b. Materials. A 588 word biographical passage (23 sentences) about the American navigator and mathematician Nathaniel Bowditch (1962) was used. Two judges constructed 37 topics. Three of the topics were general (e.g., Nathaniel Bowditch's early childhood), 11 were intermediate (e.g., Nathaniel Bowditch's first job and major decision about school), and 23 were specific in that they were intended to refer to each sentence uniquely (e.g., the number of foreign languages that Nathaniel Bowditch studied).

c. Procedure. Each subject received 37 copies of the passage in

which each sentence was separated by one space from the next
sentence. One topic appeared at the top of each copy of the passage.
A line was provided to the right of each sentence for the subject to
indicate, with a *l* or *0*, whether or not the subject would try to learn
that sentence if he were asked to learn the sentences related to that
topic.

Subjects were run individually, proceeding at their own pace. Half
of the subjects received the topics in the order of general to specific,
the other half received the topics in the order of specific to general.
Immediately after the topic-sentence matching task, subjects were
given a surprise short answer completion test that tested for the
recall of the specific factual content in the passage (e.g., dates of
birth, courses of study, and so on). Recall was scored for 62 factual
items.

   d. Results and Discussion.   Our primary interest was in selecting
topics for use in learning directions, for Experiment 3, that would
accurately locate sentences. The mean number of sentences detected
as relevant to the topics varied as a function of whether they were
general ($\overline{X}$ = 10.5), intermediate ($\overline{X}$ = 3.6) or specific ($\overline{X}$ = 2.4). For
use in Experiment 4, we selected 22 specific topics intended to refer
to the 22 experimental sentences to be used in the later experiment.
The mean proportion of subjects who correctly identified each
sentence, given its relevant specific topic, was .90 (*SD* = .16). The
mean proportion of sentences incorrectly identified was .07 (*SD* =
.06). An uncertainty analysis (Garner, 1965) was conducted using
the specific topic-sentence matrix of detection probabilities. Assuming that subject's responses were all equiprobable, the maximum
joint uncertainty (based on the marginal probabilities) for this matrix
was 8.83 bits. The obtained joint uncertainty was 6.72 bits. The
difference between these two, the contingent uncertainty, was 2.11
bits. This is a measure of the amount of correlation between topics
and sentences, that is, how well the sentences were located by the
topics. The total uncertainty in the sentences was 4.41 bits, and since
2.11 bits could be predicted on the basis of the specific topics, about
48% (2.11 bits/4.41 bits) of the variability in locating sentences
could be attributed to the effect of topics. On the basis of these data,
we anticipated that the topics could be used successfully to direct
subjects to learn certain subsets of sentences from the text. On the
other hand, our topics did not perfectly locate the intended sentences. We could think of only one way of making reference to
sentences more specific, namely, by referring to the exact words used
in sentences of the text. This manipulation was included in Experiment 3.

Two other characteristics of subjects' assignment of topics to sentences are worth noting. First, we looked at the average hits (sentences correctly detected as relevant to a topic) and false alarms (sentences that were called relevant when, according to our criterion, they should have been irrelevant to a topic) for the first and last 13 topics that subjects saw. For half of the subjects these included general and intermediate topics, for the other half of the subjects these included specific topics. For the two groups of subjects, the item set was reversed for the first and last half of their search task.

The probability of hits on the relevant sentences was relatively stable across the first ($\overline{X}$ = .90) and last ($\overline{X}$ = .89) part of the text. The probability of false alarms, however, changed from the first ($\overline{X}$ = .18) to the latter half of the text ($\overline{X}$ = .07); t (18) = 4.16, $p < .01$. Thus, subjects were better able to reject irrelevant sentences after prolonged exposure to the text than in the early portions of the search task. Apparently, subjects had learned something that transferred to later discriminative behavior.

We also analyzed the relationship between subjects' ability to discriminate sentences and subsequent recall. A subject might be either above or below the median on hits and false alarms in relation to other subjects in his group. We so categorized subjects on the basis of the first 13 topics viewed. For the seven "accurate" subjects, who were above the median on hits and below the median on false alarms, mean recall was .73. Mean recall for the other 13 subjects was .59; t (18) = 2.2, $p < .05$. These data suggest that recall was related to the precision with which subjects initially responded to the topic-sentence relations in the text. Unfortunately, we had no independent learning data on the subjects to determine if discriminative abilities transferred to the learning of other text material.

2. Experiment 3

Armed with the data on subjects' ability to locate sentences in the text using topics as a point of reference, a study was conducted to determine whether learning outcomes depend upon the precision and directness of reference to sentences in a text that are to be learned. "Precision" was varied by referring to the first few words or to the topics of each of the sentences to be learned. "Directness" was varied by telling subjects which sentences had to be learned, or which sentences did not have to be learned. One reason for the present study was to avoid learning directions that directly repeated textual information that would be tested at a later time.

a. Subjects. One hundred and thirty college undergraduates participated as a classroom exercise.

b. Materials. The same biographical passage was used as in Experiment 2. There were two sets of learning directions. One set referred to 11 of the sentences in the passage, and the other set referred to 11 other sentences. One sentence, extraneous to either set of learning directions, which summarized that the historical figure discussed in the passage was famous, was left in at the end of the passage. This sentence was irrelevant to both sets of learning directions.

Four types of experimental learning directions were constructed: (*a*) Word-Positive—*Learn the information in all of the sentences that begin as follows* . . . ; (*b*) Word-Negative—*Learn the information in all of the sentences* except *those that begin as follows* . . . ; (*c*) Topical-Positive—*Learn the information in all of the sentences that relate to the topics below* . . . ; and (*d*) Topical-Negative—*Learn the information in all of the sentences* except *those that relate to the topics below.* . . . For the word directions, the first few words in the relevant sentences were given in a numbered list. The list of beginnings of sentences was in the same order as the sentences in the text. For the topical directions, the topics were given in a numbered list in the same order as the topically related sentences in the text.

c. Procedure and Design. Subjects from seven classes were randomly assigned to experimental conditions. The experiment was conducted in class. A printed booklet containing instructions, learning directions, and the reading passage was given to each subject. Subjects were directed to learn the information in the sentences, depending on the experimental group that they were in. They were permitted to look at the learning directions along with the text. Subjects were not informed that they would be tested later on all of the information in the passage.

Ten minutes were allowed for study. After one hour of subsequent class activities, subjects were given the same short-answer recall test employed in Experiment 2.

Although analyzed in the design, for the sake of simplicity differences between sets of learning directions and location of information in the text will not be discussed. Four groups of 24 subjects received the experimental learning directions in Word-Positive, Word-Negative, Topical-Positive, or Topical-Negative form. A Control Group of 34 subjects was directed to learn the entire text. The dependent measure for each subject was the proportion of factual items correctly filled-in for the questions relevant to and incidental to the learning directions. For the Control Group no such distinction was possible.

TABLE I

MEAN PROPORTION CORRECT ON COMPLETION POSTTEST
FOR EXPERIMENT 3[a,d]

| | Condition | | | | |
| | Word | | Topical | | |
Posttest items	Positive	Negative	Positive	Negative	Control
Relevant	.67[b]	.49	.55	.53	.50
Incidental	.39	.19[c]	.47	.45	.50

[a]Means based on 34 subjects for control group; 24 subjects for other groups.

[b]Significantly higher than control mean; Dunnett's test, $p < .05$.

[c]Significantly lower than Control (Dunnett's test) and lower than all other means (Newman-Keuls test); $p < .05$.

[d]From Frase & Kreitzberg (1975). Copyright 1975 by the American Psychological Association. Reprinted by permission.

d. Results and Discussion. Table I shows the mean proportion correct for each group of subjects. The first question to be answered by these data was whether the use of topical reference to the sentences would result in significant improvements in learning above the Control Group. Although for all of the experimental groups there was a significant difference in recall between the information in sentences relevant to and incidental to the learning directions, it can be seen that the effects of the learning directions were confined entirely to the Word-Direction Groups. Significant facilitation and inhibition of learning occurred with word directions but not with topical directions.

Word directions were apparently precise enough to permit subjects to execute higher learning study activities while topical directions were not. For positive directions, the cues defined by the learning directions signal where to study, but they do not signal where not to study. For negative directions, the cues signal where not to study, but they do not signal where to study. Both types of word cues (positive and negative) produced changes in learning which the topical directions did not. That is, for word directions both positive and negative (suppressed incidental recall) learning outcomes differed significantly from the Control Group scores. For topical directions, no significant differences were observed between the experimental and control groups. One particularly interesting finding from this experiment was that indirect reference to the sentences to be learned (negative-word directions) did not facilitate relevant learning. Knowing what to learn, by exclusion, is apparently not a sufficient condition for learning. The significant suppression of incidental learning for the negative-word directions can be interpreted as a shift of rehearsal activities away from items tagged as irrelevant by the learning directions. These data seem to be in agreement with the results of other experiments (Bjork, 1970) on the effects of instructions not to learn.

We had thought that the use of topical learning directions might result in processing a text for deeper semantic content and that this activity could aid recall. On the contrary, the more precise, but less informative, word directions (they departed more radically from the test items used) resulted in the only condition which was significantly higher than the Control Group.

Perhaps the reason why some learning directions do not function effectively is that they entail activities which do not contribute to learning. In Experiment 3, for instance, negative learning directions might entail searching which detracts from the time available for rehearsal activities. This assumes that the Topical and Negative-Word Direction Groups differ in significant ways from the Topical-Positive Group, perhaps in the strategies employed by subjects to conform to the task demands. Comments elicited from the subjects in Experiment 3 gave no cause for concern about the time allotted for reading. All subjects indicated that they had more than enough time to read and study the passage. Evidently, precise and direct reference to information to be learned is required if learning is to be efficient.

We are presently seeking to answer the question of whether the complexity of activities in which a subject engages while reading affects acquisition. Some preliminary results follow. In one study the topics analyzed in Experiment 2 were used to determine whether searching a text for one or four topics was more efficient. The topics used in this study were sampled in such a way that they might refer to a narrow or somewhat broader range of sentences. These topics were selected from the specific and intermediate topics (described in Experiment 2). The hypothesis was that searching for sentences relevant to four topics would entail multiple comparisons of each sentence (once encoded). This task is relatively complex, although it might result in longer residence time for an item in short-term memory. On the other hand, searching for the sentences relevant to one topic also entails encoding the sentences once, but it does not entail multiple checks for individual sentences.

Fourteen high-school students were run individually under the one- and four-topic search. The topics were printed at the top of the passage (described in Experiment 2), and subjects could refer to them at will. The subject's task was, as rapidly as possible, to place the number, representing the topic(s) at the top of the page, next to the sentences to which the topics related. Nothing was said about a later recall test. Subjects were run individually, and their search time was recorded after completion of the task. The subjects engaged in two minutes of counting backward before taking the short-answer retention test used in Experiments 2 and 3.

Results indicated that, for the one-topic search, subjects indicated that 30% of the sentences were relevant to their topic, and 56% of the sentences were relevant for the four-topic search; t (26) = 3.13, p < .01.

Mean time for the one and four topic groups did not differ significantly, although the one-topic search group averaged 309 sec and the four-topic search averaged 377 sec.

Overall recall for the one- and four-topic groups did not differ. The mean proportions correct were .27 and .20 respectively. A measure of learning efficiency (posttest items correct divided by time) was .06 for the one-topic search, and .03 for the four-topic search; t (26) = 3.0, p < .01.

The proportion of test items correct that were not related to the topics (as indicated by subjects' response sheets) yielded a mean of .29 for the one-topic group, and a mean of .24 for the four topic group. This difference was not significant. Thus, "incidental" recall was not at all suppressed for the one-topic group, even though there was a larger set of incidental items for the one-topic group than for the four-topic group. The one-topic group recalled significantly more of the items that were related to the topically relevant sentences ($\overline{X}$ = .36) than did the four-topic group ($\overline{X}$ = .19); t (26) = 2.62, p < .05. There were relatively fewer items in this set for the one-topic group than for the four-topic group. In summary, the one-topic groups recalled somewhat more of all of the items in the text.

These data are encouraging from the standpoint of exploring how the complexity of activities in which a subject engages might affect his ability to recall what was read. Some processing operations elicited by components of the text might inhibit the acquisition of other information in the text. Studies suggest that complex sentences may take up more short-term memory than simple sentences, hence materials presented immediately after complex sentences may be poorly recalled (Savin & Perchonock, 1965). An alternative interpretation (Foss & Cairns, 1970) is that complex sentences require more rehearsal activities (but not more storage). Both hypotheses imply that the occurrence of complex processing activities during reading may limit the storage of subsequent text information, at least when subjects are reading in a paced task. This hypothesis was tested in the following experiment.

C. INTERSENTENCE RELATIONS AS A UNIT OF PROCESSING CONTROL

1. Experiment 4

a. Subjects. Twenty-four college age female clerical employees from Bell Laboratories participated.

b. Materials. The text consisted of three paragraphs of nine lines each, describing various characteristics of a fictional country. The middle three sentences of each paragraph were the critical experimental sentences designed to elicit different processing activities. The first and last part of each paragraph contained three facts (such as the names of the major products of the country) which could be tested for recall. The critical experimental sentences took three forms: (1) *Independent Sentences,* describing a set of three unique items of information about the country; (2) *Class Inclusion Sentences* of the form *All the farmers are wealthy. The wealthy people live in the north,* and (3) *Temporal Relation Sentences* of the form, *The Tuts came to Osia before the Boks. The Clons came after the Boks.*

The critical sentence types were completely counterbalanced across the three paragraphs, and the sentences preceding and following the critical sentences were also counterbalanced.

A posttest was constructed consisting of short answer completion items testing each of the 18 items of information mentioned in the text.

c. Design and Procedure. Subjects were run individually. The text was presented on slides, three lines at a time at a rate of 10 sec per slide. Subjects were given an example passage that explained the three different kinds of content that might be encountered. Subjects were told that class-inclusion relations and temporal order of events should be carefully evaluated and all of the inferences and ordering of temporal events should be learned. Examples of each type of content were given.

The design was a 3 × 2 within-subjects analysis of variance of the number of items of information recalled. The factors were: (1) *Processing Mode* (independent sentences, class inclusion sentences or temporal relation sentences interspersed within paragraphs), and (2) *Location* of the content to be recalled (preceding or following the critical sentences).

d. Results and Discussion. The interaction between Processing Mode and Location of content was significant; $F (2, 46) = 3.35, p <$ .05. The data showed that the information following the complex relational sentences was poorly recalled. Mean errors were .55 for the information following the relational sentences, and .32 for the information following the independent sentences. There were no differences in recall for the information preceding the critical sentences. These results suggest that when encountering complex information, subjects tend to maintain that information in short-term memory and to forestall subsequent inputs.

Of course, an important component of ordinary reading activities was absent in the Experiment 4, namely, the reader's optional adjustment of reading rate to accommodate variations in text complexity. Consequently, Experiment 4 was run again with a new sample of 24 college undergraduates who read the text under unpaced conditions. No differences were observed between recall among the experimental conditions.

The marginal level of significance in Experiment 4 encouraged us to replicate those results. Consequently, a third study was run with another group of 24 clerical employees. We were unable to replicate the results of Experiment 4, and so the validity of the hypothesis that subsequent inputs are limited by complex processing requirements of a text must be considered doubtful. Certain modifications in the design of the critical sentences may reveal the expected effects. For instance, increases in the amount of complex content that precedes other content should magnify the predicted differences. It might also be that material that is perceived by the reader to be relatively important would be more effective in limiting subsequent inputs. In any case, the failure to replicate the findings of Experiment 4 was disappointing, but the general experimental focus merits further exploration.

Experiment 4 reinforces my general impression that it is more difficult to induce clear-cut learning effects based upon changes in text characteristics than it is to induce such effects through clearly defined learning directions. But sometimes learning directions or questions function in unanticipated ways.

For instance, in one study (Frase, 1968) different types of questions were constructed which were intended to induce varying
amounts of text processing. The text contained eight sentences
describing the names and occupations of four men (2 X 4 = 8
sentences). Questions presented along with the text, which subjects
were to answer by reading, varied in the following ways. A *Specific*
question asked, for instance, *When was Jack born?* A *Comparative*
question asked, *Is Jim older than Jack?* A *General* question asked
When were the men in the paragraph born? The assumption was that
only one sentence would have to be encoded with the specific
question, two sentences with the comparative question, and four
sentences would have to be encoded with the general question. The
expectation was that overall recall of sentences would increase as
more text was encoded.

Before conducting the learning study, 60 undergraduates were used
to obtain data on whether the questions mapped onto the text in the
expected manner. These subjects were instructed to underline the
words in the paragraph that would compose a complete sentence
giving the information needed to answer the questions. Six different
questions were used (two each from the Specific, Comparative and
General categories). Each subject saw only one question. The mapping data confirmed the prediction that the number of words underlined would increase from specific to general questions; however,
they also revealed a significant tendency for subjects in the General
Groups to disregard portions of the sentences. For instance, instead
of underlining four sentences required by the general question,
subjects would underline only the response terms that directly answered the question. For instance, if the question were, *What jobs do
the men in the passage hold?* subjects would underline *pilot, policeman, butcher,* and *engineer.* Thus, the associations between the
names and occupations might not be encoded for the General Group.
These data suggested that the original assumption about the encoding
advantages of the more inclusive questions might be faulty. For the
specific questions, the associations between names and dates were
relevant, but not for the general questions.

In a subsequent study, 84 undergraduate educational psychology
students were given 20 sec to read the paragraph in order to answer
one question. The question was located directly above the passage.
One-third of the subjects answered a specific question, one-third a
comparative question, and one-third a general question. After reading, subjects were given a multiple-choice test that required the

correct pairing of each name in the passage with each date of birth and occupation.

Overall recall was 4.75, 4.25, and 3.25 for the Specific, Comparative, and General Groups respectively; F (2,81) = 4.35, $p < .05$. The same relative ordering of the groups was also obtained for the one age or occupation test item appropriate to the Specific Group. Presumably this information would be subsumed by the comparative and general questions, according to the original hypothesis. For the Specific Group, 82% of the subjects correctly answered the specific test item, 61% in the Comparative Group, and 39% in the General Group; X^2 (2) = 10.8, $p < .01$.

The results of these studies (see, also, Experiment 3) suggest that the form of the questions have rather precise effects on the encoding of items from a text. The problem is to characterize adequately the specific behaviors and content that are required to satisfy task demands.

A related study conducted by Rothkopf and Kaplan (1972) also shows that control over learning is lost unless specific definition of to-be-tested content is given to the reader. They studied the effects of specificity of learning directions on subsequent recall. Specific and general learning directions were employed in their experiment. The two types of learning directions always referred to the same number of sentences in the text, but one general objective corresponded to several specific objectives. For instance, a general objective would be, *Learn the physical appearance of the two kinds of type faces discussed.* The corresponding specific objectives would be, *Learn the physical appearance of Italic type* and *Learn the physical appearance of Roman type.* Rothkopf and Kaplan found that the specific objectives produced substantially higher recall of the sentences relevant to the objectives than did the general objectives. Also, recall of all sentences was higher when specific objectives were used than when subjects merely tried to learn the text without directions about the relevant content.

In conjunction with Robert Kaplan, at Bell Laboratories, a recent study was conducted to determine whether the distance of related information in a text and the requirement to integrate that information might affect the amount of incidental learning. The hypothesis was that subjects who must search out related sentences in a text should recall more of the information that is incidental to their learning directions than subjects who do not have to search, or who search less. Another question to be answered was whether complex questions (that require integrating information from two sentences) produce strong direct instructive effects. That is, given a complex question for which subjects can easily locate the relevant content, are subjects better able to answer that question at a later time than subjects who merely study the passage? The finding that incidental learning is improved with greater search activity would be consistent with the results of Frase and Silbiger (1970), but the question remains as to what class of directions can produce effective search. The findings of Frase (1968) suggest that some learning directions entail restrictive encoding.

2. Experiment 5

The present study involved four experimental groups, and four matched control groups that studied the passage without any special learning directions. For the experimental groups, one group received *Simple* learning directions that required subjects to learn the information in single text sentences. The three other experimental groups were given *Complex* learning directions that required making comparisons between information from two text sentences. The two relevant sentences were separated by four text sentences for one complex group (this group will be referred to as the Complex-4 Group). The two relevant sentences for another complex group were separated by nine sentences in the text (this group will be referred to as the Complex-9 Group). For the other complex group the sentences relevant to the learning direction were separated by 19 sentences (this group will be referred to as the Complex-19 Group).

a. *Subjects.* Two-hundred and eighty-six high school students participated. Thirty subjects were used to determine whether subjects could locate the information relevant to the learning directions, 64 subjects were run to determine the level of posttest performance without reading the experimental text, and the remainder of the subjects were randomly assigned to the four experimental and four matched control groups (24 subjects in each group).

b. *Materials.* The experimental passage consisted of six paragraphs of 10 sentences each. Each paragraph contained information about the different planets in the solar system. Each of the 10 sentences within a paragraph described a different characteristic of the planet. The same sequential order of characteristics was used in each paragraph. For example, the fifth sentence in all paragraphs gave the orbital speed of the planet discussed in that paragraph.

The learning directions were in the form of instructional objectives. There were three sets of directions. First, a set of 20 Simple directions was constructed that required learning only one text sentence. For instance, if a text sentence gave the number of years that Mars takes to orbit the sun, the Simple direction might be, *Learn how many years Mars takes to orbit the sun.* These 20 directions were divided into two subsets of 10 directions for purposes of experimental control.

Second, a set of 20 Complex directions was constructed such that each direction required comparing information from two sentences. For instance, a Complex direction might be, *Learn how many more days Venus takes to orbit the sun than Mercury.* These 20 directions were also divided into two subsets. The order of paragraphs in the text was altered so that the sentences needed to conform to the learning directions were separated by either nine (Complex-9 Group) or 19 (Complex-19 Group) sentences in the text. The complex learning directions for these two groups were exactly the same.

Third, for Complex-4 Group, another set of 20 directions was constructed that required combining information from two sentences *within* paragraphs. These two sentences were separated by four other sentences. Two subsets of these directions were also created. Since the Complex-4 directions required relating information about a particular planet, they were not matched to the directions used for the other complex direction groups. The Complex-4 directions were, for example, *Learn how many satellites surround the planet that takes 11 years to orbit the sun.*

Two tests were constructed. All items were four-alternative multiple choice. Two forms of randomly sequenced items were used. The first test assessed recall for the information required by the learning directions. This meant that the item forms differed for the simple and complex direction groups. For instance, for the complex learning groups, test items were of the complex form (they presumably involved encoding two text sentences). Half of these items were relevant to the learning directions that subjects had seen, half were incidental (did not involve the specific comparison that the learning directions required). The control groups received the same test items that their corresponding experimental group received. In addition to the test items that corresponded to the experimental condition, for the complex groups there were ten test items that tested for simple (single sentence) information that was not subsumed by the learning directions. These items were included so that the recall of individual sentences by the complex groups could be compared to the recall of the control groups. These test items were identical for each Complex experimental group and its control.

A second test was constructed especially for the complex groups. The second test required the recall of information from single text sentences. For the complex groups, these test items could be categorized into those that were subsumed by (or relevant to) the learning directions and those that were incidental to the learning directions.

c. Procedure and Design. The subjects participated during the first two class periods of the day, in groups of about 30 subjects per room. Subjects in each room were randomly assigned to treatments. The experimental materials were in envelopes that were marked with large numerals showing the sequence in which they were to be opened.

The complex treatments received three envelopes containing (1) directions and a passage, (2) the first test, and (3) the second test. The Simple Groups did not receive the third envelope. The Control Groups received the same envelopes and materials as their corresponding experimental groups, except that the experimental directions were eliminated from the first envelope. The control subjects were told to learn the information in the passage. Subjects recorded the time that they started and completed each envelope.

Analyses of variance of the proportion of correct responses to the first and second test were conducted. A number of analyses were conducted, which are perhaps best summarized in the results in the following section. Of primary interest was whether the experimental groups showed strong direct instructive effects and whether incidental learning was improved as a function of the dispersion of information in the text.

d. Results and Discussion. Regardless of test item type (simple or complex), the average proportion correct for the 64 subjects who had not read the passage was .33.

The mean proportion of correct locations of the sentences containing the relevant information was .96 for the Complex-9 Group, and .91 for the Complex-19 Group. The form of the directions used for the Complex-4 Group was not as precise; the proportion of correct locations averaged .67 for the Complex-4 Group.

Table II shows the proportion of correct responses for the first and second tests. Several analyses of variance were performed, but only a limited number of planned comparisons were made. For Test 1, relevant and incidental learning on test items of the type seen as learning directions were analyzed separately. Relevant items tested for information that subjects had been directed to learn. Incidental items tested for information that subjects had not been directed to learn. Incidental items were the same type as those subjects had been directed to learn (i.e., for the simple groups the items were simple, for the complex groups the items were complex). For the complex groups, an additional analysis was conducted on the recall of single sentences (Simple Test Items). These are referred to as Incidental Simple Test Items in Table II because they were unrelated to the information entailed by the learning directions.

For Test 2, all test items required information contained in single sentences. Information entailed by the learning directions is referred to as Relevant in Table II. Information that was not required by the learning directions is called Incidental.

The four experimental groups scored higher ($\overline{X}$ = .57) than their controls ($\overline{X}$ = .46) on relevant learning; F (1,160) = 9.30, $p < .005$. The dispersion conditions did not interact with the experimental/control group differences. The simple groups (experimental and

TABLE II

PROPORTION OF CORRECT RESPONSES ON MULTIPLE-CHOICE
TESTS FOR EXPERIMENT 5[a]

	Complex test items			Simple test items		
	Experimental groups			Experimental groups		
	Relevant	Incidental	Control	Relevant	Incidental	Control
Test 1						
Simple	none	none	none	.75	.54	.57
Complex-4	.51	.45	.48	none	.50	.54
Complex-9	.53	.38	.42	none	.43	.60
Complex-19	.48	.37	.42	none	.46	.58
Test 2 (all items tested for information in single sentences)						
Complex-4				.52	.45	.49
Complex-9				.50	.41	.51
Complex-19				.50	.48	.53

[a]N = 24 for each group. For Test 1, "relevant" refers to information that subjects were directed to learn. For Test 2, "relevant" refers to information subsumed by the complex learning directions.

controls combined) scored higher than the complex groups combined; t (160) = 5.12, $p < .001$. The Complex-4 Groups were not superior to the Complex-9 and Complex-19 Groups combined, nor was the Complex-9 Group superior to the Complex-19 Group. These comparisons indicate that there were test item effects for relevant learning. The lack of difference between the Complex-9 and -19 Groups suggests that the dispersion of information had little effect.

For incidental learning (performance on the type of test item that the experimental groups had seen during reading), control and experimental groups did not differ. Simple groups scored higher than the complex groups; t (160) = 3.78, $p < .001$. The Complex-4 Groups were higher than the Complex-9 and -19 Groups combined; t (160) = 1.87, $p < .05$. The Complex-9 and -19 Groups did not differ. Again, there appears to be evidence for differences between test item types, but no difference due to the dispersion of information in the text. If there were effects of dispersion, the Complex-9 and -19 Groups should differ. Since the experimental groups performance on incidental test items (of the same type as seen during reading) was not elevated, there was also no evidence for a transfer effect of the learning directions.

Recall for information in single sentences on Test 1 (Simple Test Items) was lower for the complex experimental groups ($\overline{X}$ = .46) than for their controls ($\overline{X}$ = .57); F (1,120) = 9.92, $p < .005$. For the experimental groups, the dispersion conditions had no significant effect upon incidental learning of the single text sentences. To summarize, there was evidence for depressed learning of incidental sentences on Test 1, but no evidence for dispersion effects.

For Test 2, comparisons of the experimental and control groups performance showed no difference on recall of the information subsumed by the learning directions, nor on incidental information. It is possible that the delay in testing between Test 1 and Test 2, and recall attempts during Test 1, could obscure differences between the experimental and control groups on Test 2.

The time data showed that the distance of the related information in the text affected total reading time for the experimental groups; F (3,62) = 4.27, $p < .025$. For the Simple, Complex-4, -9, and -19 Groups, the mean reading times (in minutes) were 7.61, 6.53, 8.11, and 12.46, respectively. Newman-Keuls tests showed that the Complex-19 Group differed ($p < .05$) from all others. Times were not recorded by some of the subjects.

What do these results show? First, they show that simple learning directions are likely to result in higher relevant recall than complex directions. These results held for the control groups, as well as the experimental groups, hence they appear to reflect test item differences. There was no direct evidence for dispersion effects: the matched Complex-9 and -19 Groups did not differ.

Although there were direct instructional effects (the experimental groups outperformed the controls on Test 1 relevant learning), Test 1 also revealed depressed recall of incidental text sentences for the complex groups. Apparently, the comparative directions used in the present study represent a minimal involvement with the text content. Although the time data revealed that subjects were spending more time with the text in the Complex-19 Group, simple incidental learning was not higher for this group than for the Complex-9 Group, and its simple incidental learning was below the control group. In short, readers who had to search out and relate sentences across 19 sentences spent more time with the text but they did not learn additional sentences.

In order to facilitate recall for text components, the reader must be constrained to respond meaningfully to the set of sentences tested later. How to exert this control over reading is a difficult problem that entails specifying the relations in a text that might be used as a basis for control. The problem is one of specifying content structure. One set of studies (Frase, 1969), used the logical relations of class inclusion as a basis for controlling subjects' processing. Readers were constrained to respond actively to the relational structure in passages by having them determine if certain inferences followed logically from the texts. The passages were designed with a simple structure that asserted inclusion relations between five classes. This required five sentences of the form A's are B's, B's are C's, and so on. The structure, then, could be diagrammed as a simple linear sequence, A →B→ C→ D→ E, in which the arrows represent the relation "is a member of," and the letters stand for the verbal classes mentioned in the texts. Items that would be selected as memory inputs with different problems (e.g., A, B, and C would be selected for the problem *Are A's C's?*) and the overall level of incidental recall could be predicted on the basis of the structural analysis. Graph theory was used to catalogue the number of times each verbal class should be encoded during problem solution, and to determine the number of ways in which each problem could be solved.

The assumption was that learning could be predicted if two things were known: (a) the rules that characterize the critical conceptual relations in the text, and (b) how subjects' reading behaviors map onto those rules (the basis upon which the subject responds to the text). It was predicted, and confirmed, that the retention of verbal information from the passage would be a function of the number of times a subject encoded that information during the reasoning established by the task requirements.

In short, given an adequate model of the readers' semantic processing activities, it is possible to make accurate predictions about what will be remembered. In order to do this kind of process analysis, elaborate information is needed about the characteristics of content.

The problem areas for research on prose learning, however, go beyond the performances required during learning. They also involve retrieval phenomena, as shown by Anderson and Biddle (Chapter 3 in this volume). Aside from the types of retrieval processes entailed by the use of questions, the organizational characteristics of text can influence the performances that subjects are capable of after reading. For instance, studies of organization have been conducted by altering the order of sentences in a text. Several studies have examined the learning of information generated from a matrix in which names and attributes are conceived as superordinate lexical items, and the attribute values are tabular entries. Sentences are then generated from different combinations of names, attributes and attribute values. For instance, *The ship Encounter* (NAME) *had a hull* (ATTRIBUTE) *constructed of wood* (ATTRIBUTE VALUE), or *The ship* Winslow (NAME) *was rigged* (ATTRIBUTE) *as a ketch* (ATTRIBUTE VALUE) are two sentences that might be produced from the table of contents. Sentences can be grouped into clusters according to the names or they can be grouped according to the attributes. Alternatively, the sentences might be randomized. One simple hypothesis is that redundant patterns of information—grouping the sentences according to the names or attributes in the content—permits more efficient coding and retrieval of the information. Studies show that the random sequence of sentences results in poorer comprehension and recall than the organized sequences (Frase, 1973).

Precisely how text organization can aid recall was studied by Myers, Pezdek, and Coulson (1973). They found that recall was better when sentences were grouped according to the attributes than when they were grouped according to the names. The authors concluded that different strategies of retrieval are available to subjects with the two organizations. With the name organization, subjects learn sets of unrelated attribute values, such as speeds and sail plans. The attribute organization results in groups of related attribute values, such as several speeds, and subjects can capitalize on this

greater semantic redundancy by using a serial order retrieval scheme
for recall. Contrary results, however, were obtained by Schultz and
Di Vesta (1972), but Frase (1973) was able to show that the semantic
redundancies of the attribute values, as proposed by Myers *et al.*
(1973), could account for the tendency of subjects to profit from
one organization over another. When these semantic associations
were balanced in the two organizations, name versus attribute, there
was no advantage for either organization (Frase, 1973). Thus, any
organization, name, or attribute, might improve recall over a randomized list of sentences, but the semantic relations among sentences resulting from the two organizations also have to be considered.

   If organization affects retrieval performance, it may be that tests of
verbatim recall will not reveal important differences among text
organizations. For instance, Frase (1970) had one group of adult
subjects learn a text in which the sentences were arranged in logical
order. For another group, the sentences were not so ordered. He
predicted that both groups should be able to recall the sentences
equally well since the very same sentences had to be learned in the
two organizations. The logical ordering, however, should enable
subjects to derive inferences more easily. The data confirmed these
predictions. Evidently the sequence of verbal information can determine the way in which information is stored and consequently alter
subjects' ability to produce new combinations of that information at
a later time. This hypothesis was followed up in a subsequent study
(Frase, 1973) in which adults learned information grouped according
to the names or attributes (as in the Myers *et al.* study) of several
concepts. All subjects were required to learn the text until they
could recall it perfectly. Then they were given a test that required
integrating the information that had been learned. For instance, if a
subject had learned *The ship Encounter had a wooden hull* and *The
ship Encounter was rigged as a ketch,* an integration test item would
ask, *What kind of hull did the ketch have?* The results of the
integration test showed that subjects' ability to answer test items
depended upon whether the test items required combining information that was close or far apart in the text. The two organizations
resulted in different patterns of correct responding on the test items
because the information was organized differently in the two texts.
Text organization was apparently reproduced in memory. If two
items were not in adjacent "locations" in memory, then a subject
had difficulty combining them. In short, the analysis of the activities
that are required to answer a test question depended upon an

analysis of the characteristics of the content and some assumptions about how that information is represented in memory.

In general, the data from these several studies on encoding and retrieval suggest the importance of a match between what the subject is trying to do, the characteristics of the text that he is reading, and the test items that he is later required to answer. For instance, as well as the retrieval effects observed in Frase (1973), the data showed that the order of mention of names and attributes within sentences and the topical nature of the paragraph should be compatible. For instance, it was found that adults incorrectly associated concepts and their attributes in recall if sentences mentioned the name of the concept first but the paragraphs each discussed a particular attribute. Incorrect associations were reduced if the first thing mentioned in each sentence referred to the topic of the paragraph. Furthermore, if the learning directions given to subjects before reading contained a list of attributes, but each paragraph mentioned only one attribute of a concept, more incorrect associations were formed than if the list of attributes matched the list mentioned in each paragraph of the text. In short, two sources of mismatch might occur for the reader: a mismatch between the sentence and the paragraph, and a mismatch between the directions given to the reader and the text content that he encounters. Any mismatch requires additional processing operations on the reader's part. The trick is to determine what kind of mismatch produces transfer and what kind merely interferes with learning.

D. QUESTIONING AS SELF-CONTROL

At this point, I would like to review briefly two final studies that concern an important, but little-addressed problem. A number of studies have shown that providing questions or learning directions along with a text can improve recall. Yet a desirable aim of instruction is to encourage independence in the learner, to make him capable of controlling his own learning. The problem is to find out what subjects can do on their own.

The two studies, reported in Experiments 6 and 7, explored whether subject-generated questions aid learning and, more specifically, whether consequent learning outcomes resemble those which occur when questions are instructor-imposed. In particular, we were interested in whether producing or answering a question would differentially facilitate the learning of information that is incidental to the questions that subjects generate or whether the questions that subjects create have primarily a direct instructive effect. We were also interested in the type and range of coverage of subjects' questions.

In Experiment 7, we attempted to replicate the results of Experiment 6. In Experiment 6 the subjects worked in pairs. In Experiment 7, they worked alone, and we attempted to modify the types of questions that they constructed by directing them to make up few or many questions about difficult information or information that they would not normally be tested upon.

1. Experiment 6

a. Subjects. Sixty-four high school seniors and juniors were paid for their participation. Sixteen of these subjects were used to obtain information on the difficulty of posttest items, leaving 48 for the experimental conditions.

b. Materials. A 1218-word biographical passage about Nathaniel Bowditch (Bowditch, 1962) was used. The passage was divided into three sections, each approximately 400 words long. For the posttest, short answer questions were constructed which involved the recall of specific facts. Thirty questions for each of the three sections of the text were recorded on tape for the posttest, with 15 sec allowed for a written response after each question.

c. Procedure and Design. Forty-eight subjects were assigned to 24 tutorial pairs in the order in which they volunteered. A printed booklet containing the passages and instructions was given to subjects. The first page of the booklet informed subjects that they were to learn a biographical text for a later test and that they would be tested on the entire text. These instructions explained that the subjects would be required to ask their partner questions on one-third of the text, their partner would ask questions on another third of the text, and they would study on their own on another third. The instructions on the first page of the booklet told subjects to ask questions that would help on a posttest, but no specific directions were given about the number or type of questions to be asked. Answerers were required to respond verbally with as direct an answer as possible, without requests for additional clarification. The questioner was allowed to reply yes or no as feedback to the answer given by this partner.

Each page of the booklet contained either instructions or one-third of the text. Each of the three parts of the text were preceded by a page containing specific directions about what the subject was to do with the text on the following page. Subjects in a pair worked together, completing one page of the booklet at a time, without going back. Each subject engaged in only one activity (e.g., asking questions) on the first third of the text, then went on to the second third and engaged in an alternate activity (e.g., answering questions) then went on to the last third and a different activity, (e.g., studying). The order in which subjects engaged in questioning (Q), answering (A), and studying (S), was counterbalanced. Subjects in a pair were yoked, that is, when one asked questions the other member of the pair was required to answer. Subjects in a pair engaged in condition S on the same section of the text.

Subjects were seated across from each other with a tape recorder between them. They recorded the time from a digital clock when they began and after they completed each section of the reading passage. The tape recorder was kept running throughout the session.

After the experiment, subjects were given an answer sheet on which they wrote answers to the 90 tape-recorded posttest questions (which were given in the order in which that information appeared in the text). Two scorers independently evaluated a typed transcript of subjects' questions. For each posttest question, related to the part of the text for which subjects had generated or answered questions, a decision was made as to whether that question could be answered on the basis of the questions (and related answers) that a particular subject-pair had produced. Posttest questions that were related to questions asked by a particular subject are referred to as T (targeted) items for that subject and his partner; posttest questions that were not related to questions generated by that subject-pair are referred to as NT (nontargeted) items. The correlation between the two raters' assignment of posttest items to these two categories was .95. The other set of posttest questions, related to the material that subjects studied alone, are referred to as S questions.

Sixteen independent subjects (run individually) engaged in condition S only in order to obtain an estimate of the relative difficulty of the test items under conditions in which subjects were not in a tutorial situation.

The basic design was a 6 X 3 analysis of variance (six orders in which the conditions were administered, and the three Q, A, S conditions), with repeated measures on the last factor. Other analyses, comparing recall for T, NT, and S items, were also conducted.

   d. Results.   Full data were available for only 38 subjects because of tape failures. The mean number of questions generated by subjects was 8.97 per section of text, or one question every 1.68 sentences. The average probability that a posttest item would be targeted was .33, .33, and .37 for sections 1–3, respectively. More than 99% of the 341 questions generated by subjects required locating specific items of information, that is, the majority of questions required verbatim answers.

There was no significant correlation between item difficulty and the probability of targeting (as ascertained by correlating the difficulty of each item obtained from the 16 subjects who merely studied the entire passage with the percentage targeting an item in the Q condition). Also, the item difficulties obtained from the 48 experimental subjects on the study trial correlated highly with the difficulties obtained from the independent group of 16 subjects. The correlation between the two sets of difficulties for the three sections of text were .88, .84, and .92, respectively (N = 30 items).

Mean total recall scores for A, Q and S conditions were 54.1%, 52.4% and 46.8%, respectively; F (2,84) = 7.19, $p < .01$. Conditions A and Q differed from S (Neuman-Keuls test, $p < .01$), but not from each other. Mean proportion of T and NT items recalled for each subject is shown in Table III.

A one-way analysis of variance comparing all five of the means in Table III revealed significant differences; F (4,148) = 10.5, $p < .001$. Recall on the two sets of T items was significantly higher than all other means, which did not differ from each other (Newman-Keuls test, $p < .01$).

Times for conditions A, Q and S were 7.99 min, 7.99 min, and 4.0 min; F (2,84) = 115.99, $p < .001$.

TABLE III

MEAN PROPORTION CORRECT ON
POSTTEST FOR EXPERIMENT 6[a]

	Condition		
Item	Answer	Question	Study
Targeted	.67	.70	
Nontargeted	.49	.52	.50

[a]N = 38

2. Experiment 7

One purpose of Experiment 7 was to determine whether the findings of Experiment 6 would be replicated if subjects were not in a face-to-face tutorial situation. Another purpose of Experiment 7 was to vary the number of subject-generated questions through verbal directions.

Finally, an attempt was made to control the type of questions which subjects constructed. In Experiment 6, there was no relationship between the difficulty of a test item and whether subjects targeted that item. Thus, some questioning was devoted to items of information that were easily recalled even without the benefit of questioning. Higher posttest payoff might be expected from targeting test items which are relatively difficult and for which relative improvements can be great.

a. Subjects. Sixty four college freshmen were paid for their participation.

b. Materials. The same text and test items were used as in Experiment 6, except that only the first two (instead of three) sections of text were employed. For purposes extraneous to the present study, the text appeared in two different formats. In this experiment, the 60-item short answer posttest (30 items per page) was in written form.

c. Procedure and Design. Subjects were run in small groups. Four different sets of instructions were written, two relating to the number of questions which were to be constructed (either 5 or 10 questions) and two relating to the type of question to be constructed (either no special instructions, or instructions to construct questions about "hard-to-remember facts and things that you wouldn't normally expect to be tested on"). These four sets of instructions are referred to as the "5-Question," "10-Question," "None," and "Difficult" instructions respectively.

Subjects were required to write the questions that they constructed, and they were also instructed to indicate which line (or lines) of text contained the answer to each question, so that the relationship between their questions and the posttest items could be determined. Subjects recorded the time that they completed each section of text.

Each subject engaged in question construction on one page of text and in study on the other page. The order of these activities was counterbalanced.

After completing the task, subjects wrote short answers to the 60 written posttest questions (which appeared in the order in which that information had occurred in the text).

The design was a 2 × 2 × 2 × 2 × 3 analysis of variance, with repeated measures on the last factor. The factors were (1) passage format (ordinary text or sentence form), (2) number of questions (5 or 10), (3) type of questions (none or difficult instructions), (4) order of activities (study 1st or 2nd), and (5) condition of posttest item (T, NT, or S, as in Experiment 6). Only the most relevant data are reported below.

d. *Results.* Both the number of questions and the type of question instructions had significant effects on the number of posttest items targeted. The 5-Question condition targeted 29% of the posttest questions; the 10-Question condition targeted 47% of the posttest questions; F (1,48) = 59.1, $p < .001$. When no difficulty instructions were given, subjects questions targeted 36% of the posttest items; when instructions to construct difficult items were given, subjects targeted 41% of the posttest items; F (1,48) = 5.09, $p < .05$.

As in Experiment 6, the difficulty of T and NT items did not differ significantly. There were no significant differences among any of the experimental groups on mean difficulty of T items. Verbal instructions concerning difficult and unimportant information did not result in the anticipation of more difficult posttest items.

The mean proportion correct *total* recall in condition S was .53, .60 when constructing questions; F (1,48) = 10.81, $p < .005$. The mean proportion correct for the T, NT and S posttest items were .72, .55 and .53, respectively; F (2,96) = 28.63, $p < .001$. As in Experiment 6, scores on NT items did not differ from S posttest items.

The 10-question condition resulted in somewhat higher learning than the 5-question condition, but comparisons between these groups were not significant, nor was there a significant tendency for the NT items to be better recalled under the 10-question condition than under the 5-question condition.

Subjects averaged 6.39 minutes when studying, 13.25 when constructing questions; F (1,48) = 56.72, $p < .001$. The difference in time spent constructing 5 questions ($\overline{X}$ = 10.97) as opposed to 10 questions ($\overline{X}$ = 15.53) was significant; F (1,48) = 10.79, $p < .005$. Type of questions did not influence time.

e. *Discussion of Experiments 6 and 7.* Experiments 6 and 7 showed that engaging in question production, whether individually or in a tutorial situation, facilitated recall more than just studying. More interesting, learning effects in both experiments were confined to posttest items that were directly related to the questions that the subjects had constructed. Recall for incidental information was neither depressed nor facilitated by questioning activities.

Question construction took more time than studying. On the average, about twice as much time was spent questioning than in study.

The range of coverage of subjects' questions was not great, compared to the exhaustive posttest (30 items per page). About two-thirds of the posttest items were not targeted in Experiment 6. The range of coverage was modified in Experiment 7 by directing subjects to construct 5 or 10 questions, but the instructions to construct difficult questions also resulted in targeting more posttest items. Subjects thus responded to the "difficult" instructions by producing questions which entailed more content. The results suggest that subjects were less responsive to the fine characteristics of content (which may contribute to test item difficulty) than they were to its more obvious characteristics (such as the number of facts).

Without belaboring these data, the results indicate that subjects' self-questioning activities affect their recall, and that the effects are confined primarily to items of information that are directly relevant to the focus of their questioning.

IV. Conclusion

In the present chapter, a broad range of experiments has been reviewed, some more, some less precise, with the intention of characterizing important factors in prose processing. The conceptual model presented in the introduction was intended to provide a framework within which this research might be viewed. Up to now, the goal of our research has been to develop a general picture of the areas in which future research might profitably concentrate and to explore some methodologies that could be of help.

A. ATTENTION AS A MULTIDIMENSIONAL CONCEPT

The concept of attention lies at the heart of this research. The conceptual model in Fig. 1 was intended to summarize performances that may themselves be components of what we ordinarily refer to as "paying attention" to text. But unless we adopt the notion that attention is only a state of heightened activation, a clearer conception of the factors that give direction to that activation is essential. For instance, the reader whose activities entail the encoding of individual words (for instance, making simple comparisons of dates in a text) may be highly activated, but the focus of his activities may have little bearing on the kinds of performance that will be later required of him.

Figure 1 was, in part, intended to suggest that if we clarify the stimulus factors that control the activities of reading, then we will make useful discoveries about learning from prose. Current research encourages a more precise understanding of the adaptive adjustments and learning outcomes that result from alterations in the reader's set to respond.

B. READING GOALS

A broad interpretation of "goal-directed" reading entails some representation in memory of intended learning outcomes and the performances that achieve that end. The research shows that the factors that control text processing are complex, but a proper conception of these behaviors reveals that they have precise effects. For instance, Experiment 2 showed that the precision of responding to topic-sentence relations in a text may change with exposure to the text. Perhaps "reading" changes with reading.

Experiment 1 showed that if the reader's processing activities elaborated (mapped onto) specific semantic properties in memory, learning outcomes were considerably higher than when only general properties were elaborated. These effects were not due to the retrieval cues provided by the learning directions.

Other research (Frase, 1973) indicates that the match between the reader's goal and the information in the passage can affect the associations that are formed among items from a text and also that the match between components within the text (for instance, the match between the order of information in sentences and paragraph content) affects those associations.

Experiment 3 also confirmed the importance of precision of the match between learning directions and items in a text, and it showed how negative as well as positive learning outcomes can be brought under stimulus control. In general, this matching process, and its effects upon learning, deserves closer experimental examination.

C. PROSE PROCESSING—A NEGATIVE OR POSITIVE VIEW?

Much of the research on prose learning has been directed at the factors that raise the level of recall. Yet the research (for instance,

Experiment 5), indicates that it might be useful to consider reading from the standpoint of what performances inhibit learning. They might be performances required during reading or during testing. The deleterious effects of a mismatch between the reader's goal, components of a text, and the requirements for posttest performance is a case in point (Frase, 1973).

When a reader performs several operations in a sequence, perhaps not all contribute equally to memory. One example is the tentative data that searching a text for sentences related to one topic might be more efficient for storage than searching for sentences related to four topics. Perhaps the number of encodings is the critical component for retention. At this stage of research, we do not know.

Research (Frase, 1969) shows that if a reader is constrained to encode class inclusion relationships among sentences, memory is strongly affected. On the other hand, encoding comparative relations (Frase, 1968) (Experiment 5) may be a semantically trivial exercise.

And so we come to the problem of specifying the semantic relations that are available in a text. These units can provide a basis for the reader to control his activities. Given the variability of semantic environments represented by ordinary discourse, there appears to be no simple way in which this can be done. For instructional purposes, for instance, what is required is a task analysis that relates desired learning outcomes to the significant performances that are required of a reader in a specific task. The prospects for a truly general model of text processing thus seems poor. At present, it is perhaps even rash to propose, as in Fig. 1, a conceptual model of the performances in which a reader might engage, because performance in a particular reading task entails task-specific process analysis, including precise characterization of the relevant semantics of the text.

D. COMMENTS ON RESEARCH FOCUS

One major point of this chapter has been to show that activities occur, or can be made to occur, during reading that influence the range and form of the text components that are represented internally by the reader. Experiments 6 and 7 suggest that self-control of these activities is possible. Reading activities are prior to other behaviors that may be involved in, for instance, answering a question on a posttest. The activities of encoding and relating test questions to memory are themselves a significant aspect of recall performance. That we should study reading activities primarily by means of recall tests seems, in retrospect, rather odd. New and better research methodologies are needed. Time to perform different activities (e.g., McConkie *et al.*, 1973), or to perform the same activities with different styles of text, may provide useful data. By studying these processes we need not neglect memory, but we may discover more precisely what factors provide effective and ineffective supports for memory and other learning outcomes.

REFERENCES

Anderson, R. C. Control of student mediating processes during verbal learning and instruction. *Review of Educational Research*, 1970, 40, 349–369.

Atkinson, R. C., & Shiffrin, R. M. The control of short-term memory. *Scientific American*, 1971, 225, 82–90.

Ausubel, D. P. *The psychology of meaningful verbal learning.* New York: Grune & Stratton, 1963.

Ausubel, D. P. *Educational psychology: A cognitive view.* New York: Holt, 1968.

Bjork, R. A. Positive forgetting: The non-interference of items intentionally forgotten. *Journal of Verbal Learning and Verbal Behavior*, 1970, 9, 255–268.

Bormuth, J. R. *On the theory of achievement test items.* Chicago: University of Chicago Press, 1970.

Bowditch, N. *American practical navigator.* Washington, D.C.: U.S. Gov. Printing Office, 1962.

Bransford, J. D., & Franks, J. J. The abstraction of linguistic ideas. *Cognitive Psychology*, 1971, 2, 331–350.

Carroll, J. B. On learning from being told. *Educational Psychologist*, 1968, 5, 5–10.

Carroll, J. B. *Learning from verbal discourse in educational media: A review of the literature.* Report RB-71-61. Princeton: Educational Testing Service, 1971.

Carroll, J. B., & Freedle, R. O. (Eds.) *Language comprehension and the acquisition of knowledge.* Washington, D.C.: Winston, 1972.

Chapanis, A. Prelude to 2001: Explorations in human communications. *American Psychologist*, 1971, 26, 949–961.

Cromer, W. The difference model: A new explanation for some reading difficulties. *Journal of Educational Psychology*, 1970, 61, 471–483.

Crothers, E. J. Memory structure and the recall of discourse. In J. B. Carroll & R. O. Freedle (Eds.), *Language comprehension and the acquisition of knowledge.* Washington, D.C.: Winston, 1972.

Duell, O. K. Effect of type of objective, level of test question, and the judged importance of tested materials upon posttest performance. *Journal of Educational Psychology*, 1974, 66, 225–232.

Foss, D. J., & Cairns, H. S. Some effects of memory limitation upon sentence comprehension and recall. *Journal of Verbal Learning and Verbal Behavior*, 1970, 9, 541–547.

Frase, L. T. Learning from prose material: Length of passage; knowledge of results, and position of questions. *Journal of Educational Psychology*, 1967, 58, 266–272.

Frase, L. T. Some unpredicted effects of different questions upon learning from connected discourse. *Journal of Educational Psychology*, 1968, 59, 197–201.

Frase, L. T. A structural analysis that results from thinking about text. *Journal of Educational Psychology Monograph*, 1969, 60(6, Pt. 2).

Frase, L. T. Influence of sentence order and amount of higher level text processing upon reproductive and productive memory. *American Educational Research Journal*, 1970, 7, 307–319.

Frase, L. T. Integration of written text. *Journal of Educational Psychology*, 1973, 65, 252–261.

Frase, L. T., & Kammann, R. Effects of search criterion upon unanticipated free recall of categorically related words. *Memory and Cognition*, 1974, 2, 181–184.

Frase, L. T., & Kreitzberg, V. S. Effect of topical and indirect learning directions on prose recall. *Journal of Educational Psychology*, 1975, 67, 320–324.

Frase, L. T., Patrick, E., & Schumer, H. Effect of question position and frequency upon learning from text under different levels of incentive. *Journal of Educational Psychology*, 1970, 61, 52–56.

Frase, L. T., & Silbiger, F. Some adaptive consequences of searching for information in a text. *American Educational Research Journal*, 1970, 7, 553–560.

Frederiksen, C. H. Effects of task-induced cognitive operations on comprehension and memory processes. In J. B. Carroll & R. O. Freedle (Eds.), *Language comprehension and the acquisition of knowledge.* Washington, D.C.: Winston, 1972.

Gagné, R. M. Learning and instructional sequence. In F. N. Kerlinger (Ed.), *Review of research in education.* Vol 1. Itasca, Ill.: Peacock, 1973.

Garner, W. R. *Uncertainty and structure as psychological concepts.* New York: Wiley, 1965.

Glaser, R., & Resnick, L. B. Instructional Psychology. *Annual Review of Psychology*, 1972, 23, 207–276.

Griggs, R. A. Logical errors in comprehending set inclusion relations in meaningful text. Report No. 74-7, Indiana University, Mathematical Psychology Program, 1974.

Hochberg, J., & Brooks, V. Reading as intentional behaviors. In H. Singer & R. B. Ruddell (Eds.), *Theoretical models and processes of reading.* Newark, Del.: International Reading Association, 1970.

Huey, E. B. *The psychology and pedagogy of reading.* New York: Macmillan, 1908. (Republished: Cambridge, Mass., MIT Press, 1968.)

McConkie, G. W., Rayner, K., & Wilson, S. J. Experimental manipulation of reading strategies. *Journal of Educational Psychology*, 1973, 65, 1–8.

Meyer, B. J. F., & McConkie, G. W. What is recalled after hearing a passage. *Journal of Educational Psychology*, 1973, 65, 109–117.

Montague, W. E., & Carter, J. F. Vividness of imagery in recalling connected discourse. *Journal of Educational Psychology*, 1973, 64, 72–75.

Morasky, T. L., & Wilcox, H. H. Time required to process information as a function of question placement. *American Educational Research Journal*, 1970, 7, 561–567.

Myers, J. L., Pezdek, K., & Coulson, D. Effects of prose organization upon recall. *Journal of Educational Psychology*, 1973, 65, 313–320.

Patrick, E. M. Prose learning: Induced question and response rehearsal, and question repetition. Unpublished manuscript, University of Massachusetts, 1968.

Peterson, R. G., & McIntyre, C. W. The influence of semantic "relatedness" on linguistic integration and retention. *American Journal of Psychology*, 1973, 86, 697–706.

Robinson, F. P. *Effective study.* New York: Harper, 1961.

Rothkopf, E. Z. Some conjectures about inspection behavior in learning from written sentences and the response mode problem in programmed self-instruction. *Journal of Programmed Instruction*, 1963, 2, 31–46.

Rothkopf, E. Z. Some theoretical and experimental approaches to problems in written instruction. In J. Krumboltz (Ed.), *Learning and the educational process.* Chicago: Rand McNally, 1965.

Rothkopf, E. Z. The concept of mathemagenic activities. *Review of Educational Research,* 1970, 40, 325–336.

Rothkopf, E. Z., & Bisbicos, E. E. Selective facilitative effects of interspersed questions on learning from written materials. *Journal of Educational Psychology,* 1967, 58, 56–61.

Rothkopf, E. Z., & Kaplan, R. Exploration of the effect of density and specificity of instructional objectives on learning from text. *Journal of Educational Psychology,* 1972, 63, 295–302.

Savin, H. B., & Perchonock, E. Grammatical structure and the immediate recall of English sentences. *Journal of Verbal Learning and Verbal Behavior,* 1965, 4, 348–353.

Scandura, J. *Structural learning.* Vol. 1. *Theory and research.* New York: Gordon & Breach, 1973.

Schultz, C. B., & Di Vesta, F. J. Effects of passage organization and note taking on the selection of clustering strategies and on recall of textual materials. *Journal of Educational Psychology,* 1972, 63, 244–252.

Thomas, E. L., & Robinson, H. A. *Improving reading in every class: A sourcebook for teachers.* Boston: Allyn & Bacon, 1972.

ANALYSIS AND SYNTHESIS

OF TUTORIAL DIALOGUES[1]

Allan Collins, Eleanor H. Warnock,[2] and Joseph J. Passafiume

BOLT BERANEK AND NEWMAN INC., CAMBRIDGE, MASSACHUSETTS

I.	Introduction	49
II.	A Brief Description of Scholar	50
III.	Analysis of Tutorial Dialogues	54
	A. Methodology	54
	B. Tutorial Strategies	56
IV.	Synthesis of Tutorial Dialogues	74
	Comparison of Computer and Human Dialogues	75
V.	Discussion	84
	A. Comments on Dialogue Analysis as a Method	84
	B. The Analytic-Synthetic Approach	85
VI.	Summary	86
	References	87

I. Introduction

How does the tutor adapt his teaching to the individual student? This is like asking how a debater wins an argument or how a thief eludes a policeman: so much depends on what the other guy does that any experimental manipulation could distort the process beyond all recognition. We decided to study the question by recording actual dialogues between tutors and students, and looking at one aspect at a time in different dialogues. This method we call *Dialogue Analysis*.

[1] This research was sponsored by the Personnel and Training Research Programs, Psychological Sciences Division, Office of Naval Research, under Contract No. N00014-71-C-0228, Contract Authority Identification Number, NR No. 154-330. Reproduction in whole or in part is permitted for any purpose of the United States Government.

We would like to thank Richard W. Pew, Daniel N. Kalikow, and Mario Grignetti for their tutoring; Nelleke Aiello for debugging of Tutorial mode; Donald A. Norman for several useful suggestions on an earlier version of the paper; and especially the late Jaime R. Carbonell for his many ideas, in addition to the SCHOLAR program.

[2] Present address: Center for Human Information Processing, University of California, San Diego, La Jolla, California.

There were two aspects of tutoring we initially wanted to look at. One ability of a human tutor is that he builds on what the student already knows. Because a tutor carries on a dialogue with the student, he can question him about his previous knowledge. Then he can teach new material by relating it to that previous knowledge.

Another ability of the tutor is that he can respond directly to student errors. If the student makes a mistake, the tutor can question him to diagnose the confusion and can provide relevant information to straighten it out. Hence, in the tutorial dialogue, the information taught can be directed against the existing confusions, rather than against what the teacher anticipates might be a typical student's confusion.

These two abilities of the tutor, coupled with the capability of responding to the student's questions, make the tutor's role worth modeling in a computer. We are attempting to develop such inter-active capabilities in a computer program called SCHOLAR so that, like the tutor, it can function in a responsive way to the student's knowledge, his misconceptions, and his questions.

Our approach has been to look first at the strategies that human tutors use in interacting with students. The analysis of tutorial strategies is akin to the protocol analysis of Newell and Simon (1972) or the analysis of children's speech by Brown and his colleagues (R. Brown, 1970, 1973). Based on this dialogue analysis, we are trying to approximate these strategies within SCHOLAR so that it can respond to each student as an individual.

II. A Brief Description of SCHOLAR

In analyzing the tutorial dialogues, we have used SCHOLAR (Carbonell, 1970a, 1970b, 1971) as a kind of filter. That is, we have selected those aspects of the dialogues that we can see how to program in SCHOLAR.

To understand SCHOLAR enough to follow the analysis, it is easiest to compare a small part of the data base with a dialogue between SCHOLAR and a student, based on that piece of data base. SCHOLAR's main data base is on South American geography (Fig. 1). The program is basically independent of the subject matter, and in fact there is also a second data base on procedures for using the ARPA Computer Network. The data base is a semantic network (Carbonell, 1970b; Collins & Quillian, 1972; Quillian, 1968), which

CAPITAL
   SUPERORDINATE (I0)
      CITY
      PLACE (I0)
         OF (I0) GOVERNMENT
   APPLIED/TO (I4) COUNTRY STATE
   EXAMPLES (I2) $EOR BUENOS/AIRES LIMA
      MONTEVIDEO BRASILIA GEORGETOWN
      CARACAS BOGOTA QUITO SANTIAGO ASUNCION LA/PAZ

SANTIAGO
   SUPERORDINATE (I0) CITY CAPITAL
   POPULATION (I3)
      APPROX (I0) 2,200,000
   LOCATION (I0)
      IN (I0)
         CHILE (I0) CENTRAL
      LATITUDE (I4) − 33
      LONGTITUDE (I5) − 71

CHILE
   SUPERORDINATE (I0) COUNTRY
   LOCATION (I0)
      IN (I0)
         SOUTH/AMERICA (I0) SOUTHWESTERN
      BORDERING/COUNTRIES (I1)
         NORTHERN (I2) PERU
         NORTHEASTERN (I2) BOLIVIA
         EASTERN (I1) ARGENTINA
            BOUNDARY (I2) ANDES
      COAST (I1)
         WESTERN (I1) PACIFIC
            ON (I0) HUMBOLDT/CURRENT
         SOUTHERN (I3) ANTARCTIC
   CAPITAL (I0) SANTIAGO
   REGIONS (I1) $L CENTRAL/VALLEY ATACAMA/DESERT SOUTHERN/ANDES
   PEOPLE (I2)
      LANGUAGE (I0) SPANISH
      RELIGION (I2)
         PRINCIPAL (I0) CATHOLICISM
      POPULATION (I3)
         APPROX (I0) 9,000,000
   CITIES (I3)
      PRINCIPAL (I0) $L SANTIAGO VALPARAISO CONCEPCION
         ANTOFAGASTA ARICA VINA/DEL/MAR PUNTA/ARENAS IQUIQUE

Fig. 1.   Three partial entries from SCHOLAR's geography data base.

means that information about any concept is stored in terms of other concepts entered in the data base.

The information is extensively cross-referenced. This can be seen by looking at the three entries shown: Chile has Santiago as a value for two different attributes, Cities and Capital. Santiago has for its Superordinate two values, City and Capital. Chile occurs under Santiago as a value for Location. Capital has City as a Superordinate and Santiago as an Example.

The entry for Location under Chile illustrates another aspect of the data base, called *embedding*. Under the attribute Location there are several subattributes, among which is Bordering-Countries. But under Bordering-Countries there are the subattributes Northern, Northeastern, and Eastern, each of which has a different value. Embedding describes the nesting of attributes or values, which can go down as deep as is necessary to describe a property to any degree of specificity.

In the data base there are also tags, such as the (I0) after Location and the (I1) after Bordering-Countries. These tags are called *importance tags* or *irrelevancy tags* (I-tags), and they vary from 0 to 6. The lower the tag, the more important the piece of information. But they add up as you go down to lower embedded levels. Thus, under Location in Chile, Southwestern South America has an I-tag level of 0, Bordering-Countries an I-tag level of 1, and the Northern Bordering-Country an I-tag level of 3. These I-tags are used in a number of ways by the program, as we will describe below.

In carrying on a dialogue with a student, SCHOLAR is guided in its questioning by an internal agenda. The agenda determines what topics are to be discussed and how much time is to be spent on each topic. It operates as a pushdown list. If the overall topic is South America, SCHOLAR must generate a topic (e.g., Chile) and then a more specific subtopic (e.g., Topography of Chile). In the version of SCHOLAR shown in Fig. 2, the subtopics are generated on a random basis, weighted for importance in terms of I-tags.

Figure 2 shows a dialogue between an earlier version of SCHOLAR and the second author. An actual dialogue with a high-school student is shown later on, in the section on Synthesis of Tutorial Dialogues.

In the first exchange shown in the dialogue, SCHOLAR asked about the cities in Chile. The student answered with two names, one of which was incorrect. SCHOLAR corrected the student by indicating which of her answers were not stored.

The next two questions by the student illustrate an important use of the I-tags. The first of the two, "Where is Santiago?" produced

WHAT ARE THE PRINCIPAL CITIES IN CHILE?

SANTIAGO AND BUENOS AIRES

"SANTIAGO" IS FINE. YOU COULD ALSO MENTION VALPARAISO, CONCEPCION, ANTOFAGASTA, ARICA, VINA DEL MAR, PUNTA ARENAS, AND IQUIQUE.
I DON'T THINK "BUENOS AIRES" IS CORRECT.

WHERE IS SANTIAGO?

SANTIAGO IS IN CENTRAL CHILE.

TELL ME MORE ABOUT THE LOCATION OF SANTIAGO

THE LATITUDE OF SANTIAGO IS −33 DEGREES
THE LONGITUDE IS −71 DEGREES.

WHAT IS THE MOST IMPORTANT DIFFERENCE BETWEEN SANTIAGO AND ANTOFAGASTA?

THE PRIMARY DIFFERENCE IS:
SANTIAGO IS IN CENTRAL CHILE
BUT
ANTOFAGASTA IS IN NORTHERN CHILE

IS VALPARAISO A CITY IN CHILE?

I THINK I HAVE ALREADY TOLD YOU ABOUT IT.

YES

Fig. 2. Illustrative dialogue between an earlier version of SCHOLAR and student. (Student inputs are between asterisks.)

information down to a level of 1 with respect to I-tags. On the second question, "Tell me more about the location of Santiago," SCHOLAR looked for information at levels 2 and 3. Because it found nothing there, it then looked for information at levels 4 and 5, where it found the latitude and longitude. It is possible to go on asking for more, and getting information that is less and less relevant until the information runs out.

The student then asked about the most important difference between Santiago and Antofagasta. The subroutine that handled this question looked for common attributes under both Santiago and Antofagasta in the order of importance in terms of I-tags. It first checked the Superordinate, but the values were the same for both (i.e., City). Then it came to Location where the values were different and printed this out as the most important difference.

The final question by the student, about Valparaiso, referred to information SCHOLAR had told her earlier. At that time, SCHOLAR had left a temporary tag in the data base on this piece of information. Then, when the student raised the question again, SCHOLAR recognized that they had discussed it previously, and pointed that out.

This dialogue is intended to give the flavor of the SCHOLAR system. The program itself is described in much more detail in Carbonell (1970a, 1970b, 1971). In Section IV we will describe the tutorial version of SCHOLAR, which incorporates what was learned from the analysis of human tutorial dialogues. Here, we have tried to give enough background to understand the dialogue analysis described in the next section.

III. Analysis of Tutorial Dialogues

A. METHODOLOGY

In order to determine in general terms what is involved in modeling a tutor's teaching strategy, we collected tape recordings of four tutors discussing South American geography with several different students. In all, we tape-recorded ten dialogues with different combinations of the four tutors and six students. The two principal tutors each tutored in four of the dialogues. Both have extensive teaching experience at the college level, though neither has taught geography. The third and fourth tutors each taught only one session, and did not prepare nearly as extensively as the first two tutors. The students were employees at BBN. Two of the students had read material on South American geography and the rest had not. The students varied widely in their sophistication about geography. In all the sessions, the tutors could point out different places on an unlabeled map of South America. In most of the sessions, the tutors conducted the dialogues in the manner that they thought would be most effective. However, in two cases, the tutors tried to limit themselves (like SCHOLAR but not too successfully) to questions that would evoke specific answers, such as names or lists of things. Because of the differences in the tutors' preparation and teaching methods, and in the students' preparation and sophistication, the dialogues varied widely.

We did not attempt to analyze a large sample that could be generalized to most tutors and students but instead tried to analyze a few tutors in depth. Our aim was to assess the individual tutorial strategies of people we considered to be good teachers. It was necessary to study a tutor with several different students in order to be able to abstract the commonalities in his approach. The second tutor was also first author of this paper. This was done because it is a little easier to analyze what processing a tutor must have gone through to arrive at a given output, given that something is known about what he has stored and what he does not have stored. However, the analysis in this paper centers on the strategies used by the first tutor, and the strategies of the other tutors are presented primarily for comparison.

Natural data of this kind are assiduously avoided by psychologists because of the difficulty in analyzing what is collected. But as Newell and Simon (1972) have shown with protocol analysis, it is possible to analyze such data in terms of a computer model. Our use of dialogue analysis is distinct from their work in three ways. First, we do not perform an exhaustive analysis of the dialogue. Rather, we study one particular aspect at a time throughout the dialogue (e.g., error correction strategies). Second, in protocol analysis, a person is usually performing a nonverbal task (e.g., playing chess) and being forced to verbalize his thinking. By contrast, in our dialogue analysis, the verbalization is inherent in the task of carrying on a dialogue, and recording does not create any interference with the task. Third, there is more of an inferential process in our analysis of dialogues than in Newell and Simon's analysis of protocols. Because the tutorial strategies are not verbalized by the tutor, they must be inferred from what he says.

There are two points related to our methodology worth making here, because of the inferential nature of such analysis. First, we will present samples of the raw data from which we have derived our descriptions so that the reader may compare our descriptions with his own analysis. Second, since our descriptions of tutorial strategies are realizable in SCHOLAR or in other computer programs, our hypotheses can be tested in terms of how well they can produce new dialogues that look like tutor-student dialogues. This, of course, is Turing's (1950) test for evaluating computer programs. It is also in essence the same procedure used to evaluate any psychological model. That is, the test comes down to a comparison between the model's prediction (the computer output) and the human data actually obtained.

It should be emphasized that in undertaking this experiment we had little idea of what we might find. Basically, we only had a framework in terms of SCHOLAR for analyzing the dialogues. In this sense, SCHOLAR acted as an information-processing model of the tutor. The need for synthesis in the program directed our analysis,

and the results of the analysis determined our synthesis in the
SCHOLAR program.

B. TUTORIAL STRATEGIES

There were a number of different aspects of the way the tutors ran
the dialogues in order to tailor the discussion to the individual
student. The four most important aspects are discussed here: topic
selection, the interweaving of questioning and presentation, reviewing by the tutor, and the tutor's response to errors.

1. Topic Selection

The tutors appeared to generate topics as they went along rather
than following a prespecified agenda. The topics taken up by the
tutors in the dialogues were clearly not generated on a random basis.
In some cases the topics were selected by moving from place to place
on the map. But more generally topic selection seemed to follow the
structure of the tutor's knowledge about South American geography.
This showed up in the fact that the pattern of topics selected looked
rather like an outline for a course.

Figure 3 shows parts of a dialogue with the first tutor. The
organization of the dialogue can be seen in the outline of topics
derived from the dialogue, shown in Fig. 4 (page 64). We will
compare this organization to the organization found in other dialogues involving both this tutor and other tutors. Then we will
describe our hypothesis as to how tutors select topics.

The first two tutors generally indicated the organization they were
following by their comments when they introduced a new topic. In
the dialogue shown in Fig. 3, the first sentence established the overall
topic, South America, and the third sentence introduced the first
subtopic, Names-and-Locations-of-Countries.[3] This subtopic came up
first in almost all the dialogues, probably because it is the most
important property of South America.

The second subtopic in the dialogue shown was introduced by the

---

[3] There are two kinds of topics: *attributes*, such as Names-and-Locations-of-Countries or
Geographical-Features, and *values*, such as South America or Cape Horn. We have adopted
the convention of hyphenating an attribute when it appears as a topic to indicate that it is
to be read as a unit. A subtopic is never simply Geographical-Features or Cape Horn but the
entire embedded chain up to the main topic (e.g., Cape Horn as a Geographical-Feature of
South America).

1. T. We are going to talk about South America today. Now in order to begin, it would be helpful if I had some idea of what you know about South America to start with. So I wonder if you can tell, for example, do you know the name of that country? (*points to Brazil*)
2. S. Brazil.
3. T. How about this one? (*points to Argentina*)
4. S. Argentina.
5. T. Can you name the rest of them?
6. S. Chile. (*points to Chile*) Peru. (*points to Peru*) The Guianas. (*points to Guianas*)
7. T. Do you know which ones are which?
8. S. No.
9. T. OK, we'll work on that. How about this one? (*points to Venezuela*) (*not heard by student*)
10. S. Is this Ecuador? (*points to Colombia*)
11. T. Which one? This one? (*points to Ecuador*)
12. S. Right here. (*points to Colombia*)
13. T. No, that's not Ecuador.
14. S. Oh dear!
15. T. Ecuador is near there. This is Ecuador. (*points to Ecuador*) Ecuador is much smaller than this country. (*error correction*) That is the one that connects to Panama. (*hint*)
16. S. No.
17. T. That's Colombia.
18. S. Colombia.
19. T. OK, and this is Ecuador. (*points again to Ecuador*) That leaves a few.
20. S. Is this Uruguay? (*points to Paraguay*)
21. T. No.
22. S. Is it Paraguay?
23. T. This is Paraguay. (*points to Paraguay*)
24. S. That has to be Uruguay. (*points*)
25. T. And that's Uruguay. (*points*)
26. S. And Venezuela? (*points to Bolivia*) (*not heard*)
27. T. You can remember Uruguay because it's so close to Argentina and sort of part way between Brazil and Argentina on the coast. (*error correction*)
28. S. Oh.
29. T. OK, that means you don't know what this one is? (*points to Bolivia*)
30. S. Is that Venezuela?
31. T. No, that's Bolivia. (*error correction*)
32. S. Bolivia.
33. T. Now, we've got everything except Venezuela and there must only be one left (*points to Venezuela*)
34. S. I never would have guessed. (*ironic*)
35. T. That covers the major countries of South America. How about some of the geographical features. What things do you remember most about the layout of South America?

Fig. 3. A dialogue between the first tutor and a student.[4] (*continued*)

---

[4] The comments in parentheses are by the authors. The dialogue is verbatim except for a few minor grammatical changes to make the text into intelligible sentences.

36. S. The Cape. Is that Cape Horn? (*points to Cape Horn*)
37. T. That's Cape Horn. Right at the base of South America is Cape Horn. Right about there. (*points to tip*)
38. S. Where all the shipping used to go around there, many years ago.
39. T. That's right, and some of the explorers. Remember the names of any of the explorers?
40. S. H'm. Magellan.
41. T. There's even something in between there, called the Straits of Magellan.
42. S. Balboa. (*ignored by tutor because didn't hear*)
43. T. Down in there somewhere. (*points to Straits*)
44. S. Right down there.
45. T. OK. How about rivers or mountains, or mountain ranges?
46. S. Amazon.
47. T. The Amazon. Where do you think that is?
48. S. It's in here. (*points to mouth*)
49. T. Right, that's the Amazon. This map isn't too good, but the Amazon penetrates all the way back into here (*points into Peru, Colombia*) and there's lots of feeders.
50. S. Tributaries.
51. T. Tributaries or feeders into the Amazon. And it's the biggest river in terms of volume in the world. OK. How about some other land features that might be of interest?
52. S. The mountains in through here. (*moves along upper coast of Pacific*)
53. T. In through there? (*pointing*)
54. S. H'm An . . . (*tries to think of name*)
55. T. You're close.
56. S. Andes.
57. T. Yeah, the Andes. The Andes run all the way down and they sort of spread out here (*points to Bolivia*) and into Chile. Down into Chile.
58. S. Oh, into Chile.
59. T. So the Andes sort of define that coast almost. And they have some of the highest mountains in the world. And one of the highest mountains in the world is in Argentina.
60. S. In Argentina? (*echoic*)
61. T. It's called Aconcagua.
62. S. I've never heard of it.
63. T. It's the highest mountain in North and South America. It's in the Argentine Andes. It's right there. (*points*)
64. S. That means "with water." (*In Spanish "con" means "with" and "agua" means "water", but her inference is wrong. The tutor probably did not understand, and so ignored it.*)
65. T. Now, an interesting dividing point between Uruguay and Argentina is the Uruguay River which is this river running right down here. (*points to it*) Then there's also another river.
66. S. That's right on the border of Argentina.
67. T. On the border of Argentina and Uruguay.
68. S. And Brazil.

Fig. 3. (*continued*)

69. T. Yes. It forms the border with Brazil as well as the border with Uruguay down here. And there's another river off here, which sort of all comes together in the estuary. This is the Parana River.
70. S. The Parana River.
71. T. And those two come together in an estuary. Do you know what an estuary is?

. . .

85. T. Whereas this kind of a mouth (*pointing to Orinoco*) is called a delta, where it sort of filters through. It's a branching of the river at the foot, built up by the silt that's carried down the river. The other large river in South America is the Orinoco. It's right here.

. . .

93. T. Now, one thing you probably haven't been exposed to is the climate and the regions of South America from the point of view of the nature of the terrain and those kinds of things. First, there's the equator. Do you know where the equator runs?

. . .

(Beginning of discussion of individual countries)

115. T. Maybe now we'll take up the countries one at a time. Let's think about Argentina for a while. While we're working on Argentina, let's review and see if we can remember the countries that surround it.
116. S. All right.
117. T. What would this country be? (*points to Chile*) (*review*)
118. S. Chile
119. T. Chile. (*then he points to Bolivia*) (*review*)
120. S. That's Bolivia.
121. T. Good. (*points to Paraguay*) (*review*)
122. S. Paraguay.
123. T. Paraguay. (*points to Uruguay*) (*review*)
124. S. And that's Uruguay.
125. T. Uruguay, and this one? (*points to Brazil*) (*review*)
126. S. That's Brazil and this is the Uruguay River.
127. T. Good.
128. S. And then this is the Parana river.
129. T. Gee. Very good.
130. S. And there's an estuary there.
131. T. And there's an estuary there. And there's an island off the tip of what cape? (*review*)
132. S. Cape Horn.
133. T. And the name of that island? Do you know that?
134. S. No.
135. T. That's Tierra del Fuego.

(The discussion continued on Argentina and other countries.)

two sentences in line 35: "That covers the major countries of South America. How about some of the geographical features?" Under the attribute Geographical-Features, the tutor and student discussed Cape Horn, the Andes, and the three major river systems. The topics that the first tutor brought up under Geographical-Features of South America in two other dialogues partially overlapped those in the dialogue shown. In one case he took up the two major lakes, in addition to the Andes and the three major river systems; in the other case he talked only about the three major river systems. The variation in the subtopics discussed under Geographical-Features is evidence for the notion that the subtopics covered are not prespecified as part of a plan but rather are facts stored under the topic in the tutor's data base. The only plan seems to be to cover the most important information stored under each topic.

The first tutor took up both topics mentioned above (i.e., Names-and-Locations-of-Countries and Geographical-Features) in three of his four dialogues. The other top-level attributes which the first tutor brought up under South America in different dialogues were Climate-and-Terrain-in-Different-Regions (once), Minerals-of-South-America (twice), and Population-Characteristics (once). We think that the topics selected reveal the structure of his information about South America, and that the frequency with which they were selected reflects their relative importance in his mind.

It is interesting to note that all these topics also came up as subtopics in discussing specific countries (except that Names-and-Locations-of-Countries was changed to Bordering-Countries). See, for example, the outline in Fig. 4 where Geographical-Features occurs as a topic under Argentina. This would indicate that the structure of this tutor's data base at the level of individual countries was parallel in part to the structure at the level of South America.

The second tutor showed a slightly different structure of information about South America. In contrast to the variety of topics that the first tutor discussed as top-level attributes under South America, the second tutor apparently had only two major divisions of information under South America. The first division might be called Geophysical-Information, and included names of bodies of water, names of countries, the location of the equator and the extent of the tropic zone, and what he called Land-Features, namely the mountains and rivers. The second division he referred to as Geopolitical-Information, and included information about the population, governments, and history of South America.

The other two tutors, each of whom ran one session, showed less organization of South American geography than the first two tutors. This is probably because they spent less time beforehand organizing the information in their own minds. Part of what a tutor must do to prepare (if we may speculate) is to create a number of intermediate concepts like Geographical-Features in his data base, under which he groups the various facts he has stored. Hence, the less his preparation, the less structure there will be among the topics he discusses with the student. The degree of structure in the dialogue appears to be one of the characteristic features of a good tutoring strategy.

The tutor discusses information under the current topic or sub-topic mostly in order of *importance.* When he has exhausted all the important information under a subtopic, he pops back up to the previous topic. (It is this strategy that produces the outline.) For example, in the dialogue of Fig. 3, the tutor popped back up to Geographical-Features several different times, in lines 45, 51, 65 and 85. The pop-up is usually accompanied by a pause for thinking, where the tutor might say "O.K." or "now," as he did in three of the pop-ups (lines, 45, 51, and 65) to Geographical-Features.

Though the tutor picks topics mainly according to importance, *context* influences his selection in two ways. An answer given by the student or a piece of information presented by the tutor may become the new topic for a period of time. For example, when the student answered Cape Horn in line 36 to the question about Geographical-Features, Cape Horn became the topic for several minutes of discussion. If the student had not named Cape Horn, the tutor probably would not have mentioned it at all under this topic. He did not bring it up in the other two dialogues in which he discussed Geographical-Features of South America. The discussion of Cape Horn took place not because the tutor regarded it as the most important Geographical-Feature of South America, but because the student brought it up.

But even when the student gives an expected answer, as with the Amazon and the Andes in lines 46 and 56, or when the tutor himself introduces a topic, as with Aconcagua, the Uruguay River, or the Orinoco River in lines 61, 65, and 85, it usually becomes the subtopic for a while. When this happens, properties of these sub-topics come up, such as the fact that the Amazon has a large volume, that are less important than things discussed subsequently, such as the fact that the major mountain range is called the Andes. Hence going deeper into each of these subtopics for a period of time distorts the process from taking up topics purely in the order of their importance. This is the major way that context affects the discussion.

Every property that comes up in discussing one topic can in this way potentially provide the next topic, and topics may thus follow contextually related sequences. This method of selecting topics exhibits all the aspects of tracing paths in a semantic network (Quillian, 1968). But tutors do not follow contextual sequences endlessly. When context leads the discussion to topics that are not very important, tutors pop up to more important topics. Context does, however, tend to dominate selection of topics in this way where the material is not highly structured, as with the third and fourth tutors. Because they did not prepare and thus did not create a structure of intermediate concepts for grouping related facts (i.e., intermediate concepts such as Geographical-Features or Geopolitical-Information), they did not show this pattern of popping-up out of context to more important topics as much as the first two tutors did.

Context also affects the tutor's choice when he is popping up to select a new topic. In this situation he tends to pick a new topic that is related to a previous topic. For instance, when the tutor was talking about a major river system that included the Rio de la Plata (an estuary), he was led into a discussion of the difference between estuaries and deltas. During this discussion he pointed out (without naming the river) the particularly large delta of the Orinoco River. Then when he popped up out of the Rio de la Plata system to select a new topic in line 85, he selected the Orinoco. This selection was almost inevitable after its delta had been discussed. Another clear example occurred in a different dialogue where he was discussing Bolivia and mentioned tin as its major source of income. When he popped up out of Bolivia as a topic, he selected Minerals-of-South-America as the new topic for several minutes.

There is a variation on this kind of contextual influence. When the tutor is discussing individual countries one at a time (as did the first tutor at the end of the dialogue shown), he goes from country to country, each time picking a neighboring country that has not yet been discussed. This is a kind of map-guided contextual selection, where relative importance is overridden by context. Tutors seem never to go from country to country in anything like their order of importance. A map-guided strategy can also be used to select Geographical-Features of South America. The fourth tutor, for example, started following along the coast from Cape Horn to the Rio de la Plata, and then to the mouth of the Amazon, and so on.

The selection strategy described here is relatively easy to formalize, though it is impossible to predict which topics will be selected unless the current state of the data base is known perfectly. The selection is also at the mercy of whatever topics the student raises. In its simplest form it can be described by the following set of rules, which are to be applied cyclically:

1. When the topic is an attribute (e.g., Geographical-Features), select the most important unused value under the current topic. When the topic is a value (e.g., South America or Cape Horn), select the most important attribute and value under the current topic. (Context affects this selection by temporarily increasing the importance of topics that are related to the previous topics discussed).

2. If the attribute and value selected are below some criterion level of importance, which indicates that all the important information under the current topic has been exhausted, then pop up from the current topic to the previous topic in the pushdown list of topics, and start again at Rule 1. (The criterion level appears to depend on some combination of importance weighted by the time available. Factors affecting the criterion are discussed in the next section.)

3. The attribute and value selected are above the required level of importance, so formulate a question about the value of the attribute, or present the attribute and value to the student. (What determines whether there is a question or a presentation is discussed in the next section.)

4. Add new topics to the pushdown list of topics. (This is the major way context affects the selection of topics.) When the current topic is an attribute, the new value is added to the top of the pushdown list. When the topic is a value, first the new attribute and then the new value are added.[5] If the student gives an unexpected correct answer, his value is used instead of the value from the data base in adding to the pushdown list. If an answer is incorrect, an error correction strategy, discussed later, takes over temporarily.

[5] In SCHOLAR's data base there are embedded attributes, as for example Bordering-Countries is embedded under Location in Fig. 1. For such cases the rules must be modified as follows: Rule 1 selects an entire embedded chain of attributes plus the associated value. Rule 4 adds the value and each of the embedded attributes separately to the pushdown list of topics. Thus Northern Bordering-Countries might be followed by Western Bordering-Countries as a topic, when the embedded attribute Northern is replaced by Western. Such embedding of attributes also occurred with the tutors. For example, for the first tutor in the dialogue shown, the subattributes Rivers and Mountains were apparently embedded under Geographical-Features of South America, and the subattributes Religion and Language under Population of Argentina (see Fig. 4).

```
South America
    Names and locations of countries
        Brazil (Q), . . . , Venezuela (P)
    Geographical features
        Cape Horn (Q)
            Location
                Southern tip (Q)
            Explorers who sailed past Cape Horn
                Magellan (Q)
            Geographical feature
                Straits of Magellan (P)
    Rivers
        Amazon (Q)
            Location and extent
                Brazil (Q)
                Peru and Colombia (P)
                Tributaries to the south (P)
            Volume
                Largest in the world (P)
    Mountains
        Andes (Q)
            Location and extent
                Venezuela (P), . . . , Chile (P)
            Shape
                Same as coastline (P)
            Height
                Some of highest in the world (P)
            Peaks
                Aconcagua (P)
                    Height
                        Highest in Americas (P)
                    Location
                        Argentina, at mid-point (P)
    Rivers
        Rio de la Plata system (P)
            Subparts
                Uruguay River (P)
                Location
                    Between Uruguay, Argentina, and
                    Brazil (P)
                Parana River (P)
                Location
                    Argentina (P)
                Estuary (i.e., Rio de la Plata ) (P)
                    . . .
```

Fig. 4. An inferred outline of topics for the dialogue of Fig. 3 in quasi attribute-value form.[6]

[6] The letters in parentheses denote how each piece of information was brought up (see text). Q denotes a question by the tutor that the student answered correctly. P denotes a

Orinoco (P)
  Location
    Venezuela (P)
  Mouth
    Delta (P)
       . . .

Countries
  Argentina (P)
    Bordering countries (review by tutor)
      Chile (Q), . . . , Brazil (Q)
    Geographical features
      Rio de la Plata System (S)
        Subparts
          Uruguay River, Parana, Estuary (S)
      Cape Horn (Q)
        Island
          Tierra del Fuego (QP)
      Chaco (P)
        Location and extent
          Northern Argentina, Paraguay (P)
        Terrain
          Semi-arid plain (P)
        Population density
          Relatively unpopulated (P)
        Extent (reiterated by tutor)
          Into Paraguay and Bolivia (P)
  Population
    Religion
      90% Catholic (P)
    Language
      Spanish (P)
        Exception to Spanish-speaking
          Guianas (Q)
          Brazil (QP)
            Language
              Portuguese (P)
  Climate
    Temperate (P)
      Because of
        Latitude (P)
      Definition
        Average temperature around 60° (Q)
        Warm season and cold season (QP)

presentation by the tutor without any preceding question. QP denotes a question by the tutor, which the student failed to answer, and so the tutor presented the correct answer. S denotes the occasional cases where the student volunteered a piece of information.

5. The top item on the pushdown list of topics becomes the next topic.

Let us briefly explain how these five rules would operate to account for the topics selected by the first turor in a portion (lines 35–45) of the dialogue in Fig. 3. In line 35 the tutor popped up by Rule 2 from the subtopic Names-and-Locations-of-Countries to the top-level South America. By application of Rule 1, where the topic is a value (South America), the tutor selected Geographical-Features as the attribute, and probably either the Amazon or Andes as the value. The attribute and value selected were quite important, so no pop-up occurred by Rule 2. Then using Rule 3, a question was formulated about the property selected ("How about some of the geographical features?"). When the student gave an unexpected correct answer, Cape Horn, it replaced the Amazon or Andes, as prescribed by Rule 4. At that time both Geographical-Features and Cape Horn were entered on the pushdown list of topics by application of Rule 4 and Cape Horn became the new topic by Rule 5.

Skipping to line 39, the tutor formulated a question about the attribute Explorers-Who-Sailed-Past-Cape-Horn, to which the student gave the expected answer, Magellan. At this point, the tutor might have discussed Magellan or other explorers who sailed past Cape Horn, such as Drake, but he did not. He popped up from both these topics by Rule 2, back to Cape Horn. Applying Rule 1 with Cape Horn as the topic, he next selected a Geographical-Feature of Cape Horn called the Straits of Magellan. Here the selection in Rule 1 appears to have been influenced by the previous mention of Magellan, since the tutor picked the Straits of Magellan rather than the more important Geographical-Feature called Tierra del Fuego, which was the one he selected later when he returned to Cape Horn in lines 131–136. After presenting (by Rule 3) the Location-of-the-Straits-of-Magellan, there was a series of pop-ups by Rule 2 through the Straits of Magellan, Geographical-Features-of-Cape-Horn, and Cape Horn itself back up, to Geographical-Features-of-South-America. The tutor probably did not know any more about the Straits of Magellan, but he might conceivably have popped back to one of the other two topics. For example, he might have mentioned Tierra del Fuego, or other facts about Cape Horn, such as its proximity to Antarctica. He presumably rejected these topics by Rule 2 as not important enough, though there may be some overriding mechanism that governs when to pop up in this way, such as using up too much time on Cape Horn as a topic.

The five rules will produce an outline of topics very much like that shown in the Fig. 4, given a highly structured data base. For a data base that lacks a hierarchical structure in which the tutor can continually pop up, these rules will produce a wandering discussion, because context will dominate the selection of topics.

We do not argue that these rules describe perfectly how the tutor selects topics. For example, the rules in unmodified form cannot handle what happened once when the first tutor took up the entire Andes under Argentina, after he had forgotten to mention them earlier under Geographical-Features. Also, the tutor may forget what a previous topic was, because it gets too far down in his pushdown list. But we would argue that these rules, or something like them, are the predominant determinants of topic selection.

2. The Interweaving of Questioning and Presentation

One of our a priori questions about the dialogues was how tutors would combine the questioning of the student and the presentation to him of new material. As should be apparent from the dialogue in Fig. 3, the tutor does not simply ask questions first to find out what the student knows and then present new material that the student has not included in his answers. Nor does the tutor follow the "programmed learning" strategy of presenting some information, then asking questions about it, and then presenting some more information and asking questions about that, and so forth. Instead, there is an intricate interweaving of questions and presentation that is tied to the structure of the topics that are selected.

One striking fact about the tutor's questions is that they often occurred when the tutor had popped back up from a lower level. If the outline of the topics in Fig. 4 is compared to the corresponding dialogue, it can be seen that there is a consistent pattern as to where the questions occurred. To facilitate the comparison, the topics that were brought up as questions are indicated by a Q in the outline, and those brought up as presentations are indicated by a P. Occasionally, a topic, labeled QP, was raised as a question, but because the student did not give a correct answer, the tutor provided the answer. It can be seen that in general the questions occurred at the top levels of the outline and at the initial topics within each level rather than at the later topics. We think this was because the top-level topics and the initial topics within a level were the most important topics. Because the tutor thought the student was likely to know about them, he asked about them rather than presenting them as new material.

As an explicit theory of the interweaving of questioning and presentation, we would argue that when the tutor thinks the student may know the answer, he introduces the topic as a question rather than presenting the information. The tutor's evaluation of whether the student will know the answer is made using an a priori estimate of the sophistication of the student, which is refined on the basis of the answers and information the student provides as the dialogue progresses. This evaluation by the tutor of the student's sophistication would be based on something like SCHOLAR's I-tags. As the student answers some questions and fails to answer others, both the answers and failures will have levels of importance with respect to the top-level topic, South America, in the tutor's own data base. It might turn out, for example, that the student can always answer questions where the importance level of the answer is from 0 to 2, sometimes answer when 3 or 4, and never answer when 5 or more. Then it would be a sensible strategy to assume that the student knows information with a level less than 2, to ask questions if the information has a level of 3 or 4, to present information if the level is 5 or 6, and to omit information if the level is 7 or more. In other words the tutor uses a simple one-parameter model of the student.

The student's ability to answer will correspond quite well with the tutor's ranking of importance. This is because there is common cultural agreement as to what is important and what is not, and learning typically proceeds from the more important to the less important. There are sometimes exceptions, as when a person happens to have learned much more about one particular concept than about other similar concepts. In that case, the tutor will revise his simple model by adding to it another estimate of the student's sophistication with respect to the particular concept the student has special knowledge about. In this way the tutor can keep refining his model of the student throughout the dialogue.

We have suggested above that there are four categories of information, the boundaries of which vary depending on the sophistication of the student. These categories are shown in Fig. 5, with examples of the kinds of information that would fall into each one for the student in the dialogue of Fig. 3. The first category is what the tutor assumes the student knows. The first tutor never asked any of the four students what South America was, but he might have if the student had been, say, a child of seven. The second category is made up of facts that the tutor tries to elicit with appropriate questions, as with the Amazon and the Andes in the dialogue. In the third category are those facts he does not bother to try to elicit with

Categories of information	Examples from the dialogue in Fig. 3
1. Information the tutor regards as very important, which he assumes the student knows, and so does not ask about.	South America is a continent. South America is south of North America.
2. Information the tutor regards as important, which he thinks the student may or may not know, and therefore asks about.	The Andes are the major mountain range in South America. The Amazon is a large river in South America.
3. Information the tutor regards as somewhat less important, which he thinks the student probably does not know, and so he presents the information to the student.	The Parana is a large river in South America. The highest mountain in the Andes is Aconcagua.
4. Information the tutor regards as still less important and too much beyond the student's level of sophistication to be worth presenting.	The Paraguay River is a tributary of the Parana River. Manaus is a port half-way up the Amazon River.

Fig. 5. The different categories of information that determine what questions are asked and what information is presented.

questions, because he does not think the student will know them. Instead, he presents the information to the student, as he did with the Paraná River and Aconcagua in the dialogue, because he thinks the student should be able to assimilate these facts. The fourth category consists of those facts that he does not even present, because they would be more than the student could learn. We infer the existence of a fourth category because some facts are presented to more sophisticated students that are not presented to less sophisticated students. The two facts shown in the figure were presented to the second student, who was quite sophisticated in geography, but not to the student in the dialogue in Fig. 3. We assume the levels of these categories move higher or lower together with respect to the tutor's own scale of importance depending on his estimate of the student's sophistication.

This description of the tutor's evaluation of the student is related to the problem which Norman (1973) refers to as the Empire State Building Problem. As he points out, the answer to "Where is the Empire State Building?" depends on where a person asks the question. In Russia the appropriate answer might be "The United States"; in England it might be "New York City"; and in New York City it might be "On 34th Street." Norman suggests that to answer such a question appropriately, "it is necessary to have a model of the knowledge of the listener." What we are presenting here is a fairly simple mechanism by which a person can adjust the level of his answer (or in our case, his question or presentation) to the level of sophistication of the other person. In terms of the Empire State Building Problem, the strategy would work as follows: People have various pieces of information stored about the location of the Empire State Building, with various levels of importance. By estimating how sophisticated the other person is (Norman suggests that where he is is one criterion for estimation), an appropriate answer can be selected. The appropriate answer would have a low I-tag for a Russian, a higher tag for an Englishman, and a still higher tag for a New Yorker. Of course, it might turn out that a Russian questioner had spent several years in New York, but his reply would quickly reveal his knowledge about New York. Any misestimate of a person's sophistication can be corrected by evaluating the level of the information he provides in his reply.

We mentioned in the first paragraph of this section that the tutorial strategy for interweaving questions and presentation is quite different from the strategy employed in programmed learning, on which most CAI systems are based. The programmed learning strategy involves presenting small amounts of information and then asking questions about that information. Because this strategy cannot be geared to the prior knowledge of the student, most programs using it start at a fairly low level. For this reason the student often finds himself going over material he already knows, which is boring. But for a less sophisticated person the same material might be too difficult. Even when the material is at about the right level, the student is giving answers based on material recently presented to him. Thus, he often winds up half parroting what he has just read, a mode of recall that Craik (1970) and Madigan and McCabe (1971) have shown leads to little or no long-term retention.

In contrast, the questioning in the tutorial strategy precedes the presentation of material. The questioning determines what the student knows about a particular topic, and then semantically related material is presented which goes a little beyond the level of knowledge the student has shown in answering the questions. Thus the tutor can build onto the knowledge the student already has, without going beyond what the student can assimilate. This is an essential aspect of the way the tutor gears his teaching to the level of the student.

3. Reviewing by the Tutor

When the first tutor finished his discussion of South America as a whole in Fig. 3 (line 115) and had started discussing each individual country, he asked the student a whole series of questions in review (lines 117–131). There are two separable aspects to this kind of reviewing: reiteration and review questions.

By reiteration we refer to repeated passes through the same topics. It is systematic and it has to do with the overall organization of the session. The repeated passes may involve review questions or introduction of new material. Review questions refer to the tutor's questions about material covered earlier. Review questions sometimes occurred in the framework of systematic reiteration; they also frequently arose when an old topic came up in a new context.

Reiteration often occurred in the dialogues (as in the one shown) when the tutor went over much of the same material discussed under South America, but on a country-by-country basis. In going through a second time, he questioned the student about some of the old material (though tutors sometimes omitted these questions), and at the same time he added related new material, such as that about Tierra del Fuego (line 135). He could have discussed such topics in relation to South America as a whole on the first time through, but this would have increased the amount of new information for the student to assimilate on the first pass. By reiterating in this way the tutor can approximate what Norman (1973) refers to as "web teaching."

As Norman describes it, the object of web teaching is to establish a coarse web of interrelated material that is well integrated with previous knowledge. When this is done, new pieces of information can be added by tying them to the original web framework. The process can be repeated over and over, adding more and more detail each time. In addition to helping the student assimilate the new information, web teaching follows an order in which the most important information is taught first and information that is successively less important is taught on later passes. If the teaching is not completed for some reason, the most important information will still have been covered. And on later passes the material reviewed will be the more important information taught on earlier passes. For these reasons, web teaching is probably the most effective method of teaching.

Review questions about previously discussed material did not occur on a systematic basis in the dialogues. For instance, the tutors did not review most of the questions that the student missed during the session. Nor did review questions occur at a systematic place in the dialogue, such as at a fixed time after a question that was not answered. The point at which review questions did occur frequently was when a topic discussed earlier came up in another context. This usually happened during a second pass through material discussed earlier, but not always. In one case, for example, a region extending into two countries was mentioned first in discussing one and then a review question was posed later in discussing the other.

The example in Fig. 3 is unusual in that there was a whole series of review questions, whereas more commonly there were only one or two review questions at a time. In the series of six review questions the student had answered three correctly earlier, and these three could well have been omitted. This tutor did not ask many review questions in any of the dialogues, and he clearly was not systematically reviewing information he had told the student earlier.

The second tutor used review questions more frequently and seemed to come back more often to questions that the students could not answer earlier. But he too only re-asked a question when the topic came up in another context. The percentage of his review questions which the student had not answered before (eleven of thirteen in the dialogue counted) was higher than for the first tutor, but he did not exhibit perfect memory either. The other two tutors asked very few review questions. None of the tutors followed what is probably the best strategy in asking review questions, that is, reviewing all those topics where the information has been provided by the tutor and not reviewing those topics where the information has been provided by the student.

4. The Tutors' Response to Errors

One of the two aspects of tutorial strategies that we initially planned to investigate was how the tutor dealt with errors. Before we looked at the dialogues, we thought that the tutor might respond to an error by questioning the student to determine the underlying misconceptions that produced the error. None of the tutors responded in this way, perhaps because the errors were all obvious ones. Interestingly enough, each of the three tutors who were faced with errors by students responded to the errors in a somewhat different pattern.

The error correction strategy that the first tutor used most often was to point out which of two things was which, and then to provide distinguishing characteristics. This can be seen in two cases during the naming of countries at the beginning of the dialogue shown in Fig. 3 (lines 13–15 and 21–27). In the first example, the tutor corrected the student's confusion between Colombia and Ecuador (line 15). For Ecuador he pointed out that it was the smaller country, and for Colombia that it connected with Panama. (The latter fact was offered as a hint by the tutor to see if he could elicit the correct answer.) In the second example (lines 21–27) the student confused Paraguay and Uruguay, and again the tutor provided some properties of Uruguay that could be used to distinguish Uruguay from Paraguay. Providing one or two distinguishing characteristics between the correct answer and the wrong answer was the essence of the first tutor's strategy for correcting errors.

Like the first tutor, the second tutor usually provided a distinguishing property to undo a student's confusion, but in addition, he frequently asked a question about the student's wrong answer as well. Three examples of this tutor's correction of errors are shown in the fragment of the dialogue at the bottom half of Fig. 6. In the first example, the student identified Sao Paulo as Santos in line 2, but the

---

1. T2. Do you know what city this is? (*points to Sao Paulo*)
2. S. I think it's Santos.
3. T2. No. Which one is Santos? (*error correction*)
4. S. No. The other one is Santos. Right here. (*points to Santos*)
5. T2. Yeah. The port city.
6. S. The port city. Right. And I can't remember what that is. (*points to Sao Paulo*)
7. T2. Now this is the second largest city in South America. (*hint*)
8. S. Buenos Aires. . No, that's in Argentina.
9. T2. No, Buenos Aires is the largest and that's down in Argentina. (*error correction*)
10. S. The second largest. And it's the former capital of Brazil.
11. T2. No, this is the former capital of Brazil. (*points to Rio*) Do you know what city this is? (*error correction*)
12. S. Yes, Rio de Janeiro.
13. T2. That's Rio de Janeiro and this (*points*) is Sao Paulo, and it's almost twice as big as Rio.

Fig. 6. Fragment of a dialogue where the second tutor corrected a student's errors.

tutor did not tell him the correct name until line 13. Before providing the correct answer, the tutor asked where Santos was (line 3),
and then mentioned the distinguishing property that Santos was the
port city (line 5). The second example occurs in lines 8 and 9, where
the student mentioned Buenos Aires and then corrected himself. The
student's self-correction precluded a question about Buenos Aires
("No. Where is Buenos Aires?"), but the tutor still pointed out that
Buenos Aires was the largest city, not the second largest city. In the
third example (lines 10–13), the student suggested that the city in
question, Sao Paulo, was the former capital, while the former capital
in fact was Rio. Here again the tutor formulated a question about
Rio and also provided the distinguishing property that Sao Paulo was
much larger than Rio.

The strategy of responding with a question about the wrong answer
was probably used to help the student remember the distinction.
Presumably, by generating the correct answer himself, the student
would remember it better. In contrast, the first tutor probably would
have responded to the first error (line 2) by telling the student where
Santos was and mentioning the same distinguishing property as the
second tutor (i.e., that Santos was the port city for the city in
question).

The third tutor encountered only six errors in his one dialogue, and
no obvious strategy emerged other than pointing out the error. In
five of the six cases, he followed just the minimal strategy of giving
the correct answer. In the sixth case he, too, used the strategy of
providing a distinguishing property in a case where the distinction (in
particular, between Uruguay and Paraguay) was difficult to remember.

By providing distinguishing characteristics, the tutors were directly
combatting the students' confusions. The strategy is a good one,
because the essence of discrimination learning is finding properties
that may be used to distinguish the two things in the future.
Providing distinguishing characteristics is another aspect of a good
tutoring strategy.

IV. Synthesis of Tutorial Dialogues

Based on our analysis, we have implemented tutorial stratigies
similar to those described for human tutors, in a Tutorial Mode of
SCHOLAR. We have not always simulated the analysis exactly; this
was not because it was impossible, but rather because the structure

of SCHOLAR made it easier to use different means to accomplish the same basic objectives. In this section, then, we will try to emphasize in what ways we have captured these strategies in SCHOLAR, and in what ways they have been altered in the implementation.

Figure 7 illustrates the Tutorial Mode in SCHOLAR with an annotated transcript of a dialogue between a high-school student and SCHOLAR. The transcript has been retyped to save space, but it is verbatim. The high-school student had no particular familiarity with computers or with SCHOLAR. She was given examples of the types of questions she could ask, but otherwise she was essentially naive. This is a typical dialogue with a well-motivated student. One of the more impressive aspects of SCHOLAR is that it can carry on a reasonable conversation with someone who knows practically nothing about it.

COMPARISON OF COMPUTER AND HUMAN DIALOGUES

The comparison of the machine dialogue in Fig. 7 and the human dialogue in Fig. 3 should be made in terms of the aspects we have tried to model in SCHOLAR: topic selection, the interweaving of questioning and presentation, reviewing, and error correction. We will discuss each of these aspects below.

The comparison should not be made in terms of wording or naturalness. Though these are relevant considerations for judging SCHOLAR, we should emphasize that it will be a long time before any machines are as flexible as humans in the use of language. On the other hand, in spite of this limitation, generative CAI systems like SCHOLAR may be useful already for tutoring such topics as geography or electronics (J.S. Brown, Burton, & Bell, 1975).

1. Topic Selection

Tutorial Mode of SCHOLAR (hereafter called SCHOLAR) selects topics according to the five rules given in Section III, B, as modified to handle embedded attributes (see footnote 5, p. 63). Like the tutor, SCHOLAR takes up topics in the order of their importance, and it discusses each subtopic that comes up during the dialogue for a little while before going on to more important topics. But there is more variability from dialogue to dialogue in the topics that the human tutor brings up. Or, put in the opposite light, SCHOLAR is more thorough about covering all the major subtopics under any topic.

WHAT IS CHILE?	This is the most important property of Chile. (A tutor would suppress it on the assumption that the student knows the answer.) In evaluating the answer, it looks for "country", ignores the rest
COUNTRY IN SOUTH AMERICA	
VERY GOOD.	
CORRECT OR INCORRECT? CHILE IS IN NORTHERN SOUTH AMERICA.	Location is the next most important attribute under Chile
INCORRECT	The student answers correctly, so SCHOLAR will go deeper into Location
YOU ARE CORRECT.	
CHILE IS IN SOUTHWESTERN SOUTH AMERICA.	
THE EASTERN BORDERING COUNTRY OF CHILE IS —.	This is the most important Bordering-Country of Chile
I DON'T KNOW	
THE ANSWER IS: ARGENTINA.	
THE BOUNDARY OF THE EASTERN BORDERING COUNTRIES OF CHILE IS THE ANDES.	Since the student has missed the question, SCHOLAR presents some related information about Bordering-Countries
THE NORTHERN BORDERING COUNTRY OF CHILE IS PERU.	
THE NORTHEASTERN BORDERING COUNTRY IS BOLIVIA.	
WHAT IS THE CAPITAL OF CHILE?	SCHOLAR would have gone on to ask about Coasts under Location, but it has run out of time for Location, so it goes to the next attribute, Capital
WHAT ARE SOME CITIES IN CHILE	
THE PRINCIPAL CITIES OF CHILE ARE SANTIAGO, VALPARAISO, CONCEPCION, ANTOFAGASTA, ARICA, VINA DEL MAR, PUNTA ARENAS, AND IQUIQUE.	
NOW YOU CAN EITHER ANSWER MY QUESTION OR ASK A NEW ONE.	The student gets some help, though without directly asking SCHOLAR's question
SANTIAGO	
VERY GOOD.	
IS THE FOLLOWING TRUE OR FALSE? SANTIAGO IS IN CENTRAL CHILE.	Because the student is right, SCHOLAR goes into the data base entry for Santiago to ask more questions. (To go into an entry, the entry must have the main topic as a Superpart, i.e., it must be part of Chile.)
TRUE	
THAT'S FINE.	

THE REGIONS OF CHILE ARE —.

I DON'T KNOW

THE ANSWER IS: THE CENTRAL VALLEY, THE ATACAMA DESERT, AND THE SOUTHERN ANDES.

THE CENTRAL VALLEY IS IN CENTRAL CHILE. IT IS ON THE COAST OF THE PACIFIC.

THE ATACAMA DESERT IS IN CHILE AND PERU. IT IS BETWEEN THE PACIFIC AND THE ANDES MOUNTAINS.

SCHOLAR has run out of the time allotted to Capital and so goes on to Regions. Time is allocated on the basis of the number of top-level attributes and their I-tag weights

Since the student does not know any Regions, SCHOLAR gives the correct answer, plus some information about two of the Regions

WHAT IS THE LANGUAGE OF CHILE?

SPANISH

YOU ARE CORRECT.

Language is under the top-level attribute Population. SCHOLAR goes on to Population not because of time but because the student doesn't know any Regions.

WHAT IS THE PRINCIPAL RELIGION OF CHILE?

I DON'T KNOW

THE ANSWER IS: CATHOLICISM.

That's all SCHOLAR knows about Language, so it goes on to Religion, which is at the same level as Language under Population. The rest of the information about Religion is above the I-tag level for the first pass, so no related information is printed

IS IT TRUE THAT THE MINERALS OF CHILE ARE VERY IMPORTANT?

WHAT ARE SOME OF THE MINERALS?

THAT WAS MY QUESTION.

THE MINERALS ARE VERY IMPORTANT. THE PRINCIPAL MINERALS ARE COPPER, IRON, SILVER, COAL, NITRATES, AND IODINE.

The time allotted to Population is used up, so SCHOLAR goes on to Minerals under Products

SCHOLAR understands this as asking about the Minerals, so it points out that it has just asked about them

(The dialogue continues through the rest of the first pass)

(continued)

Fig. 7. An annotated transcript of a dialogue between tutorial mode of SCHOLAR and a high-school student. (The student's inputs are between asterisks.)

THE EASTERN BORDERING COUNTRY OF CHILE IS —.

I DON'T KNOW

THE ANSWER IS: ARGENTINA.

THE BOUNDARY OF THE EASTERN BORDERING COUNTRIES OF CHILE IS THE ANDES.

THE NORTHERN BORDERING COUNTRY OF CHILE IS PERU.

THE NORTHEASTERN BORDERING COUNTRY IS BOLIVIA.

On the second pass, SCHOLAR skips to the first piece of information the student missed earlier

Since the student misses it again, the same related information as before prints out. SCHOLAR knows that this information was presented earlier, and we may revise SCHOLAR so that it asks about the related information here instead of presenting it again

WHAT ARE THE REGIONS OF CHILE?

CENTRAL VALLEY ATACAMA DESSERT AND THE ANDES

"CENTRAL VALLEY" AND "ATACAMA DESERT" ARE FINE.
YOU COULD ALSO MENTION THE SOUTHERN ANDES.
I DON'T THINK "DESSERT" IS CORRECT.

THE ATACAMA DESERT IS IN CHILE AND PERU.
IT IS BETWEEN THE PACIFIC AND THE ANDES MOUNTAINS.

THE SOUTHERN ANDES ARE IN SOUTHWESTERN SOUTH AMERICA.
THEY ARE IN ARGENTINA AND CHILE.

The student missed this the first time. A new answer evaluation module points out that the Andes is right but more specifically it is the Southern Andes

SCHOLAR recognizes Atacama as the Atacama Desert and does not understand Dessert

Why it gives related information about the Atacama when the student has gotten it right is a mystery

IS IT TRUE THAT THE CENTRAL VALLEY IS IN CENTRAL CHILE?

YES

VERY GOOD.

CORRECT OR INCORRECT?
THE CENTRAL VALLEY IS ON THE COAST OF THE PACIFIC.

INCORRECT

WRONG.

THE CENTRAL VALLEY IS ON THE COAST OF THE PACIFIC.

Because the student has named the Central Valley, SCHOLAR goes into the entry for Central Valley to ask questions about it. Like the tutors, SCHOLAR will go off and discuss what the student answers

This is all the information it has about the Location of the Central Valley, so no related information is given

Fig. 7. (*continued*)

IS IT CORRECT TO SAY THAT THE CLIMATE OF THE CENTRAL VALLEY IS TEMPERATE?

WHAT IS TEMPERATE?

TEMPERATE CAN BE CONSIDERED A PART OF A CLIMATE.

YOU MAY ASK MORE QUESTIONS IF YOU WANT TO.

IS TEMPERATE VERY WARM CLIMATE?

I DON'T KNOW WHAT IT MEANS FOR VERY TO HAVE TEMPERATE.

FEEL FREE TO ANSWER THE QUESTION YOU DIDN'T ANSWER BEFORE.

I DON'T KNOW

THE ANSWER IS: TRUE.

THE CLIMATE OF THE CENTRAL VALLEY IS MEDITERRANEAN.

This is a failure on our part to get around to defining Temperate properly in the data base. It is for this kind of question that the interactive ability of SCHOLAR should be most useful

This question is beyond SCHOLAR's capability to analyze, but it seems to have tried anyway. More usually it would say "I don't understand your question"

This is a related fact about the Climate

(The dialogue continues on through the second pass and part of a third.)

In selecting subtopics under the main topic, SCHOLAR always picks the most important top-level attribute that has not yet been discussed. Then it goes down into the information under that top-level attribute, always picking the most important subattribute until it finds a value. Near the beginning of the dialogue shown in Fig. 7, SCHOLAR went from the main topic Chile, to the top-level attribute Location, down into Bordering-Countries, further down into Eastern, until it found the value Argentina. It then formulated a question about the eastern bordering country of Chile. In going from Bordering-Countries to Eastern, it chose Eastern rather than Northern because of a difference in I-tag values. At each embedded level of the data base, SCHOLAR is always choosing the most important branch, as determined by I-tags. (See Fig. 1 for data base on Chile.)

Of the two ways we suggested that a tutor is influenced by context, SCHOLAR incorporates one and not the other. The major effect of context in the human dialogues was that each subject that came up in the discussion was potentially the next topic. This occurs in SCHOLAR just as the five rules provide. Perhaps the best example in Fig. 7 is in the two cases where SCHOLAR asked about the regions of Chile. The first time, the student could not name any regions, so SCHOLAR told her their names, plus a few relevant facts about two of them. Then it went on to other topics. The second time, near the end of the fragment shown, the student correctly named the Central Valley and the Atacama Desert, so SCHOLAR began asking a series of questions about each of these (after it had provided a little information about the Southern Andes, which she had missed). Thus, the answers that the student happens to give determine the topics that SCHOLAR will take up. This parallels the situation in the dialogue in Fig. 3, where the student mentioned Cape Horn in answer to the question about Geographical-Features and Cape Horn became the topic for several minutes of discussion.

The second way that context appeared to influence the human dialogues was in the selection of a new topic after popping up from the previous topic. This does not occur at all in Tutorial Mode, though something like it occurs in the original SCHOLAR (Carbonell, 1970a, 1970b), where the random selection of topics is biased toward selecting a new question on any topic which the student brings up in a question. A more elaborate scheme might change I-tag values depending on context (see Carbonell & Collins, 1973). But Tutorial Mode makes its selections on the basis of fixed I-tag values, and this accounts for its inflexibility, or perhaps the thoroughness, in selecting topics.

The decision as to when to go down deeper on a given topic as against when to pop up to a new topic is determined by several conditions. These are the criteria referred to in Rule 2 of the five rules. The tutors appeared to take both importance and available time into consideration in deciding when to pop up. There is no way to tell from the dialogues how they combined the two, so we have adopted a complicated trade-off, with no theoretical implications. Briefly the scheme is this: Time is allocated to each of the top-level attributes in proportion to its importance. When the time allocation is used up, there is a pop-up and the next most important concept is selected. There is also a cutoff level in terms of importance (currently set at an I-tag level of five). Pop-ups also occur when the student misses a question, but that is discussed in the next section. If a pop-up occurs because of a missed question or an I-tag cutoff, any extra time left is added to the allocation for the next topic.

2. Interweaving of Questioning and Presentation

Like the human tutor, SCHOLAR starts off questioning the student. Then it presents some new information related to what he already knows. The object is to tie the new material into the old, and to give the student as much information as he can assimilate at one time.

This is achieved in SCHOLAR by a somewhat different strategy from the one described for tutors. SCHOLAR does not form a model of the student, other than to build an event memory of who said what during the dialogue. It does not estimate the student's sophistication or operate with the four categories described for tutors. Instead it starts out asking questions, going down to deeper and deeper embedded levels until either the student cannot answer correctly or one of the criteria for popping up is met. When the student cannot answer a question, SCHOLAR presents two or three related facts that are embedded within that attribute or at the same level, and then backs up to the level above the question missed.

There are three major ways that this produces a different kind of dialogue from the human dialogues. First, SCHOLAR will ask questions about all its important information (e.g., "What is Chile?"), whereas a tutor would skip over any information he assumed the student would know.

Second, the tutors sometimes presented information when they brought up new topics, as did the first tutor when he discussed the Uruguay River and the Orinoco River. SCHOLAR, on the other hand, will always introduce a new topic with a question. Tutors therefore tended to talk for longer periods of time without asking any questions than does SCHOLAR.

Third, SCHOLAR pops up more often than the tutors, because of the time cutoff. Thus the pace of the conversation was more leisurely in the human dialogues, because the tutors would go into most topics in more detail. On the other hand, SCHOLAR covers a greater variety of topics, because time pressures always force it to move on to new topics. It would be easy to relax the time constraint, but it is not obvious which is the better strategy.

3. Reviewing

We distinguished two aspects of reviewing in our analysis of dialogues—reiteration and review questioning. In Tutorial Mode we modeled the tutor's behavior in both respects.

Reiteration is essential to the strategy of web teaching, which we think may be the most effective method of teaching. Therefore, we set up Tutorial Mode to allocate time so as to provide for at least two passes through the material. If there is time left at the end, it goes through more passes. Reiteration by the human tutors usually occurred by having a first pass on South America and a second pass on each country. In SCHOLAR, we are teaching about each country individually, and so each pass covers the same material.

We could have set the I-tag cutoff higher on each subsequent pass in order to go into the material in more depth. However, this effect occurs anyway, for two reasons. Time is saved on the second pass by skipping over material that has already been answered correctly, and so SCHOLAR has more time to use up. Also, the students miss fewer questions on later passes. For both these reasons, there are fewer pop-ups on the later passes, and the material is covered in more depth.

With regard to review questions, SCHOLAR follows the optimal strategy we described in the analysis. That is, it asks about information the student missed earlier, and it skips over information the student knew earlier. But when the student misses the same question twice, SCHOLAR prints out the same few related facts each time. A better strategy might be to ask about these facts the second time through, rather than to present them again. However, if the student answers the question correctly the second time, SCHOLAR will in fact ask about the related facts that were presented earlier.

Like the tutors, SCHOLAR sometimes returns to a topic discussed earlier, at times other than on a second or third pass. This happens when the same topic comes up in a different context. For example, the Pampas might come up first under Regions of Argentina, and later as a Plain under Topography of Argentina. Just as in a second pass, SCHOLAR will repeat those questions that the student missed the first time, and will skip over those questions that he answered the first time. Hence, SCHOLAR also asks review questions independent of reiteration.

4. Error Correction

On the basis of the analysis of the dialogues, we have developed a sophisticated answer-evaluation and error-correction module[7] that says "No" only if it can find some basis for distinguishing the student's answer from the correct answer. It then tells the student the basis for distinguishing the two in order to correct the student's confusion. Several sample outputs are shown in Fig. 8.

[7] This module was designed and implemented by Nelleke Aiello, with the help of Susan Graesser.

THE EASTERN AND CENTRAL PLAIN OF ARGENTINA IS —.

CHACO

NO.

THE NORTHERN PLAIN OF ARGENTINA IS THE CHACO. THE EASTERN AND CENTRAL PLAIN OF ARGENTINA IS THE PAMPAS.

IS THE CHACO IN CHILE?
NO.

THE CHACO IS IN ARGENTINA, PARAGUAY, AND BOLIVIA, NOT IN CHILE.

ARE THE ANDES A REGION IN CHILE?
WELL, YOU'RE ALMOST RIGHT.

MORE SPECIFICALLY, A REGION OF CHILE IS THE SOUTHERN ANDES.

Fig. 8.   Examples of output from new answer evaluation module.

The first example illustrates the output when the two things confused are stored under the same top-level attribute in the data base. In this case, SCHOLAR first checked that the Chaco and the Pampas were not the same. Then, since the Chaco, as well as the Pampas, was stored as a Plain under Argentina, SCHOLAR printed out the information stored under Argentina about the Chaco, as the most relevant distinction.

The second example also concerns the Chaco, and illustrates the fact that true/false questions by the students require the same processing (but usually different comments). Here the mismatch with the Chaco occurred on the basis of the countries it was part of, and this distinction was pointed out. The distinction here is different from the one in the first example, though both examples involve the location of the Chaco.

The third example illustrates how the module handles a slight mismatch, like the one that occurred in the dialogue of Fig. 7. Southern Andes is stored as a region of Chile, and it has the student's value, Andes, as a Superpart. In the search for a distinction between the two, the module found this relation, gave a weak yes, and indicated the more specific value that was stored.

There are a large number of possible outcomes from this module, but these are described in detail elsewhere (Collins, Warnock, Aiello, & Miller, 1975). The few examples shown here illustrate that the processing involved in deciding that a student's answer is wrong leads to the most relevant distinction. Being told about that distinction can help the student to distinguish the two things in the future.

V. Discussion

Because this is in part a paper on methodology, we would like to conclude it with some comments about the method of *dialogue analysis* and the general approach of mixing computer synthesis with psychological analysis.

A. COMMENTS ON DIALOGUE ANALYSIS AS A METHOD

We have not attempted to make a complete analysis of the dialogues we collected. One could derive much more information from the dialogues and at the same time treat them more systematically than we have here. But we are frankly interested in the dialogues from an applied point of view, and a finer-grain analysis could cloud the important aspects behind a myriad of detail. Therefore, we have only looked at those aspects that seemed particularly relevant to the way the tutor relates his teaching to the individual student.

There are many other questions that could be investigated using dialogue analysis. In the limited setting of tutorial dialogues one could ask the following questions, for example: (1) On the basis of the percentage of correct answers on a post-test, what variables of the dialogue affect whether or not the student remembers what he was told? (2) What types of questions (e.g., true/false, multiple choice, "WH-" questions, etc.) do tutors use and what types do students use? (3) If given instructions to do so, can the tutor keep reviewing all the facts that were covered in, say, the session's first half-hour, until the student recalls each fact at least once? (4) What differences in strategies do tutors use to teach different kinds of knowledge such as factual knowledge, functional knowledge, procedural knowledge, and visual or pictorial knowledge? These examples illustrate some of the variety of ways dialogues can be analyzed; question 1 involves relating dialogues to other data, question 2 involves tallying different cases that meet given conditions, and question 3 involves putting boundary conditions on a participant's behavior. Answers to any of these questions would be helpful to us in building a computer system to tutor students.

Another way we have used dialogue analysis is to study the use of inference by tutors and students. We investigated this directly in one session by having the student with the most knowledge about South American geography ask difficult questions of the second tutor. The difficulty of the questions often forced the tutor to make inferences on the basis of his incomplete knowledge. This analysis is reported elsewhere (Carbonell & Collins, 1973; Collins *et al.*, 1975).

Beyond tutorial dialogues there are many other kinds of conversations which might be explored with dialogue analysis. For example, it would be very useful, in constructing information retrieval systems, to analyze conversations where a person tries to find out from an expert what references exist on a given topic in his field. By looking at the ways that the two people resolve the issue of just what kind of information the person is after, we would have a much better idea of how to organize information retrieval systems and what kinds of interaction would be useful. Another question one could investigate, taken from psychology, is the problem of reference (see Olson, 1970). To study this problem, one could set up dialogues to see the different ways that people refer to a given object in conversation with people from different backgrounds and in different situations. Or, given the concern with ambiguity among linguists (e.g., Chomsky, 1965), it would be profitable to study in what conversational situations ambiguities appear and how they are then resolved.

A great many questions about language are in fact questions about dialogues, because language by its very nature involves communication between people. And yet, most research on language, whether in psychology, linguistics, or artificial intelligence, does not even consider the possibility of looking at actual human conversation. An important exception is in the field of language acquisition, particularly the innovative work of R. Brown (1970, 1973). But traditional laboratory methods in experimental psychology greatly restrict the kinds of questions that can be asked about language. In particular, nothing of an interactive nature can be studied with the present laboratory methods, even though interaction is what language is about. The methods themselves force psychologists to pay attention to limited aspects of language.

B. THE ANALYTIC-SYNTHETIC APPROACH[8]

The underlying philosophy in this paper is that the most useful way to analyze how people perform a given task is in synthetic terms, that is, in terms of how that performance could be built into some kind of machine. At the same time, the most productive way to

[8] The approach described here comes down to us from Ross Quillian, and through him from Allen Newell and Herbert Simon.

try to synthesize a machine to perform a task that humans now perform requires systematic analysis of how people perform the task.

Suppose, for example, that one wanted to formulate a theory of how to build houses. Following a purely analytic approach, one might collect data from watching people build houses, such as the mean and standard deviation of the number of bricks that make up walls, or the order in which the bricks are put in the walls. These variables have something to do with building houses, but not very much. On the other hand, to follow a synthetic approach, you could try to build a house yourself, working out the problems either in advance or as you go along. You might get somewhere this way, but houses are fairly complicated, so you would have a lot of problems and probably not much house. What we are advocating is that it is better to watch people building houses for a while, then run home and try out what you think you saw, and when that falls down, run back and see what you did wrong, and so on. You can object that it would be simpler just to ask one of the workers how to build a house. But when it comes to problems in science, there is no one to ask.

As this example might suggest, the reason that the synthetic approach to analysis pays off is that it forces one to pay attention to the relevant variables. The reason that the analytic approach to synthesis pays off is that it helps avoid a lot of mistakes. The combined approach might be called the teeter-totter theory of scientific method.

VI. Summary

In this paper we attempted to analyze the strategies by which tutors adapt their teaching to individual students, so that we could synthesize these strategies in a computer system called SCHOLAR. To find out what strategies tutors use, we tape-recorded dialogues between various tutors and students on the topic of South American geography. Because SCHOLAR is a well-defined program, it was possible to analyze such ill-defined naturalistic data in terms of the structure and processing of information in SCHOLAR. We analyzed the dialogues concentrating on one aspect at a time. Based on our analysis, we proposed several hypotheses about how the tutor relates his teaching to the individual student. We also showed a student-computer dialogue which illustrates how in modified form we have implemented some of these strategies in SCHOLAR. We further argued that the analytical method employed here could be extended to a wide range of conversational situations. This method (Dialogue Analysis) would permit psychologists to study questions about the interactive aspects of human language processing that cannot even be considered with traditional laboratory methods.

REFERENCES

Brown, J. S., Burton, R. R., & Bell. A. SOPHIE: A step toward a reactive learning environment. *International Journal of Man-Machine Studies*, 1975, in press.

Brown, R. *Psycholinguistics*. New York: Free Press, 1970.

Brown, R. *A first language: The early stages*. Cambridge, Mass.: Harvard University Press, 1973.

Carbonell, J. R. AI in CAI: An artificial intelligence approach to computer-aided instruction. *IEEE Transactions on Man-Machine Systems*, 1970, MMS-11, 190–202. (a)

Carbonell, J. R. Mixed-intiative man-computer instructional dialogues. Doctoral dissertation, Massachusetts Institute of Technology, 1970. (b) (Also Bolt, Beranek & Newman Report No. 1971.)

Carbonell, J. R. Artificial intelligence and large interactive man-computer systems. *Proceedings, 1971 IEEE Systems, Man, and Cybernetics Group Annual Symposium, Anaheim, California*, 1971.

Carbonell, J. R., & Collins, A. M. Natural semantics in artificial intelligence. *Proceedings, Third International Joint Conference on Artificial Intelligence, Stanford, California*, 1973, 344–351. (Reprinted in *American Journal of Computational Linguistics*, 1974, **1**, Mfc. 3.)

Chomsky, N. *Aspects of the theory of syntax*. Cambridge, Mass.: MIT Press, 1965.

Collins, A. M., & Quillian, M. R. How to make a language user. In E. Tulving & W. Donaldson (Eds.), *Organization of memory*. New York: Academic Press, 1972.

Collins, A. M., Warnock, E. H., Aiello, N., & Miller, M. L. Reasoning from incomplete knowledge. In D. G. Bobrow & A. M. Collins (Eds.), *Representation and understanding: Studies in cognitive science*. New York: Academic Press, 1975.

Craik, F. I. M. The fate of primary memory items in free recall. *Journal of Verbal Learning and Verbal Behavior*, 1970, **9**, 143–148.

Madigan, S. A., & McCabe, L. Perfect recall and total forgetting: A problem for models of short-term memory. *Journal of Verbal Learning and Verbal Behavior*, 1971, **10**, 101–106.

Newell, A., & Simon, H. A. *Human problem solving*. Englewood Cliffs, N. J.: Prentice-Hall, 1972.

Norman, D. A. Memory, knowledge, and the answering of questions. In R. L. Solso (Ed.), *Contemporary issues in cognitive psychology: The Loyola symposium*. New York: Halsted Press, 1973.

Olson, D. R. Language and thought: Aspects of a cognitive theory of semantics. *Psychological Review*, 1970, **77**, 257–273.

Quillian, M. R. Semantic memory. In M. Minsky (Ed.), *Semantic information processing*. Cambridge, Mass.: MIT Press, 1968.

Turing, A. M. Computing machinery and intelligence. *Mind*, 1950, **59**, 433–460. (Reprinted in E. A. Feigenbaum & J. Feldman (Eds.), *Computers and thought*. New York: McGraw-Hill, 1963.)

ON ASKING PEOPLE QUESTIONS
ABOUT WHAT THEY ARE READING[1]

Richard C. Anderson

UNIVERSITY OF ILLINOIS AT URBANA-CHAMPAIGN, CHAMPAIGN, ILLINOIS

and

W. Barry Biddle

DEPARTMENT OF EDUCATIONAL PSYCHOLOGY
UNIVERSITY OF ILLINOIS AT URBANA-CHAMPAIGN, URBANA, ILLINOIS

I.	Introduction	90
II.	Direct and Indirect Consequences of Questions	91
III.	Conditions under Which Adjunct Questions Are Facilitative	93
	A. Repeated versus New Criterion Test Items	93
	B. Position of Questions	94
	C. Timing of Questions	94
	D. Response Mode of Questions	96
	E. Effects of Feedback	98
	F. Is an Overt Response Required?	99
	G. Motivation and Adjunct Questions	100
	H. Nature of the Questions	100
	I. Other Factors	103
IV.	Explanations for the Indirect Effects of Adjunct Questions	103
	A. Specific Transfer	104
	B. Are Questions Necessary?	104
	C. Must the Questions Be Relevant to the Text?	105
	D. The Mathemagenic Hypothesis	105
	E. Indirect Review Hypothesis	108
	F. Arousal	109
V.	Toward an Account of the Direct Effects of Questions	109
	A. Experiment 1	112
	B. Experiment 2	116
	C. Experiment 3	120
	D. Experiment 4	124
VI.	General Discussion	126
VII.	Practical Educational Implications of Questioning Techniques	127
	References	129

[1] The research reported herein was supported by the Navy Personnel Research and Development Center and Advanced Research Projects Agency under Contract N61339-73-C-0078.

I. Introduction

This paper is about the effects of asking people questions during or shortly after exposure to text passages. The concern is not so much with performance on the questions as it is with the consequences of the questions for learning and remembering. Knowledge about questioning has obvious implications for education. This is one reason questioning techniques are interesting, and one reason they have been extensively investigated by educators and educational psychologists. It will probably come as a surprise to persons who work in other areas that during the past decade alone there have been over seventy papers reporting experiments on the effects of questions. One need not have a directly practical goal, however, to be interested in research on questioning. The research gives a valuable perspective on natural language understanding and human information processing, a somewhat different perspective from that which one can get from experiments within popular basic research paradigms.

That asking people questions about what they are reading can increase learning and retention was already known just after the turn of the century, as studies reviewed by Gates (1917) indicate. Gates' own research showed substantial benefits from "active recitation" on the learning of both serial lists of nonsense syllables and short factual prose passages. Jones (1923–1924) had subjects read three text selections and shortly thereafter complete one of two cloze-type tests covering the selections. A day later all subjects took both tests. Scores on the repeated test were twice as high as scores on the test taken then for the first time. Numerous investigators since that time have investigated the effects of questions. The recent wave of interest was stimulated by the work of Rothkopf (1965, 1966), though Hershberger (1964; Hershberger & Terry, 1965) was independently doing similar research during the same period.

The rather bulky literature on questioning has never been thoroughly reviewed or adequately synthesized. This is one of the purposes of the present paper. Studies in which the medium was film or lecture have been included along with those involving text. We undoubtedly have not seen reports of all the studies that have been done, even all of the recent ones. Many experiments are described only in unpublished theses, technical reports, or convention papers. Others appear in obscure journals, or their relevance is not apparent because they were mainly concerned with unrelated issues. Nevertheless, a number of conclusions are clearly warranted on the basis of studies reviewed here, and it has been possible to identify points of theoretical or practical importance about which not enough is known to draw a conclusion. Also reported are several original experiments designed to evaluate a model of the "direct" effects of questions and a report of an attempt to use questioning techniques in an ongoing instructional program.

The remainder of this paper contains discussions of (*a*) the kinds of effects of questions, their magnitude and consistency, (*b*) the conditions under which questioning facilitates learning, (*c*) an appraisal of the explanations which have been proposed to account for the effects of questions, and (*d*) a brief evaluation of the practical educational implications of questioning techniques.

II. Direct and Indirect Consequences of Questions

Let us begin by clarifying terminology. The questions answered in connection with the text will be called *adjunct* questions; these are sometimes labeled inserted, embedded, or experimental questions. The items on the criterion test generally divide into two types. First, the adjunct questions are usually given again. We shall refer to them simply as *repeated* questions. Others have called them intentional questions or relevant questions. Second, the criterion test may contain *new* items. These new items are typically unrelated to the adjunct questions in the sense that learning the answers to the adjunct questions could not improve performance on them. New test items are sometimes called incidental or irrelevant items.

Both *direct* effects, in which the group that receives adjunct questions outperforms the reading-only control group on repeated criterion test items, and *indirect* effects, in which the questioned group does better than the control on new test items, have been found. The now classic study of Rothkopf (1966) illustrates both kinds of effects. College students read a twenty-page, 5,200-word selection from a book on marine biology. Two questions were asked either before or after each two- or three-page passage. The questions were of the completion type requiring a one or two word answer. People who received adjunct questions did substantially better than controls on repeated criterion test items regardless of the position of the questions in relation to the relevant text passage. People who answered adjunct questions after, but not before, the relevant passage also showed a small but significant advantage on new test items.

Table I summarizes all of the experiments we were able to find that included a reading-only control group. A study was counted as positive or negative according to whether there was any difference, no matter how small, between the questioned group and the non-questioned control. An experiment was placed in the no difference column only if the means were exactly equal, or if the investigator reported no significant difference and did not provide means. Where there was more than one condition or more than one measure of achievement, they were averaged to obtain a single value. Some studies are represented in every row in Table I, others in only one or two.

It is apparent that adjunct questions presented after the sections of prose to which they are related consistently facilitate performance on repeated criterion test items. Though the impact is somewhat less consistent, taking each experiment to be an independent observation, a sign test shows that adjunct questions after sections of text significantly more frequently have a positive than a negative effect on new test items as well, $z = 2.70$, $p < .01$. This is an important fact since, when studies are considered one at a time, the effect on new items is often nonsignificant, and it is possible to quibble about the appropriateness of the tests of significance used in some of the studies which have reported significant results (cf. Ladas, 1973).

To get a rough idea of the size of the effects, the difference in each experiment between the means of the questioned and nonquestioned groups was divided by the maximum possible score. Again, when there was more than one group or more than one measure an average value was calculated. Based on the thirty-five experiments for which figures were available, the average increment from questions after the relevant passages was .132 on repeated and .034 on new criterion test items, respectively. This means, for instance, that if the proportion correct on repeated criterion test questions were .50 for the subjects who read a text without adjunct questions, the subjects who got questions would be expected to average .63.

The direct effect of questions asked after passages appears to be about four times as great as the indirect effect. The advice to the practical educator is obvious: Ask questions during the course of instruction about each point it is important for students to master, rather than depend upon a general, indirect consequence from questioning.

Nevertheless, the aggregate indirect benefit is probably greater than the direct benefit. Only the points of information about which adjunct questions are asked could be directly affected, whereas presumably every point in the text could be indirectly influenced. For instance, suppose that a text selection contains 400 more or less

TABLE I

NUMBER OF STUDIES SHOWING FACILITATION
FROM ADJUNCT QUESTIONS

Question condition	Comparison of questioned group with reading-only control		
	Positive	No difference	Negative
After passage			
Repeated	37	2	1
New	26	4	9
Before passage			
Repeated	10	1	3
New	4	1	13

independent "idea units." Assume 20 questions are inserted in the text. There is a criterion test consisting of the 20 old and 20 new items, each of which tests a single idea unit. Projecting on the basis of previous research, adjunct questions would be expected to have a direct effect worth 2.6 units. While the measured indirect benefit would be just .7 units, when considered in the aggregate it would be about 14 units, and certainly greater than the direct benefit.

With respect to adjunct questions asked before the passages containing the answers, a sign test again indicates a consistent direct effect, that is an effect on repeated criterion test items, $p < .05$. Questions asked before the relevant passage more frequently inhibit than facilitate performance on new criterion test items, $p < .05$. The mean increment in proportion of repeated items correct was .108 and the mean decrement in new items, $-.028$, computed in the manner described above.

III. Conditions under Which Adjunct Questions Are Facilitative

A. REPEATED VERSUS NEW CRITERION TEST ITEMS

In studies which have made the comparison, people have always done better on repeated than new criterion test items, usually a great deal better. However, it has not been the practice to counterbalance the sets of items, so there is the remote possibility of a systematic bias favoring the repeated questions.

B. POSITION OF QUESTIONS

It may be inferred from data already summarized that questions asked after the relevant passage are more facilitative than questions asked beforehand. Experiments directly comparing adjunct questions in different positions confirm this inference. In 16 of 17 such experiments, questions placed after passages resulted in better performance on new criterion test items than questions placed before passages. In most of the individual studies this contrast was statistically significant. With respect to repeated criterion test items, these studies showed an effect regardless of question position, though there was a trend for it to be somewhat stronger and more consistent when the questions were asked afterward. Hereafter, unless otherwise indicated, we shall be talking only about questions inserted *after* the relevant passages.

C. TIMING OF QUESTIONS

A half a dozen studies have investigated the timing or frequency of questions. Typical is a study by Frase (1968b). A 2,000-word passage concerning the life of William James was divided into 20 paragraphs of 10 lines each. Subjects answered either one question after each paragraph, two questions after every two paragraphs, and so on. Pooling over repeated and new criterion test items, since this factor did not interact with the timing of adjunct questions, the trend favored frequent questioning. Experiments by Frase (1968a), Frase, Patrick, and Schumer (1970), both of which also employed the William James selection, found better performance on repeated criterion test items when adjunct questions were inserted after one paragraph than after five paragraphs. The same result appeared on new criterion test items in the former study. In still another experiment using the William James material, Frase (1967) found that people who answered adjunct questions after two paragraphs did better on repeated test questions than people who answered the adjunct questions after either one or four paragraphs. There was no difference in performance on new test questions. Turning to a different investigator using different text selections, Boyd (1973) found higher scores on repeated test items when adjunct questions were placed after each paragraph of Department of State Background Notes on Bahrain and Botswana than when inserted after every five paragraphs. Scores on new test items were unaffected.

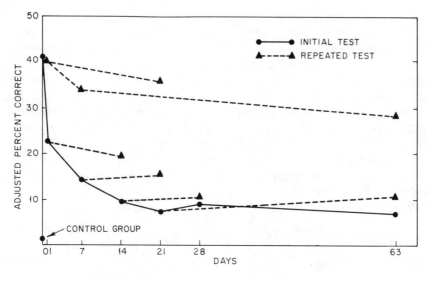

Fig. 1

In the studies reviewed so far the timing of questions was confounded with the number of questions asked at any given point. Either one question was placed after each paragraph or a batch of them after every two to five paragraphs. Eischens, Gaite, and Kumar (1972) employed a procedure which made the number of questions independent of timing. Sets of three difficult questions were selected for the first, fourth and seventh pages of a nine-page, 1,350-word text on the history of Quebec. For different groups of subjects the sets of questions were inserted after the first, fourth, and seventh pages; the second, fifth, and eighth pages; or the third, sixth, and ninth pages. In other words, either zero, one, or two pages intervened between information and the questions asking about that information. On the test 48 hr later, which consisted of just the nine previously asked questions, performance declined sharply as a function of the number of intervening pages.

To summarize, it would appear that the closer the question to the information it asks about, the higher the performance when that question is repeated later on the criterion test. It should be emphasized, however, that adjunct questions can have pronounced effects on repeated test items even when batched after lengthy passages (R. C. Anderson & Myrow, 1971; Sones & Stroud, 1940). Spitzer (1939) had 3,600 sixth graders read a 577-word passage about a United States Department of Agriculture Experimental Station. At various times thereafter groups of subjects received a 25-item multiple-choice test covering the passage. At no time were the students told the answers to any of the questions. The solid line in Fig. 1 traces the performance of groups the first time they received the test. The dashed lines represent performance on the test for the second or third time. While the greatest benefits were from taking the test immediately, they were still substantial when it was given a day or even a week later.

No effect of the timing of adjunct questions on new test items has been clearly demonstrated.

D. RESPONSE MODE OF QUESTIONS

Many investigators have employed either short-answer/completion or multiple-choice questions, so it is possible to get an impression of whether the mode of the questions makes a difference simply by sorting the studies. Table II shows the increment over the reading-only control group, averaged across all experiments, depending on the mode and position of the questions. Included in the short-answer tabulation are several studies which show that attempting to free recall a passage facilitates later attempts at free recall (Clark, 1940; Raffel, 1934; Van Matre, Aiken, Carter, Shennum, & Thomas, 1974). In every case the adjunct question mode and criterion test mode were the same. The figure in parentheses is the number of studies upon which the mean is based. As can be seen, both the direct and indirect effects are much stronger when short-answer questions are used.

This seems like a good place to emphasize the limitations of a "box score" review of the literature. It cannot be assumed that different studies are comparable. With respect to the experiments summarized in Table II, for instance, there is at least one possible bias. The studies of experienced investigators have generally involved short-answer tests whereas the studies reported in unpublished doctoral theses more frequently have entailed multiple-choice items. The point is that while sifting the literature can give a preliminary indication of whether a factor is important, there is no substitute for a direct experimental test.

We know of three studies that have compared short-answer with multiple-choice questions. In each case the two kinds of items were

TABLE II

AVERAGE PROPORTION BY WHICH QUESTIONED
GROUP EXCEEDS READING-ONLY CONTROL
GROUP ON THE CRITERION TEST AS A
FUNCTION OF THE MODE AND
POSITION OF ADJUNCT QUESTIONS

Question condition	Mode of questions	
	Short answer	Multiple choice
After passage		
Repeated	.201(9)	.089(13)
New	.070(11)	.020(14)
Before passage		
Repeated	.201(5)	.060(7)
New	−.019(6)	−.041(7)

in one-to-one correspondence, differing only with respect to the presence or absence of a set of response alternatives. Roderick and Anderson (1968) had high-school students and college undergraduates study either a 3,400-word programmed text or 1,800 words of ordinary text on classical conditioning. Immediately thereafter half the subjects completed a short-answer test followed by a matched multiple-choice test. A week later everyone received the tests. Taking the initial test had a much more pronounced effect on the delayed short-answer test than on the delayed multiple-choice test. Anderson and Myrow (1971) obtained similar results in a study involving a 2,240-word passage describing a fictitious primitive tribe. Again, adjunct short-answer and multiple-choice questions answered after reading the entire passage had a substantially greater impact on the short-answer than the multiple-choice portion of the test given a week later.

Frase (1968a) did not find a difference between short-answer and multiple-choice adjunct questions, but there is reason to discount his result. An elaborate design was employed. The other factors included the position and timing of the adjunct questions and whether the criterion test items were new or repeated. Therefore, the study may not have provided a sensitive test of the mode-of-question factor. Probably more important, in the light of studies to be reviewed below, short-answer and multiple-choice criterion test items were not differentiated in the analysis of the data.

Research on programmed instruction confirms and further illuminates the effects of question mode. Williams (1963) found no overall
difference in criterion test performance between a group of college
undergraduates who completed a "constructed-response" (i.e., completion and short-answer) version of a lengthy psychology program
and a group that completed a multiple-choice version. Both of these
groups did better than groups that read the program with the blanks
filled in. The constructed-response group scored higher than the
multiple-choice group on criterion test items which required the
student to respond with novel, technical terms. Williams (1965)
replicated these findings in an experiment in which sixth graders
received a zoology program. There was no difference between program modes on the multiple-choice section of the criterion test, but
the group that received the constructed-response program was superior on the short-answer section. As predicted, the constructed-
response program was significantly better when the test items required a novel, technical term as the answer, whereas the versions of
the program did not differ with respect to items that could be
answered with familiar vocabulary.

While it is possible to produce facilitation on repeated criterion test
items with multiple-choice adjunct questions, the evidence seems to
be conclusive that the effects are stronger with short-answer questions. Short-answer questions also tend to have a greater influence
than multiple-choice questions on new criterion test items, though
this cannot be regarded as definitely established.

A straightforward interpretation of the facts about response mode
is that adjunct questions primarily act on the retrievability of information, rather than on decisions about information once retrieved.
Under this interpretation it is the response mode of the criterion test
that is important. Another possibility is that short-answer and multiple-choice questions make different processing demands when inserted in text, thereby differentially affecting study activities. Were
this the case it would be the response mode of the adjunct questions
which was important. At the present time, there is no way to choose
between these explanations since in every study completed to date
the mode of the test items has paralleled the mode of the adjunct
questions.

E. EFFECTS OF FEEDBACK

Several experiments have studied the effects of providing feedback
in connection with adjunct questions. By "feedback" is meant dis-

playing the correct answer after the subject has had an opportunity to respond. Feedback markedly enhances performance on repeated criterion test items, regardless of the position of the adjunct questions (Frase, 1967; Maccoby, Michael, & Levine, 1961; Michael & Maccoby, 1961; Rothkopf, 1966; Throop, 1971). Incidentally, though, feedback has been provided in less than one third of the adjunct questioning studies, and the direct effect on repeated test items can be very substantial even when it is not given (cf. McGaw & Grotelueschen, 1972; Rothkopf, 1966; Spitzer, 1939).

In three experiments (Frase, 1967; Michael & Maccoby, 1961; Rothkopf, 1966) the subjects who had received feedback did slightly, but not significantly, less well on new test items than the appropriate control subjects who were questioned but got no feedback; in the other studies cited above those who got feedback did slightly better.

F. IS AN OVERT RESPONSE REQUIRED?

If in one category are placed all of the experiments in which subjects were requested to make an explicit, written response to adjunct questions and in another category those studies in which either covert, mental answers were permitted or the description of procedure was ambiguous, it is apparent that both the direct and indirect effects of adjunct questions are more consistent when the subject must make an overt response.

A number of programmed instruction experiments have compared overt responding, covert responding, and reading without questions or blanks to be filled. When care has been taken to design the programs so that the person must study the critical material in order to answer correctly, the requirement to make overt responses has proved facilitative (R. C. Anderson, 1967; Holland & Kemp, 1965; Kemp & Holland, 1966).

One experiment has studied the type of response required to answer adjunct questions. Michael and Maccoby (1961) showed a 14-min film to 1,029 high school juniors and seniors in 49 classrooms. The film was interrupted three times for "participation sessions" during which questions were asked. The mean proportion correct on repeated criterion test items for control subjects who saw the film without questions was .53, while subjects who mentally composed answers averaged .66, and those who wrote answers averaged .70. There were no differences among the three conditions on new test items.

G. MOTIVATION AND ADJUNCT QUESTIONS

There is some indication that background motivation, which would affect both questioned and nonquestioned subjects, reduces the increment in performance due to adjunct questions. Maccoby *et al.* (1961) argued that they had previously failed (Michael & Maccoby, 1961) to get an effect from adjunct questions on new test items because the film was intrinsically interesting. It was about civilian defense against atomic bombing, and the study (the date of the report notwithstanding) was completed shortly after Russia had exploded its first nuclear device. Maccoby *et al.* (1961) showed a "dull educational film" tracing the history of world map concepts to 993 air force trainees. In addition to the usual improvement on repeated test items, adjunct questions had a small but significant effect on new items, but it appeared only when the test was not announced in advance. As predicted, announcing the test in advance washed out the indirect questioning effect.[2] Frase *et al.* (1970) gave subjects either 0¢, 3¢, or 10¢ for each answer correct on the criterion test. The difference between questioned and nonquestioned groups was a decreasing function of the amount of the incentive.

Motivation to answer the adjunct questions correctly appears to enhance questioning effects. Rothkopf and Bloom (1970) and Rothkopf (1972) compared written adjunct questions, embedded after every six pages of a 100-page geology text, with the same questions asked orally by a person. In each experiment, high-school students who were asked oral questions did better on both repeated and new criterion test items. The sensible interpretation is that having a person ask the questions increased the incentive to study carefully.

H. NATURE OF THE QUESTIONS

Educational research workers generally do an inadequate job of characterizing the questions included in their tests (R. C. Anderson, 1972). It is not astonishing, therefore, though still embarrassing, that even in research on questioning there is often little information about what sorts of questions were asked and how these questions related to the text. Based on the descriptions of the few investigators who have provided unequivocal information, inference from the

---

[2] It is questionable whether this is a generalizable finding. Many studies have obtained indirect facilitation even when the test was announced to everyone in advance.

sketchy characterizations provided by others, and information in the appendices of theses, the typical adjunct question (and criterion test item) probably involves a statement lifted in close-to-verbatim form from the text. A key word or phrase—usually a proper name, technical term, or measured quantity—has been deleted. The task is to supply the deleted element or select it from among a list of alternatives. There have been no guidelines for deciding which sentences ought to serve as the basis for questions, or which elements of the chosen sentences should become the response terms (cf. Bormuth, 1970). Everybody has been flying by the seat of his pants.

There are two reasons for being interested in questions which require more than recall of specific "facts." First, the practical educator is, or should be, more concerned with whether students understand concepts and principles than whether they can recall details. Second, as will be explained at length in the following sections of this paper, the most persuasive theory is that adjunct questions affect criterion test performance by influencing the processing activities of readers. If one subscribes to the view that there are various possible levels of processing (cf. R. C. Anderson, 1970; Craik & Lockhart, 1972), it stands to reason that questions which require comprehension of the text will promote deeper processing, and therefore more learning and better remembering, than questions that can be answered on the basis of surface features.

Several studies (e.g., Berliner, Shavelson, Ravitch, & Loeding, 1973) have gotten positive results with "higher order" questions. However, we shall review here just the two studies we know of that have employed both questions requiring comprehension and closely comparable verbatim questions.

Watts and Anderson (1971) asked 300 high-school seniors to answer an adjunct question after reading each of five 450-word passages explaining a psychological principle. A set of questions for a passage was prepared according to the following recipe: Given the name of the principle, the subject had to select an example from among a list of four possibilities. In half the questions the correct alternative repeated an example used to illustrate the principle in the text. The remaining questions entailed new examples different from any described in the text. Subjects received one question of one of the types after each passage.

To make concrete the distinction between repeated- and new-example questions, there was a passage about displacement. An example of displacement which appeared in the text and a repeated-example question was, "John failed to make the basketball squad because he

was too small so he practiced hard to win a cheerleader's position."
The example of displacement which appeared in one of the "application" questions was, "When punished for sucking his thumb
Timmy stopped that habit but spent hours chewing gum given him
by his grandmother." The distractors used in any set of repeated-
example and new-example questions were constructed in such a
manner that they could be freely exchanged among questions without affecting the relationship between the distractors and the correct
alternative.

Subjects in the Watts and Anderson (1971) study who received
adjunct new-example questions performed significantly better overall
on the criterion test than all other subjects, including subjects that
received the otherwise identical questions that repeated examples
from the text. The latter group showed no advantage over a group
which got adjunct questions requiring identification of the name of
the psychologist associated with each principle or the reading-only
control group. Especially noteworthy was the performance on criterion test items involving new examples, different for each subject
from any he/she had seen before in either the text or an adjunct
question. The mean proportions correct on these items were .67, .53,
.45, and .50 for new-example, repeated-example, name, and reading-
only groups, respectively.[3]

Felker (1974; see also Dapra & Felker, 1974) generally confirmed
the findings of Watts and Anderson. Introductory psychology students read fifteen 20-line passages drawn from a book on operant
and respondent conditioning. Before or after each passage the subjects answered a multiple-choice adjunct question, either a verbatim
or a comprehension one. "Verbatim questions required rote memory
or recognition of exact words from the text. Comprehension questions were paraphrases of text statements and required responses that
implied understanding of the literal message contained in the prose
and the ability to abstract and apply information to new situations
[p. 12]." Each verbatim question was selected to be equivalent in
content and focus to the adjunct comprehension question associated
with the same prose segment. One of the criterion measures was a
"problem solving" test in which the subject had to write short essays

[3] The previously unencountered, new-example test items discussed here were not "new" in
the sense used throughout the rest of this paper. Quite the contrary for the new-example
adjunct question groups. Since the adjunct questions and the test items involved different
examples of the same principles, the semantic content, though not the surface form, was
repeated. Thus, according to the usage elsewhere in this paper, these items are most
appropriately classified as repeated.

applying principles and concepts explicated in the text to new situations. Here is an example:

> You have conditioned a friend to remove his hand from a control stick whenever a red light comes on by shocking his hand several times a few seconds after the red light. You now want him to unlearn this response. That is, you do not want him to remove his hand automatically whenever the red light comes on. *Briefly* describe how you would make your friend unlearn this response. [p. 34]

One point was scored for each of the following: listing the CS, listing the UCS, listing the CR, indicating that the CS should be presented without the UCS, indicating that there should be several nonpairings, and stating that the CS eventually will not elicit the CR. On five such essays the group that got adjunct comprehension questions after the relevant passages averaged .59 of the possible points. The pooled proportion for the remaining groups, which differed negligibly, was .46. There were no differences among conditions on two additional criterion tests, one of which involved new multiple-choice verbatim items, the other new multiple-choice comprehension items.

Of practical interest is the fact that adjunct questions can do more than increase the accuracy with which people are able to repeat strings of words. Of both theoretical and practical interest is the indication that adjunct questions which entail paraphrase and application of principles and concepts to new situations may be especially facilitative, particularly when the criterion test makes similar demands.

I. OTHER FACTORS

Neither the total length of the text, the topic, the age of the subject, nor the medium of presentation (text, taped lecture, film) seem to matter much. At least, positive results from adjunct questions have been obtained over a range of each of these factors. However, a review of the literature by Rosenshine (1974) indicates that no clear conclusions are warranted regarding the extemporaneous oral questions of live teachers in ordinary classroom settings.

IV. Explanations for the Indirect Effects of Adjunct Questions

The primary interest in adjunct questions has been with their indirect effects. Just about all of the mechanisms that have been proposed have tried to account for indirect effects. We will first look at these explanations.

A. SPECIFIC TRANSFER

One of the first explanations that comes to mind for the indirect facilitation produced by adjunct questions is a possible specific instructive effect, that is, that learning the answer to one question could give the answer to another. Rothkopf's (1966) experiment discounted this explanation. He emphasized that "The EQs [adjunct questions] were selected so as to minimize transfer of training from the portions of text underlying these 14 questions to the material underlying the remaining 25 [criterion] items [p. 242]." More important, a transfer evaluation group was included in the study. The subjects took one form of the criterion test and then were drilled on the adjunct questions until they could answer each correctly. There was no gain in performance on an alternate form of the criterion test from having mastered the adjunct questions and answers. This substantiates the claim that facilitation observed in other groups was not due to transfer. Rothkopf and Bisbicos (1967) included similar controls.

Although Rothkopf found no direct transfer effects from inserted questions, it cannot be safely assumed that such effects do not exist. His results indicate that direct transfer is not sufficient to explain the indirect effects of questions. However, there are indications that other investigators may not have generated questions in the same careful manner. No other studies have included control groups to check empirically for transfer. Therefore, some of the facilitative effects that have been reported on new criterion items may have been due to transfer.

B. ARE QUESTIONS NECESSARY?

Another possible explanation of the effects on new criterion test items is that the questions simply identify the important material or in some way review it for the student. Is it necessary to use a question format or will a review statement perform the same function? Bruning (1968) directly compared review statements with adjunct questions. For each section of the reading passage a pair of review statements was prepared. One statement was related to material on the criterion test and the other was unrelated to the criterion test. A question was constructed from each statement by deleting a key term. The questions produced significantly better criterion test performance than statements. All of the groups except the one receiving criterion-irrelevant statements performed better than the read-only control group. This study indicates that both the questioning procedure and review statements do facilitate retention of text material, but that a question is superior to an expository statement with the same content.

C. MUST THE QUESTIONS BE RELEVANT TO THE TEXT?

Bruning's study suggests that the interrogatory format is at least in part responsible for the facilitative effects of adjunct questions. But do the adjunct questions need to be related to the material being read? Perhaps a question provides a break that gives release from fatigue or boredom. Two studies (McGaw & Grotelueschen, 1972; Rothkopf, 1972) have addressed this issue. Both included groups who were asked questions irrelevant to the text material as well as various groups asked relevant questions and a read-only control group. McGaw and Grotelueschen used items from a personal opinion scale for their irrelevant questions. Rothkopf (1972) presented a lengthy earth-science passage via rear projected slides. An example of an irrelevant question, which was asked orally, was, "Is the focus of the slide projector satisfactory?" In neither experiment was the irrelevant-question group better than the read-only control.

D. THE MATHEMAGENIC HYPOTHESIS

What this hypothesis says is that readers who encounter questions will begin to process the text more thoroughly in order to be able to answer succeeding questions. "Mathemagenic" is a word coined by Rothkopf. It is derived from the Greek roots *mathema*—learning, that which is learned—and *gignesthai*—to be born. Mathemagenic activities, then, are the activities that give birth to learning.

Rothkopf and Bisbicos (1967) visualized the mathemagenic explanation of questioning as follows:

> The most plausible conception is a kind of adaptive evolution of mathemagenic behaviors, with questions providing selective contingencies. Mathemagenic behaviors, according to this view, are extinguished and dropped if they do not result in learning the skills necessary to answer the experimental

questions. On the other hand, mathemagenic behaviors which preceded successful performance on experimental questions would be strengthened. As a consequence the SA [shortly after relevant passage] treatments would be more likely to result in the acquisition of adaptive (i.e., successful) mathemagenic responses than the SB [shortly before relevant passage] or the NOEQ [No Experimental Question] conditions [p. 60].

There are several lines of evidence consistent with the mathemagenic hypothesis. First, it handles neatly the fact that questions before the passage have a negative effect on new criterion test items: readers tend to hunt for the answers to the adjunct questions, paying less attention to the rest of the text.

Second, if subjects who receive adjunct questions are paying closer attention they should spend more time studying the text, especially later sections, than nonquestioned subjects. This expectation generally has been confirmed (Morasky & Wilcox, 1970; Rothkopf, 1965; Rothkopf & Bloom, 1970). Corrozi (1970) found, as he had predicted, that the indirect facilitation from adjunct questions disappeared when time constraints were placed on the reader. Morasky (1972) observed more fixations and regressions per paragraph on the part of subjects who received questions after paragraphs than on the part of those who received no questions or questions before paragraphs.

The most subtle evidence for the mathemagenic hypothesis is that adjunct questions can selectively facilitate the learning of restricted categories of text information. Rothkopf and Bisbicos (1967) asked some subjects adjunct questions that could be answered with either a common English word or a technical term. Others always received questions that required measured quantities or proper names as answers. On new name and measure criterion test items, those who had gotten name and measure adjunct questions did best. This effect was most pronounced on items relating to the second half of the text. The same trends appeared with respect to new common word and technical term criterion items on the part of those who had received this type of adjunct question, although the differences here were small and not statistically significant. Such effects as did appear were due mainly to the technical term items. The failure to get selective effects with common-word questions can be plausibly explained. Most of the words in a text are common ones. Even if subjects were aware that they were being asked questions involving common words it may have been a practical impossibility to attend differentially to them.

Quellmalz (1972) attempted to replicate Rothkopf and Bisbicos

(1967) employing proper name and application-to-new-example questions. She hypothesized that if selective facilitation were operating, performance on new criterion items involving text information relevant to the class of text-embedded questions would gradually improve over the passage, while performance on new items based on text information of the other type would decrease. Quellmalz believed that changing the class of adjunct questions halfway through the passage would provide a more rigorous test of selective facilitation. Readers would be required to shift the focus of their attention, and performance on the second class of information would build up gradually in the second half of the passage. For half the subjects, questions requiring as answers names of persons were used for the first half of the text, and questions requiring application of principles were employed for the second half. The assignment was reversed for the remaining subjects.

Quellmalz's subjects did substantially better on new-name items for the section about which they had been asked name questions and substantially better on new-application items for the section about which they had been asked application questions. Performance was further broken down into items related to the first nine and second nine pages of each half of the text. Following Rothkopf and Bisbicos, Quellmalz had expected to find greater enhancement on the second nine pages, but the advantage was nearly as great on the first nine pages. The distinctiveness of the two classes of questions may explain the failure to find a gradual focusing on the relevant material. The subjects probably were able to recognize the shift in type of question immediately and adapt their study strategies accordingly.

The mathemagenic hypothesis was originally couched in behaviorist terms. Over the years the language has become increasingly cognitive. Looking at just the adjunct-questioning literature, there is no strong reason to prefer a cognitive to a behaviorist account. The behaviorist version is somewhat embarrassed by the lack of an identifiable reinforcer to "shape inspection behavior." The obvious candidate is feedback following the adjunct questions; however, feedback has a negligible effect on new test items. One could suppose that the feeling of certainty a person has that he has answered a question correctly gives rise to "self-reinforcement." That seems to us to be grasping at nonbehavioral straws.

Most investigators have waved in the direction of the mathemagenic hypothesis when rationalizing research on adjunct questions, but pitifully few could actually be said to have tested on implication from the theory. Like many areas of educational research, this one is infected with a mindless empiricism. We do not need another demonstration that adjunct questions "work." Surely serious application of questioning techniques in the real world of instruction will require knowing why they work and under what conditions.

E. INDIRECT REVIEW HYPOTHESIS

Frase (1967) has suggested that adjunct questions placed after a passage may cause a person to review mentally the material he/she has just read. While a number of findings are generally consistent with this hypothesis, it was first directly supported in a clever experiment by McGaw and Grotelueschen (1972). The heart of the procedure was the choice of three questions for each page, such that two dealt with the same material while the third was derived from unrelated material. The two "matched" questions were constructed so that neither could be answered from knowledge of the other. The following is an example of a paragraph and the questions developed from it:

> Then from the surveying ship Bulldog, examining a proposed northern route for a cable from Faroe to Labrador in 1860, came another report. The Bulldog's sounding line, which at one place had been allowed to lie for some time on the bottom at a depth of 1260 fathoms, came up with 13 starfish clinging to it [p. 581].

The two matched questions were:

> (a) The surveying ship which recovered starfish from a depth of 1260 fathoms in 1860, was exploring a route for a cable from Faroe to ———.
> (b) The surveying ship ———, which recovered starfish from a depth of 1260 fathoms in 1860, was exploring a route for a cable from Faroe.

The third, "unmatched" question from the same page required the name of an Arctic explorer. One of the matched questions was inserted in the text. The other matched question and the unmatched question appeared only on the criterion test.

McGaw and Grotelueschen found, relative to the reading-only control, better performance on matched than unmatched criterion items. The effect was strongest on items drawn from pages immediately preceding adjunct questions. Rothkopf and Billington (1974) have replicated these findings.

The fact that performance is enhanced on criterion items matched to the adjunct questions implies some form of mental review (naturally the procedures prevented actual, physical review). However, the research has not yet clarified whether the critical part of the matching relationship is spatiotemporal contiguity or topical-semantic similarity.

Not all of the facts about the effects of questions on new test items can be reasonably accounted for by the indirect review hypothesis. To handle all the data, it would appear necessary to postulate at least two processes, a "forward," mathemagenic process and a "backward," review process.

F. AROUSAL

Natkin and Stahler (1969) have suggested that questions may arouse subjects. Following Kleinsmith and Kaplan (1964), they predicted relatively better performance on a delayed than an immediate criterion test. Half their subjects got adjunct questions in connection with a preliminary passage. The purpose of this maneuver was to habituate the subjects and, hence, reduce the arousal potential of questions. They did find, as predicted, that habituated subjects who received adjunct questions in connection with the target passage did better on the immediate criterion test but worse on the delayed criterion test than nonhabituated subjects. However, Watts (1973) has failed in two large experiments to replicate these findings.

Bull (1971) compared adjunct questions rated in a pilot study as having high- or low-arousal value. Groups receiving these questions did not differ significantly from each other or from control groups.

Based on the evidence now available, arousal does not seem to be a promising construct for explaining the effects of adjunct questions.

V. Toward an Account of the Direct Effects of Questions

Even though the direct effects of questions are invariably more robust, it is the indirect effects which have captured the lion's share of the attention of research workers in recent years, perhaps precisely because the indirect effects are subtle and nonobvious. The purpose of the research reported in this section was to study further the large and obvious direct effects of questioning.

The general working hypothesis was that an adjunct question sets the occasion for mental review and further cognitive processing of text information. When the quiz question happens to make contact with temporarily-stored information, it is theorized that there is some probability that this information will be transferred into long-term, semantic memory. A question would not be expected to affect information already in long-term memory. Nor, of course, could a question alone influence information that had not been learned at all. Presumably when the adjunct questions are inserted a few at a time after short segments of text the direct effect of the questions is a confluence of the mathemagenic process discussed in the preceding section and the hypothesized review process. The questions were batched at the end of the passage in the studies reported here in order to rule out a mathemagenic interpretation.

The specific hypothesis was that the direct effects of questioning will be enhanced when the questions require semantic encoding of the information. Verbatim and paraphrase questions were compared. The idea was that paraphrase questions after the passage would occasion meaningful processing of the text information in temporary storage whereas verbatim questions could be processed in terms of orthographic or phonological features. It was expected, therefore, that people who initially got paraphrase questions would perform better on the criterion test than people who initially received verbatim questions.

There is a really strong case that procedures which make probably semantic encoding facilitate learning from sentences and discourse (cf. Barclay, 1973; Bobrow & Bower, 1969). For instance, R. C. Anderson and Kulhavy (1972) asked college students to study one-sentence definitions of a series of unfamiliar words. Students who created and said aloud a sensible sentence containing each defined word did markedly better on a test that involved identifying appropriate uses of the words than students who read each definition aloud. The point is that it cannot be assumed, to paraphrase Gertrude Stein, that rehearsal is rehearsal is rehearsal. The character or quality of the rehearsal is crucial (cf. Craik & Watkin, 1973). That stage-encoding or levels-of-processing notions may have application in the arena of questioning is suggested by a couple of studies reviewed earlier (Felker, 1974; Watts & Anderson, 1971).

The theory sketched so far may seem to make unusual and unsupportable assumptions about the time course of memory. The shortest intervals investigated in research on questioning have been in the neighborhood of a minute (see section on the timing of questions). Short-term memory is thought of in durations of a few seconds. Indeed, there is evidence which suggests that memory for the literal, surface form of a message persists for about the duration of a clause, or a sentence at most (Jarvella, 1971; Jarvella & Herman, 1972;

Sachs, 1967). If memory for surface features is so transient, how could questions asked several minutes after exposure to discourse make contact with such information?

The first answer to this question is that there is experimental evidence that under some conditions information coded in acoustic or articulatory form can be remembered for a relatively long time (cf. R. C. Anderson, 1971; Glanzer, Koppenal, & Nelson, 1972; Posner & Warren, 1972). Common experience supports the same conclusion. Everyone has learned a poem or song in a foreign language, which he/she can repeat despite having not the slightest idea of what it means.

To suggest that surface information can be available minutes after exposure to text is not to imply that the whole message is coded like a tape recording. A more reasonable view is that, while much of a message may be semantically coded, fragments may remain stored in more superficial form. Perhaps that which is semantically coded provides a framework that keeps the nonsemantically coded portions accessible.

The final issue investigated in this series of experiments was whether answering a question causes a person to get the meaning from a communication or whether, on the other hand, it merely causes him/her to learn the surface form of the message. This is an issue that ought to be raised with respect to any instructional treatment. It is especially relevant to an evaluation of the direct effects of questioning, since in most previous studies the criterion test has repeated the initial questions in literal, verbatim form. It would not be unreasonable to suppose that the direct effect of questions entails nothing more than rote learning of the ortho-graphic-acoustic features of the initial questions. Half of the subjects in the experiments reported herein received a criterion test in which each question was a paraphrase of a question answered earlier. For these subjects, in other words, the test repeated the semantic content but not the lexical form of the initial questions. If the direct effect of questions is one of learning meanings, these subjects would do better than control subjects on the semantically equivalent new questions, whereas to the extent that the effect is simply a matter of learning surface forms the people who got the initial questions would have an advantage only on criterion test questions that had been repeated verbatim.

In the first experiment the subjects received a set of verbatim or paraphrase questions either immediately after reading the passage or after a 20-min filled interval. A week later everyone took the criterion test. The predictions were (*a*) that persons who got the paraphrase quiz would do better on the criterion test than those who received the verbatim quiz and (*b*) that persons who completed an immediate quiz would do better on the test than people who took it after a 20-min interval, because after an interval the information which potentially could have been affected by a quiz would no longer be available.

A. EXPERIMENT 1[4]

1. Method

a. Subjects. Participating were 240 sophomores, juniors, and seniors from the high school in a farming community in central Illinois.

b. Materials. Two versions of a 550-word passage on army ants were written. The versions were identical except for 15 important sentences or clauses which were judged to convey the main ideas of the text. Each important sentence or clause in one version was paraphrased in the other version; that is, it was written to be equivalent in meaning to the sentence in the first version but to contain no substantive words in common, except technical terms for which it was difficult to find synonyms. For instance, one version of the passage contained the following important sentence: *To a great extent the colony's cohesion results from secretions from the queen that are attractive to the workers.* The matched sentence in the other version was, *The greatest factor in keeping the nest together is chemical odors from the queen that the workers find pleasant.*

A multiple-choice test item was prepared for each important sentence. A segment of the sentence was removed. The remainder was transformed into a question. The deleted segment served as the correct answer choice. To complete the item, three plausible wrong answer choices were invented. The items constructed for the matching sentences from the two versions of the passage were in one-to-one correspondence. Equivalent segments of the sentences served as correct response alternatives. The same three distractors were employed. The end result was that each form of the test contained verbatim items with respect to one of the versions of the passage and paraphrase items with respect to the other.

[4] John Surber ran this experiment; he also made important contributions to Experiments 2 and 3. Claire Lieberman and Peter Zych assisted in each of the first three experiments.

c. Design and Procedure. The design entailed four orthogonal factors. Subjects read one of the two versions of the passage; completed a verbatim quiz, a paraphrase quiz, or no quiz; and a week later took a verbatim or paraphrase delayed test. Half of the subjects who took the quiz did so immediately after reading the passage, the remainder after 20 min. Subjects were stratified *ex post facto* into three levels of verbal ability on the basis of the Wide Range Vocabulary Test (French, Ekstrom, & Price, 1963). No-quiz subjects worked on additional aptitude tests to fill the time taken by the quiz.

The experiment was run in the school cafeteria in two shifts of about 120 subjects. Subjects were assigned to conditions simply by distributing randomly-ordered stacks of booklets containing the experimental material. Instructions mimeographed on the first page of the booklet stated that the passage should be read carefully, that no notes should be taken, that the reader should stop at the end of the passage or when told to stop, and that a test would be given. Instructions preceding the quiz emphasized that no one should look back at the passage. Color coding of the pages in the experimental booklet made it easy for the three assistants who were monitoring the students to make sure this direction was followed. Not even the teachers were informed that a delayed test would be given a week later. Ample time was allowed for every subject to complete every phase of the experiment.

2. Results

Tables III and IV contain mean proportions correct on the quiz and test under the various conditions which prevailed in the experiment. Overall, students who received a quiz averaged .62 on the criterion test whereas those who did not receive one averaged .55, $t(238) = 3.16$, $p < .01$. However, two specific hypotheses could not be confirmed in the form outlined earlier. First, students who took the immediate quiz averaged .64 on the test as compared to .60 for the people who completed the quiz 20 min after reading the passage, which is not a significant difference, $F(1,125) = 2.34$, $p = .13$. Second, to our considerable surprise, the delayed test mean for the groups that got a verbatim quiz was actually higher than the mean for the groups that received a paraphrase quiz, though not significantly so, $F(1,125) = 2.26$, $p = .14$.

Performance was substantially better on the verbatim than the paraphrase quiz, $F(1,125) = 22.87$, $p < .01$, and also better on the verbatim than the paraphrase test, $F(1,181) = 5.63$, $p < .05$.

TABLE III

UNWEIGHTED MEAN PROPORTIONS
CORRECT ON THE QUIZ

	Time of quiz	
Form	Immediate	Delayed
Verbatim	.80	.72
Paraphrase	.64	.63

There was a larger difference between scores on the verbatim form of the criterion test (considering just control subjects who were being exposed to questions for the first time) and the verbatim form of the immediate quiz than between scores on the paraphrase forms of the test and immediate quiz, $t(149) = 3.76$, $p < .01$. In other words, performance declined more sharply over the retention interval on verbatim than paraphrase questions.

There was a significant Form of Quiz X Form of Test interaction, $F(1,125) = 6.40$, $p < .05$. Scores on the delayed test were highest when the test form matched the quiz form. Also appearing, however, in the analysis of the quiz scores, was a significant Time of Quiz X Form of Quiz X Form of Test interaction, $F(1,125) = 5.79$, $p < .05$. Since the delayed test had not been administered yet, this must mean that the groups were not initially equivalent, presumably because of a random perturbation. If differences among groups on the quiz were

TABLE IV

UNWEIGHTED MEAN PROPORTIONS
CORRECT ON THE CRITERION TEST

	Form of test	
Quiz condition	Verbatim	Paraphrase
Immediate verbatim	.74	.61
Immediate paraphrase	.58	.62
20-Min verbatim	.64	.56
20-Min paraphrase	.60	.60
No quiz	.59	.51

discounted, the interaction involving delayed-test scores would largely disappear.

Verbal ability affected both quiz performance, $F(2,125) = 30.34$, $p < .01$, and delayed test performance, $F(2,181) = 26.86$, $p < .01$. Also obtained were significant effects for Passage and Passage X Ability. These will not be discussed.

3. Discussion

We had confidently expected the paraphrase quiz to facilitate delayed test performance more than the verbatim quiz. The fact that the trend of the results ran in the opposite direction caused us to revise our theory. It is now argued that the process by which a quiz question enhances delayed retention involves two stages. First, the question must permit retrieval of information from "temporary" memory.[5] Second, the question must instigate meaningful processing of the information so as to transfer it into long term, semantic memory. This theory can be expressed in the following equation,

$$P(D) = k + (1 - k)rt,$$

which says that the probability of a correct response on the delayed test, $P(D)$, equals the proportion of items of information the person already knows, k, either information he knows beforehand or learns from reading the passage, plus an increment due to taking the quiz. The increment consists of that information not already known which the questions cause the person to retrieve, r, from temporary, phono-logical memory and transfer, t, into long-term, semantic memory.

Below are estimators for the three parameters, letting C be the mean proportion correct of the no-quiz control group, and Q_j and F_j be the proportion correct for the jth group on the quiz and criterion (final) test, respectively.

$$\hat{k} = C$$

$$\hat{r}_j = \frac{Q_j - C}{1 - C}$$

$$\hat{t}_j = \frac{F_j - C}{Q_j - C}$$

---

[5] We will say "temporary" rather than "short-term" because we are hypothesizing longer lived memory than most theorists who have used the expression "short-term."

The parameters were calculated for the present data using simply the mean quiz and delayed test scores, pooling over the two forms of the test. Obtained were values of r of .48 and .20 and values of t of .42 and .58 for the verbatim and paraphrase quiz groups, respectively. From the perspective of the model there is a measure of support for our original contention that paraphrase questions would be better than verbatim questions at promoting the transfer of information into long term storage. On the other hand, verbatim items proved vastly better at evoking retrieval of the information to begin with. It is not difficult to understand why. Temporary memory is largely phonological in character. A matching phonological string can be produced given a verbatim cue but not a paraphrased one.

The augmented theory further illuminates the effects to be expected from the timing of questions. Only verbatim questions can tap a large proportion of the information in temporary memory; so, the length of the interval between reading the passage and answering the questions should be important only for performance on verbatim questions. In the analysis already reported which failed to show an effect due to the timing of the quiz, the verbatim and paraphrase quiz groups were pooled. The picture changes when just the groups that received a verbatim quiz are considered. There was a significant difference between immediate and 20-min verbatim quiz scores, $t(85) = 2.57$, $p < .05$. Also significant was the difference in test scores of the groups that had received immediate and 20-min verbatim quizzes, $t(85) = 2.33$, $p < .05$.

B. EXPERIMENT 2

A main purpose of the second experiment was to test a nonobvious prediction from the theory developed during the postmortem on the first experiment: an optimum treatment should be a verbatim quiz followed by a paraphrase quiz. According to the augmented theory a verbatim question allows retrieval of phonologically coded information in temporary memory. Thus primed, the information is more likely to be accessible for meaningful processing instigated by the paraphrase question. The net result should be an increased likelihood that the information will get into permanent storage.

1. Method

Four hundred and twenty-two freshmen from a suburban high school read one of the two forms of the army ant passage and then completed a verbatim quiz, a paraphrase quiz, a verbatim quiz twice, a paraphrase quiz twice, a verbatim quiz followed by a paraphrase quiz, or paraphrase quiz followed by a verbatim quiz. One control group neither read the passage nor took a quiz. Another control group read the passage but did not receive a quiz. A week later everyone took a verbatim or paraphrase test. Subjects were stratified *ex post facto* into three levels of verbal ability. Procedures were the same as in Experiment 1.

2. Results

Performance on the quizzes and test is summarized in Tables V and VI. The initial analysis of the data involved four planned, orthogonal comparisons. It was expected, first, that reading the text would improve test performance. The mean proportion for groups exposed to the text was .53. The proportion for the control group that took the test without an opportunity to study the passage was .34. This difference is significant, $t(420) = 8.28$, $p < .01$.

Second, as expected, students who received a quiz averaged higher on the delayed test than students who did not receive a quiz, $t(329) = 1.71$, $p < .05$, though the difference was not very big, just .54 for the quiz groups as compared to .49 for the no-quiz group.

Third, the groups that completed two quizzes had a criterion test mean of .56 while the mean for the groups that completed one quiz was .49, an advantage for the two-quiz condition which had been predicted, $t(278) = 2.52$, $p < .01$. However, it happens that the groups that received one quiz performed worse (though not signifi-

TABLE V

UNWEIGHTED MEAN PROPORTIONS
CORRECT ON THE QUIZZES

Forms	Position of quiz	
	First	Second
Verbatim, verbatim	.69	.71
Verbatim, paraphrase	.71	.62
Verbatim	.64	–
Paraphrase, verbatim	.56	.56
Paraphrase, paraphrase	.61	.58
Paraphrase	.53	–

TABLE VI

UNWEIGHTED MEAN PROPORTIONS CORRECT
ON THE CRITERION TEST

	Form of test	
Quiz condition	Verbatim	Paraphrase
Verbatim, verbatim	.64	.52
Verbatim, paraphrase	.64	.56
Verbatim	.56	.41
Paraphrase, verbatim	.51	.54
Paraphrase, paraphrase	.54	.52
Paraphrase	.54	.45
No quiz	.50	.48
No passage, no quiz	.34	.34

cantly so) on the first quiz than did the two-quiz groups. This means the groups were not equivalent to begin with. Thus, it remains to be seen whether two quizzes are actually better than one.

The fourth and most interesting prediction was that students who received a verbatim quiz followed by a paraphrase quiz would do better on the criterion test than students who received other combinations of two quizzes. The prediction was confirmed, $t(183) = 1.73$, $p < .05$. The verbatim-paraphrase group averaged .60 on the test whereas the other two-quiz groups averaged .54.

One element of the argument that a verbatim quiz followed by a paraphrase quiz would maximally enhance delayed test performance was that the verbatim quiz would "prime" information so as to make it more accessible to the paraphrase questions. This contention was tested directly. The performance of the verbatim–paraphrase group on the paraphrase quiz was compared to the performance of the three groups that began with a paraphrase quiz. The latter groups averaged .57 whereas the verbatim–paraphrase group averaged .62. While in the predicted direction, the difference fell short of being significant, $t(178) = 1.41$.

The parameters of the model outlined earlier were computed for the groups that received just one kind of quiz. (It was not clear how to proceed with the mixed quiz conditions.) The values of r and t were .34 and .24, respectively, for the verbatim and verbatim–verbatim groups, and .16 and .31 for the paraphrase and paraphrase–paraphrase groups. These figures show the same trends as the ones obtained in the first experiment.

Students averaged .68 on the first verbatim quiz but only .57 on the first paraphrase quiz, $F(1,208) = 19.01$, $p < .01$. Similarly, the proportion on the verbatim form of the delayed test was .57 whereas the proportion on the paraphrase form was .50, $F(1,208) = 7.75$, $p < .01$. Performance was only slightly higher on the verbatim than the paraphrase second quiz, however, $F(1,138) = 1.44$. As already indicated, scores on the paraphrase quiz improved when preceded by a verbatim quiz. On the other hand, scores on a verbatim quiz were lower when it followed a paraphrase quiz. Verbatim scores dropped more from the first quiz to the delayed test (again considering the performance of only no-quiz subjects) than did paraphrase scores, $t(227) = 3.40$, $p < .01$.

As in the first experiment, students did somewhat better on the test when the form matched the form of the quiz, though this time the interaction was not significant, $F(1,208) = 3.04$, $p = .08$.

Verbal ability affected performance on the first quiz, $F(1,208) = 24.54$, $p < .01$, the second quiz, $F(1,208) = 28.17$, $p < .01$, and the test, $F(1,208) = 19.09$, $p < .01$. The only other F significant at the .05 level was for a five-way interaction involving second-quiz scores as the dependent variable.

3. Discussion

One of the most interesting findings of the first two experiments was a large and significant difference between verbatim and paraphrase quizzes, but a very small difference between the two forms of the test a week later (considering only no-quiz subjects).

Discounting guessing and previous knowledge, the assumption is that a person can answer a paraphrase question only if he has semantically encoded the relevant text information, whereas a verbatim item can be answered if the information has been encoded either semantically or phonologically (see R. C. Anderson, 1971, 1974). The second experiment included a control group that answered the questions without reading the passage. The difference of the scores of this group and the scores on the immediate quiz of the groups that did read the passage gives the amount of information acquired from reading, which was 34% for the group that got the immediate verbatim quiz but just two thirds as large, 23%, for the group that got the immediate paraphrase quiz. The conclusion would appear to be that one third of the "knowledge" that resulted from reading the passage depended upon asking questions which reinstated the exact language of the text. In simple, old fashioned terms, there was evidently a lot of rote learning going on.

Is there any escape from this conclusion? One alternative interpretation can be ruled out on the basis of the design and procedures. The fact that performance was higher on verbatim than paraphrase forms of quizzes and tests definitely cannot be attributed to the differential difficulty of the two forms, since the versions of the passage and forms of the quizzes and tests were counterbalanced. What was a paraphrase item for one subject was a verbatim item for the next.

Another possibility is that every proposition that was learned at all was semantically encoded. If, however, some of the paraphrases were rough the proposition still might not have been retrievable. (Inadequate paraphrase might also be a reason for failing to confirm our original hypothesis that paraphrase questions would enhance criterion test performance more than verbatim ones.) The only standard for the semantic equivalence of the sets of questions employed in the first two experiments was the intuition of the experimenters.

We began with the idea that a paraphrase quiz would lead to better test performance than a verbatim quiz. This hypothesis turned out badly. What we had overlooked in formulating the hypothesis was that information in temporary memory is phonologically coded, making it accessible to a verbatim question but relatively inaccessible to a paraphrased one.

An augmented theory seemed to turn out well. The data from both experiments described thus far supported the view that a verbatim question is more likely to allow retrieval of information from temporary memory whereas, once retrieved, a paraphrase question is more likely to instigate transfer of the information into long term, semantic memory. The second experiment confirmed a prediction from the theory: a verbatim quiz followed by a paraphrase quiz optimally facilitated delayed retention. Consistent with the dual-coding theory was the fact that performance was much higher on verbatim than paraphrase questions immediately after reading the passage and the fact that verbatim scores declined more sharply over the retention interval than did paraphrase scores.

C. Experiment 3[6]

This experiment involved two methodological innovations. First, the matched text sentences (upon which the adjunct questions and

---

[6] Experiment 3 was run by Bonnie Armbruster.

test items were based) from the two versions of the army ant passage were normed for semantic equivalence by a group of high-school students. Second, a pretest was given in an attempt to get control over an irrelevant source of variance. Whenever life-like materials are used, subjects will have varying degrees of pre-experimental knowledge.

The retrieve and transfer explanation of the direct effects of question which received a measure of support in Experiment 2 assumes that questions act on information that is stored in relatively temporary, close-to-surface form. However, the information could not be in working memory; otherwise it would not require priming by a verbatim question; it would already be accessible to a paraphrased probe. From this it follows that if paraphrase questions were inserted very shortly after exposure to the relevant text sentences, while the information was still in working memory, the retrieval stage would be bypassed. The result would be a direct advantage for paraphrase over verbatim questions. This hypothesis was investigated in Experiment 3.

1. Method

a. *Subjects.* The subjects were 356 juniors enrolled in American history classes in a suburban Chicago high school.

b. *Materials.* The army ant passages and tests were augmented with five additional items. Then versions of the passages were prepared in which the matched sentences were numbered. Eighty-eight students from a small town high school examined both passages and rated the numbered sections for equivalence in meaning. Only one pair had an average rating of worse than similar in meaning. This pair, and three others that up to one fifth of the students said they could not rate because they weren't sure they understood the constituent words, were eliminated. The remaining 16 pairs had a mean rating of 1.5 on a four-point scale in which "1" meant very similar in meaning.

c. *Design and Procedure.* The adjunct questions were either inserted after brief paragraphs or batched at the end of the passage. The order of the adjunct questions was the same whether they were inserted or batched. The other factors were form of passage, form of adjunct questions (verbatim or paraphrase), form of criterion test (verbatim or paraphrase), and level of verbal ability. Control groups received either no adjunct questions or neither the passage nor the adjunct questions. The day before the passage was presented all subjects took a verbatim pretest. The criterion test was administered a week after the passage. On every occasion in which tests or adjunct questions were given, subjects were exhorted not to guess wildly. In all other respects the procedure was the same as that of the previous experiments.

2. Results

Table VII displays the results on the adjunct questions. The measure is the proportion correct given a wrong response on the pretest. As can be seen, performance was better on inserted than batched questions, $F(1,214) = 18.96$, $p < .01$, and better on verbatim than paraphrase questions, $F(1,214) = 34.40$, $p < .01$.

Verbal ability made a difference, $F(2,214) = 22.06$, $p < .01$. There was also a significant Form of Questions X Ability interaction, $F(2,214) = 7.13$, $p < .01$. There was relatively little difference in performance on verbatim questions of students of high, average, and low ability, whereas on paraphrase questions performance fell off sharply as ability declined.

Table VIII contains mean proportion correct on the criterion test, given an error on the pretest, as a function of quiz condition. Not surprisingly those who read the passage performed much better than those who did not. More interesting was the fact that there was a large and significant, $t(322) = 3.58$, $p < .01$, increment due to receiving adjunct questions. However, neither the position, $F < 1$, nor the form, $F(1,214) = 1.90$, $p = .17$, made any difference.

Confirming the results of the first two experiments, there was a steeper drop in verbatim than paraphrase scores over the retention

TABLE VII

UNWEIGHTED MEAN PROPORTION
CORRECT ON AN ADJUNCT
QUESTION GIVEN AN
ERROR ON THE PRETEST

	Form of questions	
Position	Verbatim	Paraphrase
Inserted	.92	.80
Batched	.83	.70

TABLE VIII

UNWEIGHTED MEAN PROPORTION CORRECT
ON CRITERION TEST GIVEN ERROR
ON THE PRETEST

Quiz condition	Form of test	
	Verbatim	Paraphrase
Inserted verbatim	.72	.53
Inserted paraphrase	.60	.61
Batched verbatim	.73	.58
Batched paraphrase	.59	.61
No quiz	.52	.50
No passage, no quiz	.14	.14

interval, $t(186) = 3.30$, $p < .01$. This analysis involves the one-week scores of the control subjects and the scores on the batched adjunct questions.

The form of question, form of test interaction was significant, $F(1,214) = 10.47$, $p < .01$. As in Experiments 1 and 2, scores were highest when the wording of questions matched the wording of the test.

Verbal ability had the usual influence on performance, $F(2,214) = 24.95$, $p < .01$. Otherwise the only significant effects involved form of passage. These are uninteresting and will not be discussed.

3. Discussion

There was no support for the notion that paraphrase questions asked shortly after segments of prose would facilitate performance on a delayed criterion test. A precondition was met: people did do better on paraphrase questions when they were inserted rather than batched. But this gain did not eventuate in an increment on the criterion test.

It is possible that the verbatim pretest enhanced the effect of the verbatim adjunct questions. This might explain why people who received paraphrase questions did not surpass people who got verbatim questions; however, it could not explain the failure of those who got inserted paraphrase questions to surpass those who got batched paraphrase questions.

One point seems almost axiomatic: a treatment will have less effect on questions a person is able to answer beforehand than on ones he/she cannot answer. The ω^2 for treatment in an analysis which included both the no-quiz and the no-passage/no-quiz control groups was .65 when the dependent variable was a right answer on the criterion test given a *wrong* answer on the pretest, but only .11 when the dependent variable was a right answer on the criterion test given a *right* answer on the pretest. The moral is that experiments using real prose can be made more sensitive by employing conditional measures.

Another point which would appear to be self-evident is that an adjunct question could not have a direct effect unless the reader is able to answer it correctly. The data showed this was true. The probability of a right answer on the criterion test, R_3, given a wrong answer on the pretest, W_1, and a right answer to the adjunct question, R_2, pooled over all quiz groups was .69. In contrast, $P(R_3 | W_1 W_2)$ was .22, which is just about chance performance on a four-alternative, multiple-choice test.

D. EXPERIMENT 4[7]

The idea with which we have been working is that an adjunct question will facilitate long-term storage if it permits retrieval of temporarily stored information and evokes further processing. It has been assumed that verbatim questions are better at promoting retrieval whereas paraphrase questions are more likely to cause "deep" semantic encoding. This theory received some support in Experiment 2, in which it was found that a verbatim quiz followed by a paraphrase quiz maximally facilitated criterion test performance.

Experiment 4 again investigated the efficacy of what we came to call the "piggyback" treatment. As will be detailed in the last section of this paper we have developed a "study management system" that entails giving computer-administered quizzes after short reading assignments. A number of difficult questions, involving either paraphrase or application of concepts and principles to new examples, were identified. For each of these a verbatim priming question was written. The experiment sought to determine whether the priming

---

[7] This experiment was run by Stephen Alessi. Edward Wietecha, Bonnie Armbruster, and Bruce Dalgaard assisted.

questions would improve subsequent performance. A positive result would support the retrieve-and-transfer theory and also be of practical interest.

1. Method

a. Materials. Those items which 60% or more of the students answered incorrectly during the first semester the study management system functioned were screened for flaws. Selected were 41 of these questions, hereafter called "target items," spread over 16 chapters of an economics text. Verbatim priming questions corresponding to the target items were prepared in the following way. The target items were examined to determine the portion of the text from which they were drawn. A verbatim summary statement of the text passage was produced. The verbatim question was developed from the summary statement.

b. Design and Procedure. The experiment was run in the semester following the one in which the items were selected. The target items were divided into two sets. Approximately half of the 77 undergraduates enrolled in the computer-managed sections of the course were assigned at random to receive a verbatim priming question just prior to each related target item in the first set but did not receive a priming question for any item in the other set. The assignment was reversed for the remaining subjects. The procedure was implemented by the computer system. As far as we can tell, this was a completely invisible experiment; that is, none of the subjects was aware of any experimental manipulation.

2. Results and Discussion

The mean proportion correct on primed target items was .58. The figure for nonprimed target items was .59. On the verbatim priming questions subjects averaged .75, so there was room for an effect to show itself. Some of the target items were included in later examinations, but in the light of the data already reported it seemed pointless to analyze performance on them. The target items were sorted into ones upon which a positive priming effect appeared and ones in which the effect was negative. A graduate student in economics was unable to see any difference between the two groups or their companion priming questions.

VI. General Discussion

The set of experiments described here failed in its major objective, which was to give rise to a theory of the direct effects of questions. To be sure, adjunct questions did enhance criterion test performance, and since the questions came after the entire passage, this must mean—almost by definition—that some sort of mental review process is involved. However, we were unable to provide an illuminating account of how this process might work. The retrieve-and-transfer hypothesis got off to a promising start but then came upon hard times. There is the favorable outcome of Experiment 2, but unless that can be replicated the hypothesis is best regarded as a nice idea that didn't work.

Still somewhat puzzling is the fact that paraphrase questions did not give better results than verbatim questions. The principle that procedures which induce meaningful processing facilitate learning cannot be doubted. Perhaps paraphrase does not induce sufficiently "deep" processing, or maybe the processing must be instigated at the time of initial encoding rather than retrospectively as is the case when questions appear after the passage. An experiment completed in this laboratory suggests that if either of these possibilities is correct, it is more likely to be the former (Surber, Anderson, & Stevens, 1975). Lists of verbatim or paraphrase "objectives" were provided to guide study of text. Groups who received objectives did better than the reading-only control group on a multiple-choice criterion test, but there was no difference as a function of the type of objective. Another possible explanation is that verbatim questions evoke meaningful processing in about the same measure as ones which are paraphrased. Finally, it could be that the benefits of paraphrase have to do with the retrievability of information and that, therefore, an advantage did not appear in these experiments because multiple-choice criterion tests were used. In this regard, it is worth mentioning again that Felker (1974) got a big increment from adjunct comprehension questions on an essay test, but no difference with a multiple-choice test (see however Swenson & Kulhavy, 1974).

In the previous studies showing a direct questioning effect the questions have been repeated in literal form on the criterion test. This fact leaves open the possibility that the effect is trivially specific. The first three experiments were designed to see if the effect would appear when the items in the final test repeated the semantic content but not the lexical form of the initial questions. In every case performance on the criterion test was highest when the wording of the items matched the wording of the adjunct questions. Further analysis indicated that when the wording did not match there was a small but nonsignificant advantage over the reading-only control in Experiments 1 and 2. In Experiment 3, the most sensitive in the series, this contrast was significant, $t(194) = 2.10$, $p < .05$. The conclusion would appear to be that some but not all of the direct questioning effect depends upon reproducing the specific language of the adjunct questions.

Perhaps the most important findings of the present research were that in every experiment verbatim scores were significantly higher than paraphrase scores when the questions were asked immediately after reading the passage, and that verbatim scores declined more over a one-week interval than did paraphrase scores. The most plausible interpretation of these facts is that there are at least two kinds of memory code, a close-to-surface code with a relatively short memorial half life, and a more permanent semantic-based code. It should be stressed, especially, that the surface code must be much longer lived than previous research would suggest (see also R. C. Anderson, 1971, 1974).

It might be argued that verbatim and paraphrase scores were different because of roughness of paraphrase. To check this possibility the data from Experiment 3 were analyzed further. The differences in performance between verbatim and paraphrase questions in each of the sixteen matched pairs was correlated with the ratings of semantic equivalence obtained in the norming study. The correlations were .18, .26, and .25 for the inserted questions, batched questions, and one-week criterion items (no-quiz group only), respectively. While these coefficients are positive, not much of the variance is accounted for. Consider also that the proportion correct on the verbatim question exceeded the proportion correct on the paraphrase question for 15 of the 16 pairs in both the inserted and batched groups. Anyway, even if some of the verbatim-paraphrase difference were attributable to lack of semantic equivalence, this would not explain the consistently obtained interaction between the form of the questions and retention interval.

VII. Practical Education Implications of Questioning Techniques

Currently in operation at the University of Illinois is a computer-based study management system that attempts to take practical advantage of questioning techniques (see T. H. Anderson, Anderson,

Dalgaard, Wietecha, Biddle, Paden, Smock, Alessi, Surber, & Klemt, 1974). Here is how it works. The student signs on at a computer terminal and receives a four- to eight-page reading assignment. Upon completing the assignment in a nearby work space, the student again signs on. This time he/she takes a quiz consisting of at least four questions. If he/she gets 75% or more of the questions right the student receives feedback on any that were missed and then has the option of receiving the next assignment. If he/she fails the quiz, the student is directed back to the text for further study. Following an initial assignment or a failed quiz, there is a 7-min programmed delay before a quiz may be taken or retaken. The quizzes themselves are not graded but a quota of them must be passed before graded exams may be taken.

The study management system is now in its third semester of operation in an introductory economics course. Nearly 300 questions based on 25 chapters of the required text are presented in 63 quizzes. An experiment showed that the system (just the study management component) produces significant gains in student achievement on hourly and final examinations and also significant improvements in student attitudes toward the course and the quality of instruction. The system has been installed in a community college history course as well, but we have no hard data about its effectiveness there.

Our present design might better be called a course management system, for study management is just one of its components. Students are expected to acquire basic concepts and information from individual reading. Their attention to the material is maintained and their progress monitored by the already functioning study management system. Lectures and standard quiz sections have been scrapped. The time of instructors, saved because lecturing and routine review are no longer required, has been invested in remediation for students having trouble mastering the core curriculum, and a smorgasbord of topical, activity-oriented seminars and special projects. A student dissatisfied with his/her performance on a graded examination has the option of trying again. Able, hard-working students may complete the course before the end of the semester or, alternatively, elect extra credit for extra work. The computer is employed to manage study activities, administer achievement tests on-line, schedule seminars and individual tutorial sessions, and keep course records.

REFERENCES

Anderson, R. C. Educational psychology. *Annual Review of Psychology*, 1967, **18**, 129–164.

Anderson, R. C. Control of student mediating processes during verbal learning and instruction. *Review of Educational Research*, 1970, **40**, 349–639.

Anderson, R. C. Encoding processes in the storage and retrieval of sentences. *Journal of Experimental Psychology*, 1971, **91**, 338–340.

Anderson, R. C. How to construct achievement tests to assess comprehension. *Review of Educational Research*, 1972, **42**, 145–170.

Anderson, R. C. Substance recall of sentences. *Quarterly Journal of Experimental Psychology*, 1974, **26**, 530–541.

Anderson, R. C., & Kulhavy, R. W. Learning concepts from definitions. *American Educational Research Journal*, 1972, **9**, 385–390.

Anderson, R. C., & Myrow, D. L. Retroactive inhibition of meaningful discourse. *Journal of Educational Psychology Monograph*, 1971, **62**, 81–94.

Anderson, T. H., Anderson, R. C., Dalgaard, B. R., Wietecha, E. J., Biddle, W. B., Paden, D. W., Smock, H. R., Alessi, S. M., Surber, J. R., & Klemt, L. L. A computer based study management system. *Educational Psychologist*, 1974, **11**, 36–45.

Barclay, J. R. The role of comprehension in the remembering of sentences. *Cognitive Psychology*, 1973, **4**, 229–254.

Berliner, D. C., Shavelson, R. J., Ravitch, M. M., & Loeding, D. Individual differences in the effects of adjunct questions on learning from prose material. Paper presented at the annual meeting of the American Educational Research Association, New Orleans, March 1973.

Bobrow, S. A., & Bower, G. H. Comprehension and recall of sentences. *Journal of Educational Psychology*, 1969, **80**, 455–461.

Bormuth, J. R. *On the theory of achievement test items.* Chicago: University of Chicago Press, 1970.

Boyd, W. M. Repeating questions in prose learning. *Journal of Educational Psychology*, 1973, **64**, 31–38.

Bruning, R. H. Effects of review and testlike events within the learning of prose material. *Journal of Educational Psychology*, 1968, **59**, 16–19.

Bull, S. G. *The effect of prequestions that arouse epistemic curiosity on long term retention.* (Doctoral dissertation, University of Oregon) Ann Arbor, Mich.: University Microfilms, 1971. No. 72-909.

Clark, K. B. Some factors influencing the remembering of prose material. *Archives of Psychology*, 1940, **36**, No. 253.

Corrozi, J. F. *The effects of reading time, type of question, and instructional format on short- and long-term retention of relevant and incidental prose material.* (Doctoral dissertation, University of Delaware) Ann Arbor, Mich.: University Microfilms, 1970. No. 71-6465.

Craik, F. I. M., & Lockhart, R. S. Levels of processing: A framework for memory research. *Journal of Verbal Learning and Verbal Behavior*, 1972, **11**, 671–684.

Craik, F. I. M., & Watkins, M. J. The role of rehearsal in short-term memory. *Journal of Verbal Learning and Verbal Behavior*, 1973, **12**, 599–608.

Dapra, R. A., & Felker, D. B. Effects of comprehension and verbatim adjunct questions on problem-solving ability from prose material: Extension of the mathemagenic hypothesis.

Paper presented at the American Psychological Association Annual Convention, New Orleans, Feb. 1974.

Eischens, R. R., Gaite, A. J. H., & Kumar, V. K. Prose learning: Effects of question position and informational load interactions on retention of low signal value information. *Journal of Psychology*, 1972, **81**, 7–12.

Felker, D. B. *The effects of question type and question placement on problem solving ability from prose material.* Pittsburgh: American Institutes for Research, 1974.

Frase, L. T. Learning from prose material: Length of passage, knowledge of results, and position of questions. *Journal of Educational Psychology*, 1967, **58**, 266–272.

Frase, L. T. Effect of question location, pacing and mode upon retention of prose material. *Journal of Educational Psychology*, 1968, **59**, 244–249. (a)

Frase, L. T. Some data concerning the mathemagenic hypothesis. *American Educational Research Journal*, 1968, **5**, 181–189. (b)

Frase, L. T., Patrick, E., & Schumer, H. Effect of question position and frequency upon learning from text under different levels of incentive. *Journal of Educational Psychology*, 1970, **61** 52–56.

French, J. W., Ekstrom, R. B., & Price, L. A. *Kit of reference tests for cognitive factors.* Princeton, N.J.: Educational Testing Service, 1963.

Gates, A. I. Recitation as a factor in memorizing. *Archives of Psychology*, 1917, **6**, 1–104.

Glanzer, M., Koppenal, L., & Nelson, R. Effects of relations between words on short-term storage and long-term storage. *Journal of Verbal Learning and Verbal Behavior*, 1972, **11**, 403–416.

Hershberger, W. A. Self-evaluating responding and typographical cueing: Techniques for programing self-instructional reading materials. *Journal of Educational Psychology*, 1964, **55** 288–296.

Hershberger, W. A., & Terry, D. F. Delay of self-testing in three types of programed text. *Journal of Educational Psychology*, 1965, **56**, 22–30.

Holland, J. G., & Kemp, F. D. A measure of programming in teaching-machine material. *Journal of Educational Psychology*, 1965, **56**, 264–269.

Jarvella, R. J. Syntactic processing of connected speech. *Journal of Verbal Learning and Verbal Behavior*, 1971, **10**, 409 –416.

Jarvella, R. J., & Herman, S. J. Clause structure of sentences and speech processing. *Perception & Psychophysics*, 1972, **11** 381–384.

Jones, H. E. The effects of examination on permanence of learning. *Archives of Psychology*, 1923–1924, **10**, 1–70.

Kemp, F. D., & Holland, J. G. Blackout ratio and overt responses in programmed instruction: Resolution of disparate results. *Journal of Educational Psychology*, 1966, **57**, 109–114.

Kleinsmith, L. J., & Kaplan, S. Interaction of arousal and recall interval in nonsense syllable paired-associate learning. *Journal of Experimental Psychology*, 1964, **67**, 124–126.

Ladas, H. The mathemagenic effects of factual review questions on the learning of incidental information: A critical review. *Review of Educational Research*, 1973, **43**, 71–82.

Maccoby, N., Michael, D. N., & Levine, S. Further studies of student participation procedures in film instruction: Review and preview covert practice, and motivational interactions. In A. A. Lumsdaine (Ed.), *Student response in programmed instruction.* Washington, D. C.: National Academy of Sciences—National Research Council, 1961.

McGaw, B., & Grotelueschen, A. Direction of the effect of questions in prose material. *Journal of Educational Psychology*, 1972, **63**, 586–588.

Michael, D. N., & Maccoby, N. Factors influencing the effects of student participation on verbal learning from films: Motivating versus practice effects, feedback, and overt versus covert responding. In A. A. Lumsdaine (Ed.), *Student response in programmed instruction*. Washington, D.C.: National Academy of Sciences—National Research Council, 1961.

Morasky, R. L. Eye movements as a function of adjunct question placement. *American Educational Research Journal*, 1972, 9, 251–261.

Morasky, R. L., & Wilcox, H. H. Time required to process information as a function of question placement. *American Educational Research Journal*, 1970, 7, 561–567.

Natkin, G., & Stahler, E. The effects on adjunct questions on short- and long-term recall of prose materials. *American Educational Research Journal*, 1969, 6, 425–432.

Posner, M. I., & Warren, R. E. Traces, concepts, and conscious constructions. In A. W. Melton & E. Martin (Eds.), *Coding processes in human memory*. Washington, D.C.: Winston, 1972.

Quellmalz, E. *Effects of three characteristics of text-embedded response requirements on the development of a dominant focus in prose learning*. (Doctoral dissertation, University of California at Los Angeles) Ann Arbor, Mich.: University Microfilms, 1972. No. 72-13672.

Raffel, G. The effect of recall on forgetting. *Journal of Experimental Psychology*, 1934, 17, 828–838.

Roderick, M. C., & Anderson, R. C. A programmed introduction to psychology versus a textbook-style summary of the same lesson. *Journal of Educational Psychology*, 1968, 59, 381–387.

Rosenshine, B. Teacher competency research. Urbana: Bureau of Educational Research, University of Illinois, 1974.

Rothkopf, E. Z. Some theoretical and experimental approaches to problems in written instruction. In J. D. Krumboltz (Ed.), *Learning and the educational process*. Chicago: Rand McNally, 1965.

Rothkopf, E. Z. Learning from written instructive materials: An exploration of the control of inspection behavior by test-like events. *American Educational Research Journal*, 1966, 3, 241–249.

Rothkopf, E. Z. Variable adjunct question schedules, interpersonal interaction, and incidental learning from written material. *Journal of Educational Psychology*, 1972, 63, 87–92.

Rothkopf, E. Z., & Billington, M. J. Indirect review and priming through questions, *Journal of Educational Psychology*, 1974, 66, 669–679.

Rothkopf, E. Z., & Bisbicos, E. E. Selective facilitative effects of interspersed questions on learning from written prose. *Journal of Educational Psychology*, 1967, 58, 56–61.

Rothkopf, E. Z., & Bloom, R. D. Effects of interpersonal interaction on the instructional value of adjunct questions in learning from written material. *Journal of Educational Psychology*, 1970, 61, 417–422.

Sachs, J. Recognition memory for syntactic and semantic aspects of connected discourse. *Perception & Psychophysics*, 1967, 2, 437–442.

Sones, A., & Stroud, J. Review with special reference to temporal position. *Journal of Educational Psychology*, 1940, 31, 665–676.

Spitzer, H. F. Studies in retention. *Journal of Educational Psychology*, 1939, 30, 641–656.

Surber, J. R., Anderson, R. C., & Stevens, K. V. Instructional objectives and learning from text: A cautionary note. Paper presented at the annual meeting of the American Educational Research Association, Washington, D.C., April 1975.

Swenson, I., & Kulhavy, R. W. Adjunct questions and the comprehension of prose by children. *Journal of Educational Psychology*, 1974, 66, 212–215.

Throop, S. T. *Effect of density, position, evidence, sex, and grade upon recall of questions representing Bloom's six classes.* (Doctoral dissertation, University of Akron) Ann Arbor, Mich.: University Microfilms, 1971. No. 72-4054.

Van Matre, N. H., Aiken, E. G., Carter, J. F., Shennum, W. A., & Thomas, G. S. *Learning from lecture: Investigations of study strategies involving note taking.* Technical Report NPRDC TR-75. San Diego: Navy Personnel Research and Development Center, 1974.

Watts, G. H. The "arousal" effect of adjunct questions on recall from prose materials. *Australian Journal of Psychology*, 1973, 25, 81–87.

Watts, G. H., & Anderson, R. C. Effects of three types of inserted questions on learning from prose. *Journal of Educational Psychology*, 1971, 62, 387–394.

Williams, J. P. Comparison of several response modes in a review program. *Journal of Educational Psychology*, 1963, 54, 253–260.

Williams, J. P. Effectiveness of constructed-response and multiple-choice programing modes as a function of test mode. *Journal of Educational Psychology*, 1965, 56, 111–117.

THE ANALYSIS OF SENTENCE PRODUCTION[1]

M. F. Garrett

MASSACHUSETTS INSTITUTE OF TECHNOLOGY, CAMBRIDGE, MASSACHUSETTS

I.	Introduction	133
II.	Speech Errors: The Corpus	137
III.	Speech Errors: The Analysis	140
IV.	Sound Exchange Errors	143
V.	Word and Morpheme Exchanges	148
VI.	Stranded Morphemes, Shifts, and Exchanges	154
VII.	Fusions and Substitutions: Semantic Errors	172
VIII.	Summary	175
	References	177

I. Introduction

When one is speaking, one is thinking;[2] the problem of language production has often been thought of as determining what necessary relations hold between the former and the latter. However, no attempt will be made here to wrestle with such hoary issues as whether the structure of language determines general cognitive structure. Rather, it is taken as a point of departure that there exists a nonlinguistic representational system in terms of which significant cognitive functions can be performed (for recent discussions of this and related issues, see Fodor, 1975; Fodor, Bever, & Garrett, 1974, Chapter 7).

Given this assumption, we may raise the more tractable problem of *sentence* production. That is, we distinguish between the general problem of language production, which must include message formu-

[1] The research reported here was supported in part by NIMH grant HD 05/68-02,03,04. Some of the work was done in collaboration with S. R. Shattuck and her contribution is gratefully acknowledged. This paper was written while the author was a Senior Research Fellow of the Australian-American Educational Foundation (Fulbright-Hayes program) at Monash University, Melbourne.

[2] Barring appeals to certain chimerical pathologies and rote recitation or reading.

lation, and the specific problem of sentence production, which may be viewed as *translation* process (Fig. 1).

We assume that somewhere in the recesses of our central nervous system an interaction takes place among our current motor and perceptual experiences, our stored information, our motivational systems, and, doubtless, sundry other variables. That interaction gives rise to what we might call a "communicative intention"— hereafter *message*. In some manner, that message must be translated into a set of instructions sufficient to guide our articulatory apparatus.

Beyond knowing that some translation exists—there is nothing so clear as that we do not think with our lips or velum—what can be said of the translation process(es)? If we first focus on the form of messages when they are uttered, we can begin to explore some aspects of the translation process.

Constraints on the form of utterances which are to count as sentences are determined by formal linguistic analyses. How does this bear on the translation process we wish to analyze? We know that whatever models of the translation process we may postulate, one thing they must do is to distinguish among all the meaningfully distinct messages. In mapping from any of the indefinitely many possible messages $M_1, M_2, M_3, \ldots M_n$ onto an utterance, the translation process must preserve the bases for computing distinctions among $M_1, M_2, M_3, \ldots M_n$ if communication is to take place. Thus, the translation process must preserve whatever aspects of the manifest form of sentences can be shown to contribute to their semantic interpretation. That is tantamount to the claim that the structural descriptions of sentences must be preserved by the translation process, for virtually all the structural features encompassed by the surface phonological description and the underlying and surface syntactic descriptions of sentences[3] can be shown to contribute in one way or another to their semantic analysis. Thus, the structural analyses assigned to sentences by an adequate grammar provide one powerful constraint on the formulation of models of the translation process from messages to utterances.

[3] Excluded from this claim are "intermediate" syntactic trees and underlying phonological descriptions. This is not because these aspects of structural descriptions are taken to be less well motivated linguistically, but only because they cannot be given a prima facie defense on grounds of maintaining distinct representation of semantically distinct utterances. The relevance of such levels of representation to the processes of producing or comprehending sentences must appeal to other empirical support, some of which is mentioned or discussed in subsequent portions of this paper.

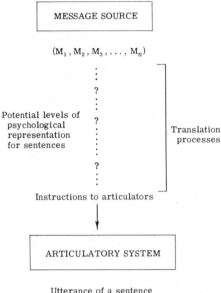

| MESSAGE SOURCE |

$(M_1, M_2, M_3, \ldots, M_n)$

Potential levels of psychological representation for sentences

Translation processes

Instructions to articulators

| ARTICULATORY SYSTEM |

Utterance of a sentence

Fig. 1

But even though this constraint on the character of possible production models is a very powerful one, it tells us less than we might wish about the computational procedures which will effect the translation. For example, we know that the structural descriptions for sentences express regularities in the distribution of a variety of structural types—sounds, syllables, words, phrases and phrase types, sentences and sentence types. Such structural distinctions must be recoverable from the output of the translation process (if they are semantically relevant), but the way in which they are reflected in the information flow which gives rise to that output is an open question. We know for example that the structural analysis of sentences requires that "words" be decomposed into more elementary meaning bearing elements (morphemes); but the computational system may take account of this in a variety of ways. In particular, there may or may not be an independent, phonological representation of bound morphs in the computational vocabulary of the production system. Thus although the analysis of the word "bigger" must mark it as the comparative form of the adjective "big," that analysis may not be reflected in the existence of an element "comparative:—er" in the processing vocabulary (though this phonetic fact would still be inferrable from the phonetic arrays assigned to "big" and "bigger"). Similarly for many other aspects of phonological and syntactic structure. One more example, of a syntactic sort, may suffice to make the point clear. If one compares certain varieties of complex nominals in English, for example, "peanut butter," "brick layer," "cast iron," "fog horn," "used car sales man," "college students," "elderly ladies," and so forth, one quickly sees, even with a rough attempt at a uniform periphrastic treatment of them, that they embody a wide range of syntactic and semantic relations, (indeed virtually the full syntactic possibilities of the language; see Lees, 1960) all of which will have to be reflected in the analysis which the production system assigns to them if their appropriate use is to be explained. But, though "elderly ladies" must be analyzed, roughly, as "ladies who are elderly" and "brick layer" as "one who lays bricks," both, either, or neither of these might be represented in the processing system by their constituent words, the stipulation of what grammatical relations hold between them and the derivational processes required to yield their surface forms. Alternatively, both, either, or neither might be entered in their derived form as elements of the computational vocabulary in the same way as words like "dog," "symbol," or "apricot." The alternatives sketched do not begin to exhaust the possibilities, of course, but for our purposes it is enough that the compatibility of structural descriptions with a variety of computational procedures be appreciated.

The final point that should be made on this aspect of the analysis of sentence production is that, even were we to have good evidence about the vocabulary of the computational system that mediates the translation from messages into their realization as instructions to the articulatory system, we would still be unsatisfied. For one would want to be able to characterize the information flow in the system in terms of interactions between the various structural types represented in the computational vocabulary. It would, for example, be important to know whether there were "stages" or levels in the processing which correspond to the distinct linguistic types characteristic of semantic, syntactic, and phonetic descriptions of sentences. It is entirely consonant with our acceptance of structural descriptions as constraints on translation models that there should be *no* stage in the processing at which the "decisions" are primarily syntactic or semantic. That is an empirical question about information flow in the system.

How does one go about assessing the behavior of speakers in order to provide answers to the sorts of questions raised above? How do we discover what sorts of structure are computed on-line by the speaker, and in what sequence? Such questions are not easily amenable to experimental attack (although there have been a few useful efforts, some of which I will take up in the discussion section). On the one hand, we are handicapped by our inability to control or manipulate the input to the sentence production system (messages) and, on the other, by the arduousness of analyzing the experimental results (large amounts of "spontaneous" speech). The recourse for people interested in language production processes has, largely, been to "observational" techniques, and, in particular, to the study of various sorts of departures from ideal speech (e.g., nonfluencies and speech errors of a variety of types); and that is the approach adopted for the work described in this paper. This is not because I doubt the possibility or need for specifically experimental enquiry into production processes. It is, rather, because I feel both that experimental enquiry can be better undertaken against a background of empirically supported working hypotheses and that the study of speech errors is a good way to generate and support such hypotheses. For, as has often been observed, speech "errors" have a powerful claim to face validity as indicants of the on-line processing that underlies speech. Beyond this, the study of speech errors is a larger enterprise than might be imagined on initial consideration. Thus, despite the interest of several investigators past and present, much remains to be determined about the nature and explanation of the several ways in which "natural speech" departs from the idealization of prose or the precision of formal address.

II. Speech Errors: The Corpus

There are a variety of departures from normally fluent speech which could count as "errors"; for example, hesitations, changes of mind, repetition of sounds or words, and so forth. The data I will be discussing, however, concerns less common, but by no means rare, error types. Consider the entries in Table I. Each of the varieties of error listed has a single example given, and that example is, perforce, one which involves only one of the several types of linguistic elements that appear in speech errors. But each of these error patterns (e.g. addition, exchange, etc.) does have exemplars for nearly every linguistic type (e.g., sounds, morphemes, words, etc.). It is evident that the sorts of errors represented in Table I are *not* part of the

TABLE I

SOME PATTERNS OF SPEECH ERRORS

---

a. Addition:
   "I don't see **any many** paddocks around here."
   (intended either *any* or *many* but not both)
b. Deletion:
   "I'll just get up and mutter _intelligibly."
   (intended *unintelligibly*)
c. Substitution:
   "At low speeds it's too **light.**"
   (intended *heavy*)
d. Complex addition:
   "The one **exPosner** experiment that. . . ."
   (intended *Posner*)   .
e. Complex deletion:
   "That would be _having like Harry."
   (intended *behaving*)
f. Shift:
   "That's so she'll be ready in case she decide_ to hits it."
   (intended *decides to hit it*)
g. Exchange:
   "Fancy getting your **model renosed.**"
   (intended *nose remodeled*)
h. Fusion:
   "At the end of todays **lection.** . . ."
   (intended *lecture* or *lesson*)
i. Double whammy:
   "He's a **laving runiac.**"
   (intended *raving lunatic* or *maniac*)

---

same class of events as hesitations, changes of mind, or "sloppy articulation" (as that characteristic of inebriated, hurried, or very casual speech). These sorts of errors occur (although not exclusively) in fluent speech, and although they may well be affected by changes of communicative intention on the part of speakers, they are not readily interpretable as the simple consequence of having abandoned one form of expression in mid-utterance in order to shape another nearer to intent's desire. These errors represent cases in which either all and only the intended elements of the speaker's utterance appear, but in the wrong order, or some intended element is missing, or some element not intended intrudes in one way or another.

These error types are illustrative of those in an error corpus of some 3400 errors I gathered, together with my colleague S. R.

Shattuck, principally over the past 3½ years. The errors are with minor exceptions, all from spontaneous speech, and all are (a) those observed by myself or S. R. S., or (b) those reported by our friends, colleagues, and students.[4] For most of the errors, as much was recorded (written down) of the utterance surrounding the error locus as was consonant with the preservation of friendships or the exigencies of the recording situation. In the sections that follow I will report some aspects of the analysis of that corpus (hereafter called "MIT corpus"), and an interpretation of its apparent regularities. Relatively little discussion is offered of errors of sound structure (see however Fromkin, 1971; Shattuck, 1974); the primary focus is on syntactic processes and their relation to semantic and phonological variables.

There are a number of methodological caveats to be entered before discussing the structure of the error types. First of all, there will rarely be any mention in what follows of the statistical significance of such differences as I may call attention to. There are a number of good reasons for this. For the most part, the behavior of speech elements that I have tried to interpret has virtually binary conditions—either a certain class of speech errors is conditioned by a given structural variable, or it is not sensitive to that variable at all. This is not to say that one cannot find "statistical error patterns," nor that such may not be of importance. It is only to say that I have avoided their interpretation for the most part (only occasionally succumbing to the temptation of the implications of "trends"). This fastidiousness is prompted by an appreciation of the hazards of "naturalistic" data collection and the paucity of reliable information on the frequency of occurrence of elements of the language at levels higher than sound elements or "word forms" (and even there the information is primarily orthographically based). Even if one had standards against which to assess error frequencies, one could not be assured that the corpus one has amassed provides a reasonable basis for inferring the incidence of different error types. The "sampling" must be decidedly nonrandom given the reasonable assumption that certain sorts of errors are perceptually more salient than others.[5]

---

[4] Errors were accepted from contributors other than myself or S.R.S. but the "source" of all errors was recorded. Subsequent analysis shows no apparent basis for distinguishing among the errors contributed by others and those observed by myself or S.R.S. so far as the generalizations discussed in this paper are concerned.

[5] For example, there is a clear difference in the sensitivity of myself and S.R.S. to vowel errors. I rarely hear them unless they are metathesized. In general, it seems likely that vowel changes will be less readily noted than consonantal changes for most listeners.

Similarly there are very likely contributions of situational and individual variability in speakers. Since a large proportion of the errors are those committed by myself and my most frequent colleagues, considerable caution is indicated in interpreting differences in the incidence of different error types. I believe that one is on somewhat firmer ground, however, in discussing the apparent interactions between structural features of sentences and a particular error type, given a fairly large number of errors and very pronounced differences within the class in its sensitivity to given structural constraints.

III. Speech Errors: The Analysis

As the preceding remarks may suggest, my approach to the analysis of speech errors departs in some measure from that of most previous investigators. This is true in two primary respects: (1) a focus on syntactic variables rather than sound structure, semantics, or motivational processes, and (2) a focus on constraints on particular error types rather than on the existence of errors involving particular linguistic types. Roughly, in what follows I will be interested in generalizations concerning limitations on the range of movement of various linguistic types, the nature of immediate environmental determinants of errors, and the relevant description of elements which are (apparently) interacting, and I will be exploring the implications of such generalizations for a characterization of sentence production as a succession of quasi-independent "levels" or stages of processing activity. We will begin by loosely characterizing some of the properties of speech errors that emerge from past research and then proceed, through emendations and exceptions based on the current data, to some working hypotheses about sentence production.

One of the most striking regularities encountered on first reading through a set of speech errors, especially those involving sound elements, is the degree to which interacting elements occur in similar environments, both positionally and, to some extent, phonetically. Errors such as the following

(1) *So while you do the cooking, Bill snovels show, does he?* (shovels snow)

(2) *The little burst of beadan is.* . . . (beast of burden)

(3) *You're not a poojin pitter-downer* . . . *(are you)*? (pigeon putter-downer)

(4)   *That's an easer-eagy sentence.* (eager-easy)
(5)   *Children interfere with your nife lite.* . . . . (night life)
(6)   *I think I met someone who had a spet pider.* (pet spider)
(7)   *There's a lot of flee floating anxiety.* . . . . (free floating)
(8)   *The straight lawn drawn through.* . . . . (line drawn)
(9)   *We will go down to the sound roof proo.* . . . . (sound proof room)

illustrate the tendency of word initial segments to exchange with, or intrude into, other word initial positions, and correspondingly for medial and final segments;[6] and they are more likely to do so when the elements preceding or following those positions are phonetically similar (Fromkin, 1971; Mckay, 1970). These examples also illustrate another powerful condition on elements that interact: namely, that they be themselves similar in certain aspects. In particular, for sound errors, identity as consonant or vowel seems crucial; consonants exchange with other consonants but not with vowels, and conversely. There are virtually no plausible exceptions to this generalization in the MIT corpus and none that I am aware of in published reports of other error corpora. So far as these varieties of sound errors are concerned, these two generalizations seem secure: interacting elements are similar to each other, and their environments are also similar. Their application to other types of errors involving other linguistic elements is, as we shall see later, sometimes straightforward, sometimes obscure.

A third general aspect of these sorts of errors is what might be termed the preservation of phonological well-formedness. Nearly every investigation of speech errors has remarked upon the rarity of error outputs which violate the constraints on sequencing of sounds in whatever language is being spoken. Thus, in English, one simply does not find movement errors which yield, for example, illegal initial clusters like /sd/ or /sg/;[7] this in spite of the fact that such clusters are perfectly pronounceable and, indeed, regularly occur in casual speech (e.g.,/sdən/for *it's done* or /sgʌnə/ for *it's going to*,

---

[6] This might be couched (and has been) as a syllable-position constraint. The data, however, do not really seem to distinguish between a syllable structure constraint, on the one hand, and the joint effects of constraints on word (or morpheme) position and the vowel/consonant identity of exchanged elements, on the other (see later in text). See Shattuck (1974) for some discussion of this point.

[7] Though no such errors occur in the MIT corpus, this is apparently because they are rare, not that they are "impossible"; for example Kermit Shaefer's recorded collection of TV and radio errors contains the following: . . . *forks and spoons* . . . *sforks and sfoons* . . .

etc.). There seems to be either an aspect of the articulatory program which prevents such errors from occurring or an editing function which selectively picks up errors that violate sequencing constraints before they are emitted, thus barring them from the error corpus. On the current evidence, there is not any very satisfactory way to decide which of these is in fact the correct account (although I will argue below that there are some grounds for adopting a modified editing view).

The fourth, and final, general remark I wish to make in this preliminary characterization of speech errors concerns the role of prosodic features of sentences. There is a clear relation between the involvement of a speech segment in an error and both word and phrasal stress. Boomer and Laver (1968) reported that the majority of the sound errors they analyzed[8] involved an intrusion from the tonic word of a major phrase group ("phonemic clause"). And further, they observed that the two syllables involved in an error interaction were metrically similar for at least two degrees of stress; for example, the two syllables were either both weak or both salient, usually the latter, but rarely was one weak and the other salient. McKay (1970) has observed similar sorts of effects in his analysis of the corpus of German speech errors collected by Merringer (1908). Fromkin's (1971) report of her own corpus of errors and my analysis of the MIT corpus are also consonant with Boomer and Laver's generalizations. One of the things we will explore here is the degree to which these relations between stress features and errors may be accountable in terms of planning systems at the syntactic and morphological levels.

In short, where there is an error interaction involving two elements of the intended utterance, as those in examples (1)–(9), such elements

(10) a. occur in similar environments, both with respect to word (or syllable) positions and preceding or following phonetic elements;

b. are similar to each other both phonetically and prosodically;

---

[8] Boomer and Laver's corpus consisted of 200 errors; 100 were tape-recorded and 100 from written records. Their errors, judging from the examples they provided, were not just exchanges, but included what I have called shifts and complex additions (e.g., their *frunds have been frozen*, would be a shift in my terminology if the second underlined element had been omitted; as it stands, it is a complex addition).

    c.   will very likely involve the tonic word of a major phrase group;

    d.   will yield from their interaction a phonologically permissable sequence.

It will be clear from a comparison of the errors in (1)–(9) with the categories given in Table I that these generalizations do not cover the full range of error phenomena, nor, it should be pointed out, do they exhaust the claims that can be made of such "interactive errors" themselves. They are, however, well-supported generalizations and they provide an initial illustration of the sorts of descriptive and environmental constraints on error interactions that we may expect to find at levels other than that of sound structure.

IV.   Sound Exchange Errors

The first errors from the MIT corpus that we will examine in some detail are those like examples (1)–(5). These are *full exchanges* (i.e., enough of the utterance was completed by the speaker to allow unambiguous determination of the complementary elements and their positions) of separate segments of the intended utterance. Exchange errors of every sort (i.e., those involving morphemes, words, or phrases as well as those involving sounds) are of paramount importance in our analysis for a number of reasons. They first of all provide us with an unambiguous instance of the simultaneous existence of temporally discrete elements of the intended utterance; and second, to the extent that the error interacts with the intervening structures and elements, we may also argue for their simultaneous existence. Thus, such errors enable us to make inferences both about the size of the units over which production processes are normally integrated, and about the structural properties of those units. It is, therefore, of considerable importance to establish the character of such errors.

We remarked earlier that our results were generally compatible with those of previous analyses both with respect to the stress of interacting elements and the prominent role of the tonic word of major phrase groups; this is very strikingly the case for the pure sound exchange errors. Of the total of 137 such errors in the MIT corpus, almost all (92%) were interactions between two salient sylla-

TABLE II

SOUND EXCHANGE ERRORS

A. Stress Relations

	Exchanges within words	Exchanges between words	Total
Word stress			
Salient/salient	8	118	126
Weak/weak	0	1	1
Weak/strong	7	0	7
Indeterminate	3	0	3
Phrase stress			
Tonic word	12	94	106
Other	4	15	19
Indeterminate	2	10	12

B. Syntactic Relations

	Within clause	Between surface clauses
Form class preserved	21	2
Form class changed	89	7
Totals:	110	9

bles, and the large majority involved the tonic word (80%) of a major phrase (see Table II).[9]

At this level of description our results reinforce those of Boomer and Laver and others. There is, however, another powerful constraint on sound exchanges which may be related to the results for stress relations, and which may lead us to a reinterpretation of their significance. That constraint, as it is reported in Table II, is a

[9] The within-word exchanges are not included in the analysis of the syntactic relations. Note that the exceptions to the word stress regularity are all within-word exchanges. This may indicate that such errors are the consequence of different processing mechanisms than are other exchanges. Note further that the exceptions to the tonic word involvement are usually interactions between two modifiers of the tonic word.

syntactic one: the interacting elements of an exchange, with very rare exception,[10] are both members of the same surface clause.

This fact relates most obviously to another conclusion reached by Boomer and Laver. They analyzed their error corpus in terms of tone groups (or "phonemic clauses") which are units defined by a single tonic center and certain junctural phenomena characteristic of the boundaries of major phrase groups. Boomer and Laver found not only that the tonic word was usually involved in the errors they analyzed, but that it usually interacted with a word from its tone group, and hence, the results in Table II would be seen in their terms as an effect of tone groups. Thus, the findings of stress involvement at word and phrase levels coupled with the limiting effects of tone group boundaries conspire to suggest a prosodically defined encoding unit, and at the same time, an account of these sound errors in terms of neural correlates of the physical differences representing stress variations. Boomer and Laver's remarks are certainly in this spirit, [11] "but McKay (1969, 1970) has been most explicit on this point. He attributes the intrusion of error elements to the level of activation of speech motor units, with " . . . stressed elements taking a higher level of subthreshold activation than unstressed ones [McKay, 1970, p. 40] ." If this sort of account is correct, it is important, for it suggests both a hypothesis about the planning in speech and it provides a mechanism which accounts for a significant error type. There is, however, an alternative account of these same facts, as the classification in Table II suggests; namely, that they are a consequence of the syntactic and morphological structure which underlies prosodic features. What can be done by way of discovering which of these levels of description is the preferred one for accounts of error interactions, and by hypothesis, for the existence of particular varieties of planning in the sentence production system?

Two preliminary points might be made. First, the account of errors in terms of stress-correlated levels of activation in the motor system would lead one to expect only errors of anticipation to occur.

---

[10] The sound exchange exceptions to the clausal constraint are usually clause adjuncts (e.g., *Did you get yoursev socks, Clease?*") or idioms; e.g., *With this wing, I thee red.* (Surprisingly, Fromkin reports an error in a variant of the same idiom, *With this wing, I do red.*) In these respects the clause exceptions for sound errors differ from those for word exchanges.

[11] My interpretation of Boomer and Laver's remarks may be too strong. They speak of "neurophysiological prominence" of stressed elements, and of the "strength" of representations. These remarks do not necessarily commit them to a motor level of representation.

Though we have yet to discuss them, there are numerous nonexchange sound errors that appear to be perseveratory, for instance, example (9) and (f) in Table I), and a different account would be necessary for them. Similarly, one would expect that in exchange errors the higher stressed element should follow the lower stressed one in the intended output. Though this tends to be true by the report of most investigators, and it is true of the MIT corpus (62% of the cases where stress of the exchanged elements differs are anticipatory), it is by no means so impressive a regularity as the other constraints we have been discussing.

Second, if physical level of stress is the significant variable in precipitating speech errors, one might expect to find a greater incidence of errors in sentences with emphatic or contrastive stress than in sentences with normal stress, for normal stress variations are much less impressively reflected in actual acoustic energy differences than are emphatic and contrastive stress. It is difficult properly to evaluate this expectation since one has no good idea of the relative incidence of the relevant sentence types in normal conversation. In any event, there is no striking support for this prediction in the MIT corpus.

Though these sorts of observations might give one pause, they are, of course, by no means sufficient to render untenable the interpretation that motor correlates of physical stress differences are a major causal factor in these sorts of speech errors. There is, however, another set of observations which does seem to conclusively rule out that sort of explanation. We need to recall another of the strong generalizations about errors which was noted above; namely, that the result of an error interaction is phonologically well formed. This constraint is, in fact, a good deal more general than the examples used to present it might suggest. For not only are the sequencing constraints honored, but so too are various stress regularities and phonetic accommodations of elements to their error-induced environments.[12] To illustrate briefly:

(11) a. Vowels are restored or reduced when the deletion or addition of an intended element requires; e.g.,

　　　　easily　　　　　　　　　　*easy*
　　　　/isɬi/ *enough*　　　　→ /izi/ *enoughly*
　　　　　　　　　　　　　　　easuh
　　　　　　　　　　　　　　↛ /izɬ) *enoughly*

---

[12] Examples of one or another kind of accommodation are reported by most observers. In the MIT corpus there are about 20 cases where an accommodation is clearly demanded by an error and in every case it occurred.

b. The phonetic form of an indefinite article accommo-
    dates to its environment; e.g.,
    an aunt's money   → *a money's aunt*
                                    ↛ *an money's aunt*
    (see also Fromkin, 1971)
c. The phonetic forms of tense and number morphemes are
    appropriate to the stems to which errors attach them;
    e.g.,
    . . . add/z/ up to   → *add up/s/ to*
                                    ↛ *add up/z/ to*
    (see also Fromkin, 1971)
d. Word stress is appropriate to the error forms resulting
    from syllable movements, additions or deletions; e.g.,
    treméndously   → *trémenly*
    specifícity   → *specífity*
    compúted   → *cómputated*
    marsúpials   → *musárpials*
e. Phrasal stress is preserved; e.g.,
    . . . stop beating your heád against a brick wall
                              → *. . . brick against a heád wall*
    . . . avoid the trée pruning → *trúe preening*
    (see also Boomer and Laver, 1968).

These examples and those given earlier all indicate a late condition
on output which insures that the actual uttered form will be phonologically acceptable (although it may depart markedly from "sensi-
bleness" or syntactic well-formedness). This conditioning of the
output must occur *after* the level at which the errors occur, and must
be either prior to or identical with the level at which particular
phonetic forms are being translated into motor commands.[13] But that
fact presents an insupportable problem for the view that it is interactions among the motor elements underlying utterances which account for errors, and, in particular, for the prominence of stress
factors in error regularities.

It is undeniable that there is a level of representation of speech
events in the motor system at which there is a reflection of physical
differences of output energy in levels of neural activity; subglottal air
pressure does rise prior to the emission of a stressed syllable, and
thoracic and laryngeal muscle groups will reflect this. But, it is

---

[13] The suggestion of an ordering of error types by ordered levels of processing can be
taken as an "editing" explanation of accommodations, as opposed to a view that they are
somehow antecedently prevented.

equally certain to be fatuous to look for such a correspondence at much higher levels; my intention to speak softly surely does not have a notably lesser level of neural excitation than does my intention to speak loudly. One may legitimately wonder at what point the iso-morphisism breaks down between these two extremes. One thing we can be confident of, however, is that for speech, that point must fall somewhere before the level at which accommodations like those of (11) (*a*)–(*e*) take place, for all those are cases in which errors have demonstrably occurred prior to the realization of the particular phonetic form of the elements involved in the error.

Put another way, if the neural correlates of physical differences between stressed and unstressed speech elements were the primary causal factor in movement errors, one would expect those differences to appear as features of the emitted error elements. But that is precisely what we do not find. Rather, it appears to be the position which an element occupies within an independently specified struc-ture which endows it with the detail of its physical form.

We may regard the foregoing discussion as the first step in a contrast of the notion of "forcible intrusion" with that of "descrip-tive error" as ways of accounting for speech errors. The former notion stresses the physical concomitants of structural features and exploits their differences of "strength" in explanations of the etiol-ogy of errors. The latter notion relates structural differences to planning differences and the consequent opportunities for interac-tion among similarly described elements of the ultimate speech event. The evidence that we have so far considered indicates that the regularities of stress involvement in errors should not be accounted for by an appeal to a notion like forcible intrusion, and that we should consider them further aspects of the importance of similar-ities in the description of interacting elements, that is, as intimately related to the generalizations in (10) (*a*) and (*b*). Two things suggest that we should look to syntactic descriptions for the relevant anal-yses. One is the fact that prosodic features are determined by surface syntactic descriptions, and the other is the powerful constraint exerted on sound exchange errors by surface clausal structure. What one needs is additional independent evidence both for the operation of the clausal constraint and for the existence of a specifically syntactic processing level which could give rise to it.

V. Word and Morpheme Exchanges

The most obvious place to begin looking for such evidence is with exchanges involving elements that have themselves syntactic features:

TABLE III

WORD AND COMBINED FORM EXCHANGES

	Within clause	Between clause
Form class preserved		
Independent words	67	17
Combined forms	13	3
Form class changed		
Independent words	13	0
Combined forms	29	1
Totals:	122	21

morphemes, words, and phrases. Very little can be made of phrase exchanges, for they are too rare; exchanges of words and morphemes, however, are relatively frequent. In the MIT corpus there are 143 such errors that are unambiguously exchanges between words or parts of words that are morphemes. There are an additional 72 errors in which the words are in incorrect serial order, but because the misordered elements are adjacent, one cannot determine whether an exchange has taken place, or simply a shift in the location of a single word. These three classes of word movement errors (exchanges of independent forms, exchanges of combined forms, and "exchanges" of adjacent forms) turn out to have quite different properties, and these differences provide us with a basis for evaluating the role of syntactic factors in sentence production.

Table III presents the distribution of the first two of these three error types with respect to clausal structure and form class; examples (12)–(19) are typical of these error categories.

(12) *Slips and kids—I've got* **both** *of* **enough.**
     (intended: *enough of both*)
(13) *I broke a* **dinghy** *in the* **stay** *yesterday.*
     (intended: *stay in the dinghy*)
(14) *Although* **murder** *is a form of* **suicide,** . . .
     (intended: *suicide is a form of murder*)
(15) *I've got to go home and give my* **bath** *a hot* **back.**
     (intended: *back a hot bath*)
(16) *McGovern favors* **pushing busters.**
     (intended: *busting pushers*)

(17) *I hate working on two*-**word letter**s.
      (intended: *two-letter words*)
(18) *It just* **sound**e*d to* **start**.
      (intended: *started to sound*)
(19) *Oh, that's just a* **back truck**i*ng out*.
      (intended: *truck backing out*)

If one simply looks at the total frequencies of between- and within-clause errors, it is apparent that the clausal constraint we observed for sound exchanges is also present for word forms. There are, however, differences in the behavior of sound errors and word errors with respect to that constraint.

We note first of all that even though the word exchanges are predominantly between members of the same surface clause, this restriction is not quite so sharply drawn as for the sound errors (7% sound exceptions versus 15% for word exceptions). But what is more interesting is that these exceptions to the clausal constraint appear to be disciplined. In particular, such exceptions are almost invariably interactions between words of the same form class. If one compares Table II with Table III, one finds no apparent form class effect for sound exchanges, but a strong one for word exchanges that span clauses (and perhaps for those within clauses as well). This immediately suggests two things: (a) though both sound and word exchanges show sensitivity to clausal structure, they may do so for somewhat different reasons, and (b) the description which governs interactions between words in different clauses is one that includes at least their form class designation, while that for sound interactions does not. There are a number of aspects of these two possibilities which deserve exploration.

The most obvious first question is whether the form class constraint so evident for the between-clause errors is, in fact, restricted to such errors and, hence, whether we are entitled to infer that form class designations are only relevant to a level of planning at which elements of more than a single clause are being manipulated. A look at Table III suggests that this is very likely not true, for there is indication that form class is preserved both between and within clauses for exchanges between independent words. Of the 80 such within-clause exchanges, 84% preserve form class. This contrasts sharply with the pattern for those exchanges in Table III which involve combined word forms, as well as with the pattern for sound errors. For the combined form exchanges, within-clause errors show the reverse tendency; 70% of these errors violate form class (this is similar to the pattern for sound exchanges—see Table II).

In a limited way, these results provide what we were looking for, namely, an indication that elements (words) with specifically syntactic properties (e.g., form class) show a clausal constraint, and thereby justify the attribution of both the clausal limitation on the excursion of sound exchanges and their prosodic involvement to a syntactic level of sentence production processes. This resolution of the apparent facts is, however, unsatisfactory in a number of respects. Most glaringly, it does not countenance the existence of a class of word exchanges (the combined forms) which do not observe the form class restriction. To this must be added the difference in the behavior of sound errors with respect to clause boundaries and form class. When sound errors do transcend the clausal limitation, there is no indication of a change in their respect for form class (seven of nine such errors change form class). This distinguishes them from the word exchanges, where the form class restriction on interclause errors is virtually absolute (extending even to the combined forms, although there are really too few cases to make a firm judgment).[14] Thus, simply to attribute limitations on sound exchanges to the manifest existence of a syntactic level of processing would be to ignore an inconsistency in the behavior of the putatively syntactically organized elements with respect to our diagnostic variable, form class.

The inference that one is tempted to make from all this is that the very strong form class constraint observed for between-clause errors is, in fact, not solely the consequence of the distinct clausal membership of the elements involved, but is instead a characteristic of the level of processing at which most word exchanges take place. But this suggests that the combined forms are exchanged at a different level of processing than are the independently occurring word forms, and *that* is surprising, for, as the examples in (12)–(19) indicate, these errors are, barring the differences which define their initial classifica-

---

[14] It should be obvious that the error classifications that are being explored are classifications in terms of superficial properties (e.g., the presence of a bound morph) that may be reasonably supposed to be *diagnostic* of syntactic processes. The absence of such a diagnostic variable does not preclude the occurrence of a given error at a different level than the typical one. Hence, the frequencies of the error types are not "pure," but reflect some potential overlap in levels.

TABLE IV

FREQUENCY OF EXCHANGE ERRORS BY CHANGE IN FORM CLASS
AND DEGREE OF SEPARATION IN WORDS

Error type		0	1	2	3 or more	Σ
Sound exchanges	Form class same	6	15	2	0	23
	Form class diff.	45	41	7	2	96
Combined-form	Form class same	9	5	1	1	16
Exchanges	Form class diff.	20	8	2	0	30
Independent word	Form class same	–	37	30	17	84
exchanges	Form class diff.	–	12	1	0	13

tions, seemingly very similar. Indeed, the combined forms are almost always free forms, that is, the permuted elements are not bound morphemes but forms that can occur grammatically as independent words.

The theoretical seat becomes, at this point, uncomfortably warm. We seem well on the way toward claiming not one, but two syntactically organized levels of sentence production processes. The empirical thread from which these speculations depend is admittedly a slender one, but there is one immediately available property of these errors which suggests that we ought not resist this particular proliferation of theoretical entities.

It appears that, though all are clause limited, sound exchanges, and combined and independent word exchanges nevertheless "span" different intervals. So far, our discussion has been in terms of the interactions between errors and certain structural variables and in terms of the type of interacting elements. We now add to those variables the notion of degree of separation in the intended utterance. This might be expressed temporally (a measure for which we have no data at present), or in terms of the number of intervening elements—phones, syllables, morphemes, or words; since we will be comparing the three error types, discussion here is in terms of word separation.[15] Table IV provides the frequencies of errors for each of

---

[15] A distance measure in terms of syllables would not change the comparison except to magnify the distance of the word exchanges. This is because the words that intervene between the elements of a combined form or sound exchange are closed class (and almost always single syllables) while those intervening between independent word exchanges are often open class (although not often multisyllabic).

the error types at varying degrees of separation. The comparison is vexed by the fact that the number of independent word exchanges is indeterminate for 0 degrees of separation. I will argue below that, in fact, Table IV represents the frequencies of these types fairly well as it stands (i.e., that there are very few 0-degree exchanges of independent words). But for the moment, we may simply confine our attention to those errors of 1 degree or more. It is very clear that the likelihood of an error spanning two or three elements is greater for the word errors than for the sound or combined form exchanges ($p <$ .05, χ^2 for both the word versus sound and the word versus combined forms comparisons). What seems equally clear is that these longer error spans are confined to elements of a common form class for word exchanges.[16]

I have ventured onto dangerous ground in this comparison of the spans of different error types—and been properly punished by the necessity of resorting to a statistical defense of the distinction. Nowhere is one more at the mercy of the undoubted vegaries of sampling in this research than in comparisons of the incidence of different error types.[17] Nonetheless, in this case, the risk may prove justified by the conclusions I will argue for subsequently. I believe the clear implication of the differences among the error types we have been discussing, with respect to form class and error span, is the existence of two processing levels for word forms, one under "real

[16] The effect of distance on form class might be taken to explain the failure of combined form and sound exchanges to honor form class. That would, I think, be mistaking a symptom for the disease. Consider: (a) even at 1 degree of separation the word exchanges are predominantly form class preserving, and (b) clause-spanning errors of 0 and 1 degree are form class preserving. What appears likely is that the form class constraint and the clausal constraint are diagnostic of processing levels, and so too are the types of error elements involved (sounds, combined forms, and words); but none of these are definitionally related to a processing level. Thus, for example, we may reasonably expect some errors which involve combined forms (especially those which cross clause boundaries) to occur at the level characteristic of word exchanges and vice versa.

[17] This is particularly true for the present argument since I am using differences in error spans as an indication of differences in processing. For example, one might reasonably expect an "editing" function to catch long span errors more often than short span errors, thus excluding most of the latter from our analysis (which is based on completed errors). It is certain that there is such an editor, for incomplete exchanges/anticipations (one cannot tell which it might have been) are much more frequent than are complete ones. But though one might readily grant that an editor would be "length sensitive," it would still be left open why such an editor would more often pass long word exchanges than long combined-form exchanges. Similarly, why should both the long and the short-word exchanges show the same properties? Most important, however, is the fact that an analysis of the *in*complete exchange/anticipations shows the same patterns as the analysis of the complete ones (making the best guess one can about the likely nature of the completed error).

time" constraints and, hence, affected by adjacency of elements in the intended output, and one under "functional" constraints, and, hence, primarily sensitive to the structural relations upon which form class distinctions among the words of the intended output are attendant. These points may be more elaborately stated as follows:

(20) a. Exchanged words that are (relatively) widely separated in the intended output or that are members of distinct surface clauses will serve similar roles in the sentence structures underlying the intended utterance and, in particular, will be of the same form class. These exchange errors represent interactions of elements at a level of processing for which functional relations are the determinant of "computational simultaneity"; similarity of the descriptions that govern the selection among elements at this level is assumed to determine error interactions.

b. Exchanged elements that are (relatively) near to each other and which violate form class represent interactions at a level of processing for which the serial order of the elements of an intended utterance is the determinant of computational simultaneity. Similarity of left and right adjacent elements both phonetically and syntactically, as well as similarity of the elements themselves, is assumed to determine the likelihood of error interactions.

The facts about production errors which we have discussed to this point are not by themselves sufficient to sustain the claims of (20) (*a*) and (*b*). There are, however, a variety of other regularities of production errors which indicate the truth of something like these generalizations. We turn now to a systematic discussion of such additional properties of errors as bear on (20) (a) and (b) and on related claims.

VI. Stranded Morphemes, Shifts, and Exchanges

A somewhat unexpected consequence of the preceding analysis has been the postulation of two levels of nonphonological structural processing. That postulation rests primarily on the failure of words that are combined with bound morphs to show the same error behavior as independently occurring words, both with respect to form class and span of error movement. In (20) (a) and (b), these facts have been interpreted as the reflections of a planning level in which structural relations among words are being manipulated, as opposed to one in which the serial deployment of lexical and grammatical formatives is being worked out. (We leave open for the moment the question of how sound errors fit into this system.) The data we wish to consider now strengthen the basis for claiming the existence of these two processing levels and provide some further indication of their character.

We will begin by a closer examination of the structures in which the various error types occur. We note first of all that a striking regularity of the sound errors converges with a "definitional" property of the combined forms: they are both restricted to open-class elements (primarily to nouns, verbs, and adjectives). Since, barring some pronouns and elements of the auxiliary expansion, closed-class words are not inflected or combined, the combined form errors will necessarily involve only open-class words. It is significant that sound exchanges are similarly restricted, but in one particular respect, word exchanges are not. Only two of the 137 sound exchanges in the MIT corpus involve closed-class items (a qualifier, "few," and a subordinate conjunction, "until"); twenty of the 97 word exchanges involve closed classes. The most interesting for present purposes are the ten that exchange prepositions (the remaining ten such exchanges are distributed: six between pronouns, two between determiners, one between the elements of a complementizer, and one between a negative and a temporal qualifier). Their interest lies not simply in the closed versus open contrast, although that has its significance, but in the fact that these closed-class elements of word exchanges, like the open-class ones, come from corresponding positions within their respective structures. But the open-class items of sound and combined-form exchanges do *not* show any such parallelism of structure; they are typically interactions between the head of a construction and one of its modifiers. (For this contrast, see the earlier examples (1)–(9), (12)–(19), and (21)–(28), following; the elements that have been permuted are boldfaced.

(21) *I have to fill up the* **gas** *with* **car**.
(22) *Prior to the operation they had to shave all the* **head** *off my* **hair**.
(23) *She donated a* **library** *to the* **book**.
(24) *Older men* **choose** *to* **tend** *younger wives.*
(25) *. . . which was parallel* **to** *a certain sense,* **in** *an experience. . . .*
(26) *Everytime I put one of these buttons* **off**, *another one comes* **on**.
(27) *she* **sings** *everything she* **writes**.
(28) *. . . read the newspapers,* **watch** *the radio, and* **listen to** *T.V.*

The parallelism of structure is most strikingly evident for the word exchanges that cross clause boundaries, but even the within-clause exchanges show strong correspondence, usually involving two similarly placed words from distinct phrases. These phrases are quite often, for example, the noun phrases (NPs) of direct and indirect objects, or the NPs from a direct object and an adverbial phrase, or from successive adverbial phrases. This contrasts with the dominant pattern for sound or combined-form errors, in which the interacting elements are members of the same phrase. These differences in the structural features of the error types are summarized in Table V.

There are two aspects of this contrast which bear on the characterization given in (20) (a). One, the similarity of structural roles played by exchanged words, speaks for itself. The other turns on the fact that both verbs and prepositions are (relatively) frequently involved in the word exchanges. The prepositions are of particular interest since they do not enter into sound exchanges at all (nor, obviously into combined form exchanges). Both prepositions and verbs are important determinants of the relations between phrase types. It seems fairly clear that the sorts of structures typically involved in a sound or combined-form exchange are different from those of word exchanges, and that the nature of this difference is consonant with a characterization of the processing level at which word exchanges take place as one in which the functional relations between the words within constructions, and of the relations between the constructions themselves, are paramount.

It should be recognized that the facts about the error types we have just been discussing are not independent of the earlier observations about form class and error span. Though it is perfectly possible for adjacent element exchanges, or exchanges of one degree separation, to involve different phrases, it is clear that an increase in the separation of error elements will increase the likelihood of distinct phrases being involved. And, similarly, the likelihood that an error will involve elements of the same form class is decreased if both are members of the same phrase. Thus, one should see the error span and form class properties of exchanges on the one hand, and the structural properties in Table V on the other, as different, but closely related reflections of the same causes.

In the discussion thus far, we have focussed most attention on the level of processing described in (20) (a). There remain two principal issues to be dealt with before attempting to relate the predominantly syntactic processes now under examination to the more general framework of sentence production. These are (a) the character of the

TABLE V

STRUCTURAL SUMMARY FOR EXCHANGES[a]

Types of structures in which exchanges occur	Error class		
	(n=119) Sound	(n=46) Comb. form	(n=97) Word
Within NPs (or Pred. Phrase)	85	19	19
Names (e.g., *Sen Diago, Jahn Honcock,* Treato Seaty)	13	4	—
N and N (e.g., *cheeps and twirts*)[b]	9	2	4
Nominal Compounds (e.g., *skay pale; pre-truning*)	25	6	1
Adj (Adj) N (e.g., *stilthy finking drunk; sollow hound*)	25	5	—
N of N (e.g., *bate of dirth*)[b]	10	2	15
Pred. Phrase: (Adv Adj)	3	—	—
Between NPs	6	7	45
NP V NP	2	4	8
V NP (prep) NP	4	3	37
Between V and Pred. (or Subj. Phrases)	19	16	4
V NP, or V Adj Phrase or Adv Phrase (e.g., *he was slowing shides; that would pick in steoples mind*)	14	9	3
NP V (e.g., *you should have your brekes chācked*)	5	7	1
Between closed classes *not* in NPs	—	—	12
V *Prep* NP *Prep* NP	—	—	10
V (VP) *Adv Adv*, or V *comp.* NP*comp.* VP	—	—	2
Between clauses	9	4	17
Relatives	2	1	2
Complements	3	3	4
Conjunctions	—	—	11
Clause adjuncts (e.g. *Helf, Helf, the wolp is after me*)	4	—	—

[a]The errors used as examples consist mostly of sound errors simply because the other error types have ample numbers of illustrations in the text.
[b]May be better analyzed as *NP* and *NP* or *NP* of *NP* in some cases.

level of processing outlined in (20) (b) and (b) the relation of the levels in (20) (a) and (b) to sound exchanges. We first take up the evidence relevant to (20) (b).

The errors we have been referring to as "combined form" exchanges are errors of a rather remarkable sort. They might, as a matter of fact, have been more aptly designated as "morpheme stranding" errors, for not only are the permuted elements nearly always free forms, but the elements that are left behind are as often bound morphemes, as examples: (16)–(19) and (29)–(32) show (permuted elements boldfaced).[18]

(29) . . . *but the* **clean**'*s* **two***er*.
(30) . . . *I'm not in the* **read** *for* **mood***ing*.
(31) . . . *he made a lot of money in*telephon*ing* stalls.
(32) *She's already* **trunk***ed two* **packs**.

Moreover, as the examples also attest, not just any bound morph gets stranded; it is, rather, those we might term "syntactically active" affixes; for example, tense and number morphemes, possessive morpheme, comparative morphemes, the -*er* of noun formation, and so forth. There are also a very few nonderivational morphemes and a nonmorphemic maverick or two which are intermixed in a fashion discussed below. Table VI provides a summary of these errors in terms of the sort of elements stranded by the exchange. Of the 46 errors classified as combined form exchanges, 33 involve only the bound morphs I have called "syntactically active," that is, the morphemes that are directly involved in syntactic rules (as, auxiliary elements, or possessives, or comparatives), or that affect the form class of the stem to which they are attached (as the -*er* of noun formation). Of the remaining thirteen errors, a further six also involve syntactically active bound morphs, but include as well a nonmorphemic segment (e.g., the *er* in *shoulder*), or what might be called "moribund" affixes, that is, those of dubious productivity and very likely not semantically analyzed (as, the prefixes in *along*, *install*, and *intend*).

[18] It will be apparent that the basis of classification of errors as "combined form errors" is crucial to any evaluation of the nature of stranded elements. If only errors which result in the movement of a morpheme are included, then, of course, only morphemes can be stranded. Such a classification does not require, however, that the moved elements be potentially free forms, nor that the stranded elements be bound morphs of a particular subvariety. In fact, the classification used was more conservative: an error was counted as a combined-form error just in case the permuted elements had the *form* of morphemes (i.e., could have been morphemes in a different environment), and the shorter of the two forms created by the error was the one which maintained its serial position. Thus the actual description of the elements involved in these errors is not dictated by the basis of the classification. Errors like, *errples of examors* (examples of errors), or *chainse playges* (place changes) *would* have been included had they been in the corpus. It simply turns out that no such errors were observed.

TABLE VI

SUMMARY OF STRANDED ELEMENTS IN COMBINED FORM ERRORS

No. of such errors	Type of stranded elements	Examples
9	Number only	Make it so the tree has less apples → ... apple has less trees; also (17) above
8	Tense only	It just started to sound → ... sounded to start; also (18) and (19) above
2	Tense and number	...Windows rolled up → rolls windowed up; also (32) above
6	Tense and/or number, and a derivational suffix	All the starters scored in double figures → ... scorers started. ...
4	Gerundive	O.J. is thirst quenching → ... quench thirsting. ...
3	Comparative and/or possessive	the Cognitive Center's study of ... → ... Cognitive study's Center ...; also (29) above
1	Tense and a free form	...the flashlight be smashed → ...smash light be flashed
	A syntactically active bound morph and	
4	(a) a "moribund" morph	I had intended staying → ...instayed tending; also, (g) in Table I and (31) above
2	(b) a nonmorph	My shoulders are frozen → ... frozers are shoulden
2	Two free forms	Paperback Booksmith → Paperbook backsmith
1	A nonmorph and a free form	get ready for bedtime → ... bedy for red time
3	Nonmorphs only	Cambridge Fenway → Fenwidge Camway, Seato Treaty → Treato Seaty, Lackner and Goldstein → Goldner and Lackstein
1	Moribund morph only	He didn't get along so well → ... awell so long

It is a striking fact that involvement of a moribund morph or a nonmorph in these errors is usually accompanied by a syntactically introduced morpheme. A possibly related fact is that even among the affixes I have dubbed syntactically active, the derivational affixes also do not appear alone in stranding errors, but nearly always in conjunction with a morpheme introduced by a syntactic process; the syntactically introduced morphs, on the other hand, often appear singly in errors. It almost appears that the bound morphs in the domain of syntactic rules "catalyze" the involvement of other affixal elements or of elements that have the phonetic shape of affixes (e.g., the *er* in *shoulder*, or the *y* in *epitome*). At any event, it is true that 85% of the stranding errors involve syntactically introduced bound morphs (and the exceptions are of limited sort: three could be sound errors and four of them are proper names).

It would be unwise to conclude from the preceding that strictly derivational affixes *cannot* appear alone in stranding errors. The sample of stranding errors that we have is, after all, rather small. None the less, it is surprising that when morphemic decomposition of a word occurs in an exchange, it should be so nearly restricted to cases in which that decomposition implicates syntactic processes. This suggests two things. First, the level of representation at which stranding errors take place—by hypothesis, the level described in (20) (b)—is one for which the computational vocabulary is of morphologically complete types. Thus, at this level words like *compassion*, *inept, unwieldy, preamble,* and so forth, that are undoubtedly represented in the lexicon as sequences of morphemes, are single vocabulary units, coming apart at their morphemic seams only when an error in the integration of such an element with its syntactic frame occurs. Second, as the just preceding remark in fact assumes, the nature of the stranded elements in the combined-form errors indicates that we are, in fact, dealing with a processing level for which the syntactic organization of the sentence is at issue. This is important, for without this evidence the basis for imputing specifically syntactic significance to level (20)(b) is weak. We have only the fact that *word* forms are involved in the errors to go on, coupled with the clausal restriction on the error span. On the other hand, there is a clear failure of these errors to honor the sort of structural features we have taken as diagnostic of the syntactic processes for level (20) (a).

Why should the presence of a syntactically active bound morpheme be associated with an error at the level described by (20)(b)? Precisely because the attachment of a syntactic morpheme to a particular lexical item reflects a mapping from the "functional" level to the "positional" level of sentence planning. Why should stranding errors fail to honor form class? Because that is exactly the nature of the error being made; a given pair of free forms is assigned to the wrong position within the syntactic "frame" which determines the order of their surface appearance and their form class.

Finally, why should the elements we have called syntactically active bound morphemes be stranded? Not simply because their morphemic analysis is represented at (20)(b), for after all, so too is some sound structure, and the structure of some other morphemes. A stronger claim seems required, and it is suggested by the earlier observation that the stranding errors are restricted to open class items. That might be taken not as a definitional consequence of the error classification, but as a substantive claim about processing at this level; namely, that the open class elements are being "inserted" into a grammatical framework defined by closed-class elements, including syntactically active bound morphs. Such an assumption makes a good deal of sense in light of the sort of observations we made in discussing the phenomena of accommodation, particularly the preservation of phrasal stress. For as Boomer and Laver pointed out (1968, p. 12), the appearance of appropriate phrasal stress on misplaced elements requires that the sentence processing system provide for an independent (of lexical items) specification of that stress. A syntactic frame which specifies the serial order of content words would provide a vehicle for such an independent specification. A "list" of such frames might be thought of as a part of a heuristic system for mapping from an underlying functional representation of sentences onto a representation constrained by the real time occurrence of the words.

This separation of "form" and "content" items into distinct aspects of the processing system is attractive, for it provides not only for the facts discussed above, but also accounts in a natural way for the very strong restriction on *all* exchanges that has not yet been mentioned. That restriction precludes the interchange of open- and closed-class items (even when form class is violated, this restriction is not). Further, if we assume that the syntactic morphs are parts of such structural frames, it accounts for another feature of their behavior—they do not themselves exchange. It would, of course, be perfectly possible for stranded morphs to have the characteristics we have so far described and still undergo exchange; for example, it is logically possible to have an error like *the boys shouting disturbed us* → *the boying shouts disturbed us*, but no such errors appear in the

MIT corpus. The rarity of exchanges between the final portions of words makes the firm evaluation of this "error lacuna" difficult, but, the frequency with which these elements occur as the terminal portions of words, coupled with their behavior in stranding errors and their involvement in "shift" errors (mentioned later), makes their complete absence from the corpus of such final position exchanges noteworthy. Rather than prepare a table, I have simply listed all the cases of final position exchanges in the MIT corpus (permuted sequences boldfaced).[19]

(33)   a. *Jill and Mike → Jike and Mill*
        b. *Howard and Claire → Haire and Cloward*
        c. *Structure and function → strunction and fucture*
        d. *expect and persuade → exspade and perswect*

(34)   a. *I'm about to spill beer → . . . speer bill*
        b. *I won't hit the ball hard → . . . bard hall*
        c. *you should have your sholders forward → . . . sholwards forders*
        d. *in the next ten minutes → . . . nen text*
        e. *listen to me give → . . . live me gissen*
        f. *night life → . . . nife light*

(35)   a. *the girl who called → . . . gall who curled*
        b. *a monkey's uncle → . . . monkle's unkey*

(36)   a. *the single biggest problem → . . . singest biggle*
        b. *Singer Sewing Machine → Singing Sewer Machine*
        c. *passive usage → passage usive*

Note first of all that most of these segments do not have a morphemic analysis at all, and of the cases, (36), where a morpheme is involved, it exchanges with a nonmorph, suggesting that the morphemic status of the element is irrelevant and that these are in fact sound errors. The errors in (35) (a) and (b) are especially instructive, for these are cases where the final portion of two words *does* permute, but one of them is inflected; the inflection stays behind.

---

[19] The four errors in (33) are suspect cases since either output order of the nouns is grammatically acceptable, and there is therefore no basis for classifying these as word final exchanges, rather than word initial, other than the speaker's report of his intention.

Note further that (36) (*c*) *might* have been classed as a morpheme-stranding error since both *-age* and *-ive* are morphemes (although it seems unlikely that *passive* should be so analyzed—i.e., it is a moribund morph in this case). If (36) (*c*) were so classified, it would then constitute the single case of a morpheme-stranding error which moved the final rather than the initial or medial portions of a word, and which moved bound rather than free forms.

This suggests not only that syntactically active bound morphs do not permute even when a sound exchange involving their word position occurs, but also that perhaps sound-exchange errors may be conditioned by the syntactic frames we have been discussing. (I will return to this point momentarily).

The final observation about syntactically active bound morphs concerns their involvement in what I have called "shifts"; for example, Table I, entry (f) and examples (6) and (9). Shifts in the location of a sound seem to fall into roughly two classes: those that involve nonfinal sounds and usually result in the formation or destruction of a cluster, and those that involve final sounds and are almost exclusively confined to syntactically active bound morphs. That is, one does *not* find errors like: *final sound* → *fina soundl,* or *tax restriction* → *tak restrictions,* or *end run* → *en rund.* One *does* find errors like (37)–(40), however.

(37)   *they get wierder every day* → . . . *wierd everier . . .*
(38)   *he gets it done* → . . . *get its done*
(39)   *he goes back to* → *go backs to*
(40)   *pull its genes down* → . . . *gene downs*

This difference could be a "sampling error," and claims about the nonoccurrence of a given error type have a dismaying way of being disconfirmed by the next sleepy speaker one encounters. At any event, of the 25 cases of a word-final sound shift, 25 are syntactically active bound morphs (this includes both derivational and syntactic morphs, but principally the latter). It is clear that one cannot explain this by an appeal to phonologic constraints or to a prohibition against producing nonwords. There *are* final clusters in English (if shifts were restricted to cluster formation), and sound errors yield nonwords as often as they yield word forms. There are also numerous end-ryme errors in the MIT corpus (e.g., *Wenatchie is the appital capital of the world;* . . . *and sol did Tolman; half a cuff of coffee;* etc.), so it cannot be a "constraint" against distortions of the ends of words that restricts such shifts to bound morphs. The obvious inference is that these are not sound errors at all—their status as bound morphs is related to their appearance in this error pattern.

If this is the case, it would make sense in light of the notion of a syntactic frame, of which these morphs are features. One would not expect exchanges of such morphs at the same level as exchanges of the elements (words) being fitted into the structural framework of which the bound morphs are a part. Hence, the stranding errors. But, one might very well expect to get errors of placement of these syntactic features when they are phonetically realized and attached to particular lexical items. Further, these morpheme shifts, unlike the stranding exchanges, frequently involve closed-class words—e.g., (37)–(40); 16 of the 25 shifts are between an open-class and a closed-class word, or between two closed-class words. This provides a convincing independent argument against considering these shifts as exchanges between a "zero" morph (phonetically unrealized) and a phone; for, of course, the words to which the shifts attach the bound morphs are often not capable of inflection. This involvement of closed class words in the bound-morpheme shifts is also typical of word shifts. I will presently argue (in discussing word shifts) that the shifts of bound morphemes and of free forms arise from similar processes, and that both are distinct from exchanges.

What we have discussed of the behavior of stranding exchanges and of morpheme shifts to this point seems to support the characterization offered in (20) (b) of a processing "level" constrained by the serial deployment of the lexical items in a sentence, and indicates that this is accomplished through the integration of two computationally distinct types of information—that connected with the open-class 'content" items on the one hand, and that connected with the closed-class structural elements which "define" the surface form of sentences on the other.

In the preceding discussion, I have used the behavior of sound exchanges as a touchstone of contrast with word exchanges, but have not explicitly addressed the question of how sound planning in general, and sound exchanges in particular, relate to the processing levels of (20)(a) and (b). Such comment as can be made is limited, but I will take up that issue now and at the same time summarize some of the contrasts discussed so far.

It will have been obvious that, by the diagnostic variables we have been using, sound exchanges are more akin to the combined-form exchanges than to the word exchanges. It should be emphasized that this is an empirical consequence of the error data and *not* a necessary condition on sound errors. There is no a priori reason why sound errors should not occur at any level of processing for which there exists some specification of phonetic information about lexical items. On the current evidence, one cannot rule out the possibility of sound errors at the level of word exchanges, as in (20)(a); but the assignment of morpheme-stranding exchanges and some sound errors (exchanges) to a common level is not only indicated by the facts we have, it makes a certain sort of sense as well. Consider the "facts" first, and then the sense:

	Sound	Combined form	Word
Phonetic similarity:			
of exchanged elements	Yes	(Possibly)	No
of environment	Yes	(Possibly)	No
Structural similarity:			
of exchanged elements (form class)	No	No	Yes
of environment (structural role)	No	No	Yes
Closed-class words involved	No	No	Yes
Error spans open-class words (error span frequently exceeds 1 word)	No	No	Yes
Clausally constrained	Yes	Yes	Yes

I have not commented previously on the phonetic relation between exchanged words, although the phonetic similarity of exchanged sounds and their environments has been mentioned. It is clear, however, that in this respect as in the others word exchanges contrast with sound exchanges. (There is also an indication that the combined-form exchanges are more likely to be phonetically similar than are exchanged words, especially at their final segments, i.e., the point of their attachment to stranded morphs. It is not a powerful constraint, however, if it does exist at all.) In every respect, save that of the clausal constraint, the sound exchanges and combined form exchanges are similar to each other and contrast with the word exchanges.

To this list of similarities in the behavior of sound and combined form exchanges we might also recall the pair of examples in (35). We were examining the behavior of syntactically active bound morphs, and we noted that (35)(a) and (b) were cases of word-final sound exchanges which stranded morphemes. This strongly suggests that at the point where sound exchanges occur, the bound morphs are still marked for their syntactic status. In terms of our earlier discussion, that would entail that they are still features of the "nodes" of the syntactic frame to which lexical items are attached. One other aspect of the sound exchanges which deserves stress in this connection is their apparent restriction to open-class words, especially since most other sound errors *do* include closed-class words as sources. This is somewhat surprising, barring some reason for "insulating" closed-class and open-class sound elements from interaction in exchanges. But the assumption that sound exchanges take place at the point of inserting lexical items into their "surface" structural frames, just as we have argued combined-form exchanges do, provides such a reason.

Finally, if we assume that the phenomena of phonetic accommodation cannot take place at the same level as sound exchanges and stranding errors, we need to postulate two levels at which sound-structure errors can occur. Under the current suggestion the first such level is coincident with the planning for the serial deployment of lexical items—that is, (20)(b)—and would be the point at which the phonetic consequences of syntactic variables are accommodated. Detailed phonetic regularities that are the consequence of the phonetic environment of a sound segment would be worked out at a subsequent level of phonological processing, and that level would be the locus of sound errors other than exchanges (barring the possibility of a fourth category arising out of motor interactions—like "tongue twisters" and some common word-internal errors of similar ilk; e.g., *tachistoscope* → *taskistoscope*).

This reconstruction of the role of sound exchanges also accommodates the clausal constraint displayed by such errors. It should be noted, however, that it is not necessary to assign these errors to a specifically syntactic level of processing in order to rationalize their sensitivity to a syntactic variable. For example, both their error span (an open-class word never intervenes between the source words) and the character of the constructions they occur in (see Table V) suggest that sound exchanges may very well take place in a system with units smaller than clause size. One might suppose, on these grounds, that sound-exchange interactions take place when the sound structure of the lexical items to be inserted into the hypothesized syntactic frames of level (20)(b) is specified in a limited capacity store and that store has a length of two content items. The *input* to this store might be clausally constrained such that two elements from different clauses are never simultaneously present in it. This would preclude the occurrence of interclause errors even though the size of the sound planning system was itself smaller than a clause and, indeed, even quite insensitive to syntactic processes in its internal operation. Given that combined form errors have so much in common with sound exchanges, in fact, one might even suppose that the stranding errors arise because of a misassignment of the output of the words from such a store to their positions in the syntactic frames that specify their surface order. This is no more than speculation, of course, for we have no grounds in the present error data to decide matters of such detail. It is sufficient to emphasize the point that the decision to assign sound exchanges to the level (20)(b) is compatible with the clausal constraint but not demanded by it.

There remains one more class of syntactic errors that bears in an interesting way on the issues we have been considering. Those are the "word shifts" we referred to earlier in our discussion of word exchanges. Errors such as those in (41)–(44) are evidently ambiguous as to their status—exchanges of adjacent elements, or shifts in the position of a single element.

(Elements that would be involved if an exchange is assumed are bracketed; the element presumably moved if a shift is assumed is boldfaced)

(41) *Who* (**else**) (*would*) *like one?* → *Who would else . . .*
(42) *There's* (*something*) (**very**) *peculiar about this* → *There's very something . . .*
(43) *They* (*might*) (**not**) *be too closely glued together* → *They not might be . . .*
(44) *I'll bet you* (*that*) (**what**) *he said was . . .* → *I'll bet you what that he . . .*

More than a terminological quibble is at issue here, for I wish to argue that word exchanges are typical of a level of processing at which the functional relations between vocabulary elements is at issue, while shifts are a consequence of the operations which map from a level that captures such functional relations to one that represents the serial constraints on vocabulary items, that is, that word shifts are more related to the processes of (20)(b) than those of (20)(a).

Though we cannot tell about cases like (41)–(44), we can, I believe, safely consider (45)–(50) as shifts for several reasons. Eighteen of the 72 shifts errors are like (45)–(50) in that an analysis of them as exchanges would require an exchange between a single word and a word sequence. An inspection of the properties of these errors (which I will refer to as "word/string" shifts) may help decide the unclear cases.

(45) *When the number of letters (in common) (gets) to be large* → *... letters gets in common to ...*

(46) *I've got something (to tell you) (all)* → *... something all to tell you*

(47) **(Little)** *(beads of) blood will pop out on my brow,* → *beads of little blood will ...*

(48) *If you can't figure* **(out)** *(what that) is,* → *... figure what that out is*

(49) *Who* **(else)** *(did I think) had left?* → *Who did I think else had left*

(50) *(This place is)* **(hardly)** *well run* → *Hardly this place is well run*

Consider what we would be required to claim if these were taken as exchanges. We would first of all have to accept that words may exchange with phrases, and presumably, therefore, that at some level they have similar descriptions. In principle, there is no bar to this move, and if it could be sustained for a putatively syntactic level of sentence processing it would be of considerable theoretical interest independent of our current concerns.[20] There are a number of grounds for rejecting this sort of account, however. For example, if words are exchanged with phrases in the same fashion as words are exchanged with other words (if they are, in other words, typically at the same level of description for the sentence processor), one might expect the phrase types that are exchanged with words to fulfill structurally similar roles, just as do the words in word exchanges. And, indeed, for those very few cases of clear exchanges where a single word is exchanged with a construction, this is true (e.g., *Did you ever go to the F & T with Bob* → *... to Bob with the F & T?*). Moreover, in the MIT corpus, all such cases proper names or idioms. Neither of these properties is true of the putatively exchanged elements in (45)–(50) or of the other similar cases. Even more telling, in (47)–(50) the word string that must be assumed to exchange is not even properly analyzed as a phrase. Indeed, much of the earlier discussion of bound morphemes can be seen as bearing on

---

[20] There are independent grounds for doubting that lexical and syntactic structures should be interchangeable within a given language (see Fodor, Fodor, & Garrett, 1975).

the relevant generalization here: exchanges do not take place between elements at significantly different levels of linguistic description, words do not exchange with bound morphs, sounds do not exchange with words, words do not exchange with phrases, We will thus consider the sort of errors in (45)–(50) to be shifts in the position of a single word or phrase, usually the former.

It is immediately apparent that the word/string shifts have properties (other than those just discussed) which distinguish them from exchanges and, further, that these are properties which they have in common with most of the 54 cases, like (41)–(44), that misplace single adjacent words. Consider the prominence of closed-class words. These errors more than any others seem to involve closed-class items: fourteen of the eighteen word versus word/string shifts involve apparent movement of closed-class words, and 42 of the 54 single-word cases. By contrast, only the word exchanges showed any closed-class involvement at all, and it was in a substantially smaller proportion of the errors, confined to elements in structurally similar roles. Thus, in both proportion (24% of word exchanges as against 77% of shifts) and structural role, the closed-class items of shifts contrast with those of word exchange. But it is in the contribution of adverbs to shift errors that the sharpest difference emerges. Adverbs are conspicuously absent (both open and closed class) from all exchanges, but in the shifts, 40 of the 72 errors involve misplaced adverbs or abverbials (nine of the 18 word versus string cases, and 31 of 54 single word cases). As all the preceding would suggest, form class is not preserved between the putatively exchanged adjacent words, and neither are they parts of the sort of structures typical of exchanges (e.g., noun phrases of various sorts). On every count save that of the clausal constraint (discussed later) they contrast with word exchanges.

At this point, it would seem that a prima facie case has been made for assigning all the 54 ambiguous movement cases to the shift category established by the 18 clear cases. But one may do a bit better than that if one takes seriously the arguments from diagnostic variables that we have used in the preceding several sections. We can "purge" the ambiguous 54 of just those cases which could reasonably be exchanges—of either level (20)(a) or (20)(b)—on grounds of form class and structural role. There are, in fact, twelve such cases; (51)–(54) give four that are typical.

(51) *It's just* **plain heavy** *stop-and-go traffic down there* →
    . . . just heavy plain stop . . .

(52) *Though the long* **Labor-day** *weekend ...* → *... long day-Labor week ...*
(53) *I'd like to make a credit-***card call** → *... a credit-call card*
(54) *You're not allowed to* **mix meat** *with milk* → *... to meat mix with ...*

The contrast of these with the errors of (41)–(50), and their similarity to the errors of word and, especially, combined-form exchanges is obvious.[21] Whether one confines one's attention to the presumably pristine remainder of 60 shifts or contemplates the entire set of 72, the account of this error pattern is transparent. They are predominantly instances in which a word in the surface positional string must intervene between two words that are in immediate construction at the functional level. Another way of reflecting this is to note the frequency with which movement transformations are involved in the linguistic derivation of the structures in which shift errors take place. As the frequency of adverbial involvement indicates, adverb placement will figure in the majority of the shift cases. Note, too, that these are almost entirely closed-class adverbs (qualifiers and quantifiers like *so, very, really, quite, all, else,* etc.). Moreover, the adverb-placement transformations very often occur in conjunction with other movement transforms (e.g., "*wh-* fronting," "particle movement," "question," "extraposition of relatives," etc.).

There are several very important aspects and implications of these errors which should be stressed. Note first of all the parallel between the word shifts and the bound-morpheme shifts discussed earlier. Both types of shifts seem to be strongly restricted to *syntactic* morphemes. The interpretation of the bound morphemes as features of the syntactic frames which organize the serial order of the open-class lexical formatives might thus quite reasonably be extended to the closed-class syntactic elements of word shifts as well.[22]

---

[21] If one wished to carry this bootstrap operation further, of course, the obvious move would be to sort out those combined form errors that arise at the functional level and those word exchanges that arise at the positional level. Though one is filled with an ineffable sense of tidiness when this operation is performed on the data, it does not shed any new light on the mechanisms underlying the error classes.

[22] The similarities of the bound morpheme shifts and the word shifts are perhaps stronger than I have suggested in the text. Jackendoff (1969) has argued that the bound morphs I have referred to as "syntactic" are, in fact, the only vehicles for *transformationally* altering word form. Thus, *all* the morpheme shifts, both bound and free forms, would implicate transformational placements by this argument.

Second, note that these sorts of word shifts reflect an aspect of the relations between the functional and the positional levels of representation that was hinted at in the discussion of differences among the error types in terms of error span. Elements which are near to each other in the surface form of a sentence need not be adjacent at underlying levels and conversely. If adjacency is an important determinant of the occurrence of sound exchange and combined form exchanges, one might expect to find grammatical formatives and "movable" open-class elements as the only types of elements which intervene between the source words of an exchange between sounds or combined forms. That appears, in fact, to be true. Error spans of one or two words are found for sound exchanges, but the intervening elements are closed class, grammatical formatives, or movable elements like adverbs. This is not true of independent word exchanges, for which open-class words frequently intervene between the two error positions. When this difference is taken account of, the differences in the error spans of word exchanges and sound and combined forms are even more striking.

Closely related to the preceding observation is the obvious implication that the surface position of words does not predict their "position" at the functional level of representation. Consider the error in example (41) where the actual utterance was, *Who did I think else would come?* The position occupied by the word *else* corresponds to the location it would have in an underlying description of the sentence prior to *wh-* movement in the question form. One might almost think of this error and a number of very similar ones as "failures" of movement transformations (but see later). In this same vein, we might reconsider the matter of structural parallels between the two elements of a word exchange. When the main verb and the verb of an infinitival complement change places, the parallelism of structure at the surface level is not readily apparent; but when one considers an underlying, functional level of description, the parallelism is obvious. For example, (24) would have, very roughly, the representation: *Older men tend* (for *to older men choose younger wives*).

Finally we should explicitly note that the shift errors do not violate the clausal constraint: 64 of the 72 cases of shifts are intraclause errors. Thus, it is clear that the involvement of movement operations in the processing system is very likely defined over clause-length units, just as are the operations of inserting lexical elements into their structural frames.

One should not assume that because transformations figure in the linguistic derivation of the structures in which shift errors occur that, therefore, the linguistic transforms are part of the information processing that underlies these sentences. Having noted that, however, the evidence of these errors strongly indicate that the "movement" of lexical items is involved in the mapping from the "functional" level of representation that is the result of processing referred to in (20)(a), to the "positional" level of representation that results from the processes of (20)(b).

We should at this point take explicit notice of a systematic and heretofore harmless ambiguity in the way I have used the term "level." Clearly, it may refer to both a structural representation and to the processing activity presumed to give rise to it. The shift errors simply provide the most obvious demonstration of this distinction. If we restated the implications of the preceding several sections in terms of that distinction, we would characterize the error processes of (20)(a) as attendant upon the mapping from the message level of representation to a functional level of representation; the error processes of (20)(b) would be assumed to arise from the mapping of that level onto the surface positional level given by the "syntactic frames" we discussed earlier. I will argue in the next section that there are other errors which should be assigned to the message-to-functional level mapping.

VII. Fusions and Substitutions: Semantic Errors

This discussion of semantic factors in production will be limited; it is presented primarily for purposes of contrast with the preceding discussion of errors I have deemed syntactic. The first thing of import to note is the absence of any indication that specifically semantic factors influence the exchange errors of various sorts.

One may look for semantic relations between the two words involved in a sound, combined form, or word exchange just as one looks for phonetic and syntactic relations.[23] But while the evidences

---

[23] The phonetic and semantic "indices" of similarity are my own judgments. They are conservative, and will err on the side of ignoring any "subtle" involvements of sound or meaning. Unless there was an obvious phonetic overlap (e.g., *Did you know you have a* sole *in the* hole *of your shoe?*), the case was counted as phonetically unrelated (e.g., *I left the* briefcase *in my* cigar.) Similarly for semantic cases; unless there was near synonomy or antonymy (e.g., *lion/tiger* or *car/truck*; *start/stop, on/off*) cases were counted as semantically unrelated (e.g. *car/gas, barns/cats, idea/guy* etc.)

for involvement of the latter factors are plentiful, no suggestion of a semantic relation (that is not exhausted by correlated syntactic features) is to be found. The many examples of the various error types given in the preceding discussions are quite typical in this respect. The only place where there is a hint of semantic regularity appears in the cross-clausal word exchanges. There are, however, too few such cases to make an effective assessment, and even within the small set available there are exchanges that are hard to rationalize semantically. It thus seems very likely, not only on the positive grounds of syntactic and phonological involvement in exchanges and related error types, but also on the negative grounds of no apparent semantic effects, that we are dealing with syntactic processes in exchanges.

One has only to turn to errors like those of (53)–(62) to see what a "semantic involvement" yields (see also Table I). These errors are of two sorts: *fusions,* in which two expressions destined for the same functional role are in competition, and portions of both are output, and *substitutions,* in which roughly the same circumstance yields a different word than that intended by the speaker.

(53) *I just* **snabbed** *it* (intended *nabbed it* or *snapped it up*)
(54) *Nobody gets very* **upcited** *about that . . .* (intended: *excited* or *upset*)
(55) *I don't want to* **intervere** (intended: *intervene* or *interfere*)
(56) *I don't know what the* **outshot** *of that is* (intended: *outcome* or *upshot*)
(57) *Do you want to try just a* **tab** *. . . uh, a* **dad,** *uh, Jesus! Do you want a dab or a tad of this stuff?* (speaker intended only one of the two expressions initially)
(58) *I'm chronically on the* **fringe** *of . . . on the verge of making a break.*
(59) *Now that's what I call a full* **cup** *of tea.* (speaker was commenting on an overflowing **pot** of tea)
(60) *What I've done here is torn* **together** *three . . . uh, torn apart three issues that . . .*
(61) *I have to leave in at* **least** *. . . in at most an hour.*
(62) *I would like to see it now that I've* **written** *the book—uh, read the book.*

The fact there are semantic relations between the conflated words is very clear. A discussion of the precise nature of those relations would take us beyond the scope of this paper. Two or three comments are in order, however.

First of all, recall the discussion of shift errors, in which I argued against the assumption of equivalence between words and phrases at the syntactic level of processing. In the fusion errors, however, we find fairly frequent cases like the one in (53). Thus, one might wish to argue that where semantic (message level) selection among expressions is concerned, there is a word–phrase equivalence. The indications from the errors in the MIT corpus are, however, that this is of a very limited sort. Nearly all the cases of such a conflation involve idioms or very highly practiced "formula phrases."

Second, we note that a very large percentage of the substitutions involve outright antonyms or "pragmatic" opposites (e.g., *write/read, speak/listen, see/hear* etc.),[24] while the majority of the fusions turn on a rough sort of synonomy (e.g., *athlete/player, grip/fist, bet/guess, bottles/jars, shout/yell*). And related to this, most of the cases of word/phrase conflation arise as fusions. This, plus one further point raised later, suggests that though the fusions and substitutions ought both be considered a consequence of mapping operations from messages onto the first syntactic level, they may nevertheless arise from rather different aspects of that process—roughly, that the substitutions arise from outright errors of lexical selection, while the fusions may arise from failures of an evaluation or checking procedure which determines the appropriateness of the mapping from messages to the functional level.

It is worthwhile commenting on the fact that it is a loose sort of synonomy that connects the two expressions involved in a fusion. But that approximateness is a bit deceptive in one respect: *within the context of the intended utterance,* the two words almost invariably have equal currency. That is, they will equally well convey the communicative intent of the speaker. This would seem to rule out

---

[24] The tendency for substitutions to be between opposites is true for cases (most of those in the MIT corpus) for which there is no apparent "motivational" account of the error or its direction. The so-called "Freudian" interpretations of word substitutions (e.g., *Who said that liars . . . uh that lawyers make a living by shoveling smoke?*) and sound errors (e.g., *We can make passionate love while the bed breaks, . . . I mean, while the bread bakes!*) should perhaps be tempered by such facts. For, if there is a general tendency to substitute opposites, it dictates caution in interpreting cases of such substitution where one has, antecedently, an expectation of a motivational account of some particular person's error. Similarly, for sound errors, there really does not seem to be any particular evidence that sound errors which yield words (let alone situationally apposite words) are more likely than sound errors which yield nonwords. There undoubtedly are "Freudian slips," but they may be a good deal rarer than might be supposed.

the possibility that the representation of messages consists, in part, of the vocabulary items of the language. For it is hard to see how one could accommodate the sort of situationally apposite confusions so evident in fusion errors. If messages are framed in words, all the fusion errors ought, as most of the substitutions are, to be very closely related semantically, and in particular, that relation ought to be context free.

The last point I wish to raise is one that further indicates that these errors are not message-level interactions, but are a part of the process of moving from that level to the representation level of (20)(a). Both fusions and substitutions are strongly constrained by their ultimate form class role: nouns substitute or fuse with other nouns, verbs with other verbs, and so forth. This constraint on the word substitutions seems to require an interaction at the level where syntactic relations have been at least partially formulated.

The comments I have made on the semantic errors are meant to be little more than suggestive. Their proper evaluation requires, I believe, both a clearer understanding of the syntactic processes of production and more information concerning the organization of our stored lexical information. A good deal of experimental interest in this latter area has been manifest in recent years and the evaluation of errors like those of (53)–(62) within the context of, for example, proposals for the organization of the lexicon which arise out of lexical access studies (e.g., Conrad, 1972; Rubenstein, Garfield, & Millikan, 1970) would be worthwhile.

VIII. Summary

We can conveniently draw together the several threads of the sections on the various error types in terms of Fig. 1. We might now replace some of those question marks as in Fig. 2. In the figure the various error types that have been used to motivate the postulated levels of representation are indicated.

At several points in the preceding pages I have gone beyond the data to speculate on the possible character of the processing systems under discussion. Those matters aside, it seems clear that a satisfactory reconstruction of the error data requires the postulation of two distinct levels of syntactic analysis, and that these levels will differ in that one is sensitive to the functional grammatical relations among words and phrases, while the other is primarily responsive to the integration of grammatical formatives with the serial ordering of

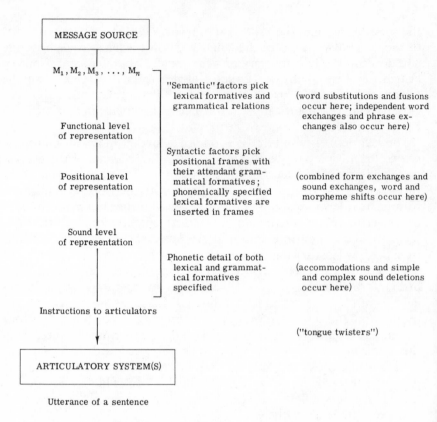

Fig. 2

"content words." Further, there is strong indication that this second level involves certain aspects of sound structure. Finally, it is clear that the clausal restriction on sound errors first suggested by Boomer and Laver is, in fact, a very much more general constraint on errors of a variety of types, and that it arises out of specifically syntactic processes. Such clausally constrained syntactic processes seem most likely to be connected with the mapping from the functional level of sentence planning to the positional one.

These and related observations about the role of motor integrations in error patterns will, I hope, prove amenable to experimental investigation. Ultimately it is only upon the results of such experimental work that detailed answers to the nature of the sentence production process can be worked out.

REFERENCES

Boomer, D. S., & Laver, J. D. M. Slips of the tongue. *British Journal of Disorders of Communication*, 1968, **3**, 2–12.

Conrad, C. Cognitive economy in semantic memory. *Journal of Experimental Psychology*, 1972, **92**, 149–154.

Fodor, J. A. *The Language of thought.* New York: Thos. Y. Crowell, 1975.

Fodor, J. A., Bever, T. G., & Garrett, M. F. *The psychology of language.* New York: McGraw-Hill, 1974.

Fodor, J. D., Fodor, J. A., & Garrett, M. F. The psychological unreality of semantic representations. *Lingusitic Enquiry*, 1975, in press.

Fromkin, V. A. The non-anomalous nature of anomalous utterances. *Language*, 1971, **47**, 27–52.

Jackendoff, R. S. Some rules for semantic interpretation for English. Unpublished doctoral dissertation, Massachusetts Institute of Technology, 1969.

Lees, R. B. *The grammar of English nominalizations.* Publ. No. 12. Bloomington: Indiana University Research Center in Anthropology, Folklore, and Linguistics, 1960.

McKay, D. G. Forward and backward masking in motor systems. *Kybernetik*, 1969, **2**, 57–64.

McKay, D. G. Spoonerisms: the structure of errors in the serial order of speech. *Neuropsychologia*, 1970, **8**, 323–350.

Merringer, S. M. *Aus dem Leben der Sprache.* Berlin: Behr's, 1908.

Nooteboom, S. G. *Some regularities in phonemic speech errors.* Annual Progress Report No. 2. Eindhoven: Institut voor Perceptie Onderzock, 1967.

Rubenstein, H., Garfield, L., & Millikan, J. A. Homographic entries in the internal lexicon. *Journal of Verbal Learning and Verbal Behavior*, 1970, **9**, 487–494.

Shattuck, S. R. Speech errors: An analysis. Unpublished doctoral dissertation, Massachusetts Institute of Technology, 1974.

CODING DISTINCTIONS AND REPETITION EFFECTS IN MEMORY[1]

Allan Paivio

UNIVERSITY OF WESTERN ONTARIO, LONDON, ONTARIO, CANADA

I.	Introduction	179
	A. Dual-Coding Theory	180
	B. Common-Code Theories	183
	C. Depth of Processing	184
II.	General Evidence on Memory-Code Distinctions	185
III.	Repetition Effects and Memory-Code Independence	186
	A. General Background	186
	B. Picture-Word Repetition Effects	187
	C. Experiments on Encoding Repetitions	191
IV.	Concluding Remarks	208
	References	211

I. Introduction

This chapter deals with the problem of memory coding. The discussion is oriented around a dual-coding approach in which the major theoretical distinction is between verbal and nonverbal memory systems. The theory assumes, among other things, that the two memory systems are functionally independent in a strong sense. This assumption has various empirical implications that will be reviewed briefly, but the major emphasis will be on one implication, namely, that independent memory systems should have additive effects on memory performance. I will report a series of recent studies in which this idea has been applied to dual-coding effects and extended to dimensions that may cut across the verbal–nonverbal distinction.

First, the dual-coding approach should be viewed in a broader context of related and contrasting ideas. It is consistent with the

[1] The author's research reported in this paper was supported by grants from the National Research Council of Canada (A0087) and the University of Western Ontario Research Fund.

increasingly popular view among memory researchers that memory is a many-splendored thing, comprised of dimensions, modalities, components, attributes, codes, and the like. Although not concerned specifically with traditional memory problems, Osgood's (1953) theory of meaning can be interpreted as the earliest systematic attempt to interpret long-term (or semantic) memory as a multidimensional process. The general idea appears in the specific context of memory research and theory in terms of modalities of memory (Wallach & Averbach, 1955), the memory trace as a multicomponent vector (Bower, 1967), and attributes of memory (Underwood, 1969a; Wickens, 1970). All such views imply that the information in memory is somehow differentiated into independent dimensions or components, which can be identified by such empirical techniques as factor analysis, release from proactive inhibition, and differential forgetting of the components. These approaches differ from dual-coding theory in that they do not assume that the verbal–nonverbal distinction has any special theoretical importance, although they agree that memory is multidimensional.

Dual coding contrasts with other recent approaches that differ among themselves in various ways but apparently share the assumption that long-term memory in particular consists of abstract representations that are neutral with respect to input modality, including the verbal–nonverbal dichotomy (e.g., J. R. Anderson & Bower, 1973; Pylyshyn, 1973; Rumelhart, Lindsay, & Norman, 1972). It differs similarly from approaches in which the major variable assumed to affect memory is the degree or depth of semantic processing an item receives (Craik & Lockhart, 1972; Hyde & Jenkins, 1969). These various approaches will be labeled common-coding theories to distinguish them from dual coding.

I will now discuss the dual-coding and common-coding approaches in more detail, together with a brief review of general evidence on relevant distinctions. The balance of the chapter will deal with a particular method of attack and related experimental data, involving encoding and repetition effects designed to reveal dimensions of memory that are functionally independent to a significant degree.

A . DUAL-CODING THEORY

The dual-coding approach distinguishes between imaginal and verbal processes. I have assumed, as a working hypothesis, that these processes involve independent but partly interconnected systems for encoding, storage, organization, and retrieval of stimulus information. The imagery system presumably is specialized for processing nonverbal information stored in the form of *images*, that is, memory representations corresponding rather directly to concrete things. Images, in short, are analog representations (Attneave, 1972; Cooper & Shepard, 1973). The verbal system, on the other hand, is specialized for dealing with linguistic units, which involve discrete, sequentially arranged informational units that are only indirectly and arbitrarily related to things, according to the conventions of a given language. The two classes of representations presumably include sensory components from various modalities. Images may be visual, auditory, or haptic or any combination of these. Similarly, the verbal system obviously must involve representational processes capable of interpreting visual or auditory input and generating speech or writing. Thus the distinction between verbal and nonverbal symbolic modalities can be regarded as generally orthogonal to the sensory modalities (Paivio, 1972). It is convenient for present purposes, however, to restrict the analysis of images to the visual modality and to treat the *functional* units of the verbal code as basically auditory-motor, or phonemic, in nature.

The qualitative distinctions extend to the way information is organized into higher order structures and how it may be reorganized or transformed. Elementary images presumably can be organized into compound images that have a synchronous or integrated spatial structure, whereas linguistic units can be extended only by concatenating them into larger sequential structures. Reorganization of the informational units in the two classes of representations is governed by their structural features. Thus dynamic visual imagery permits transformations along such visual and spatial dimensions as color, size, location, and orientation of imaged objects, whereas verbal transformations involve rearrangements of the sequential ordering of words and other linguistic units, or substitution of new units into such structures.

The theory also incorporates the idea of levels of information processing. These have been referred to elsewhere as representational, referential, and associative levels (Paivio, 1971, Chapter 3; Paivio & O'Neill, 1970), where "levels" refers to the degree of elaborative processing that is imposed on a stimulus event. Processing to the representational level involves the activation of images by nonverbal stimulus events on the one hand and of verbal representations by linguistic events on the other. The processes at this level can be regarded as corresponding in principle to Morton's (1969) concept of the logogen or Bousfield's (1961) representational response, but extended to include nonverbal as well as verbal representations. Referential processing refers to the activation of one system by the other, through some established interconnection. Thus a word may arouse an image, an object may be named, or such communication may occur entirely at an implicit level without being expressed in overt responses. The term "referential" captures the idea of a semantic relation between word and thing at the cognitive level. This does not imply a one-to-one relation between a word and a particular image. It implies instead a probabilistic relation analogous to a verbal associative hierarchy: a word may arouse different images or an object different verbal descriptions, depending upon the individual's past experiences and the context in which the referential relations occur (Paivio, 1971, p. 75). This aspect of the theory is in accord with the recent emphasis on the contextual determination of meaning (R. C. Anderson & Ortony, 1974; Bransford & Johnson, 1973; Olson, 1970). Finally, associative processing refers to the activation of associations between representational units *within* each system, so that verbal cues can activate verbal reactions in an associative chain, and aroused images activate other imaginal representations through interconnections within the imagery system.

1. Control Processes and Controlling Variables

The structural and functional features of the theory obviously need to be supplemented by assumptions concerning factors that determine the arousal of images and verbal reactions or, in information processing terms, processes that control information flow within and between systems. I have not taken any firm stand on how such processes should be conceptualized within the theory. I have simply assumed that the control processes are an intrinsic part of the representational systems themselves (e.g., Paivio, 1975) and that they are operationally defined by empirical variables that permit one to manipulate or predict the type of encoding activity that is likely to occur in a task. Thus it can be assumed that activation of nonverbal images and verbal representations is controlled by (a) the characteristics of the stimulus material to which the individual is required to respond, (b) contextual stimuli such as encoding instructions, and (c) individual differences in dispositional habits or skills related to the functioning of the two systems. The probability that imagery will be involved in a given task presumably increases with stimulus concreteness, so that it is lowest with abstract words, intermediate with concrete words, and highest with objects or pictures. Imagery is also augmented by instructions to encode items imaginally and is more likely to be used by individuals who score high on figural ability tests than by those who score low on such abilities. Conversely, verbal processing is more probable with verbal material than pictures, with coding instructions that call for linguistic rather than figural analysis or production, and with individuals who are high rather than low on relevant verbal abilities or habits.

2. Empirical Implications

The approach has implications related to the independence–interconnectedness assumptions, as well as the qualitative distinctions between images and verbal representations (e.g., see Paivio, 1972, 1974b). The independence of the two codes is the central issue here although, as we shall see, qualitative differences are also implicated by the data. Independence means that a given task might involve both imaginal and verbal systems concurrently, or one system without the other, or neither. In the case of a memory task in which the target items can be coded in either form, such as easily labeled pictures or easily imaged concrete nouns, storage and retrieval could be mediated by either images or words, or both are remembered, or both forgotten, depending on the precise conditions of the experiment. One statistical consequence of such independence is that the two codes should have additive effects on memory performance. This is the main empirical test used in the studies reported below. Additive effects of two encoding conditions suggest that the two codes are independent; nonadditivity implies nonindependence. Note also that additivity does not mean that the independent components must constribute *equally* to performance—this might be the case but it could also be that one code is mnemonically "stronger" than the other in a given task. The task that permits such inferences to be made will be described following consideration of alternative theories of memory coding.

B. COMMON-CODE THEORIES

A general alternative to the dual-coding position is that both verbal and nonverbal kinds of information are ultimately stored in some common form. Logically, it could be argued that the common code is always verbal or always imagistic. Verbal coding was in fact the common assumption of mediation theories of verbal learning, perception, and thought for several decades but few psychologists would take an extreme verbal position today. Imagery had even a longer history as the primary stuff of memory and thought prior to J. B. Watson, and there are signs of a similar emphasis in the recent literature (e.g., Bugelski, 1970; Moeser, 1974; Strømnes, 1973).

The more popular view is that the common code is some kind of abstract representation that is neutral with respect to modality. Osgood's (e.g., 1971) representational mediation process is probably the earliest version of such an abstraction. His well-known r_m-s_m process was assumed to originate from reactions to things and hence retain behavioral features that are abstract in the sense that the same set of features can be combined in various ways to represent the meanings of different perceptual or linguistic signs. Conversely, signs with similar meanings, including pictures and their verbal descriptions, presumably share the same abstract representation. Other contemporary cognitive theorists conceptualize long-term memory representations as abstract descriptions or propositions (e.g., J. R. Anderson & Bower, 1973; Chase & Clark, 1972; Pylyshyn, 1973; Rumelhart et al., 1972). These theories differ in important ways (see J. R. Anderson & Bower, 1973), but they are similar in their insistence that nonverbal and verbal kinds of information are represented in a common format in long-term memory. Reciprocally, images and linguistic descriptions of the same concept are generated from the same abstract representation. The critical implication of common-coding theories in the present context is that conceptually related images and verbal representations could not be independent memory events, since they must be generated from the same abstract structures. It follows that the effects of relevant stimuli (e.g., pictures and their labels) should be nonindependent unless one assumes some additional mechanism, such as differentiating (independent) "tags" that are stored along with the "core" representation to preserve input modality. Such alternatives will be considered in more detail later.

C. DEPTH OF PROCESSING

Still another theoretical approach relates memory performance directly to the level or depth to which a given item is processed following its presentation. Craik and Lockhart (1972) advocate such an approach, and J. J. Jenkins and his collaborators (e.g., Hyde &

Jenkins, 1973; Walsh & Jenkins, 1973) have proposed a similar process theory in which the crucial variable affecting memory is whether item processing is semantic or nonsemantic. Semantic and nonsemantic can be interpreted as corresponding to deep and superficial processing in the Craik-Lockhart approach. These alternatives differ in principle from the processing levels involved in the dual-coding model in that the depth approach includes no necessary reference to specific structural or functional differences between memory codes at any given level. Within dual-coding theory, the memory representations aroused directly by nonverbal perceptual events and by linguistic signs are assumed to be at the same (relatively superficial) level. Deeper processing is presumably involved when an interconnection is activated at the referential level, but it is equally deep whether it involves verbal coding of perceptual objects or image coding of words. Associative elaboration within either coding system is yet another kind of processing, where the cognitive activity is not necessarily deeper than in the referential case but involves representations of the same class as those aroused directly by the target stimulus (i.e., word–word associations in the case of the verbal system, and image–image associations in the case of imagery). Whereas the depth hypothesis attributes effects to the hypothetical depth or level variable, dual coding attributes effects to the number of codes activated in a given task and to functional distinctions between imaginal and verbal codes. The Jenkins *et al.* version of depth theory likewise makes no qualitative distinctions with implications for memory performance but assumes instead that memory depends on the degree to which items have been processed semantically. Differential predictions from the depth models and dual coding are somewhat problematic because of the uncertainty of defining depth of processing independent of memory performance itself, but some empirical comparison will be suggested later.

II. General Evidence on Memory-Code Distinctions

Various kinds of evidence bear on the issue of the independence of imaginal and verbal symbolic processes and their relation to semantic processes generally. A sampling of this general evidence will be reviewed briefly, followed by a more detailed examination of a specific experimental task that was used in a series of experiments to test for additive effects of different codes.

Available evidence generally suggests that nonverbal and verbal memory systems are functionally independent to a nontrivial degree. This conclusion is supported by individual difference studies which show that tests of verbal abilities load on factors that are independent of figural abilities (Guilford, 1967), as well as by tests specifically selected to measure imagery as a habit or skill (Di Vesta, Ingersoll, & Sunshine, 1971; Paivio, 1971, pp. 495–497). It is supported also by neuropsychological evidence which indicates that such linguistic skills as speech production and verbal memories are left-hemisphere functions in most people, whereas certain nonverbal abilities are controlled by the right hemisphere (e.g., Kimura, 1973; Milner, 1971; Nebes, 1974). That mental images and linguistic representations are qualitatively distinct is strongly supported by the work of Shepard and his colleagues on shape isomorphism (Shepard & Chipman, 1970) and rotation of mental images (e.g., Cooper & Shepard, 1973). Such studies show that images function as perceptual analogs to a degree of precision that cannot be readily explained in terms of verbal mechanisms or common abstract descriptions. The analog nature of nonverbal memory is supported also by research involving size comparisons of objects in long-term memory (Moyer, 1973; Paivio, 1974a).

Finally, several investigators have suggested that nonverbal and verbal memory codes may be independent on the basis of comparisons of pictures with words or imagery with verbal coding conditions in a variety of episodic memory tasks (e.g., Bahrick & Bahrick, 1971; Nelson & Brooks, 1973; Rowe, 1972; Snodgrass, Wasser, Finkelstein, & Goldberg, 1974). A similar interpretation can be given to the finding that, with sentences that are concrete and high in their imagery value, wording can be forgotten independently of meaning (e.g., Begg, 1971).

III. Repetition Effects and Memory-Code Independence

A. GENERAL BACKGROUND

Research and theory on the effect of spacing of repetitions on recall suggest a paradigm for determining more precisely whether or not the memory events aroused by different encoding conditions are independent. The literature on spacing indicates that the repeated presentation of an item benefits recall more when other items intervene between the repeated events than when the repetitions are successive (Melton, 1970; Underwood, 1969b). Various interpretations have been proposed for this interitem "lag effect" as well as the related phenomenon of memory facilitation with temporally-spaced as opposed to massed repetitions (for a recent summary, see Hintzman, 1974). Some of the alternatives will be considered later, but the most relevant one for the present analysis is an extension of Martin's (1968) theory of encoding variability. Several investigators (e.g., Bower, 1972; Madigan, 1969; Melton, 1970) have proposed that spacing encourages differential encoding of an item and that this might benefit recall, perhaps by increasing the number of retrieval cues that converge on the target item during the test trial. Especially pertinent here is the suggestion that the encodings of a repeated event will increasingly differ as a function of lag, with the difference perhaps asymptoting at a level expected for independent and additive events (e.g., Glanzer, 1969; Melton, 1970). This means that the repeated events should be nonindependent and less than additive under successive presentation conditions, when recall is lower than under spaced conditions. The theory suggests further that the recall difference between massed and spaced presentations should be reduced if differential encoding can be achieved under massed conditions.

These predictions have received some positive support from studies in which differential encoding was induced by varying the contextual cues that accompanied a repeated target item (e.g., Gartman & Johnson, 1972; Madigan, 1969; Thios, 1972). However, similar procedures have produced negative results in other studies (e.g., Johnson, Coots, & Flickinger, 1972). Results consistent with the hypothesis were also obtained by Glanzer and Duarte (1971) using bilingual subjects and bilingual word lists. The crucial result was that recall was much better under massed conditions when words were repeated in a different language than when they were repeated in the same language. The difference disappeared as interitem lag increased, as would be expected if spacing encouraged differential coding even when the item was repeated in the same language.

B. PICTURE-WORD REPETITION EFFECTS

The lag effect was explicitly used to evaluate the possible independence of imaginal and verbal memory traces in a series of experiments (Paivio, 1974b; Paivio & Csapo, 1973, Experiment 5). The critical studies involved pictures and words as items, and memory was tested by free recall. The pictures were line drawings of familiar and easily labeled objects. The words were the most commonly used names of the objects. Subjects were presented with long lists of items in which pictures were repeated as pictures (PP repetitions), words as words (WW), and pictures as words (i.e., their verbal labels) or vice versa (PW). The lists also included once-presented P and W items. The repetitions were either successive (0-lag) or separated by 24 or 48 intervening items. Different versions of the basic list were used to counterbalance the picture-word mode of the items, the occurrence of particular items under both repeated and unrepeated conditions, and so on. Following a single presentation of a given list under either incidental or intentional learning instructions, subjects recalled the items verbally. I will discuss only the standard (intentional) recall results, since this is the condition under which the lag effect has been generally obtained.

The relevant results concern the degree to which obtained recall of repeated items approximates what would be expected for independent events. It was predicted that, if pictures and words arouse independent imaginal and verbal memory traces corresponding to the same concept, additive effects would be obtained for PW repetitions even at 0-lag. Within-code repetitions (WW and PP), however, should be less than additive at 0-lag but approach additivity at long lags to the extent that spacing promotes differential encoding.

The recall level that would be expected for repeated events according to the independence hypothesis was estimated using the data for once-presented items. Thus the expected recall probabilities for PW repetitions were calculated by the formula, $P(\text{PW}) = P(\text{P}) + P(\text{W}) - P(\text{P})P(\text{W})$. This was done for individual subjects and then averaged for each experimental condition. The same procedure was followed for PP and WW repetitions. The equation involves a number of assumptions. Theoretically, it assumes an all-or-none threshold model of recall. Statistically, it assumes that the recall of pictures and corresponding words (in the case of PW repetitions) are uncorrelated. If they are correlated, and if there is item heterogeneity, the right-hand expression in the equation will be inflated due to a covariance term not included in the expression. This covariance cannot be directly calculated, but it is possible to estimate the maximum likely covariance. This was in fact done using a computer simulation program.[2] The simulation showed that, even assuming perfect correlation, expected values computed with or without the covariance differed only slightly. Since the real correlation is likely to be much

---

[2] I am grateful to Ian Spence, who worked out the implications of the problem and wrote the simulation program to evaluate its consequences.

less than unity, the unadjusted expression is a reasonable although approximate test of the independence model, and it was used in all of the experiments reported here.

The results of two experiments reported in Paivio (1974b) were completely consistent with expectations from the differential encoding and independence hypotheses. Obtained and predicted recall for PW repetitions did not differ at 0-lag, suggesting additivity and independence of the two memory codes. This was true also at long lags, except in one of several comparisons where obtained recall exceeded predicted recall. No obvious explanation can be suggested for the one exception, which suggests a *greater* than additive effect, and the conservative conclusion is that PW repetitions were at least additive under both massed and spaced presentations. Conversely, obtained WW and PP repetitions were less than additive in both experiments at 0-lag, but became additive (apparently independent) at long lags. Thus the results were in complete agreement with the dual coding theory of picture-word recall and with the differential encoding interpretation of the lag effect. The recall levels also suggested, however, that imagery contributed more than the verbal code to their combined mnemonic effect. This was indicated by the fact that once-presented pictures were consistently recalled much better than once-presented words even under incidental conditions designed to minimize implicit labeling of the pictures. Even more telling was the observation that once-presented pictures were recalled as well as successively repeated words (a picture, it appears, is worth about two words in mnemonic value), again under incidental as well as intentional recall conditions. These findings, together with the effects of encoding instructions, to be reviewed in the next section, are consistent with the assumption that images and verbal traces are additive but unequal in memory value, imagery being favored roughly by a factor of two under the conditions of those particular experiments. Why a nonverbal image should be more memorable than a verbal trace is theoretically very puzzling and we shall return to the question briefly after we have considered further data and alternative interpretations.

A Theoretical Extension to Imaginal and Verbal Encoding Instructions

The results of the item-repetition experiments permit post hoc inferences to be made concerning the effects of imaginal and verbal encoding instructions in earlier experiments (Paivio & Csapo, 1973, Experiments 2 and 3). Subjects in these studies were presented homogeneous lists of either pictures or words and were instructed either to image each item (the picture itself or the verbal label, depending on the condition) or to pronounce the name of the picture or the word. In one experiment, the encoding operations were overt. That is, subjects drew their image or wrote the name of each item during a 5-second interitem interval. In the other experiment, they imaged or pronounced implicitly and rated the ease of each kind of reaction on a 7-point scale during the interval. A free verbal recall test was given incidentally following the encoding task. The level of recall was generally higher following the overt encoding (drawing and writing) tasks than after implicit coding, but the pattern of results over conditions was the same in both experiments. Specifically, recall of words that had been verbally encoded (written or pronounced) was about half the level of recall of verbally coded pictures and imaged pictures or words. The latter three conditions did not differ significantly from each other. The results for the overt encoding experiment are presented in Fig. 1A.

What do these results mean? The fact that verbalizing to pictures and imaging to words approximately doubled recall relative to the condition in which words are verbalized is consistent with the additivity predicted by dual coding theory. However, the fact that imaging to pictures also doubled recall introduced a complication because a subject-generated repetition of the same code (i.e., image) should produce the same level of recall in that case as in the word-pronounce case—unless the image code is mnemonically stronger than the verbal code, so that repeating the image aroused by a picture is more effective than repeating the verbal code aroused by a word. But if images are mnemonically stronger than words, why was recall not *higher* under the picture-image conditions, which involved repeated arousal of a "strong" trace, than under picture-pronounce or word-image conditions, which presumably involved arousal of a weak (verbal) trace and a strong (image) trace?

The results of the picture-word repetition experiments provided a tentative resolution of the problem. Generalizations from that experiment to the encoding experiments are justified by the parallel recall results obtained in the different experiments. If we assume that picture-word repetitions are analogous to imaginal and verbal encodings of pictures and words, the overall pattern of results should be similar under the different conditions. Specifically, since the encoding experiments showed that P(image) = P(verbalize) = W(image) >

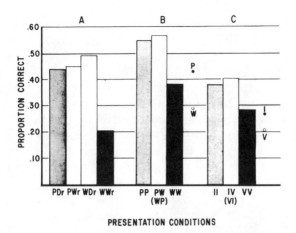

PRESENTATION CONDITIONS

Fig. 1. Correct recall proportions for A: pictures (P) and words (W) encoded by drawing (Dr) or writing (Wr); B: repeated and once-presented P and W items; and C: repeated and once-presented words encoded imaginally (I) or verbally (V) on each presentation. The data in panels A and B were adapted from Paivio and Csapo (1973, Experiments 2 and 5).

W(verbalize), then the result for repetitions should be PP = PW = WP > WW. This was exactly the case, as can be seen from the graphical presentation in Figs. 1A and 1B, which show the results for both experiments. The comparability suggests further that, just as PP recall was less than an additive combination of the individual events, imaging to pictures might result in a smaller recall increment than imaging to words or verbalizing to pictures. The latter two conditions in effect involved different encodings, one aroused directly by the target stimulus, the other by the encoding instructions, whereas imaging to pictures and verbalizing to words involved a subject-produced repetition of the same code. The differential encodings were additive, the within-code rehearsal less than additive, in their effects. The expected superiority of the picture-image, like that of the picture-picture repetition condition, failed to appear because the mnemonic potency of the image code was somewhat offset by the less-than-additive increment produced by the immediate (subjective) repetition of the same code.

C. EXPERIMENTS ON ENCODING REPETITIONS

The general hypothesis suggested by the foregoing analysis is that qualitatively different encodings, however aroused, should have additive effects on recall whereas repetition of the same memory code should be less than additive in its effect. Repetitions of pictures and words provided support for the hypothesis, and the comparable effects of imaginal and verbal encoding of pictures and words were also consistent with the generalization, although the additive (or less than additive) contributions of the implicit encodings could not be directly determined from the data. A series of experiments extended the logic entirely to repeated, implicit encodings as elicited by encoding instructions. The initial experiments involved imaginal and verbal encodings; later ones involved other semantic dimensions as well.

1. Repeated Imaginal and Verbal Coding of Words

In the first experiment of this series, subjects were presented with a list of concrete nouns, some of which were successively repeated and others presented once. The lists were mixed with respect to encoding conditions. That is, a given subject imaged to some words and verbalized (pronounced) others, so that equal numbers of items were presented once and either imaged [W(I)] or verbalized [W(V)], or presented twice and imaged on each presentation [W(I)W(I)], verbalized on each [W(V)W(V)], or imaged and verbalized successively [W(I)W(V) or W(V)W(I)]. Thus the six encoding conditions, I, V, II, VV, IV, and VI were precisely analogous to P, W, PP, WW, PW, and WP of the picture-word repetition experiments. If the effects of implicit (mental) encodings are truly analogous to the effects of perceptual events, and if the differential encoding hypothesis is relevant to such events, then the recall pattern for encoding conditions should parallel the picture-word pattern. Since the picture-word recall order was PP = PW = WP > WW = P > W, the predicted pattern for encoded word units would be W(I)W(I) = W(I)W(V) = W(V)W(I) > W(V)W(V) = W(I) > W(V). Moreover, repeated words that are encoded differently on each occurrence, as in the W(I)W(V) or W(V)W(I) conditions, should show an additive effect relative to their unrepeated W(I) and W(V) components, whereas the similarly encoded W(I)W(I) and W(V)W(V) repetitions should be less than additive.

The items and their arrangement in lists were conceptually the same as in Paivio and Csapo's (1973) Experiment 5. Seventy-two concrete nouns were arranged into 96-item lists in which 36 words occurred twice and 24 words occurred once. The visual presentation of each item was accompanied by a spoken cue either to image (I coding) or pronounce implicitly (V coding), so that the sequence of I and V and the conceptual items involved corresponded exactly to the arrangement of pictures and words in the Paivio and Csapo experiment. Thus, of the 36 repeated words, 12 would be coded both times as an image (II), 12 both times verbally (VV), and 12 once imaginally and once verbally (6 each in IV and VI sequences). Of the 24 once-presented words, 12 were coded as I and 12 as V. Four different lists of this kind were constructed to counterbalance the treatment conditions for particular items.

The lists were presented to different groups under an incidental learning condition, thereby exercising control over the way items were encoded. The items were presented at a 5-sec rate and each item was exposed for 1/16 sec. The subjects were told that the purpose of the experiment was to obtain ratings on the ease of imaging to, or pronouncing, words. The subjects understood from the instructions that when they heard "image," they were immediately to generate a mental image of the object suggested by the stimulus word, draw it mentally, and then indicate the ease of doing so by writing a number from 1 (most difficult) to 7 (easiest) in the appropriate space on the recording sheet. Similarly when they heard "pronounce" they were to pronounce the word to themselves and then rate the ease of doing so using the numerical scale. Following presentation of all items, the subjects were unexpectedly asked to recall as many of the items as they could remember, in any order, by writing the names on a sheet.

The performance data are shown in Table I as correct recall proportions for each condition, with W(I)W(V) and W(V)W(I) sequences collapsed into a single score because they did not differ significantly. The data are based on 39 subjects. A one-way repeated measures analysis of variance and Newman-Keuls pairwise comparison yielded a significant overall effect ($p < .001$) in which W(I)W(I) and W(I)W(V) did not differ significantly but both exceeded W(V)W(V) ($p < .01$). The W(V)W(V) repetitions were not recalled significantly better than once-presented words coded as I, but both were superior to W(V) ($p < .01$). Thus the order of conditions was W(I)W(I) = W(I)W(V) [or W(V)W(I)] > W(V)W(V) = W(I) > W(V), corresponding closely to the pattern observed in the earlier experiments for lists involving pictures and words in lieu of imaginally and verbally coded words. In the case of the repetition conditions, the remarkable parallel extends further to the experiment involving lists of unrepeated pictures and words coded once imaginally or verbally, as can be seen in Fig. 1, where the pertinent results of the three experiments are plotted together.

TABLE I

OBTAINED CORRECT RECALL PROPORTIONS FOR
ONCE-PRESENTED AND REPEATED ITEMS THAT
WERE IMAGED (I) AND VERBALIZED (V) AND
PROPORTIONS PREDICTED FOR
INDEPENDENT REPEATED ITEMS

	I	V	II	IV(VI)	VV
Word stimuli (N = 39)					
Obtained	.269	.177	.378[a]	.402	.282
Predicted			.447	.397	.307
Picture stimuli (N = 36)					
Obtained	.269	.241	.382[a]	.440	.361[b]
Predicted			.449	.446	.408

[a] $p < .01$ obtained versus predicted.
[b] $p < .05$ obtained versus predicted.

A comparison of the obtained values with the values that would be expected for repeated mental events if they were independent and additive provided a further crucial test of the parallel between mental events and perceptual events. As in the earlier experiments, the expected values for repetition effects were calculated using the data for once-presented items. Thus the expected probability (P) values for W(I)W(V) repetitions were calculated for individual subjects by the formula, $P[W(I)W(V)] = P[W(I)] + P[W(V)] - P[W(I)] P[W(V)]$. The same procedure was followed for W(I)W(I) and W(V)W(V) repetitions.

The mean expected proportions are presented in Table I along with the obtained values. The differences between obtained and predicted proportions were evaluated statistically using the normal curve approximation to the binomial expansion. The results showed that obtained W(I)W(I) and W(V)W(V) were lower than the expected values, although the difference was significant only in the case of W(I)W(I) ($Z = 2.99$, $p < .01$). In the case of W(I)W(V), the difference between obtained and expected values did not approach significance. Thus I and V codings of repeated items resulted in an additive effect, whereas imaging each time to repeated words was less than additive. These results correspond closely to those obtained for 0-lag picture-word and picture-picture repetitions under standard recall conditions in the previous experiments (Paivio, 1974b; Paivio & Csapo, 1973). The results for W(V)W(V) differ from their simple WW analogue in that recall was less than additive in the case of WW but not significantly so in the case of W(V)W(V). Apart from the latter discrepancy, then, the results generally parallel the recall effects resulting from imaginal and verbal coding of words and those resulting from presentation of items as pictures and words without specific encoding instructions.

2. Repeated Imaginal and Verbal Coding of Pictures

The second experiment in this series was identical to the first, except that all of the items were pictures rather than words. The interest again centered on the recall levels and additive (or nonadditive) effects of imaginal and verbal encoding reactions to the items. On the basis of the prior research and the reasoning that pictures evoke images directly, the pattern of recall levels expected as a function of the encoding conditions and repetitions would be somewhat different from that expected when the items were words. In particular, the mnemonic effect of picture-evoked imagery should override the effect of the instructionally-evoked encodings, inasmuch as all picture conditions involve direct image arousal. The previous encoding studies involving once-presented items (e.g., see Fig. 1A) had in fact already established that recall scores did not differ significantly for imaged and verbalized pictures, i.e., $P(I) = P(V)$. Thus the important question here is what will happen when the pictures are repeated with different combinations of imaginal and verbal encodings. Despite the equivalent recall for $P(I)$ and $P(V)$, differences can be predicted from the differential encoding hypothesis and the earlier studies in this series. Because $P(I)P(V)$ and $P(V)P(I)$ conditions involve different encodings of repeated pictures, the repetition effect should approach additivity. On the other hand, $P(I)P(I)$ and $P(V)P(V)$ conditions involve repetition of similarly encoded units, so the effect in each case should be less than additive. It follows that the recall levels for $P(I)P(V)$ and $P(V)P(I)$ conditions should exceed $P(I)P(I)$ and $P(V)P(V)$, and the latter two should not differ. All repetition conditions should exceed $P(I)$ and $P(V)$, which should be approximately equal in recall. Thus the predicted ranking of recall levels for all conditions is, $P(I)P(V) > P(I)P(I) = P(V)P(V) > P(I) = P(V)$.

The pictures again were line drawings of the objects labeled by the concrete words. The encoding instructions were slightly modified to take account of the fact that the items were pictures. Thus the subjects understood that when they heard the word "image," they were to imagine themselves drawing the presented picture and then rate how easy it was to detect the details of the imagined picture. When they heard "pronounce," they were to pronounce the name of the picture to themselves and then rate the pronounceability of the name. Following the incidental recall task, the pictures were shown again and the subjects wrote the names they had used to label the pictures. This information permitted the verbal recall data to be scored using the subjects' own labels for the items.

The scores for P(I)P(V) and P(V)P(I) coding sequences for repeated items again did not differ significantly, so they were collapsed into one score for the analysis. The correct recall proportions are presented in the lower half of Table I. An analysis of variance yielded a significant overall effect of conditions ($p < .001$). Among the repetition conditions, the only significant effect was that P(I)P(V) exceeded P(V)P(V) recall ($p < .05$, Newman-Keuls). Each of the repetition conditions produced higher recall ($p < .01$) than the unrepeated P(I) and P(V) conditions, which did not differ significantly. Thus the results generally conformed to the predicted pattern for pictures, the only exception being that differential encoding, P(I)P(V), did not significantly exceed P(I)P(I).

Table I also shows the expected recall proportions for repeated items on the assumption that they are independent and additive. The statistical comparisons showed that obtained recall was significantly lower than the predicted value in the case of both P(I)P(I) and P(V)P(V) ($z \geqslant .01$), but obtained and expected probabilities did not differ significantly in the case of P(I)P(V) repetitions. Thus imaginal and verbal encodings were again additive, whereas repeated imaginal or verbal encodings were less than additive in their effects. These results correspond exactly to the pattern previously obtained for successive picture-word, picture-picture, and word-word repetitions under standard recall conditions, without encoding instructions (Paivio, 1974b; Paivio & Csapo, 1973).

Theoretical Discussion. Together, the results of the two encoding experiments and the earlier picture-word studies provide strong support for the dual-coding theory of memory and cognition. They also suggest that perceptual events and analogous encoding instructions activate similar memory traces in the two systems. More specifically, the data appear to be completely consistent with the following theoretical generalizations as applied to free recall performance:

(a) imaginal and verbal memory codes are independent, (b) the image code is mnemonically "stronger" than the verbal code, (c) the two codes have the same relative mnemonic properties whether evoked directly by perceptual stimuli or indirectly by verbal instructions, and (d) successive (zero lag) repetitions of the same code, unlike dual coding, are mnemonically less than additive.

Alternative interpretations can be suggested, however, at least for some aspects of the data. That different perceptual events or encoding instructions arouse independent memory codes seems conclusive provided that one accepts the statistical additivity model as a reasonable test of code independence. The conclusion will not be debated here because it is consistent also with other empirical evidence that verbal and nonverbal memories are independent or at least distinct (see the summary in the Introduction), although obviously interconnected as well. The conclusion is theoretically important because it seems inconsistent with any theory that assumes a common long-term memory representation for conceptually equivalent pictures, images, and names. As stated earlier, such a view has been explicitly asserted or at least strongly implied by several proponents of abstract representational models (e.g., J. R. Anderson & Bower, 1973; Chase & Clark, 1972; Pylyshyn, 1973; Rumelhart et al., 1972). These theories could, of course, account for the observed independence by assuming that a common underlying representation is differentially tagged depending on whether it has been aroused by a picture or a word, or associated with a mental image rather than implicit verbalization (cf. J. R. Anderson & Bower, 1972; Bower, 1972, p. 113). However, differential tagging could not explain the superior recall for pictures and imaginally coded items without also assuming that the tags differ in their retrieval effectiveness. Unless they are deducible from other principles within the theories, such additional assumptions would render the common-coding models formally equivalent to dual coding, which simply assumes that the memory representations corresponding to the different events are independent and qualitatively different despite their conceptual relatedness.

The generalization that the image code is mnemonically "stronger" than the verbal code is, of course, open to alternative interpretations. It could be argued, for example, that every instance in which verbal recall is higher for pictures than for words, or under imagery than verbal encoding conditions, reflects the influence of uncontrolled differences in dual encoding; the further assumption of image superiority is unnecessary. Thus, without encoding instructions, pictures are more likely to be implicitly named than words are to be imaged, hence the higher recall probability in the former case. When coding is controlled so that subjects name pictures or image to words, the difference disappears, that is, $P(V) = W(I)$. In the case of the superiority of imagery over verbal coding instructions with words as items, the former, i.e., $W(I)$, involves arousal of two independent codes whereas verbal coding involves implicit repetition of the code already evoked by the word, i.e., $W(V)$. The inferior recall in the latter case results from the less-than-additive effect of implicit arousal of a redundant code, rather than from image superiority per se. Such arguments, though generally plausible, are strained in some instances. For example, the fact that words presented only once and imaged were recalled just as well as words that were repeated and pronounced on each occasion (Table I) strongly suggests a compensatory positive effect of image coding, rather than merely a negative effect due to the repeated arousal of the same code. Nonetheless, a simple dual-coding interpretation cannot be firmly excluded as a sufficient explanation of apparent image superiority in these experiments. I shall consider more compelling evidence presently.

The third generalization is that subject-generated mental pictures and implicit verbal reactions are functionally equivalent to explicitly-presented pictures and words in regard to their mnemonic value. This conclusion, like the dual-coding theory itself, assumes qualitative distinctions between the two memory codes: one code is in some sense pictorial, and the other, verbal in form. But this is not a necessary inference from the data. It could be argued instead that the pattern of results reflects different levels of processing (Craik & Lockhart, 1972). Picture presentation, imagery, and dual-coding conditions produce high recall because they involve relatively deep (semantic) processing of the input items. Repeated words or verbally coded words are remembered poorly because they are processed superficially. This analysis implies that there is nothing unique about pictures or imagery instructions. They simply promote deep processing and the same results presumably could be achieved by any procedure that induces processing depth. In terms of the related approach proposed by Jenkins et al. (e.g., Hyde & Jenkins, 1969), any conditions that encourage meaningful, semantic coding of items will produce high recall.

The next experiments in the series attempt to evaluate these various alternatives, recognizing that they are not necessarily mutually exclusive. For example, dual-coding theory does not assert that imagery is the only alternative to simple verbal coding. Words can arouse various elaborative or semantic reactions and these could enhance recall to varying degrees through differential encoding or other mechanisms. The following experiment was specifically designed to compare differential verbal coding with dual (i.e., picture-word) coding.

3. Bilingual Coding versus Picture Labeling

The experiment was done in collaboration with Andrew Yackley and Wallace Lambert at McGill University. It involved an incidental free recall paradigm patterned after the earlier encoding experiments involving pictures and words as stimuli. In this case, French-English bilinguals were presented a list containing equal numbers of pictures, French words, and English words. The words in each case were concrete nouns. The subjects were required to code these items during list presentation by writing down the name of each picture, translating each word into English, and writing down the English word. The encoding task was therefore the same in each case, namely, writing an English word. Following this task, the subjects were unexpectedly asked to recall the words they had written. Since these were all English nouns, any recall difference would be attributable entirely to differences in the input items or the processes involved in translating these into a common code.

Note, first, that this procedure permitted a choice between simple dual coding, in which the two postulated codes are assumed to have equal mnemonic value, and differential dual coding, in which the two codes presumably contribute unequally to recall. If picture labeling simply involves the arousal of two codes that are equal in memory value, recall should be equal in the picture-name and word-translate conditions, and both should be superior to monolingual coding. If the pictorial memory code is superior to the verbal code, however, the picture-labeling condition should produce the highest recall. The translation condition should be intermediate, with its superiority over monolingual coding depending on the degree to which the two languages are independent in memory.

The different possible outcomes are also relevant to the depth hypothesis. The translation of a French word into English clearly requires deep processing in the sense that the meaning of the word must be grasped if the translation is to be accurate. The process is in fact a true analog of picture naming, since both tasks involve the presentation of a stimulus to which there is a high-probability English response. There is no a priori reason to assume that the English naming of a picture is any more semantic or deep than the English translation of a French word, so no difference would be predicted from a depth approach that assumes no qualitative differences in processes that may be equally deep.

The results of the experiment were clear. Recall was highest for labeled pictures (the proportion of items correctly recalled was .51), next for translated words (.34), and lowest for copied words (.17). All differences were highly significant. They provide unambiguous evidence for the arousal of independent verbal codes in the translation condition and two qualitatively different memory codes in the picture-naming condition. These conclusions follow from the fact that translated words were recalled twice as well as copied words, suggesting that translation was at least additive in its effect. That labeled pictures exceeded translated words by as much again suggests that the nonverbal image contributed more to recall than did the alternative linguistic code in the translation condition. It is difficult to see how these results could be interpreted so directly by the depth theorists. Presumably they would have to argue that picture labeling in fact requires deeper processing than does bilingual translation. Any resort to such arguments would tend to render the depth hypothesis untestable because depth would be defined after the fact, in terms of recall performance itself. By contrast, the results were directly predicted from the dual-coding theory of independent memory codes and the empirically derived assumption that the two codes are unequal in mnemonic value.

Note, finally, that these results can be generalized to the experimental designs and encoding conditions of the earlier picture-word experiments. The recall proportions for the picture-write and word-copy conditions were very similar to those reported by Paivio and Csapo (1973, Experiment 2) for lists that were homogeneous rather than mixed with respect to the way items were encoded. Moreover, Paivio and Csapo found that imaging to words by drawing a picture resulted in recall performance equivalent to that produced by seeing a picture and labeling it. Thus it can be assumed that a word-draw condition would have exceeded the translation condition in the bilingual experiment by about as much as the picture-write condition. These experiments involved comparable overt coding responses (writing or drawing). Generalizing from Paivio and Csapo (1973, Experiment 3), the overall recall level presumably would be lower if the bilingual study were repeated with implicit coding (silent pronunciation) rather than overt (written) coding responses, but the relative pattern of differences should remain the same. This assumption remains untested, however, since no prior experiments have compared the effects of implicit and overt translation on recall.

4. Imagery versus Semantic Coding

The next series of experiments compared imagery with coding on another semantic dimension, thereby permitting an evaluation of the depth-of-processing alternative under conditions more directly comparable to those used by its proponents. Pleasantness of meaning was chosen as the encoding dimension because it consistently produced high incidental recall levels in prior experiments that compared the effects of various orienting tasks (Hyde & Jenkins, 1969, 1973; Till & Jenkins, 1973; Walsh & Jenkins, 1973).

a. *Image, Pleasantness, and Verbal Coding of Unrepeated Items.* The first experiment required subjects to encode 72 once-presented concrete nouns in different ways prior to an unexpected free recall test. The items were the same as those used in previous picture-word experiments. In one condition, each of a random sequence of 36 items was encoded imaginally and the other 36 verbally, given the words "image" and "pronounce" as prompts. The overt orienting task involved ratings of ease of imagery or ease of pronunciation on 7-point scales. The other condition required a different group of subjects to rate half the words for "pleasantness of meaning" on a 7-point pleasant-unpleasant scale, given the cue "pleasantness," and the other half on pronounceability.

Surprisingly, the two list conditions produced identical recall differences: 31% of the items were correctly recalled whether they had been encoded imaginally or in terms of pleasantness of meaning, and 17% of the pronounced items were correct in each list. Thus the facilitating effect of image coding on recall performance was indistinguishable from the effect of evaluating items on pleasantness of meaning. The general pattern was replicated in another experiment in which one-third of the list items were coded imaginally, one-third in terms of pleasantness, and one-third were pronounced. The recall percentages for the three conditions were 26, 29, and 18, respectively.

The results agree with at least three general interpretations. First, they are consistent with the depth-of-processing hypothesis. Second, imagery could account for the data if we assume that the semantic groups rated the pleasantness of the imagined referents of the concrete words. Third, imagery and pleasantness judgments might involve distinct processes which happen to be quantitatively equivalent in this particular task. The first of these, semantic depth, could be viewed as the preferred interpretation because it accounts parsimoniously for the quantitative effects of both imagery and pleasantness encodings, as well as other semantic orienting tasks (e.g., Bower & Karlin, 1974; Craik & Lockhart, 1975; Gardiner, 1974). The strong implication of the depth interpretation is that qualitative differences in encoding processes have no quantitative consequences for memory, provided that the processing in each case is equally semantic and deep. This might turn out to be correct as far as it goes, but the story would remain incomplete because qualitative distinctions may well be crucial in other tasks. To argue otherwise would be to deny the validity of a great deal of evidence that images have unique structural and functional properties (e.g., see Cooper & Shepard, 1973; Paivio, 1974a)—properties succinctly grasped by the idea that images are relatively isomorphic perceptual analogues of environmental objects and events.

Such qualitative uniqueness could be reflected in aspects of memory performance not revealed by overall accuracy scores alone. There is as yet little evidence from memory tasks directly comparable to those I have described, but some relevant findings have been reported by Simpson (1972). His data involved differences in the nature of recognition memory errors as a function of the way items had been encoded. Simpson asked different groups of subjects to encode words by generating an image to each, or a verbal association, or simply repeating the item. This encoding variable was crossed orthogonally with test conditions in which subjects chose the correct input item from a pair of synonyms (e.g., wigwam, tepee), antonyms (e.g., king, queen), homophones (e.g., profit, prophet), or unrelated pairs. On the basis of the dual-coding hypothesis, Simpson predicted that recognition errors would be highest for synonym pairs in the imagery condition (the pair members would tend to evoke similar images), antonym pairs in the verbal association condition (a pair member would have tended to evoke its distractor as an associate during the encoding task), and homophones in the repetition condition.

The results were generally as predicted in the case of imagery and verbal association conditions. In the case of repetition, homophone errors were more frequent than either synonym or unrelated-pair errors, but antonym errors were most frequent. These results have been replicated under incidental learning conditions (Simpson, personal communication), indicating that the pattern of effects is reliable. The findings are important because dual-coding theory predicted the differential error patterns under imagery and verbal association conditions, as well as the fact that imagery produced the highest recognition accuracy overall. Depth of processing might predict the general superiority of imagery on the assumption that it involves deeper processing than verbal associative coding, but nothing in the depth approach as such implies that the type of error should differ in the two conditions.

The critical implication of Simpson's results in the present context is that imaginal and verbal-associative encoding reactions may have independent memory effects, just as imagery and pronunciation appear to have. The same possibility extends to imagery and other semantic codings, including pleasantness—unpleasantness. Pleasantness judgments may be based on affective reactions, as Osgood claims (e.g., Osgood, Suci, & Tannenbaum, 1957), whereas imagery represents an independent denotative or referential reaction. This suggestion is supported by correlational data which shows that ratings of imagery are uncorrelated with evaluative ratings of nouns (Paivio, 1968). This implies that the two would have independent effects on recall when they are manipulated by instructional sets. In terms of the paradigm involved in the encoding repetition experiments described earlier, imagery and pleasantness encodings should be additive. On the other hand, to the extent that the different coding instructions arouse a common memory process, their combined effect should be less than additive.

   b. *Repeated Imaginal and Pleasantness Coding of Words.*   The idea was tested in an experiment that was precisely analogous to the image-pronounce study with repeated items. Subjects were presented a list of concrete nouns, some of which were repeated and some were not. They were instructed to image to an item and rate the ease of so doing when cued with the word "image," and to judge the pleasantness—unpleasantness of an item when cued by "pleasant." In the case of repeated items, they sometimes imaged successively [W(I)W(I)], sometimes rated pleasantness each time [W(Pl)W(Pl)], and at other times imaged to one occurrence and rated pleasantness on the other [W(I)W(Pl)]. Unrepeated items were either imaged or rated on pleasantness. The items were identical to those used in the image-pronounce study. Different subgroups received different lists which counterbalanced the item conditions. As before, recall was tested incidentally following the encoding tasks.

The correct recall proportions are shown in Table II. A comparison of the results for the imagery condition with those from the earlier image-pronounce experiment (Table I) shows highly similar values for W(I) and W(I)W(I). Moreover, Newman-Keuls tests following

TABLE II

OBTAINED CORRECT RECALL PROPORTIONS
FOR ONCE-PRESENTED AND REPEATED WORDS
CODED ON IMAGERY (I) AND PLEASANTNESS
(Pl) AND PROPORTIONS PREDICTED FOR
INDEPENDENT REPEATED ITEMS (N = 47 Ss)

	I	Pl	II	IPl(PlI)	PlPl
Obtained	.284	.340	.360[a]	.450[a]	.424[a]
Expected			.467	.523	.533

[a] $p < .001$ obtained versus predicted.

significant analysis of variance results indicated that I and Pl encoding of unrepeated items did not differ significantly, which is consistent with the equivalent recall levels obtained for the two conditions
in the experiment involving only once-presented items. Thus it can
be assumed that the results are generally reliable. In the case of
repeated items, W(I)W(I) was lower than W(I)W(Pl) and W(Pl)W(Pl),
$p < .05$, but the latter two did not differ significantly from each
other.

The values expected for repeated events according to the independence hypothesis were calculated from the scores for once-presented
W(I) and W(Pl) items. These values are also presented in Table II.
Comparisons showed that in each case the obtained values were
lower than the expected ones, $z \geqslant 3.45$, $p < .01$. Thus image and
pleasantness encoding of a repeated item, like repeated judgments of
pleasantness or imagery, resulted in an effect that was less than
additive, indicating nonindependence of the repeated memory
events.

The experiment was replicated with different arrangements of the
same items in counterbalanced lists, with almost identical results.
The only difference from the previous finding was that once-
presented items rated on pleasantness significantly exceeded recall of
once-imaged items. Otherwise, both experiments lead to the same
conclusion regarding the independence issue. The results suggest that
imagery and pleasantness encoding instructions activate a common
memory process to a significant degree. This contrasts with the
additivity and apparent independence of image and verbal (pronunciation) codings. However, it cannot be concluded that imagery and
pleasantness encodings are entirely indistinguishable in their effects.
If they were, no differences would have occurred in the level of recall

for imaged and semantically coded items, in whatever combination. The fact that repeated items coded once on imagery and once on pleasantness were recalled at least as well as repeated items coded each time on pleasantness, and both significantly exceeded twice-imaged items, suggests instead that the two encoding tasks arouse somewhat different processes. Arguments could be made for variation in semantic depth or some degree of dual coding, but a simpler explanation would be that the recall differences are due entirely to the superficial differences in the verbal tags associated with the items under imagery and pleasantness conditions. If this is true, differential coding effects should occur using instructional cues that are superficially different even when the subjective codings aroused by the different instructional cues can be assumed to be highly similar or at least correlated. On the other hand, if variation in verbal tagging is irrelevant when the underlying process is consistent, no differential coding effects should occur. The alternatives were investigated in two experiments, the first involving processes related to imagery and the second, pleasantness–unpleasantness of meaning.

5. Repeated Encodings on Correlated Dimensions

a. Imagery versus Concreteness. Group ratings of imagery and concreteness of nouns are highly correlated. The *r* value is .83 for the normative data obtained by Paivio, Yuille, and Madigan (1968) for 925 nouns, and several related measures have been found to load on a common imagery–concreteness factor (Frincke, 1968; Paivio, 1968). Thus, although careful examination can reveal subtle differences in the relations of rated imagery and concreteness to memory performance (Richardson, 1973), the two variables share a large common component. This component presumably reflects interconnections between imaginal and verbal representations, which are theoretically equated with referential meaning within dual coding theory. If this interpretation of the relation between imagery and concreteness is correct, and if the item and encoding repetitions paradigm is sensitive to such commonality, successive encodings of repeated items on imagery and concreteness should be less than additive in their effect on subsequent recall, as should repeated encoding on either of these dimensions separately. Moreover, unlike imagery and pleasantness codings, imagery and concreteness should be completely equivalent in their effects on the level of recall under repetition conditions as well as without repetition.

These predictions were tested in an experiment involving the same lists of words as in the previous repetition experiments, but the concreteness (C) instructions and encoding cues substituted as the contrast to imagery encoding. Thus equal numbers of repeated items were encoded twice as II, CC, and IC, and unrepeated items once as I or C. The instructions for I coding remained as before and those for C coding were adapted from Paivio *et al.* (1968). The emphasis in the case of C was on judging the directness with which the word refers to concrete objects. The procedure otherwise was identical to what was followed in the previous experiments.

The recall proportions are presented in Table III, with IC and CI sequences (which did not differ significantly) collapsed into a single score. An analysis of variance with conditions and subjects as factors showed that the conditions differed significantly ($p < .05$). Newman-Keuls comparisons indicated that IC and CC recall significantly exceeded unrepeated items coded once as I. No other differences were significant. The recall proportions expected on the basis of the independence hypothesis were calculated as before and are presented in Table III. The test of differences showed that the obtained scores for all repetition conditions were less than expected ($z \geqslant 2.89$, $p < .01$).

TABLE III

OBTAINED RECALL PROPORTIONS FOR UNREPEATED AND
REPEATED WORDS ENCODED ON IMAGERY (I) AND
CONCRETENESS (C) AND ON PLEASANTNESS (Pl) AND
GOODNESS (G) AND PROPORTIONS EXPECTED IF THE
REPEATED EVENTS WERE INDEPENDENT

	I	C	II	IC(CI)	CC
I-C Codings ($N = 19$)					
Obtained	.246	.298	.320[a]	.368[a]	.368[b]
Expected			.415	.466	.481

	Pl	G	PlPl	PlG(GPl)	GG
Pl–G Codings ($N = 19$)					
Obtained	.382	.311	.360[b]	.386[b]	.333[b]
Expected			.608	.573[a]	.509

[a] $p < .01$ obtained versus predicted.
[b] $p < .001$ obtained versus predicted.

The experiment was repeated with different lists involving new counterbalancings so that every item served equally often in each condition. The recall proportions were .37, .35 and .33 for II, IC(CI), and CC, respectively, and .32 and .25 for I and C. The results differed from the previous experiment only in that C recall was now significantly lower than all others which did not differ among themselves. The theoretically crucial results were that the repetition conditions were again essentially equivalent and that the obtained recall for each was substantially lower than expected ($z \geqslant 4.80$, $p <$ .001). Thus the data are completely consistent with the prediction that repeated coding on correlated dimensions would be less than additive.

b. Pleasantness versus Goodness. Judgments of the goodness of words on a good–bad scale were chosen as the correlate of pleasantness because ratings of concepts on these two scales have been consistently found to load highly on a common evaluative meaning factor (Osgood *et al.*, 1957). The design and method were identical to the previous experiments except for the encodings. Thus equal numbers of repeated words were encoded twice on pleasantness (PlPl), goodness (GG), and pleasantness–goodness or vice versa (PlG). Unrepeated words were coded as Pl or G.

The scores for PlG and GPl sequences were again justifiably combined. The recall proportions for the resulting five conditions are presented in the lower half of Table III, together with predicted scores predicted from the independence hypothesis. The analysis of variance of obtained scores yielded no significant effects. This is even more surprising than the IC experiment because it means that none of the repetition conditions exceeded unrepeated item scores. This fact alone suffices to show that the repetition must be less than additive, and this was strongly confirmed by the significance tests: in each case, obtained scores were less than expected scores ($z \geqslant 5.31$, $p < .001$). This is again as predicted for correlated codes. To evaluate the comparability of the results for imagery–concreteness and pleasantness–goodness codings, the data for the two experiments were analyzed by an overall analysis of variance with experiment as an additional factor. No significant main effects or interactions were obtained, indicating that the two experiments yielded statistically equivalent results.

Strong generalizations can be entertained because the results are fully consistent with predictions in both of the independent experiments. What they show is that encoding dimensions that are identified by nominally different encoding tags do not produce additive effects on recall if the dimensions involve a common theoretical substrate and are empirically correlated. Conversely, when the two encoding dimensions are empirically and theoretically independent, as in the case of the imagery and pronunciation, they had additive effects on recall. The generalizations are especially strong because they emerge from such different convergent operations. On the one hand, imagery and concreteness as well as pleasantness and goodness are highly correlated attributes of verbal concepts as measured by averaged group ratings. These same encoding pairs turn out to be nonindependent and less than additive in their effect on memory in the encoding repetitions experiments. On the other hand, ratings of words on imagery and pronounceability show these dimensions to be relatively uncorrelated,[3] and pairwise inclusion of these uncorrelated dimensions in the repetition experiments show them to be additive and presumably independent in their effects.

Generalizations are not so straightforward in the case of imagery and pleasantness. Factor analytic research (Paivio, 1968) suggests that imagery—concreteness and goodness are relatively independent attributes of nouns, yet the less than additive effect of repeated coding on these dimensions suggest that they are mnemonically interdependent to a substantial degree. The problem is discussed further in the following section.

IV. Concluding Remarks

This final section sums up the major theoretical and empirical implications of the research. Theoretically, the results provide support for dual coding theory, although they also implicate depth of processing and semantic coding mechanisms other than imagery. Dual coding is supported in that the procedures that define imaginal (or pictorial) coding have additive effects on recall, as though the aroused memory representations were independent. Representational distinctiveness is further suggested by the observation that imagery apparently contributes substantially more than the verbal code to their combined effect. Depth of processing cannot explain such

---

[3] Correlations have been calculated among average ratings obtained for the words in the encoding tasks used in the experiments reported here. The resulting correlations have generally ranged from zero to low positive. This is true also of unpublished data in which pronounceability ratings were correlated with rated imagery, concreteness, and goodness values for 96 nouns used in the factor analytic study by Paivio (1968).

differential effects without adding the circular argument that imagistic or pictorial memory processing is by definition deeper than verbal.

The most general principle that can be applied to the results is that encoding variation implies additivity of mnemonic effects. As in the case of processing depth, however, differential coding leaves unstated the possibility that distinct codes may contribute unequally to recall. This possibility, as manifested specifically in the apparent superiority of the nonverbal image over a simple name code, remains somewhat of a theoretical puzzle. The problem has been discussed in detail elsewhere (Paivio & Csapo, 1973), and nothing important can be added to the story on the basis of the present results. The difference in code effectiveness must lie either in interitem relations or properties of individual items and processes that they arouse. The former could operate through the positive influence of interitem organization, or the negative influence of differential interitem interference. Specifically, picture presentation or image coding could result in better organization or less interitem interference than word presentation or verbal coding. Evidence in support of both of these possibilities can be found in the literature, but memory differences have also been obtained without concomitant variation in organization or interference variables. Thus, there is no consistent evidence related to interitem properties that would account for image superiority. The properties of individual items that might explain the effects include better chunking or unitization of the nonverbal image than of the verbal representation in memory. The former may be a synchronous chunk whereas the verbal representation is a sequentially organized concatenation of elementary units that somehow utilize more memory "space" than does the image. Again, there is no firm evidence and such ideas are in fact difficult to test. It could be reasoned that, if the principle is correct, more complex verbal chunks should be more difficult to recall than less complex. No support was obtained for the prediction within the limits of the word characteristics in these experiments (Paivio & Csapo, 1973). Thus the puzzle remains and, because it does, it is tempting to entertain the possibility that uncontrolled dual coding might eventually explain the superiority of imagery over verbal conditions in these experiments—tempting because dual coding specifies a simple mechanism that would account for the difference.

The generally comparable and less than additive effects of pleasantness and imagery codings are also puzzling, especially in view of the relative independence of the two dimensions in factor analytic research (Paivio, 1968). Indeed, the average imagery and pleasantness ratings assigned to words in the encoding phase of the incidental free recall experiments reported here are also uncorrelated, as indicated by r values of .09 and .16 in two comparisons involving once-presented (and once-coded) items. Thus predictions from the semantic differential rating data to the memory task were not upheld in the case of the uncorrelated dimensions of imagery and pleasantness, although they were in the case of the correlated dimensions of imagery and concreteness as well as pleasantness and goodness.

The findings suggest a common process underlying imagery and pleasantness encodings. How should this process be conceptualized? One possibility is that the common code is imagistic in nature, so that subjects required to rate concrete words on pleasantness do so by imagining the objects suggested by the words, as do those required to rate them on imagery. Alternatively, both tasks may elicit abstract semantic processing of some kind. A third possibility is that both encoding tasks involve imagery but the pleasantness-rating task requires an additional affective judgment. This additional processing could be viewed as a deeper semantic level than visual imagery alone, thereby producing the slight memory advantage of pleasantness over imagery encoding in some of the studies. Of course, that small difference could also be interpreted as due to more superficial processing in the case of imagery because of the high concreteness–imagery values of the words used in the experiments. That is, subjects can assume that all of the words are highly concrete and accordingly rate them high on imagery without always making an effort to generate images to the items. Research is currently underway to check out some of these possibilities, for example, by using items that are lower in their imagery value.

Finally, the studies validated an empirical technique as well as providing theoretical information. The additive or less-than-additive effects of successive repetitions are apparently sensitive to coding similarities as well as differences. The procedure could be extended to any pair of encoding dimensions. For example, within connotative semantic dimensions, evaluation, potency, and activity should have additive effects on recall if a repeated word is successively coded on any two of these. In certain respects the technique resembles release from PI (Wickens, 1970). Release from PI occurs in the Peterson and Peterson (1959) paradigm when there is a shift in the encoding characteristics of the to-be-recalled set of items. There is a difference in what the two procedures reveal, however. Release from PI seems to be particularly sensitive to shifts in polarity from one end of a dimension to another, for example, from evaluatively "good" words to "bad" words. The additivity paradigm was used in the present series of studies to assess independence across encoding dimensions. The procedure presumably could be applied to bipolar distinctions on a given dimension, for example, by having subjects judge how "good" a word is on one occurrence and how "bad" on another. Release from PI and the additivity technique would be shown to tap different memory processes if less than additive effects occur when the successive encodings involve reference to different poles of the same dimension, despite the fact that such a shift produces strong release from PI.

The repetition paradigm and additivity model can also be extended to the evaluation of various degrees of intercode dependency. Clearly, repeated events need not be classified dichotomously as interdependent or independent vis-à-vis their contribution to memory. There was some suggestion in the present research, for example, that imagery and pleasantness codings might be slightly additive in their mnemonic effect. It would be useful if the degree of additivity could be precisely determined in such cases using some general metric, based perhaps on the independence model and the empirical procedures that were successful in the studies reported here.

REFERENCES

Anderson, J. R., & Bower, G. H. Recognition and retrieval processes in free recall. *Psychological Review*, 1972, 79, 97–123.
Anderson, J. R., & Bower, G. H. *Human associative memory*. Washington, D.C.: Winston, 1973.
Anderson, R. C., & Ortony, A. On putting apples into bottles—a problem in polysemy. *Cognitive Psychology*, 1975, 7, 167–180.
Attneave, F. Representation of physical space. In A. W. Melton & E. Martin (Eds.), *Coding processes in human memory*. New York: Winston-Wiley, 1972.
Bahrick, H. P., & Bahrick, P. Independence of verbal and visual codes of the same stimuli. *Journal of Experimental Psychology*, 1971, 91, 344–346.
Begg, I. Recognition memory for sentence meaning and wording. *Journal of Verbal Learning and Verbal Behavior*, 1971, 10, 176–181.
Bousfield, W. A. The problem of meaning in verbal behavior. In C. N. Cofer (Ed.), *Verbal learning and verbal behavior*. New York: McGraw-Hill, 1961.
Bower, G. A multicomponent theory of the memory trace. In K. W. Spence & J. T. Spence (Eds.), *The psychology of learning and motivation*. New York: Academic Press, 1967.
Bower, G. H. Stimulus-sampling theory of encoding variability. In A. W. Melton & E. Martin (Eds.), *Coding processes in human memory*. New York: Winston-Wiley, 1972.
Bower, G. H., & Karlin, M. B. Depth of processing pictures of faces and recognition memory. *Journal of Experimental Psychology*, 1974, 103, 751–758.

Bransford, J. D., & Johnson, M. K. Considerations of some problems of comprehension. In W. G. Chase (Ed.), *Visual information processing.* New York: Academic Press, 1973.

Bugelski, B. R. Words and things and images. *American Psychologist,* 1970, 25, 1002–1012.

Chase, W. G., & Clark, H. H. Mental operations in the comparison of sentences and pictures. In L. Gregg (Ed.), *Cognition in learning and memory.* New York: Wiley, 1972.

Cooper, L. A., & Shepard, R. N. Chronometric studies of the rotation of mental images. In W. G. Chase (Ed.), *Visual information processing.* New York: Academic Press, 1973.

Craik, F. I. M., & Lockhart, R. S. Levels of processing: a framework for memory research. *Journal of Verbal Learning and Verbal Behavior,* 1972, 11, 671–684.

Craik, F. I. M., & Lockhart, R. S. Recognition studies of short-term memory: implications. In J. Brown (Ed.), *Recall and recognition.* New York: Wiley, 1975.

Di Vesta, F. J., Ingersoll, G., & Sunshine, P. A factor analysis of imagery tests. *Journal of Verbal Learning and Verbal Behavior,* 1971, 10, 471–479.

Frincke, G. Word characteristics, associative-relatedness, and the free-recall of nouns. *Journal of Verbal Learning and Verbal Behavior,* 1968, 7, 366–372.

Gardiner, J. M. Levels of processing in word recognition and subsequent free recall. *Journal of Experimental Psychology,* 1974, 102, 101–105.

Gartman, L. M., & Johnson, N. F. Massed versus distributed repetition of homographs: A test of the differential-encoding hypothesis. *Journal of Verbal Learning and Verbal Behavior,* 1972, 11, 801–808.

Glanzer, M. Distance between related words in free recall: Trace of the STS. *Journal of Verbal Learning and Verbal Behavior,* 1969, 8, 105–111.

Glanzer, M., & Duarte, A. Repetition between and within languages in free recall. *Journal of Verbal Learning and Verbal Behavior,* 1971, 10, 625–630.

Guilford, J. P. *The nature of human intelligence.* New York: McGraw-Hill, 1967.

Hintzman, D. L. Theoretical implications of the spacing effect. In R. L. Solso (Ed.), *Theories in cognitive psychology: The Loyola symposium.* Potomac, Md.: Lawrence Erlbaum Associates, 1974.

Hyde, T. S., & Jenkins, J. J. The differential effects of incidental tasks on the organization of recall of a list of highly associated words. *Journal of Experimental Psychology,* 1969, 82, 472–481.

Hyde, T. S., & Jenkins, J. J. Recall for words as a function of semantic, graphic, and syntactic orienting tasks. *Journal of Verbal Learning and Verbal Behavior,* 1973, 12, 471–480.

Johnson, W. A., Coots, J. H., & Flickinger, R. G. Controlled semantic encoding and the effect of repetition lag on free recall. *Journal of Verbal Learning and Verbal Behavior,* 1972, 11, 784–788.

Kimura, D. The asymmetry of the human brain. *Scientific American,* 1973, 228, 70–78.

Madigan, S. A. Intraserial repetition and coding processes in free recall. *Journal of Verbal Learning and Verbal Behavior,* 1969, 8, 828–835.

Martin, E. Stimulus meaningfulness and paired-associate transfer. *Psychological Review,* 1968, 75, 421–441.

Melton, A. W. The situation with respect to the spacing of repetitions and memory. *Journal of Verbal Learning and Verbal Behavior,* 1970, 9, 596–606.

Milner, B. Interhemispheric differences in the localization of psychological processes in man. *British Medical Bulletin,* 1971, 27, 272–277.

Moeser, S. D. Memory for meaning and wording in concrete and abstract sentences. *Journal of Verbal Learning and Verbal Behavior,* 1974, 13, 682–697.

Morton, J. Interaction of information in word recognition. *Psychological Review,* 1969, 76, 165–178.

Moyer, R. S. Comparing objects in memory: evidence suggesting an internal psychophysics. *Perception & Psychophysics,* 1973, **13**, 180–184.

Nebes, R. D. Hemispheric specialization in commissurotomized man. *Psychological Bulletin,* 1974, **81**, 1–14.

Nelson, D. L., & Brooks, D. H. Functional independence of pictures and their verbal memory codes. *Journal of Experimental Psychology,* 1973, **98**, 44–48.

Olson, D. R. Language and thought: Aspects of a cognitive theory of semantics. *Psychological Review,* 1970, **77**, 257–273.

Osgood, C. E. *Method and theory in experimental psychology.* London & New York: Oxford University Press, 1953.

Osgood, C. E. Where do sentences come from? In D. D. Steinberg & L. A. Jakobovits (Eds.), *Semantics: An interdisciplinary reader in philosophy, linguistics, and psychology.* London & New York: Cambridge University Press, 1971.

Osgood, C. E., Suci, G. J., & Tannenbaum, P. H. *The measurement of meaning.* Urbana: University of Illinois Press, 1957.

Paivio, A. A factor-analytic study of word attributes and verbal learning. *Journal of Verbal Learning and Verbal Behavior,* 1968, **7**, 41–49.

Paivio, A. *Imagery and verbal processes.* New York: Holt, 1971.

Paivio, A. Symbolic and sensory modalities of memory. In M. E. Meyer (Ed.), *The third Western symposium on learning: Cognitive learning.* Bellingham, Wash.: Western Washington State College, 1972.

Paivio, A. Language and knowledge of the world. *Educational Researcher,* 1974, **3**, 5–12. (a)

Paivio, A. Spacing of repetitions in the incidental and intentional free recall of pictures and words. *Journal of Verbal Learning and Verbal Behavior,* 1974, **13**, 497–511. (b)

Paivio, A. Imagery and long-term memory. In R. A. Kennedy & A. Wilkes (Eds.), *Studies in long term memory.* New York: Wiley, 1975.

Paivio, A., & Csapo, K. Picture superiority in free recall: Imagery or dual coding? *Cognitive Psychology,* 1973, **5**, 176–206.

Paivio, A., & O'Neill, B. J. Visual recognition thresholds and dimensions of word meaning. *Perception & Psychophysics,* 1970, **8**, 273–275.

Paivio, A., Yuille, J. C., & Madigan, S. A. Concreteness, imagery, and meaningfulness values for 925 nouns. *Journal of Experimental Psychology,* 1968, **76**(1), Part 2.

Peterson, L. R., & Peterson, M. J. Short-term retention of individual verbal items. *Journal of Experimental Psychology,* 1959, **58**, 193–198.

Pylyshyn, Z. W. What the mind's eye tells the mind's brain: a critique of mental imagery. *Psychological Bulletin,* 1973, **80**, 1–24.

Richardson, J. T. E. Imagery, concreteness, and lexical complexity. Unpublished doctoral dissertation, University of Sussex, 1973.

Rowe, E. J. Imagery and frequency processes in verbal discrimination learning. *Journal of Experimental Psychology,* 1972, **95**, 140–146.

Rumelhart, D. E., Lindsay, P. H., & Norman, D. A. A process model for long-term memory. In E. Tulving & W. Donaldson (Eds.), *Organization and memory.* New York: Academic Press, 1972.

Shepard, R. N., & Chipman, S. Second-order isomorphism of internal representations: Shapes of states. *Cognitive Psychology,* 1970, **1**, 1–17.

Simpson, H. M. Effects of instructional set, encoding time, and word type on recognition memory. Paper presented at the meeting of the Canadian Psychological Association, Montreal, June, 1972.

Snodgrass, J. G., Wasser, B., Finkelstein, M., & Goldberg, L. G. On the fate of visual and verbal memory codes for pictures and words: evidence for a dual coding mechanism in recognition memory. *Journal of Verbal Learning and Verbal Behavior*, 1974, **13**, 27–37.

Strømnes, F. A semiotic theory of imagery processes with experiments on an Indo-European and a Ural-Altaic language: Do speakers of different languages experience different cognitive worlds? *Scandinavian Journal of Psychology*, 1973, **14**, 291–304.

Thios, S. J. Memory for words in repeated sentences. *Journal of Verbal Learning and Verbal Behavior*, 1972, **11**, 789–793.

Till, R. E., & Jenkins, J. J. The effects of cued orienting tasks on the free recall of words. *Journal of Verbal Learning and Verbal Behavior*, 1973, **12**, 489–498.

Underwood, B. J. Attributes of memory. *Psychological Review*, 1969, **76**, 559–573. (a)

Underwood, B. J. Some correlates of item repetition in free-recall learning. *Journal of Verbal Learning and Verbal Behavior*, 1969, **8**, 83–94. (b)

Wallach, H., & Averbach, E. On memory modalities. *American Journal of Psychology*, 1955, **68**, 249–257.

Walsh, D. A., & Jenkins, J. J. Effects of orienting tasks on free recall in incidental learning: "difficulty," "effort," and "process" explanations. *Journal of Verbal Learning and Verbal Behavior*, 1973, **12**, 481–488.

Wickens, D. D. Encoding categories of words: An empirical approach to meaning. *Psychological Review*, 1970, **77**, 1–15.

PAVLOVIAN CONDITIONING
AND DIRECTED MOVEMENTS[1]

Eliot Hearst

INDIANA UNIVERSITY, BLOOMINGTON, INDIANA

I.	Introduction	216
II.	Pavlovian Conditioning, Auto-Shaping, and Sign-Tracking	217
III.	Empirical Manipulations and Their Effects	222
	A. Type and Degree of Contingency between Stimulus and Reinforcer	222
	B. Sign Redundancy	225
	C. Type of Reinforcer	229
	D. Type of CS	232
	E. The Feature-Positive Effect in Discrimination Learning	235
IV.	Conjunctions, Contingencies, and Cognitions: Stimulus–Stimulus versus Response–Stimulus Relations	244
	A. Omission Procedures	245
	B. Stimulus-Sequence Learning and Overt Movements	253
V.	Concluding Comments	258
	References	260

If we lay aside, for the moment at least, such learning theories as Thorndike's Law of Effect and Hull's Law of Reinforcement by Drive Reduction and simply ask what [a subject] learns when confronted by a quick sequence of stimuli, $S_1 S_2$, and how he learns it, we find that he learns to take S_1 as a signal of the coming S_2, and to make preparations accordingly. If S_2 is something good, his preparation, R_1, is some form of approach; if S_2 is something bad, he prepares to avoid it, or at least "take it"; if S_2 is something of no importance to him, he prepares to disregard it, as by continuing what he

[1] The preparation of this article and the research connected with it were supported by a Guggenheim Fellowship during 1974–75 and National Institute of Mental Health Research Grant No. MH 19300. I thank Michael Browne, Greg Christoph, Stanley Franklin, Dexter Gormley, John Karpicke, Sandra Martin, Blaine Peden, Gail Peterson, Barbara Salzenstein, Edward Wasserman, and William Wolff for valuable ideas, assistance, and encouragement. An especially great debt is due Herbert Jenkins of McMaster University, whose research and thinking have influenced almost every aspect of my work on this topic. Some parts of this article contain restatements of material covered in the monograph jointly written by Jenkins and me (Hearst & Jenkins, 1974).

is doing. The preparation for S_2 depends on the response which will be made to S_2, that is on R_2. If R_2 is to be some form of acceptance, R_1 is an appropriate form of approach; if R_2 is to be adverse, R_1 makes ready for escape or avoidance; if R_2 is to be a disregard of S_2, R_1 is a beginning of such disregard. . . . We can safely say that the *motor preparation depends on the sequence of stimuli,* so that what is primarily learned is the sequence $S_1 S_2$. . . . The reinforcement theories are apt to by-pass [the trials before any conditioned response appears] but evidently the learner could not do without them [Woodworth, 1958, pp. 239–240] .

I. Introduction

Pavlovian and operant conditioning are the two basic procedures used in the experimental study of learning. They are objectively distinguished in terms of whether the occurrence of some biologically significant event depends on the subject's behavior. Pavlov's procedure involves presentations of the conditioned stimulus (CS) and unconditioned stimulus (US) independently of behavior, whereas in operant conditioning some response of the subject controls presentation or removal of the US.

This apparently straightforward operational distinction implies more than a mere procedural difference to many psychologists, who believe that different associative laws or basic processes are correlated with the two types of experimental arrangement (for reviews and discussions of two-process approaches, see Hearst [1975], Kimble [1961], Mackintosh [1974], Rescorla & Solomon [1967], and Seward [1970].) One of the most persistent of these presumed fundamental differences involves the relationship between conditioning procedures and response categories: Pavlovian conditioning is considered the technique for modifying responses of the autonomic (involuntary) nervous system, whereas operant conditioning is appropriate for modifying responses of the somatic nervous system. Accordingly, visceral and glandular responses are thought to be conditionable mainly, if not exclusively, by means of Pavlovian procedures, and skeletal movements by means of operant procedures.

The work of Neal Miller and others (see the annual volumes on *Biofeedback and Self-Control,* published by Aldine-Atherton since 1970) has already cast doubt on the belief that autonomic responses cannot be modified by operant procedures. The present chapter concerns experimental and theoretical work relevant to the second half of the above set of beliefs: are skeletal responses modifiable by Pavlovian procedures? Of course, several instances of such modification have been known to experimental psychologists for a long time.

Eyeblinks, limb withdrawals, finger flexions, and knee jerks have served as responses in successful studies of Pavlovian conditioning. However, these results are often viewed as minor, isolated exceptions to the rule that the training of skeletal movements requires application of operant conditioning procedures. After all, the argument goes, the exceptions comprise only undirected "reflexive" movements of relatively small parts of the organism and are not of great practical and theoretical significance. Coordinated, organized movements of the whole organism—"molar" acts directed at external objects—should command our attention, according to proponents of this view, and such responses are presumed to be forms of operant behavior, modifiable only by their contingent effects on the environment.

In this chapter, I will describe some research demonstrating that the establishment of stimulus-reinforcer contingencies (i.e., Pavlovian conditioning) produces powerful effects on skeletomotor activities of the whole organism. Even though the animal's behavior does not affect US delivery, an organism will move toward or away from environmental stimuli, depending on whether these stimuli are positively or negatively correlated with the reinforcer. Moreover, behavior directed at signals of impending reinforcement is surprisingly difficult to eliminate and will frequently persist even if it actually *prevents* the delivery of a scheduled reinforcer. The fact that the experimental arrangements produce directed actions and yet fulfill most of the usual criteria for Pavlovian conditioning raises serious questions about the respondent—operant distinction. The results indicate that the learning of a relationship between a stimulus and reinforcer precedes and guides skeletal movements in many situations; as the quotation from Woodworth at the beginning of this chapter suggests, a primary aspect of most, if not all, learning seems to involve the subject's registration of some correlation between environmental events.

II. Pavlovian Conditioning, Auto-Shaping, and Sign-Tracking

Although Pavlov's research emphasized the use of the salivary response, he occasionally described some of the movements of his dogs during standard salivary conditioning. Of course, in order to measure salivation by means of the fistula technique, he had to restrict the movements of his subjects; and, in a harness, they had very little opportunity to display organized, directed activity. Despite that limitation, directed movements appeared, as the following passage indicates:

> The first reaction elicited by the established conditioned stimulus usually consists in a movement toward the stimulus, i.e., the animal turns to the place where the stimulus is. If the stimulus is within reach, the animal even tries to touch it, with his mouth. Thus if the conditioned stimulus is the switching on of a lamp, the dog licks the lamp; if the conditioned stimulus is a sound the dog will even snap at the air. . . . [He appears] to eat the sound, that is, licking his lips and making the noise of chewing with his teeth as though it were a matter of having the food itself. . . . The conditioned stimulus actually stands for the food. In the case of several conditioned stimuli coming from different directions the animal turns toward each of them [Pavlov, 1941, pp. 120 and 150].

   In this description Pavlov offered some examples of the conditioning of directed movements that may occur when a CS and US are paired. Several points related to Pavlov's account seem of particular interest and will arise again during this chapter. First, Pavlov viewed his procedure as an appropriate technique for conditioning skeleto-motor behavior. In his writings he did not limit potential application of the procedure to visceral and glandular responses. Second, Pavlovian conditioning cannot be adequately characterized in terms of changes in a single response. Although the experimenter may measure only salivation, a pattern of functionally related behaviors actually develops to CS. Unfortunately, past researchers have neglected many aspects (particularly the skeletomotor ones) of an organism's "preparation" for the imminent US. Third, Pavlov's account indicates that the animal's preparatory behavior was frequently directed toward the CS, rather than toward the food dish; instead, one might have suspected that motor preparation for US would involve orientation and movement toward the source of the US. It would seem worthwhile to determine the conditions that engender orientation and approach toward the CS, rather than performance of the apparently more "adaptive" response of approaching the US. Fourth, the fact that the subjects licked and chewed the "CS," and seemed to treat it as a surrogate for food, makes one wonder whether a change in the US (e.g., to water, or to the presentation of a sexual partner) would lead to a change in the type of behaviors directed toward the CS. Fifth, suppose the subjects were *not* restrained and the CS was relatively far from the US delivery site; would subjects still attempt to approach and contact it? Or suppose that Pavlov's dog were released from its harness after standard Pavlovian training with a CS located far out of reach; when released, would the subject immediately approach and contact the CS, even though such extensive movements could never have been "instrumentally" reinforced?

Although Skinner (1948) did not describe his experiments on "superstitious conditioning" of movements as an application of Pavlov's procedures, Skinner's method actually conforms to what Pavlov called temporal conditioning, with the passage of time acting as a CS. Skinner's pigeons received grain every x seconds, regardless of their behavior in a chamber in which they could move about freely, and Pavlov's dogs received food every x seconds regardless of their behavior in the harness. Skinner reported that most of his subjects acquired stereotyped movements (e.g., pecking at the floor, thrusting the head into one of the upper corners of the chamber) even though these movements had no experimental consequence. Nevertheless, Skinner argued that conditioning in this situation was operant in nature. "The conditioning process is usually obvious. The bird happens to be executing some response as the [grain] hopper appears; as a result it tends to repeat this response [p. 168]." Additional conjunctions of response and grain serve to strengthen the response further, until it reaches a considerable state of strength.

Skinner concluded that operant conditioning usually occurs even when grain is presented "at regular intervals *with no reference whatsoever to the bird's behavior* [p. 168]." But according to operational definitions of operant versus respondent conditioning, in terms of whether a response-reinforcer contingency is present or absent, Skinner's procedure would be an example of respondent (Pavlovian) conditioning. His statement indicates a willingness to extend the concept of "contingency" to cases which involve mere conjunctions of responses and reinforcers, and he said frankly that contingency may mean nothing more than that a reinforcement follows a response. However, such an extension of the concept of contingency nullifies the operational distinction between respondent and operant conditioning, since salivation also occurs in close conjunction with food on Pavlov's temporal-conditioning procedure.

Apparently, more than just the presence of an explicit response-reinforcer contingency is involved in the psychologist's practice of labeling the conditioning of stereotyped movements as "operant" and the conditioning of salivation as "respondent." Perhaps the persistent belief that directed movements form a category of behavior that follows different laws or processes as compared to visceral or glandular behavior is responsible for continued adherence to the view that two types of conditioning are involved—even though on the surface Pavlov's and Skinner's experiments are so similar. After all, Skinner could have measured some visceral or glandular response while subjects were performing their "superstitions," or Pavlov could have recorded directed movements in his situation; should we talk about different forms of conditioning merely because of the response we happen to measure on a particular procedure? Hearst (1975) has discussed some of the traditional beliefs (e.g., voluntary behavior versus reflex action) which may contribute to the tenacity of such dual-process views, despite insubstantial evidence for distinguishing between two processes.

Even in a standard operant-conditioning situation, not only is delivery of the reinforcer contingent upon a prior response, but it is also necessarily contingent on the presence of certain cues (visual, tactual, proprioceptive, etc.) associated with the manipulandum on which the response is made. The reinforcer occurs if and only if the subject has approached and received stimulation from such cues. Perhaps the subject's behavior is directed toward the lever not so much because *pressing* the lever has been reinforced but because the lever as a *stimulus* has been associated with the reinforcer. The quotation from Pavlov suggests that subjects will direct behavior toward a stimulus associated with reinforcement. Study of the conditioning of directed movements within a Pavlovian paradigm, but with freely-moving subjects, ought to be valuable in assessing this possibility.

The first extensive study of directed actions acquired via Pavlovian procedures was performed by Brown and Jenkins (1968). In contrast to conventional research also employing pigeons, response keys, and grain reinforcement, Brown and Jenkins made grain delivery contingent only on a prior stimulus (key illumination). The key was occasionally illuminated for 8 sec and immediately followed by 4 sec of access to grain. As pairings of CS (key illumination) and US (grain) continued, birds first exhibited increases in activity to CS and oriented toward the lighted key, then began to approach it, and finally pecked at it. The first peck occurred, on the average, after 40 pairings of light and grain. Brown and Jenkins named this phenomenon "auto-shaping" and intended the term to cover the approach and contact behavior that develops toward the signal of an appetitive reinforcer; the procedure was *auto*matic, could be *auto*mated, and the pigeon could be said to have shaped it*self* to perform a response that in previous research had required the experimenter's assistance (the method of successive approximations, or "manual shaping"). Apparently the standard "arbitrary" operant, a key peck, was not so arbitrary after all, since it developed on a procedure where the response was not even required for grain.

Since Brown and Jenkins' initial work, auto-shaping has been reported in studies employing a variety of species, CSs, responses, reinforcers, and general situations. Hearst and Jenkins (1974) reviewed and evaluated the major findings, discussed the variables that affect the phenomenon, and coined a new term, *sign-tracking*, to cover auto-shaping and several other related effects.[2] Sign-tracking refers to behavior that is directed toward (e.g., orientation, approach, contact) or away from a stimulus (sign) as a result of the relation between that stimulus and a reinforcer.

Some writers have suggested that auto-shaping is a form of superstitious conditioning: pecks at the illuminated key are consistently followed by grain, despite the accidental nature of the relationship. This explanation cannot account for the very first key peck, which is dependent on a positive contingency between key illumination and grain; subjects rarely peck keys that are lit randomly with regard to grain presentations (Hearst & Jenkins, 1974). However, response-reinforcer conjunctions could be critically involved in the later increase and maintenance of auto-shaped behavior. Hearst and Jenkins described several techniques for determining whether stimulus-reinforcer or response-reinforcer relations are more important in the control of sign-tracking; some additional data concerning the relative influence of these relations will be described in the present chapter. Many of these results clearly violate the Law of Effect and generally support perception-centered theories of learning.

The bulk of this chapter will be devoted to a description of research on sign-tracking, some previously unpublished, performed at Indiana University. I shall not review other work summarized in Hearst and Jenkins (1974), nor retrace most of the theoretical discussions in that monograph, except when necessary to place the present research in perspective. Some of our experiments merely provide additional illustrations of phenomena and effects reported by researchers who employed rather different experimental settings. Other studies, however, particularly those concerning negative stimulus-reinforcer correlations, cue redundancy, learning during "observation" of stimulus-stimulus correlations, and approach versus

---

[2] The word "auto-shaping" is so popular nowadays that I shall continue to use it frequently in this chapter, as applied to situations in which no response is required and yet subjects *contact* a localizable stimulus (usually some standard manipulandum) that predicts the imminent delivery of an appetitive reinforcer.

contact as separate components of sign-tracking behavior, seem to involve relatively novel contributions to our understanding of the Pavlovian conditioning of directed movements.

III. Empirical Manipulations and Their Effects

A variety of factors affect the rapidity of acquisition, asymptotic response level, and type of behavior observed in sign-tracking situations. In addition to more extensive treatment of the factors discussed below, the effects of several other important variables are summarized in Hearst and Jenkins (1974), to which the interested reader should refer.

A. TYPE AND DEGREE OF CONTINGENCY BETWEEN STIMULUS AND REINFORCER

Most experiments on sign-tracking have examined only positive contingencies between CS and US. Wasserman, Franklin, and Hearst (1974) asked whether there was a negative counterpart to the approach and contact behavior evoked by food-predictive signals located on a pigeon's response key. Like a positive signal (CS+), a signal (CS−) that food is *not* coming is also "informative," but the event it predicts is an unfavorable one (see Rescorla, 1972, for a discussion of positive and negative contingencies in Pavlovian conditioning). Because the mere absence of pecking at CS− would not permit us to distinguish between a lack of control by CS− and a conditioned repulsion from it, we recorded not only pecks at the signal but also the bird's physical proximity to it. A pivoted floor detected whether the bird was standing on the left or right side of the chamber. Two response keys, one on either side of the chamber, were used and on a given trial either the left key or right key was illuminated.

In our first experiment, three birds were exposed to a *positive* contingency between CS and US, in which 10-sec illuminations of either key were immediately followed by 3 sec of access to grain. Three other subjects received training in which CS and US had a *negative* relation to each other: all grain deliveries occurred during the time the keylights were off and never followed key illumination by less than 33 sec or preceded key illumination by less than 20 sec. Other birds received (a) keylight-only trials (*CS-only*, no grain was ever presented), or (b) *backward* pairings of CS and US. After behavior had stabilized on one of these four conditions, some of the birds were switched to a different condition for 9–21 sessions.

All birds in the *positive* group soon began approaching and pecking the lighted key, but subjects in the other three groups hardly ever pecked it. On the basis of key pecking behavior, therefore, the birds in these three groups could not be differentiated from one other. However, measures of approach-withdrawal toward the lit key clearly distinguished among the groups (Fig. 1). Birds in the *CS-only* group and the *backward* group (not included in Fig. 1 to avoid overcrowding the figure) did not exhibit any consistent tendency to approach or withdraw from the lit key, but *negative* birds spent most of their CS time on the side of the chamber opposite the lit key. When later switched from *positive* to *negative, negative* to *positive,* or *CS-only* to *positive,* subjects showed appropriate changes in performance, although the approach and key-pecking levels reached on the positive contingency by subjects previously exposed to the negative contingency were generally lower than levels attained by subjects exposed first to the positive contingency—a result we have also obtained in several subsequent experiments.

Thus, birds not only approach and peck a spatially-shifting signal which indicates that grain is imminent, but they also position themselves relatively far from a signal that grain is not coming. These results were confirmed and extended in two other experiments reported by Wasserman *et al.*, one of which included a group exposed to random presentations of CS and US (see Rescorla, 1967); no consistent approach or withdrawal was obtained toward CS in that arrangement. The whole set of experiments demonstrated that, even though key pecking, approach-withdrawal movements, and any other behavior do not affect deliveries of CS or US, subjects still acquire consistent and relatively permanent locomotor responses that are guided by the location of stimuli which predict the presentation or nonpresentation of US. These conditioned skeletal movements are a result of exposure to associative procedures that fulfill the usual criteria for Pavlovian conditioning.

In his master's thesis, Stanley Franklin (1973) examined withdrawal from a stimulus negatively correlated with food as a function of the rate of food presentation in the absence of the stimulus. The general procedure was very similar to that used in the experiments of Wasserman *et al.*, except that each CS lasted 20 sec. Three groups of eight birds were included: one group (.37) received .37 grain presentations per min during the intertrial interval (ITI), another group (.74) received .74 grain presentations per min during the ITI, and the third group (1.48) received 1.48 grain presentations per min during the ITI. No grain was ever delivered during CS (lit key) periods, and the rate of grain delivery during the ITI was determined by the setting of a random probability generator which was sampled every 2 sec; grain was presented for 3 sec whenever a positive output from the generator occurred.

Figure 2 shows that the amount of withdrawal displayed to CS was directly related to the frequency of grain in the absence of CS. Group 1.48 displayed reliable withdrawal from CS much sooner than Group .37 and reached a significantly lower mean withdrawal level than Group .37 over the 14 sessions (t = 4.27, df = 14, $p < .001$). Although birds in Group .74 showed somewhat slower acquisition of CS withdrawal than Group 1.48, they reached essentially the same

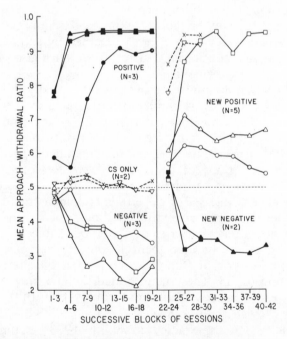

Fig. 1. Mean Approach–Withdrawal ratios over successive blocks of sessions for eight individual pigeons. The Approach–Withdrawal ratio was calculated by the formula: total time on the same side as the keylight/total trial time. A ratio of .50 would indicate that the bird's movements were not controlled by the keylight. Ratios near .00 or 1.00 would indicate very strong withdrawal or approach, respectively. Each bird was first placed on its indicated procedure for 21 sessions, and then (with the exception of one originally Positive bird, which was not tested further) switched to the Positive or Negative contingency for either 9 or 21 additional sessions. (Adapted from Wasserman et al., 1974.)

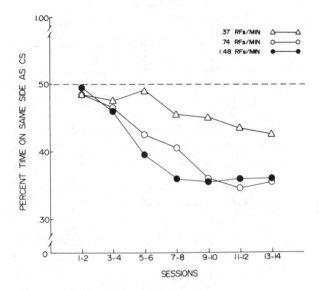

Fig. 2. Mean Approach–Withdrawal ratios (as in Fig. 1) over successive blocks of sessions for each of three groups of pigeons exposed to different rates of grain delivery in the absence of the keylight. No grain was ever delivered during key illumination (CS) periods. (From Franklin, 1973.)

asymptotic level. Group .74 also differed significantly from Group .37 in mean CS withdrawal over the 14 sessions ($t = 2.37$, $df = 14$, $p < .05$). Very little pecking of CS occurred in this experiment, even though a US could be delivered within as little as 2 sec following CS offset.

Franklin's findings support Rescorla's proposal (e.g., 1969, pp. 76–82) that in Pavlovian conditioning the amount of negative associative strength accruing to a CS negatively correlated with US is a direct function of the difference between the probability (or rate) of US occurrence in the presence versus absence of CS. Rescorla used noxious USs and a CER procedure in his work, whereas Franklin obtained analogous results with an appetitive US and a measure of active withdrawal from CS.

B. Sign Redundancy

A surprising, but extremely reliable finding furnished the starting point for Edward Wasserman's dissertation research (see Wasserman, 1973a): Auto-shaping was not obtained if keylight → grain pairings occurred in a chamber that was completely dark between trials. The

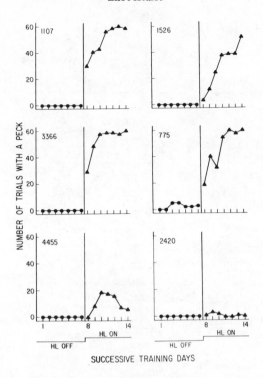

Fig. 3. Number of trials with at least one key peck during successive houselight-off (HL OFF; Sessions 1–7) and houselight-on (HL ON; Sessions 8–14) phases. There were 60 trials per day for each of the six subjects. Subject numbers are shown at the upper left of each individual panel. (Adapted from Wasserman, 1973a.)

birds did not peck at the illuminated key during trials, but engaged in various idiosyncratic behaviors (e.g., head bobbing), which were usually directed toward certain specific features of the apparatus (e.g., one corner of the chamber; the food magazine). Wasserman had expected auto-shaping to be particularly effective in a dark box, since key illumination should be especially salient against a background of no light.

Figure 3 presents data from one of Wasserman's experiments. Birds failed to acquire the key-pecking response when general chamber illumination was absent, but they began pecking the lit key when a houselight remained on throughout the session. Observation revealed that even the two birds at the bottom of the figure pecked repeatedly toward the keylight during houselight-on periods. However, these pecks did not trigger the recording equipment, since they either struck off the key surface or stopped just short of it (a common observation in our laboratory for birds who *apparently* do not auto-shape).

Wasserman invoked cue redundancy as an explanation for the houselight effect. In a dark chamber the bird could detect key illumination regardless of where it was standing or looking, since lighting of the key brightened the entire chamber; so many redundant contextual cues were available that its behavior need not be directed toward the "small" response key and was in fact usually directed toward other environmental features, as noted earlier. With continuous houselight illumination, however, the delivery of grain was unpredictable unless the bird was looking at the area near the key (and research with a variety of organisms has generally demonstrated that subjects will move to locations in which US is signaled as compared to locations in which it is not).

Later experiments (Wasserman, 1973a) confirmed and extended Wasserman's original results and interpretation. They also indicated that the houselight effect was not due in some way to the "aversiveness" of blackouts or sudden illuminations of the key, or to general inattentiveness of pigeons exposed to long periods of darkness. Wasserman's research demonstrated the importance of cue localizability in auto-shaping the pigeon's key peck. When diffuse or numer-

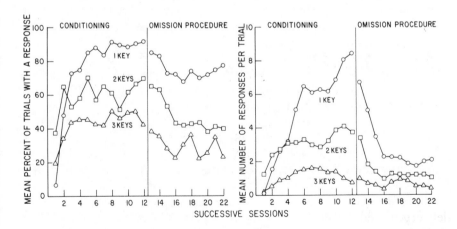

Fig. 4. Mean percent of trials with a key peck and mean number of key pecks per trial over successive sessions for three groups of pigeons. Grain deliveries were signaled by the illumination of either one, two, or three keys in the different groups. After 12 sessions of conditioning, an omission procedure was instituted on which a peck to any lighted key canceled the scheduled grain delivery on that trial.

ous predictors of US are available, key pecking does not emerge or occurs at a relatively low level.

Additional evidence in support of this type of explanation has been obtained in a recent experiment performed for control purposes in connection with research on the feature-positive effect, to be described shortly. In this experiment, the independent variable was the number of keys in a standard 3-key pigeon chamber that were lit during the 6-sec CS period preceding each food delivery. Otherwise, the procedure for the first 12 sessions was analogous to those used in conventional studies of auto-shaping: the subject's behavior had no effect on grain delivery, the chamber was continuously illuminated, 50 CSs occurred daily, the ITI was of variable duration averaging 40 sec, and grain access time was 3 sec. One group of birds had only one key lit (always the left, center, or right key for a given bird) during CS, another group had two keys lit (always the same two for a given bird), and the third group had all three keys lit. There were six birds in each group.

According to one hypothesis, the greater the number of keys lit during CS the more likely the bird is to notice the relationship between keylight onset and food, and therefore peck a key. According to the localizability-redundancy hypothesis, on the other hand, the fewer the number of cues that predict US, the stronger should be the likelihood of key pecking. Figure 4 shows acquisition curves in each group for two response measures, percent of trials with at least one peck to any key and total number of pecks to all keys per trial.

Although there was a tendency for the 1-key birds to peck less than birds in the other groups on the first day of training, the 1-key group soon exceeded and remained above the other two groups according to both response measures. These results provide support for the cue-redundancy hypothesis outlined above.

After 12 sessions of acquisition, we instituted an *omission* procedure for the final 10 sessions of the experiment. The rationale for using this procedure, and additional findings obtained with it, will be developed more fully later in this chapter. However, the reader may find the results interesting in the present context. Under the omission procedure a single peck to any lighted key *prevented* the grain delivery scheduled to occur on that trial. Williams and Williams (1969) were the first to investigate the effects of this negative response-reinforcer contingency in an auto-shaping situation; they found that birds continued to peck the key on many trials and for many sessions, even though the only consequence of key pecking was loss of a scheduled reinforcer. Results of this kind argue against the importance of response-reinforcer conjunctions in the maintenance of auto-shaped behavior, since the omission procedure eliminates key peck-grain conjunctions.

As Fig. 4 demonstrates, birds in the 1-key group continued to respond on more than 70% of the trials for 10 sessions and thus received only about 15 of the 50 reinforcements they would have obtained if they had not responded at all. The 2- and 3-key groups reached a final level of approximately 40% and 30% reinforcements lost, respectively. In all three groups there was no indication of a further decline in key pecking after the first 3 or 4 days on the omission procedure. Apparently, pairing of CS and US on 30–70% of the trials was sufficient to maintain key pecking at high levels, despite the negative correlation between key pecking and US. Declines in total response output (right side, Fig. 4) on the omission procedure were more pronounced than for the percent-trials measure, but toward the end of the experiment subjects in the three groups were still averaging 0.5 to 2.0 responses per trial.

C. TYPE OF REINFORCER

If Pavlov's belief that the CS comes to "stand for" the US is generally correct, then the topography of the behavior directed at the CS ought to resemble that elicited by the US. Jenkins and Moore (1973) compared food and water reinforcers in a variety of auto-shaping situations. They found, in general, that pecks at a water-predictive signal were irregularly spaced, sustained, and relatively weak; while the bird was pecking, its beak opened only slightly, and licking and swallowing movements were prominent. On the other hand, pecks at a food-predictive signal were evenly spaced, brief, and forceful; the bird's beak was usually open while pecking. The birds seemed to be "sipping" or "drinking" a water-predictive key and "eating" a food-predictive key. The form of the directed behavior conformed to Pavlov's notions about stimulus substitution.

Peterson, Ackil, Frommer, and Hearst (1972) developed a method for auto-shaping the rat, and they varied the type of reinforcer which the CS predicted. The CS in these rat studies was the 15-sec insertion of a retractable, lighted lever into the chamber. Lever depressions and all bare-skin contacts of the lever were recorded separately. Videotapes provided data on the topography of the responses made to CS.

In all prior auto-shaping experiments, the reinforcers were dis-

pensed from devices that evoked directed movements; food maga-
zines or water dippers had to be approached and contacted, for
example. Peterson *et al.* set out to determine whether auto-shaping
would occur with a reinforcer that did not have to be approached
and consumed: electrical stimulation of the lateral hypothalamus in
the brain. They compared behavior exhibited toward signals of
impending brain stimulation with that exhibited toward signals for
food US.

Figure 5 indicates the percent of trials with a lever contact under
various experimental conditions for a group of rats that received a
food pellet immediately after each presentation of one lever (CS+).
Another lever (CS°) was inserted randomly with respect to presentations of food or CS+. The behavior of the subject had no effect on
lever or food presentations.

During the acquisition phase (Sessions 1–10) there was a very large
increase in contacts of CS+, whereas contacts of CS° increased only
slightly. During extinction and reacquisition, contacts of CS+ rapidly
declined and recovered respectively. When the functions of CS+ and
CS° were subsequently reversed, contact behavior changed accordingly. Videotapes revealed that contacts of CS+ were almost exclusively oral and consisted mainly of licking and gnawing.

Other rats received similar treatment, except that rewarding brain
stimulation served as the US. Videotapes showed that every rat soon
began to approach and contact CS+; however, the lever was often
contacted only by the subject's whiskers, as the rat "explored" near
it. These rats seldom gnawed or licked CS+. They tended to engage in
exploratory behavior, which in many cases included fragments of the
movements that occurred when brain stimulation itself was delivered.
Thus, if an animal sniffed, "explored," or displayed certain postural
adjustments during US presentations, specific details of this behavioral pattern also appeared frequently during CS+.

In his doctoral dissertation, Gail Peterson (1972) replicated and
extended many of the findings with rats. The same topographical
differences in lever contact (licking-gnawing versus sniffing-explora-
tion) occurred reliably in between-subject and within-subject comparisons of signals for food versus brain-stimulation US. In these later
studies *all* rats (*a*) had electrodes implanted in lateral hypothalamic
sites, (*b*) were hungry, and (*c*) were attached to the electrode cable
during experimental sessions. Peterson's dissertation showed that the
topographical differences reported by Peterson *et al.* (1972) were not
due to the different dominant drives present during training of the
two separate groups or to potentiation of different patterns of

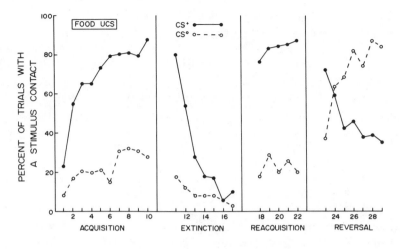

Fig. 5. Mean probability of a lever contact during successive treatments in a group of six rats trained with food as the reinforcer. During acquisition and reacquisition, CS+ signaled food whereas CS° occurred randomly. During extinction, no food was given. During reversal, CS° signaled food and former CS+ occurred randomly. (From Peterson *et al.*, 1972; copyright 1972 by the American Association for the Advancement of Science and reprinted by permission.)

behavior because of the repeated elicitation of different URs in the two situations. Like Jenkins and Moore's work with pigeons, the rat research indicated a strong resemblance between the form of the conditioned contact responses to CS and the unconditioned movement patterns elicited by the US.

Other experiments (see Hearst & Jenkins, 1974, for a review and evaluation) have also yielded resemblances between movements occurring in CS and US. There are apparent exceptions, however. For example, Wasserman (1973b) reported that baby chicks pecked a key whose illumination signaled 4 sec of overhead heat in a cold chamber, but he did not observe any pecking while the heat US was on. Nevertheless, J. A. Hogan (1974 personal communication), pointed out that pecking is part of the normal heat-seeking behavior of baby chicks toward their mother. In Wasserman's experiment the keylight served as a signal of heat-to-come and may have evoked heat-*seeking* responses, not responses appropriate to heat itself.

In any event, Pavlov's simple concept of stimulus substitution is unlikely to encompass all the results occurring in sign-tracking situations. The properties of CS and US (their localizability, size, 3-

dimensionality, and the other behaviors they naturally evoke) will undoubtedly prove crucial in determining the exact form of the behavior directed at CS. The quotation from Woodworth at the start of this chapter stated that the subject's "preparation" for US will depend on the response to US and will be somehow "appropriate" for the forthcoming US. However, it is not easy to decide what an "appropriate form of approach" would be for every type of CS and US. In fact, one could argue that pecking a key when food is about to be delivered elsewhere is a rather inappropriate form of behavior.

D. TYPE OF CS

Most successful studies of sign-tracking have involved visual CSs that are localizable and relatively brief. However, Jenkins (see Hearst & Jenkins, 1974, p. 9) has obtained some positive evidence of sign-tracking in pigeons with auditory signals. Perhaps the use of organisms that depend more on auditory or olfactory cues than pigeons do in their natural foraging behavior would result in an even greater probability of sign-tracking to cues other than visual ones (cf. Grastyán & Vereczkei, 1974).

Pigeons will not only approach and peck a single stationary signal of impending US delivery but they will also track a CS that is composed of several successive components. Dexter Gormley and I designed and constructed a 25-key (5 × 5) matrix and investigated the acquisition and maintenance of sign-tracking behavior to sequences of four successive lights, each 2 sec long, that preceded inevitable grain delivery. Pigeons tracked (pecked) a variety of patterns, "organized" (e.g., systematic horizontal or vertical series) or "disorganized" (random lights on the matrix). These results may be related to Neuringer and Neuringer's (1974) finding that pigeons, after learning to eat from the experimenter's hand, followed the hand and rapidly learned to peck a key which the hand "approached and pecked" for food. Neuringer and Neuringer suggested that under natural conditions young animals may learn to behave like their parents simply by following (tracking) parental sources of food.

In a well-designed and interesting experiment, Douglas Grant (1974), working in William Timberlake's laboratory at Indiana University, employed an unusual CS in an auto-shaping experiment with rats: the CS involved the delivery of another rat into the chamber for 10 sec. The CS rat was fastened in a crouched position on a retractable platform, and entered the apparatus sideways. Grant wanted to determine (*a*) whether rats would approach and contact a fellow rat (conspecific) that served as a CS for food and (*b*) whether the form of contact behavior would resemble feeding activity evoked by US (e.g., chewing, licking, biting), as simple application of Pavlov's notion of stimulus substitution might suggest, or would involve species-typical social behaviors normally evoked by other rats.

Four groups of five animals were tested: (1) Group *CS+*, in which each of 30 daily 10-sec presentations of the conspecific, separated by variable ITIs averaging 60 sec, was followed by delivery of a food pellet; (2) Group CS^R, which received 30 daily 10-sec presentations of the conspecific and 30 daily presentations of food, each scheduled according to independent 60-sec variable-interval (VI) schedules (in this "random control," any pairings of CS and US were accidental); (3) Group CS^S, which received 30 daily presentations of the conspecific, but no food was delivered; (4) Group CS^W, which matched the procedure of the CS+ group, except that a block of wood approximately the same size as a rat was placed on the retractable platform. Subjects were run for 11 sessions on their original procedure and then all food was discontinued (extinction). Continuous individual observation and videotape records permitted Grant to score and enumerate a great variety of behaviors occurring during CS. His data were checked for reliability by an independent observer, who also scored one session for each subject; their reliability coefficients proved very high (> .99).

Subjects presented with a predictive conspecific (Group *CS+*) eventually reached very high levels of approach and contact behavior, whereas rats in the other groups did not. Figure 6 presents curves displaying the progressive changes in different behaviors of Group *CS+* as acquisition continued and then extinction was instituted. The figure nicely illustrates the sequential development of different components of sign-tracking behavior. The first responses to attain high levels were *"change"* (defined as: "the subject alters its ongoing behavior when CS is presented, e.g., stops grooming, lifts or tilts head, freezes"), and *"orient"* ("the subject points its nose in the direction of the CS for a minimum of 1 sec"). Subsequently, *"approach"* ("the subject moves to within 1.3 cm of the CS at any time during its presentation"), *"sniffing"* ("the subject rhythmically moves its nose and vibrissae within .6 cm of CS"), and *"social contact"* (the subject paws, grooms, crawls over, or sniffs the genital area of the conspecific) all reached high levels. During extinction each type of behavior decreased, with the greatest changes occurring in the social-contact and sniff responses.

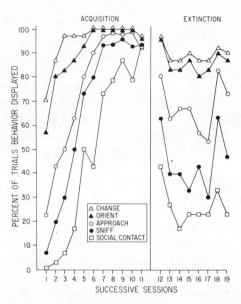

Fig. 6. Mean percent of trials on which different response categories were displayed by group CS+ toward a predictive (rat) conspecific (Sessions 1–11). During Sessions 12–19 food no longer followed presentation of the conspecific. (From Grant, 1974.)

Like other sign-tracking experiments, Grant's research demonstrated that rats will approach and contact a cue that predicts food (although it is somewhat surprising that they did not approach and contact CS^W very much). However, the form of the contact behavior that emerged toward the conspecific was social in nature, rather than a response resembling the consummatory response to food. Biting and chewing did not develop to the CS. Thus, as suggested at several points in this chapter, the properties of the particular CS are certainly important in determining the type of contact behavior exhibited toward CS. If the CS itself normally elicits behavior incompatible with appetitive consummatory behaviors or provides little support for such behaviors, contact responses will probably not resemble the URs in the situation. If the CS is "diffuse," other forms of anticipatory conditioning may occur, such as changes in general activity.

Michael Rashotte of Florida State University (1974 personal communication) has obtained results with pigeons that complement Grant's findings. When grain delivery was preceded by illumination of a visual signal imbedded in a "neutral" context (i.e., a flat rectangular wall surface), "food pecks" were directed at it, as in standard auto-shaping experiments. However, when the same signal was imbedded in a "biologically-meaningful" context (on the breast of a stuffed pigeon), aggressive behaviors were directed at it. In the latter case, there frequently appeared to be a conflict between "pecking" and "attacking" (cf. Reynolds, Catania, & Skinner, 1963). The pigeon oriented toward and approached the signal, like the sign-tracking exhibited in Grant's experiment, but the form of contact depended on the CS context.

Future studies that include detailed ethological analysis of behaviors occurring in CS, US, and the general situation seem indispensable for our understanding of sign-tracking, particularly with respect to the type of contact responses that develop toward CS. Such analyses cannot be easily automated and will require the experimenter (and his dedicated assistants) to observe ongoing sessions or to score videotapes for long periods of time. However, the rewards for such behavior by experimenters are likely to be substantial, in my opinion.

E. THE FEATURE-POSITIVE EFFECT IN DISCRIMINATION LEARNING

One of the most interesting recent findings in the field of animal discrimination learning (see Sainsbury, 1971b, for related phenomena in children) is Jenkins and Sainsbury's (1969, 1970) report of an asymmetry in the learning of discriminations that are based on the presence versus absence of a single distinctive feature. If the feature (e.g., a small green circle on the display facing the pigeon) appears on the positive (S+) trials of a successive discrete-trial *operant* discrimination, but never appears on the negative (S−) trials,[3] pigeons learn the discrimination quickly and stop responding on S− trials. However, if other birds are presented with the same two displays, but the S+ and S− conditions are reversed so that the distinctive feature appears only on negative trials, the subjects either fail to learn the discrimination or they achieve appreciably lower levels of discriminative performance than do birds trained with the feature present on positive trials. The great superiority of learning for the case in which the feature appears on positive trials has been called the feature-positive effect.

---

[3] In this chapter, I follow the convention of using S+ and S− as labels for the positive and negative stimuli in operant conditioning, and CS+ and CS− for their counterparts in Pavlovian conditioning.

In Jenkins and Sainsbury's experiments (see also Jenkins, 1973), an explicit response-reinforcer contingency was always in force; subjects had to peck the display on positive trials in order to obtain grain. Even though pecks *anywhere* on the S+ display would have produced the reinforcer, subjects (FP) with the feature present on positive trials began to peck *directly at* the feature on S+ trials before they began to eliminate responses on S− trials. In the feature-negative (FN) case, on the other hand, pecks directed at the feature disappeared; birds pecked at other parts of the display, parts common to both S+ and S− (background areas, circles of a color appearing on both S+ and S− displays, etc.). In other words, birds on both the FP and FN arrangements pecked at aspects of the display that had the highest positive correlation with the reinforcer—the feature in the former case, some common element present during trials in the latter. Therefore, learning of the FN discrimination failed to occur.

Both Herbert Jenkins and I were struck by certain similarities between the feature-positive effect and results from experiments on auto-shaping, which involves no explicit response-reinforcer contingency. In auto-shaping, pairings of CS and US produce behavior directed at the best predictor of the reinforcer, if this predictor is easily localized and not redundant. Furthermore, pairings of CS with nonreinforcement produce behavior directed away from CS. The same general effects occur on the FP versus FN discriminations. In both the feature-discrimination and auto-shaping experiments, the subjects seem to be controlled mainly by stimulus-reinforcer, not response-reinforcer correlations. Furthermore, as I shall substantiate shortly for both phenomena (see Jenkins, 1973, for the original work on this topic), the subject's registration of a positive relationship between signal and reinforcer appears to precede the emergence of a response directed at the signal.

Why should noticing that a particular environmental feature signals reinforcement produce behavior directed at that feature? Although no current theory of conditioning implies such an outcome, both the feature-positive effect and the phenomenon of auto-shaping involve exactly this result. One of the reasons why Jenkins and I coined the term "sign-tracking" was to cover both feature-discrimination and auto-shaping effects: subjects approach and often contact signals of a reinforcer and withdraw from signals of no-reinforcer.

According to this logic, the feature-positive effect ought also to appear in auto-shaping situations, where no response of the subject is required for delivery of the reinforcer. Therefore, some work in my laboratory, conducted in collaboration with Gail Peterson, was aimed at integration of the feature-positive effect and results from experiments on auto-shaping. First of all, however, we wanted to replicate Jenkins and Sainsbury's FP versus FN asymmetry in our experimental arrangement, with an explicit response-reinforcer contingency in force as in their work. Jenkins and Sainsbury had used a special square key for presenting S+ and S− displays; each quadrant of their key was separated from the others so that pecks at each quadrant could be individually recorded, thus permitting measurement of feature-tracking as the feature shifted from one quadrant to another on successive trials.

We used a more conventional display and arrangement than Jenkins and Sainsbury did. Our basic apparatus was a standard Grason-Stadler 3-key pigeon chamber and *each discrimination-learning trial consisted of illumination of all three keys.* The "feature" was a key illuminated by a color different from the color that appeared on the other two keys on feature-present trials and on all three keys on feature-absent trials. For example, an FP arrangement might involve one red key and two green keys as the S+ display (the red color shifting randomly from one key to another on successive S+ trials) and three green keys as the S− display. The two types of display would be reversed in function for the FN arrangement. As in this example, the feature was a red key for some of our birds; but half the subjects in all our experiments had a green key as the feature. Effects did not differ depending on the color of the feature, and therefore results for both colors are combined in our presentation of the findings.

In our first comparison of FP versus FN learning with these displays, birds received manual shaping, with only one key lit at a time. Initial shaping (first ten pecks, all reinforced with grain) occurred to a key (left, center, or right key, counterbalanced across subjects) illuminated with the color that was later to be the "common" color (i.e., not the "feature" color) for that bird. Then all subjects received additional continuous reinforcement (i.e., all pecks reinforced) for pecking each of the three keys, still lit only one at a time; each of the two possible colors was projected on each key in different 10-reinforcement blocks. By the end of two sessions of continuous reinforcement, all birds had received a total of 120 grain deliveries, 20 reinforcements for pecking at each of the six possible key-color combinations. During the next two sessions, only one key was still lit at a time and birds received discrete-trial operant training. A key was lit after variable ITIs averaging 40 sec, and birds terminated the keylight and received grain for the first peck at that key occurring after 5 sec of its illumination (FI 5-sec). The three keys were lit in a random order, each for a block of 10 consecutive trials and with either red or green light projected on the key during a particular block. After 20 reinforcements for pecking at each of the six possible key-color combinations, preliminary training was concluded.

Discrimination training began on the next day. All three keys were illuminated on each trial. During feature-present trials, the feature color could appear (randomly) on either the left, center, or right key; the common color appeared on the other two keys. During feature-absent trials, the common color appeared on all three keys. On positive trials the first peck *at any key* after 5 sec produced grain. Negative trials lasted 5 sec, and reinforcement was never available on these trials. As during preliminary discrete-trial training, ITIs averaged 40 sec in duration. Subjects received 30 trials per day of both S+ and S−, in a random sequence. The FP group (the feature was present on positive trials) and the FN group (the feature was present on negative trials) each included four subjects. Among a variety of measures tabulated were the number of responses occurring during the first 5 sec of S+, for comparison with the number of responses during S−, and the number of pecks at the feature key and common keys on feature-present trials. After several sessions of exposure to the FP discrimination, the subjects in that group were placed on the FN discrimination procedure, and vice versa.

Figure 7 demonstrates a feature-positive effect very similar to that obtained by Jenkins and Sainsbury (1969) in a rather different situation (compare these curves to those from Jenkins and Sainsbury's work reprinted in Fig. 9 of Hearst and Jenkins' monograph, 1974). The birds initially exposed to the FP discrimination began tracking the feature ("within positive") during the first session (i.e., they rarely pecked the common color) and mastered the successive discrimination within 4–6 sessions. Birds in the FN group soon stopped pecking at the feature ("within negative") but showed little evidence of learning the successive discrimination. On Day 12 the highest successive-discrimination ratio attained by any bird in the FN group was .58. It ought to be reiterated that birds could peck any key to obtain reinforcement on S+ trials and that they had been equally pretrained to peck all keys and all colors. Despite these aspects of the procedure, birds in the FP group very rapidly came to peck only the feature color and birds in the FN group to peck only the common color.

When switched to the FN discrimination, all the former FP subjects

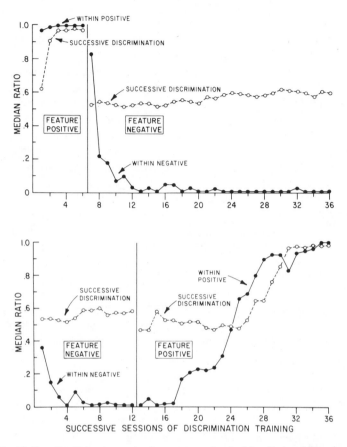

Fig. 7. Median discrimination ratios for groups trained with a distinguishing feature (key color) either on positive trials (Feature Positive) or on negative trials (Feature Negative). The index for the development of the *successive discrimination* (positive versus negative *displays*) is the ratio of responses on the positive display to total responses on both displays; this index approaches 1.0 as responses on the negative display approach zero. The index for the development of a discrimination between common and feature key colors *within* the display containing both key colors is given by the ratio of responses on the feature key to total responses on that display. On positive trials the first peck at any key after 5 sec produced grain. After initial exposure to either the Feature Positive or Feature Negative condition, subjects were switched to the other procedure.

soon stopped tracking the feature. They continued to peck the common color on both S+ and S− trials. Even after 30 sessions of exposure to the FN procedure, only one bird exhibited a successive-discrimination ratio consistently above .60; its ratio never exceeded .76, however. Subjects switched from FN to FP (lower set of curves,

Fig. 7) all performed poorly for 7–10 sessions, but eventually they all began to track the feature ("within positive") and soon afterward mastered the successive discrimination.

Every important aspect of Jenkins and Sainsbury's findings was confirmed in our experiment with 3-key displays. The FP discrimination was acquired by all subjects, whether it occurred in the first or second phase of the experiment, and each subject began to track the feature before mastering the successive discrimination. Learning of the FN discrimination, on the other hand, was poor or nonexistent, even in birds that had formerly mastered the FP discrimination and had presumably learned to "attend to" the feature. Birds directed their behavior at the color most highly correlated with grain in the situation, the feature color in the FP arrangement and the common color in the FN arrangement, even though pecks at any key or color on positive displays would have been reinforced. Apparently the presence of the feature on S− trials in the FN arrangement did not come to serve as a conditional cue that reinforcement was not available for pecking the common color. Summarizing earlier results, Hearst and Jenkins (1974) speculated that "treatment of the signal as a 'target' seems to be a more elementary form of learning than treatment of the signal as a condition for responding elsewhere."

Our next experiment was a close analog to the first one, except that no response-reinforcer contingency was in effect; the procedure was essentially a discriminative auto-shaping arrangement. After brief training to eat from the grain magazine, birds were immediately placed on either a FP or FN discrimination (n = 4 in each). The displays and other procedural details were essentially the same as in the prior experiment, except that all positive displays (CS+) terminated after 6 sec and grain was immediately delivered; all negative displays (CS−) also lasted 6 sec but were not followed by grain. No attempt was made to shape key pecking manually and key pecks had no programmed effect.

Despite the absence of a response-reinforcer contingency, the general results (Fig. 8) were very similar to those in the operant, discrete-trial experiment just described. Birds in the FP group began tracking the feature within the first session and mastered the successive discrimination within 3 or 4 sessions. When later exposed to the FN discrimination, these birds stopped pecking the feature ("within negative") and showed very little evidence of acquiring the successive discrimination. Only one of the four subjects produced a successive-discrimination ratio greater than .62 over the last five days on the FN discrimination; this subject's best daily effort was .79.

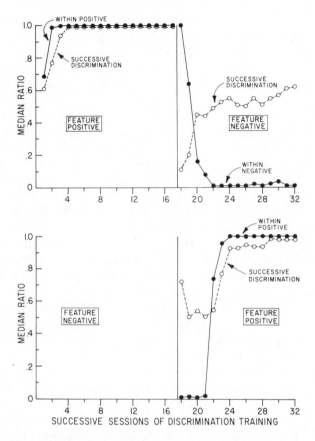

Fig. 8. Median discrimination ratios for groups placed either on Feature Positive or Feature Negative auto-shaping discriminations. All grain deliveries were independent of the subject's behavior. Other than the absence of a response-reinforcer contingency, the procedures and indices were as in Fig. 7.

Three of the four subjects initially placed on the FN discrimination pecked very infrequently and therefore no results are plotted for that group during the FN phase. However, of the 365 total pecks made to the negative display by all four birds throughout the 17 sessions of this phase, only one peck was at the feature; they pecked "common" keys, if anything, during this phase. One subject began to show evidence of learning the successive discrimination after 5 or 6 days on the FN procedure and usually attained a successive-discrimination ratio above .85 on the last 10 days of this phase. When transferred to the FP discrimination, all four birds eventually started tracking the feature and mastered the successive discrimination. The fact that these subjects generally responded so little during the prior (FN) phase is probably related to our previous observations concerning cue redundancy (see Fig. 4); auto-shaping levels are lower when three keys of the same color signal impending grain delivery than when only one does.

Therefore, even in a situation in which no response-reinforcer contingency is programmed, subjects on FP discriminations peck at the feature and master the discrimination between CS+ and CS– displays. Subjects on FN discriminations, on the other hand, rarely peck the feature or master the discrimination. The degree of positive correlation between features of the environment and delivery of the reinforcer directs behavior in the auto-shaping and feature-discrimination situations (cf. Wasserman, 1974).

One other illustration of the FP effect in a discriminative auto-shaping situation may help to demonstrate the generality of the phenomenon. In work done in collaboration with Dexter Gormley, we used a different type of feature from those studied in prior experiments. The research was conducted in the pigeon chamber equipped with a 25-key (5 × 5) matrix; the distance between the centers of adjacent keys was 3.1 cm. Four keys were lit on every trial; but on some trials all four were located in a single vertical column (for example, the second column from the left), and on other trials three lit keys were from that same column and the fourth lit key was located three columns away (the last column on the right). Different columns for the "compact" common keys and the "isolated" feature key were employed for different subjects. On feature-present trials, the positions of the three illuminated common keys and the position of the illuminated feature key in its column varied from trial to trial. Thus the subject could not learn the discrimination merely by attending to a particular key. The bird had to notice that one key was lit which was isolated from the main group of lit keys.

Four FP and four FN subjects were run. After being trained to eat grain from the magazine, the birds received 24 daily trials of both CS+ and CS–. Each trial was 8 sec long, and the ITI was variable, averaging 40 sec. All positive trials were followed by grain regardless of the bird's behavior and no grain followed negative trials.

Figure 9 displays the results of this experiment. Only half the birds in each group started pecking during the first two sessions, and therefore no data are plotted for these initial sessions. Three of the

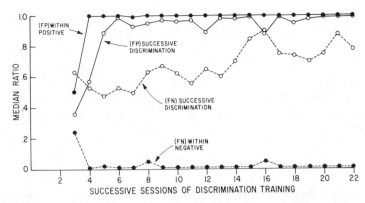

Fig. 9.   Median discrimination ratios for groups placed on either Feature Positive (FP) or Feature Negative (FN) discriminations, during an experiment in which the "feature" was an illuminated key some distance away from the main group of lit (common) keys. All positive trials were followed by grain regardless of the bird's behavior. General experimental procedures and methods for calculating the discrimination ratios were as in Figs. 7 and 8.

four birds in the FP group soon began to track (peck) the feature and mastered the successive discrimination within 4–5 sessions. The performance of the other bird was extremely variable; this subject did not peck at all during several sessions (Days 11–15), and although its successive-discrimination ratio eventually attained a consistently high level, the bird never pecked at the feature. Visual observation of this subject revealed that it first looked at the feature key on positive trials and then pecked a key in the "common" column (the only subject of all those we have tested that mastered an FP discrimination without pecking directly at the feature).

On the other hand, all birds in the FN group soon stopped pecking at the feature and subsequently showed very slow acquisition of the successive discrimination. They all attained a ratio of at least .66 on each of the last two days of training (Sessions 21–22; the range of ratios was .66 to .95). Although FN learning was still greatly inferior to FP learning, the higher levels of FN discriminative performance attained in this experiment than in all other ones conducted in our laboratory may be mainly due to the fact that the elements of the stimulus display were located closer together in this matrix arrangement than in the 3-key arrangement described above (cf. Sainsbury, 1971a, on differences in FN acquisition and asymptotic performance for *compact* versus *distributed* displays).

IV. Conjunctions, Contingencies, and Cognitions: Stimulus–Stimulus versus Response–Stimulus Relations

Evidence summarized here and in Hearst and Jenkins (1974) demonstrates that the initial acquisition of CS-directed behavior depends on the type and degree of contingency between CS and reinforcer. However, complications arise in auto-shaping and FP-discrimination situations as soon as the directed movements begin to take place with regularity; these behaviors now appear in close conjunction with the reinforcer. The eventual strength and persistence of sign-tracking may depend as much on close temporal conjunctions between the acquired *response* and the reinforcer as on the experimentally-programmed positive contingency between *signal* and reinforcer. To understand the phenomena of sign-tracking, we must try to separate the effects of stimulus–reinforcer and response–reinforcer correlations.

Two general methods have been developed to accomplish this goal. One involves arrangements in which a response–reinforcer relation is pitted against a stimulus–reinforcer relation. The omission procedure, mentioned briefly in connection with some of the research described above, exemplifies this method: the scheduled reinforcer is allowed to occur *only if* the subject does not exhibit some specified movement (e.g., approach or contact) during CS. Thus, while maintaining a positive stimulus–reinforcer correlation (all reinforcers occur immediately after the stimulus), the experimenter ensures that a reinforcer can never occur in conjunction with the specified movement (negative response–reinforcer correlation). If the response remains strong even when its occurrence can serve only to prevent delivery of the reinforcer, then a primary role for the stimulus–reinforcer correlation would be demonstrated.

The second general method for assessment of the relative contributions of stimulus–reinforcer and response–reinforcer correlations entails arrangements in which subjects are prevented from approaching or contacting CS or US while pairings of the two stimuli proceed. Prevention of such directed actions may be accomplished by, for example, inserting a barrier between the subject and the CS or US locations, or by harnessing the subject in a place from which CS or US presentations are visible but inaccessible (another possibility, which to my knowledge has not yet been attempted in a sign-tracking paradigm, would be to curarize the subject during CS-US presentations). If actual occurrences of approach, contact, and consummatory *behaviors* are not crucial either for the learning of the stimulus–reinforcer relation or for the development of tendencies to approach and contact CS, then prior "observation" of a positive contingency between CS and US should produce the immediate or very rapid appearance of approach and contact responses when CS is finally made accessible to the subjects.

A. OMISSION PROCEDURES

1. Auto-Shaped Key Pecking in Pigeons

Williams and Williams (1969) were the first to use the omission procedure in the study of auto-shaping. Employing Brown and Jenkins' basic method with pigeons, they added the contingency that any peck at the illuminated key would prevent scheduled grain. Nevertheless, pigeons continued to peck the key on many trials; they lost a large number of the reinforcers that they would have received if they had not responded. I have already mentioned some other instances of the same type of effect (see, e.g., Fig. 4).

Although the effects of the omission procedure indicate that the positive contingency between stimulus and reinforcer is much more important than conjunctions of responses and reinforcers in producing and maintaining auto-shaped key pecks, several lines of evidence indicate that response-reinforcer conjunctions do have some influence, too. Birds peck the key less frequently under the omission procedure than during regular auto-shaping (see Fig. 4). This decrement in behavior could result from (a) the fewer pairings of CS and US that occur because of the subject's failure to stop key pecking on the omission procedure or (b) the negative response-reinforcer contingency on the omission procedure. To assess the latter possibility, Schwartz and Williams (1972) employed a self-yoking procedure. Their results indicated that response-reinforcer conjunctions were influential in auto-shaping, although not of "overriding importance."

The long-box experiments of Jenkins (see Hearst & Jenkins, 1974) support Schwartz and Williams' conclusions about the relative importance of stimulus–reinforcer and response–reinforcer correlations in auto-shaping. In Jenkins' research, approach toward and pecking of a food-predictive keylight that was located 3 ft away from the grain magazine developed and persisted even though this behavior always caused complete or partial loss of food. Grain presentations lasted only 4 sec and the food tray had frequently dropped out of reach by the time the bird managed to return to it. This experimental arrangement provides a spatial parallel to Williams and Williams' (1969) procedure, since the extent of movement toward the remote CS was negatively correlated with the amount of grain obtained.

2. Components of Conditioned Movement Patterns

Sign-tracking involves a variety of movements (e.g., orientation, approach, and contact) governed by the spatial location of CS. Are separate components of this sequential pattern differentially sensitive to the omission contingency? Wessells (1974) suggested that auto-shaped key pecking may develop and persist mainly because prepecking behaviors (e.g., orientation and approach) occur in conjunction with the reinforcer. In other words, pecking is not independent of prior orientation and approach; and if orientation and approach are correlated with the reinforcer, they may bring about pecking because of the usual patterns of consummatory behavior possessed by the pigeon. Wessells was able completely to eliminate *approach* responses toward CS when such behavior was arranged to terminate CS and prevent delivery of grain. On the basis of this result, Wessells argued that response—reinforcer relations, especially those involving prepecking behavior, are more important in auto-shaping and the omission-for-pecking effect than Williams and Williams had suggested.

Wessells used only two subjects and approach responses were judged by the experimenter, rather than recorded in some automatic fashion. Michael Browne and Blaine Peden have collaborated with me on research similar to Wessells' but involving a substantial number of birds and a more objective measure of approach behavior. In our arrangement, the response key was located on the left wall of an experimental chamber, 35 cm from the grain magazine and house-light source. Whenever the pigeon entered an area within 25 cm from the key, an "approach response" was automatically recorded by means of switches beneath a hinged floor.

After brief magazine training, pigeons were scheduled to receive 50 daily trials, consisting of 8-sec illuminations of the key followed by 5-sec access to grain. Successive trials were separated by ITIs averaging 45 sec. There were two experimental procedures. On the auto-shaping procedure, key illuminations were always followed by access to grain, regardless of the behavior of the pigeon. On the omission-for-approach procedure, the keylight was immediately terminated and grain delivery canceled if the pigeon made an approach response during CS. Some birds (n = 6) were placed on the omission-for-approach procedure at the outset of the experiment and remained on it for 40 sessions. Other birds (n = 5) were first placed on the auto-shaping procedure for 25 sessions and then on the omission-for-approach procedure for 40 sessions. After completion of omission-for-approach training, the auto-shaping procedure was reinstated for 25 sessions (except for two birds in the second group). Thus, we were interested not only in examining general performance under the omission-for-approach contingency, but also in assessing possible effects of (*a*) prior auto-shaping on the sensitivity of behavior to the omission-for-approach procedure, and (*b*) prior exposure to omission-for-approach on behavior displayed during regular auto-shaping.

The mean percent of trials on which birds approached the illuminated key appears in Figs. 10 and 11 for the two groups. Each data point represents an average over a block of five successive sessions; the group means are connected by a solid line. After 20 sessions on the omission-for-approach procedure (Sessions 16–20 in Fig. 10 and Sessions 41–45 in Fig. 11), the mean percent of grain presentations lost per session because of persisting approach responses was 48% (range: 5–83%) in Fig. 10 and 49% (range: 23–82%) in Fig. 11. Even

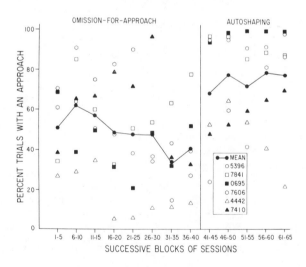

Fig. 10. Percent of trials with a key-approach response over successive blocks of sessions in a group of six pigeons that were first exposed to an omission procedure for 40 sessions. During those sessions an approach response toward CS canceled the grain scheduled to occur at the end of that trial. During the last 25 sessions (auto-shaping) all CSs were followed by grain regardless of the bird's behavior. Individual and group mean data are both included in the figure.

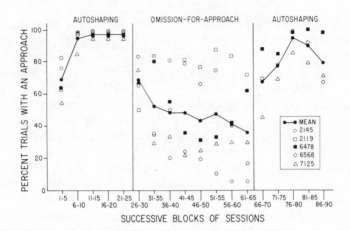

Fig. 11. Percent of trials with a key-approach response over successive blocks of sessions in a group of five pigeons that were first exposed to the auto-shaping procedure for 25 sessions and then to the omission-for-approach procedure for 40 sessions. In the last phase of the experiment three of the birds were re-placed on the auto-shaping procedure for 25 sessions. Individual and group mean data are both included in the figure.

during the final five sessions on the omission-for-approach procedure (Sessions 36–40 in Fig. 10 and Sessions 61–65 in Fig. 11), the mean percent of reinforcers lost per session was 41% (range: 14–78%) in Fig. 10 and 38% (range: 6–72%) in Fig. 11. Approach responses were never completely eliminated in any subject even though the consequence of such behavior was cancellation of a scheduled grain presentation. Since both groups lost an average of 49% of the total of 2000 reinforcers possible while on the omission-for-approach contingency, there was no apparent effect of prior auto-shaping upon subsequent behavior under the omission contingency.

When the omission-for-approach contingency was removed, that is, when auto-shaping was reinstated, the average number of trials with an approach increased for all subjects. The two groups did not differ significantly in their final levels of approach behavior under auto-shaping, which were, however, generally lower than the levels achieved by birds placed on auto-shaping at the very outset of the experiment (Fig. 11).

The omission-for-approach effect closely parallels the omission-for-pecking effect reported by Williams and Williams. Our findings do not support Wessells' conclusion that conjunctions between prepecking behaviors and reinforcers are of major importance in sign-tracking. However, Wessells' definition of an "approach response" was different from ours, and the key and grain hopper were much closer together in his experiment. Current research by Blaine Peden and me indicates that these factors may account for some of the differences in experimental results between Wessells' and our studies.

Certain components of organized anticipatory or consummatory behavior may be more susceptible than others to negative consequences like that imposed by the omission procedure. How sensitive would subtler components of sign-tracking behavior be to the imposition of an omission procedure—for example, orienting responses toward the response key (cf. Patten & Rudy, 1967)? Ethologists have observed that orientation toward a prey generally habituates much less quickly than approach and attack; perhaps orienting behavior toward CS would, therefore, be even less sensitive to its negative consequences than would approach and contact, at least in certain species and situations.

Colleagues and students of David Williams at the University of Pennsylvania have been examining effects of the omission procedure on various components of classically-conditioned movement patterns. Several of their studies employ auto-shaping situations, but, to illustrate their work, I shall give an example that involves somewhat different movements. Murray (1973) found that four separate components of the display pattern of fighting fish became conditioned to a visual CS which preceded presentation of a mirror (US) in which the fish could see itself. These components were fin erection, frontal approach, gill extension, and undulating movements (presentation of the mirror elicited this whole pattern prior to pairings of CS and US). However, different components proved differentially sensitive when, in separate groups of subjects, occurrence of a particular component prevented presentation of US. The negative contingency virtually eliminated frontal approach, but fin erection and gill extension continued to occur on a substantial number of trials even when these responses cancelled US.

This type of research seems extremely important to pursue, since it is unlikely that all parts of an organized pattern of movements will display persistence of the degree shown in Figs. 4, 10, and 11 for approach and pecking behavior in pigeons on omission procedures. Such research is related to the question of the "inhibitability" of various responses in different situations and species and to the whole topic of "involuntary behavior." Skinner (1953) wrote that evidence for the view that reflexes were involuntary "was not so much that they could not be willed as that they could not be willed against [p. 111]." Actually, "inhibitability" may prove easier to define operationally and study experimentally than the property of "elicitation" that Skinner described as characteristic of Pavlovian CSs and USs. Degree of inhibitability (measured, e.g., by use of omission procedures) could turn out to be a dimension of value in establishing categories of learning or behavior (see Hearst, 1975).

3. Feature-Positive Discriminations

The term sign-tracking is meant to encompass aspects of discrimination learning based on distinctive features, as well as the phenomena of auto-shaping. In both cases, subjects exhibit a strong tendency to direct their behavior toward that feature of the environment which has the highest positive correlation with the delivery of an appetitive reinforcer. If our belief is correct that the feature-positive effect and auto-shaping both reflect the operation of very similar basic behavioral mechanisms, then the omission procedure ought to produce effects on the learning and maintenance of FP discriminations that are analogous to those just described for auto-shaping situations. That is, subjects should persist in contacting the distinctive feature on positive trials even though such behavior cancels the delivery of a scheduled reinforcer.

Jenkins (1973) has already demonstrated an effect of this kind in the learning of FP discriminations that included an explicit response-reinforcer contingency. A peck at the quadrant of the key on which the feature (e.g., a red dot) was projected canceled the possibility of reinforcement on that S+ trial. However, pecks at the common-color dot (e.g., green) or an empty quadrant did produce grain. Birds in this FP-omission group continued to peck the feature on more than 50% of the S+ trials, which cost them more than half their potential reinforcers. Jenkins' study demonstrated that the role of the distinctive feature as a signal of reinforcement or nonreinforcement was the main factor governing the tendency of subjects to peck at it. Grain delivery could not have been strengthening a link between the feature and a response to it, because such a conjunction of events was never followed by grain. Birds must have learned the relationship between feature and reinforcer while they were pecking at other aspects of the display, and perception of this relationship was presumably responsible for behavior directed at the feature.

In my laboratory we have examined the effects of an omission contingency upon FP learning in the 3-key, discriminative auto-shaping situation described earlier in the discussion of Fig. 8. The data in that figure revealed clear differences between FP and FN discrimination learning, in a situation in which reinforcers did not depend on any behavior of the subject. In the FP case birds soon began to peck at the distinctive feature (a particular color projected on one of the three keys) and acquired the FP discrimination within a few sessions; they pecked at the food-predictive color if it was present on the display (CS+), and otherwise they did not peck (CS−).

In later research we employed an FP procedure like that used in obtaining the data of Fig. 8, but we added the provision that any peck at the feature key would cancel the grain scheduled to occur at the end of CS+ trials. Pecks at the common keys had no effect. Nine birds served in this experiment, five trained with a red keylight as the feature and four with a green keylight. There were 25 positive trials and 25 negative trials daily.

Figure 12 presents the group results from this experiment. Most birds made only a few responses during the first session, and therefore behavioral measures were unreliable and are not supplied for that session. During later sessions Fig. 12 shows, as did Fig. 8, that birds confined their responding almost exclusively to the feature key and hardly ever pecked on negative trials. Out of a maximum of 25 possible grain deliveries, the median number of daily reinforcers declined from 24.5 on Day 1 to approximately 6 or 7 on Days 5−14.

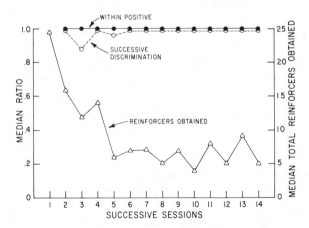

Fig. 12. Median discrimination ratios and number of reinforcers obtained over successive sessions for a group of pigeons exposed to a Feature Positive discrimination in which grain deliveries occurred at the end of each positive trial if the bird did not peck the feature key. A single peck at the feature key canceled the grain scheduled on that trial.

Only two of the nine subjects obtained more than 50% of the maximum possible number of reinforcers over the last 10 days of the experiment. Six of the nine subjects lost more than 73% of the maximum possible number of reinforcers over the same 10 days.

In *both* the FP-omission arrangement and the FN discriminations (see the description of relevant procedures and findings accompanying Fig. 8), pecks directed at the feature key are never followed by grain, whereas pecks at the other key color are followed by grain 50% of the time. Therefore, the fact that the feature signaled grain in the FP-omission arrangement and signaled no-grain in the FN arrangement provides the only plausible basis for our finding that the feature is pecked (tracked) in the former case and hardly ever pecked in the latter case. The results of Jenkins' operant study and my auto-shaping experiment demonstrate that the role of the distinctive feature as a *signal* of reinforcement or nonreinforcement is the crucial factor influencing the tendency of subjects to peck at it; *pecking* directed at the feature never occurs in conjunction with grain. Hearst and Jenkins (1974) concluded that in the FP case "pecking the feature results mainly from the perception of the feature's relation to reinforcement [p. 23]," even while a peck at a common element or some other behavior may be followed by a reinforcer. "Perception of this [stimulus-reinforcer] relationship precedes and steers behavior toward the distinctive feature [p. 24]."

4. Additional Comments on the Omission Procedure

Pigeons frequently approach and contact the signal of an impending appetitive reinforcer even when approach toward or contact of that signal prevents delivery of the reinforcer. Chicks do the same (Wasserman, 1973b). However, there remains a real question as to how general this omission effect is across species, reinforcers, responses, and experimental situations in which signtracking has been demonstrated. The persistence of behavior in the face of such negative consequences, besides providing a dramatic illustration of the strength of sign-tracking, has important implications concerning the relative strengths of stimulus–reinforcer and response–reinforcer correlations in these situations. If, on the other hand, the omission procedure were to eliminate sign-tracking behavior, a more important role for response-reinforcer conjunctions would be indicated. Some experimenters (e.g., Gamzu & Schwam, 1974) have successfully eliminated auto-shaped behavior in other organisms and situations by means of the omission procedure, and it seems certain that many additional cases of response elimination after application of the omission procedure will be reported in future research. Learning situations apparently involve an interaction between stimulus–stimulus and response–stimulus correlations or conjunctions, and the omission procedure serves as an extremely valuable assay for determining the relative importance of each. It seems time to surrender the notion that behavioral tasks can be simply classified into "respondent" or "operant" depending on the contingency the experimenter imposes on the subject. Both types of relationship are implicitly or explicitly operating in virtually all laboratory arrangements for studying learning (cf. Hearst, 1975).

The food-predictive signal in the auto-shaping and feature-positive arrangements seems to have a status very similar to that of the token or object in the situations so vividly described by Breland and Breland (1961, 1966) in discussions of the "misbehavior of organisms." In their animals, consummatory-like behaviors developed and persisted towards objects that had to be manipulated to obtain reinforcement, even though these behaviors delayed or prevented the delivery of reinforcers. For example, racoons taught to insert coins in a box for food reward began to "wash" the coins in the way they wash food. These prolonged forms of behavior delayed receipt of food; nevertheless, they became more frequent as training progressed. In many respects, these effects resemble those occurring on auto-shaping and omission procedures (see also Grastyán & Vereczkei, 1974).

B. STIMULUS-SEQUENCE LEARNING AND OVERT MOVEMENTS

A second technique for separating stimulus–reinforcer and response–reinforcer correlations in the development and maintenance of sign-tracking involves prevention of directed movements while subjects "observe" stimulus–reinforcer sequences. Can learning of such a sequence occur in the absence of overt approach and contact movements and of actual consummatory behavior during US presentation? Such problems are related to a persistent issue in learning theory, the question of what is learned. Expectancy or cognitive theories conceive learning as mainly a matter of gaining knowledge about relationships among stimuli. On the other hand, reinforcement or S–R contiguity theories conceive learning as primarily a matter of developing links between actions (responses) and stimuli. Many battles, some very heated but almost all inconclusive, were fought in the 1930s and 1940s over related topics. However, under the powerful influence of B. F. Skinner in the 1950s and 1960s, a general aversion to evaluation of theoretical issues of this kind developed and the issues were often ridiculed as "pseudo-problems." Nevertheless, in the past decade they have reappeared in various shapes and forms. Cognitive learning theories are respectable again as applied to both human and animal learning (cf. Anderson & Bower, 1973; Bolles, 1972; Estes, 1969; McGuigan & Lumsden, 1973).

The foregoing general issues are not pseudo-problems, in my opinion, but worthwhile topics for research and theory. They will not be resolved by unsubstantiated or extreme assertions from either camp, such as "knowledge is action rather than sensing." Evidence presented in this chapter indicates that sign-tracking is primarily dependent on stimulus-reinforcer correlations and represents the subject's learning of a contingent relation between two environmental events. Such an interpretation will be rejected by contemporary workers who view learning as necessarily involving the acquisition of overt (or at least potentially measurable) behaviors; animals are said to have learned to *salivate* to a buzzer and the US is believed to "reinforce" a particular *response.* Consequently, only a movement or glandular activity can be learned; a stimulus sequence cannot. However, in many cases it seems obvious that learning of some kind must have taken place before the appearance of the first measurable CR. As the passage from Woodworth heading this chapter suggests,[4] the trials before the first CR are very important for the learner; reinforcement theories are likely to ignore them or hypothesize the conditioning of incipient, covert movements (which are just about as intangible as "cognitions" or "expectancies"). A great deal of human learning apparently occurs without overt behavioral changes and without the presentation of reinforcing stimuli, and it seems likely that infrahuman organisms possess similar capabilities to some degree.

These issues are very complex and frequently difficult to express in concrete terms. Studies of sign-tracking, and the evidence that it is preceded by and maintained by the subject's registration (perception) of a stimulus sequence, can in themselves hardly resolve the general problems. However, the research to be described shortly

---

[4] Incidentally, Woodworth's (1958) last major work deserves a resurrection, in my opinion; the general principles expressed there provide a valuable framework for analyzing much of the material described in the present chapter. Woodworth's lack of dogmatism is particularly appealing.

concerning the role of overt movements in sign-tracking seems relevant to these fundamental issues in learning theory (see Hearst & Jenkins, 1974, for a detailed assessment of the relation of sign-tracking to various specific theoretical systems, e.g., those of Skinner, Thorndike, Tolman, Pavlov, and the ethologists).

An observation by Liddell, cited by Lorenz in a discussion of the innate bases of learning, is pertinent to the questions of (a) what is learned during Pavlovian conditioning and (b) whether overt movements must be followed by reinforcement in order for their likelihood to increase:

> My late friend Howard Liddell told me about an unpublished experiment he did while working as a guest in Pavlov's laboratory. It consisted simply in freeing from its harness a dog that had been conditioned to salivate at the acceleration in the beat of a metronome. The dog at once ran to the machine, wagged its tail at it, tried to jump up to it, barked, and so on [Lorenz, 1969, p. 47].

This description suggests that the progressive development of approach responses toward the signal and actual instrumental "reinforcement" of such behavior are not necessary for the later appearance of sign-tracking. The passage also indicates that a subject is learning much more than mere salivary CRs while it stands restrained in the Pavlovian harness; this other learning will be manifested when the subject is given the opportunity to display its "knowledge." Experiments on *latent learning*, most of which were performed more than 25 years ago, are based on notions of this kind, reflecting the distinction Tolman made between learning and performance.

Michael Browne's (1974) dissertation research represented an attempt to evaluate the role of overt movements and primary reinforcement in the development of sign-tracking behavior. Browne's general plan allowed pigeons to "observe" presentations of CS (keylight) and US (activation of the grain magazine), at times when access to both CS and US (in some experiments) or only to US (in other experiments) was blocked by placement of a plexiglas cover in front of the stimulus panel. After this observation period, CS and US were both made available to the subject and the development of sign-tracking was examined as a function of the type of contingency between CS and "US" which the subject had observed in the prior phase.

An early study, conducted by Browne in collaboration with John Karpicke, revealed that pigeons which had observed a positive contingency between inaccessible CSs and USs pecked CS more frequently during a subsequent auto-shaping session than pigeons which had observed zero or negative correlations between inaccessible CSs and USs (for more details of this experiment, see Hearst & Jenkins, 1974). Therefore, even though pigeons could neither peck the key nor eat during observation sessions, their subsequent behavior revealed learning of the relationship between two salient stimulus events that occurred during the observation period. Visual monitoring of the subjects during the observation phase did not indicate any consistent movements toward CS or US locations after the first few trials with the plexiglas cover in place. Thus, as judged by overt movements of the subjects, there was no consistent evidence of "learning" during the observation periods prior to auto-shaping.

In the main experiment of his dissertation, Browne first trained subjects to eat from the lighted magazine and then placed the plexiglas cover in front of the magazine only. When the food tray was raised, grain was visible to the subject but not accessible. The key always remained accessible, however, and pecks at it were recorded. For three sessions four different groups of birds, each comprising eight subjects, received about 60 daily presentations of CS and "US," programmed on the basis of either a positive, a negative (two differently treated groups; see the legend for Fig. 13), or zero correlation between illuminations of the key and presentations of visible but inaccessible grain. A fifth group ("US"-only), also with eight subjects, received only the grain presentations. Then the cover over the magazine opening was removed, three "free" grain deliveries were given, and standard auto-shaping was immediately instituted for five sessions.

Birds that had observed a positive contingency between CS and "US" pecked sooner and more frequently during the auto-shaping test sessions than did subjects in all the other groups. The median trail of the first key peck was 9.5, 27.5, 61.5, 56.0, and 83.5 for the positive, "US"-only, zero, negative-26, and negative-86 groups respectively; two-tailed Mann-Whitney U tests indicated that subjects in the positive group made their first peck significantly earlier than subjects in any of the other four groups (all p's $< .03$). Three of the positive-correlation birds actually pecked the key on the very first trial, that is, before the keylight had ever been followed by food which was consumed, whereas the earliest any subject in the other four groups pecked was on the tenth trial. Pecks at the key had occurred very infrequently (on less than 1% of the trials) during the "observation" phase that preceded auto-shaping, and the five groups did not differ significantly with respect to that measure. Figure 13

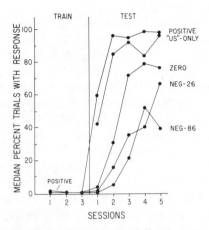

Fig. 13. Acquisition of auto-shaped key pecking over five sessions ("Test") for five experimental groups. During the preceding phase ("Train") the different groups had observed different correlations between an accessible keylight and visible but inaccessible grain: *Positive* correlation (every keylight followed by "US"), *Zero* correlation (keylights and "USs" presented according to independent 60-sec VI schedules), *Negative-26* ("USs" never occurred within a 26-sec period following onset of the 6-sec keylight), *Negative-86* ("USs" never occurred within an 86-sec period following onset of the 6-sec keylight), and "US"-only (no keylights, but "USs" presented on a 60-sec VI schedule). (From Browne, 1974.)

presents key peck data for all five groups during the observation ("TRAIN") and auto-shaping ("TEST") phases.

Browne's experiment showed that the contingency between key illuminations and visible but inaccessible grain influenced the subsequent acquisition of auto-shaped key pecking. However, it was conceivable that directed movements other than key pecking could have been acquired during the observation phase, and that learning of these movements mediated the results obtained when the key peck was subsequently auto-shaped. For example, the positive-correlation birds may have learned to approach the lighted key and the negative-correlation birds to withdraw from it.

Periodic surveillance of the subjects by the experimenter had not revealed any consistent movements toward or away from the key during the observation phase; when monitored, almost all the subjects were crouching motionless in front of the magazine. Nevertheless, because the subjects were monitored only intermittently during the observation phase, it was possible that some approach or withdrawal movements toward the key had occurred. Therefore, Browne conducted another experiment in which approach and withdrawal from the key were actually measured throughout the observation phase.

In this experiment, a 75-cm long box was used and switches beneath the floor permitted partitioning of the subject's location into three categories: near the key (approach), near the magazine, and far from the key (withdrawal). The magazine and houselight were situated in the center of the front wall, and the key was mounted on the left wall about 35 cm from the magazine.

After magazine training, two groups of six birds were exposed for three sessions to either a positive or a negative correlation between illuminations of the accessible key and presentations of visible but inaccessible grain. During this observation phase, birds in the positive group almost never stood in the part of the chamber nearest the response key and subjects in the negative group showed no tendency to withdraw from the key. Nevertheless, after the cover over the magazine was removed and all birds received keylight→food pairings (auto-shaping), the "positive" subjects approached the key significantly more often than the "negative" subjects.

Browne's experiments demonstrated that a positive relationship between two salient stimuli—key illuminations and visible grain, presented to a bird that is not permitted to reach the source of either or both of the stimuli—still results in a tendency for the subject to approach and contact the key when the barrier is removed. Subjects are apparently acquiring or registering a stimulus sequence during the observation phase rather than learning specific overt movements. This somewhat "cognitive" view seems consistent with the bulk of evidence presented in this chapter indicating that stimulus–reinforcer, rather than response–reinforcer, correlations are mainly responsible for the acquisition and maintenance of sign-tracking behavior. Such an interpretation may be helpful when applied to the analysis of imitative behavior and "vicarious reinforcement." There, too, subjects seem to learn while observing correlations between external stimulus events.

V. Concluding Comments

Contrary to prevailing opinion, it is clear that complex directed actions of the whole organism are conditionable by means of Pavlovian procedures. Subjects orient toward, approach, and often contact signals indicating that an appetitive US is imminent or highly probable, and frequently exhibit consummatory-like behavior while contacting the signal (pecking a disc whose illumination signals grain; biting and gnawing a lever whose appearance signals food). These approach and contact movements often persist indefinitely even though they are not required for delivery of the US—and even when they are actually programmed to prevent US (a violation of the Law of Effect). The degree of positive contingency between *CS* and US, rather than accidental conjunctions of the directed *responses* and US, seems to be the major factor controlling the acquisition and maintenance of such sign-tracking behavior. Moreover, there is a negative counterpart to this directed approach behavior, since subjects will generally withdraw from a signal that indicates an appetitive US is *not* coming.

Animals apparently can learn something about correlations among stimulus events, the "causal texture of the environment," even while no primary reinforcement is being delivered and even while they display no obvious changes in overt behavior; contingent CS-US pairings presented to a subject that is physically blocked from reaching the location of CS or US result in a tendency for the subject to approach and contact CS when the barrier is removed. Perception or registration of stimulus-reinforcer contingencies seem to *precede* and steer behavior toward the most reliable predictor of US in a given situation. When several cues are available that equally predict the reinforcer, the probability of sign-tracking declines compared to the case in which a single predictive feature is present.

Hearst and Jenkins (1974) pointed out that sign-tracking may operate in a variety of standard arrangements for investigating appetitive and aversive conditioning and may help to explain certain phenomena observed in studies of operant behavior, for example, behavioral contrast, positive conditioned suppression, and "observing responses." The development of sign-tracking behavior may account for some experimental effects of variations in the spatial proximity of cue, response, and reinforcer, and for difficulties often encountered in teaching conditional discriminations to young children and infrahuman organisms. However, further pursuit of these and other applications and extensions is beyond the scope of this chapter.

The situational and species generality of sign-tracking and the relative contributions of stimulus–reinforcer versus response–reinforcer correlations in a variety of experimental arrangements need evaluation in the future. Is sign-tracking a form of behavior that appears only in some infrahuman organisms, or do young children and adult humans also tend to direct their behavior toward (orient, point, reach, touch) features of the environment that provide information about impending favorable events and to direct their behavior away from features signaling unfavorable events? If so, can human beings at various developmental levels easily learn to inhibit these directed movements, when such behavior results in cancellation or delay of the favorable event?

The results of research described in this chapter and in Hearst and Jenkins (1974) imply that the operant–respondent distinction is not very helpful and may be quite misleading, because all behavioral tasks involve potential interplay between stimulus→stimulus and response→stimulus relations, even if the experimenter does not explicitly arrange them. Directed movements of the whole organism are often classified as examples of "operant behavior," but the fact that they arise during Pavlovian conditioning and are strongly controlled by stimulus–reinforcer relations makes such a classification dubious. Many responses presumed to be relatively arbitrary "representative" operants (e.g., key pecking, lever contact and depression) are apparently not so arbitrary after all; their strength, conditionability, and topography depend on the type of situation, manipulandum, species of subject, and reinforcer employed.

Although a revival of research based on the old S-S versus S-R controversy certainly seems unwarranted, in view of its relatively unproductive history and the oversimplified alternatives it offered, many aspects and residues of that controversy (e.g., the possibility of sensory-sensory learning, the necessity for reinforcement and overt behavioral change in learning, the learning–performance distinction) seem to merit earnest reconsideration today. If Skinnerians could be convinced to take more seriously a variety of problems posed by such writers as Tolman and Woodworth, and contemporary cognitive psychologists to take more seriously the contributions of workers in animal learning and conditioning, there would be benefit to all.

REFERENCES

Anderson, J. R., & Bower, G. B. *Human associative memory*. New York: Winston, 1973.
Bolles, R. C. Reinforcement, expectancy, and learning. *Psychological Review*, 1972, 79, 394–409.
Breland, K., & Breland, M. The misbehavior of organisms. *American Psychologist*, 1961, 16, 681–684.
Breland, K., & Breland, M. *Animal behavior*. New York: Macmillan, 1966.
Brown, P. L., & Jenkins, H. M. Auto-shaping of the pigeon's key peck. *Journal of the Experimental Analysis of Behavior*, 1968, 11, 1–8.

Browne, M. P. Autoshaping and the role of primary reinforcement and overt movements in the acquisition of stimulus-stimulus relations. Unpublished doctoral dissertation, Indiana University, 1974.

Estes, W. K. New perspectives on some old issues in association theory. In N. J. Mackintosh & W. K. Honig (Eds.), *Fudnamental issues in associative learning*. Halifax, Can.: Dalhousie University Press, 1969. Pp. 162–189.

Franklin, S. Negative correlations between a signal and food: Variations in rate of food presentation in the signal's absence. Unpublished master's thesis, Indiana University, 1973.

Gamzu, E., & Schwam, E. Autoshaping and automaintenance of a key-press response in squirrel monkeys. *Journal of the Experimental Analysis of Behavior*, 1974, **21**, 361–371.

Grant, D. L. Anticipatory behavior (auto-shaping) in rats to the presentation of another rat predicting food. Unpublished B.A. honors thesis, Indiana University, 1974.

Grastyán, E., & Vereczkei, L. Effects of spatial separation of the conditioned signal from the reinforcement: A demonstration of the conditioned character of the orienting response or the orientational character of conditioning. *Behavioral Biology*, 1974, **10**, 121–146.

Hearst, E., & Jenkins, H. M. *Sign-tracking: The stimulus-reinforcer relation and directed action*. Austin, Tex.: Psychonomic Society, 1974.

Hearst, E. The classical-instrumental distinction: reflexes, voluntary behavior, and categories of associative learning. In W. K. Estes (Ed.), *Handbook of learning and cognitive processes*. Hillsdale, N.J.: Lawrence Erlbaum Associates, 1975.

Jenkins, H. M. Noticing and responding in a discrimination based on a distinguishing element. *Learning and Motivation*, 1973, **4**, 115–137.

Jenkins, H. M., & Moore, B. R. The form of the auto-shaped response with food or water reinforcers. *Journal of the Experimental Analysis of Behavior*, 1973, **20**, 163–181.

Jenkins, H. M., & Sainsbury, R. S. The development of stimulus control through differential reinforcement. In N. J. Mackintosh & W. K. Honig (Eds.), *Fundamental issues in associative learning*. Halifax, Can.: Dalhousie University Press, 1969. Pp. 123–161.

Jenkins, H. M., & Sainsbury, R. S. Discrimination learning with the distinctive feature on positive or negative trials. In D. Mostofsky (Ed.), *Attention: Contemporary theory and analysis*. New York: Appleton, 1970. Pp. 239–273.

Kimble, G. *Hilgard and Marquis' conditioning and learning*. (2nd ed.) New York: Appleton, 1961.

Lorenz, K. Z. Innate bases of learning. In K. Pribram (Ed.), *On the biology of learning*. New York: Harcourt, 1969. Pp. 13–93.

McGuigan, F. J., & Lumsden, D. B. *Contemporary approaches to conditioning and learning*. New York: Winston, 1973.

Mackintosh, N. J. *The psychology of animal learning*. New York: Academic Press, 1974.

Murray, C. S. Conditioning Betta splendens. Unpublished doctoral dissertation, University of Pennsylvania, 1973.

Neuringer, A., & Neuringer, M. Learning by following a food source. *Science*, 1974, **184**, 1005–1008.

Patten, R. L., & Rudy, J. W. Orienting during classical conditioning: Acquired vs. unconditioned responding. *Psychonomic Science*, 1967, **7**, 27–28.

Pavlov, I. P. *Lectures on conditioned reflexes*. Vol. 2. *Conditioned reflexes and psychiatry*. (Translated by W. H. Gantt) New York: International Publishers, 1941.

Peterson, G. B. Auto-shaping in the rat: Conditioned approach and contact behavior toward signals of food or brain-stimulation reinforcement. Unpublished doctoral dissertation, Indiana University, 1972.

Peterson, G. B., Ackil, J., Frommer, G. P., & Hearst, E. Conditioned approach and contact behavior toward signals for food or brain-stimulation reinforcement. *Science*, 1972, **177**, 1009–1011.

Rescorla, R. A. Pavlovian conditioning and its proper control procedures. *Psychological Review*, 1967, **74**, 71–80.

Rescorla, R. A. Conditioned inhibition of fear. In N. J. Mackintosh & W. K. Honig (Eds.), *Fundamental issues in associative learning*. Halifax, Can.: Dalhousie University Press, 1969. Pp. 65–89.

Rescorla, R. A. Informational variables in Pavlovian conditioning. In G. H. Bower (Ed.), *The psychology of learning and motivation*. Vol. 6. New York: Academic Press, 1972. Pp. 1–46.

Rescorla, R. A., & Solomon, R. L. Two-process learning theory: Relationships between Pavlovian conditioning and instrumental learning. *Psychological Review*, 1967, **74**, 151–182.

Reynolds, G. S., Catania, A. C., & Skinner, B. F. Conditioned and unconditioned aggression in pigeons. *Journal of the Experimental Analysis of Behavior*, 1963, 6, 73–74.

Sainsbury, R. S. Effect of proximity of elements on the feature-positive effect. *Journal of the Experimental Analysis of Behavior*, 1971, **16**, 315–325. (a)

Sainsbury, R. S. The "feature positive effect" and simultaneous discrimination learning. *Journal of Experimental Child Psychology*, 1971, **11**, 347–356. (b)

Schwartz, B., & Williams, D. R. The role of the response-reinforcer contingency in negative automaintenance. *Journal of the Experimental Analysis of Behavior*, 1972, **17**, 351–357.

Seward, J. P. Conditioning theory. In M. Marx (Ed.), *Learning: Theories*. New York: Macmillan, 1970. Pp. 49–117.

Skinner, B. F. "Superstition" in the pigeon. *Journal of Experimental Psychology*, 1948, **38**, 168–172.

Skinner, B. F. *Science and human behavior*. New York: Macmillan, 1953.

Wasserman, E. A. The effect of redundant contextual stimuli on autoshaping the pigeon's keypeck. *Animal Learning and Behavior*, 1973, **1**, 198–206. (a)

Wasserman, E. A. Pavlovian conditioning with heat reinforcement produces stimulus-directed pecking in chicks. *Science*, 1973, **181**, 875–877. (b)

Wasserman, E. A. Stimulus-reinforcer predictiveness and selective discrimination learning in pigeons. *Journal of Experimental Psychology*, 1974, **103**, 284–297.

Wasserman, E. A., Franklin, S., & Hearst, E. Pavlovian appetitive contingencies and approach vs. withdrawal to conditioned stimuli in pigeons. *Journal of Comparative and Physiological Psychology*, 1974, **86**, 616–627.

Wessells, M. G. The effects of reinforcement upon the prepecking behaviors of pigeons in the auto-shaping experiment. *Journal of the Experimental Analysis of Behavior*, 1974, **21**, 125–144.

Williams, D. R., & Williams, H. Auto-maintenance in the pigeon: Sustained pecking despite contingent nonreinforcement. *Journal of the Experimental Analysis of Behavior*, 1969, **12**, 511–520.

Woodworth, R. S. *Dynamics of behavior*. New York: Holt, 1958.

A THEORY OF CONTEXT
IN DISCRIMINATION LEARNING[1]

Douglas L. Medin

THE ROCKEFELLER UNIVERSITY, NEW YORK, NEW YORK

I. Introduction 263
II. Units of Analysis in Discrimination Learning 264
    A. What Is Learned? 264
    B. Stimulus Description 267
III. Basic Notions of the Context Theory 269
    A. Context Change 269
    B. A Theory of Context in Discrimination Learning 270
    C. Further Predictions of the Context Model 281
    D. Summary 293
IV. Extensions of the Context Model to Selective Learning 295
    A. Attention Assumptions 296
    B. Predictions of the Context Model with Assumptions Concerning Attention 297
V. Discussion and Summary 303
    References 304
    Appendix 310

I. Introduction

Discrimination learning is a fundamental concept in psychology. It is hard to imagine a world where variability in behavior would not to some extent be associated with environmental events. Differential stimuli must be perceived (discriminated) to influence behavior, and the study of the process by which changes in behavior become correlated with changes in environmental stimuli defines the domain of discrimination learning.

[1] This research was supported by U.S. Public Health Service Grant MH25134-01 and a grant from the Office of Education (OEG 2 710532). This research is based, in part, on a paper presented at a conference on discrimination learning models held at Rockefeller University in April, 1973, and supported by the Mathematical Social Science Board.

At an initial stage in any theoretical analysis of discrimination learning two fundamental questions arise: (1) what is learned when an organism masters a discrimination, and (2) how should the stimulus situation be described? Both of these questions provoke a number of related subquestions, answers to which represent key choice points in theory construction. In this chapter, I propose to review briefly current discrimination-learning theories in light of these two questions, with the aim of demonstrating an important weakness in them. Following that, a new theory addressed to this weakness and drawing on concepts from research on memory processes will be presented and its predictions assessed. Finally, some modifications of the theory designed to account for phenomena from research on selective attention in learning will be developed and evaluated.

II. Units of Analysis in Discrimination Learning

A. WHAT IS LEARNED?

Consider an educated rat running in a T-maze on a brightness discrimination task. On each trial the rat runs down to the choice point. On some trials the reward is on the left and on others reward is on the right. When the reward is on the left, a black stimulus is on the left at the choice point and a white stimulis is on the right; when reward is on the right, the black stimulus is on the right and the white is on the left. We observe an experienced rat make a correct response at the choice point on each of a series of trials even though the reward varies in position from trial to trial. How should one describe the rat's performance? We can think of the rat as learning which stimuli to approach and which to avoid or, alternatively, view the rat as learning when to make one response (go left) and when to make another response (go right). The former view will be referred to as stimulus selection and the latter as response selection.

Before developing these two points of view it will be useful to introduce the two main variants of discrimination-learning problems, the simultaneous and the successive discrimination paradigms, both shown in Fig. 1. The letters B and W stand for black and white. The panel on the left illustrates the example we used of the simultaneous discrimination paradigm, where the reward is associated with one stimulus value (in this case, black) regardless of its position. For the successive paradigm shown in the right panel, the stimuli on each trial are identical and the position of the reward depends on which of

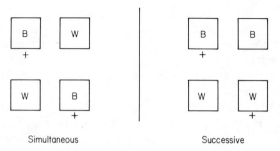

Simultaneous   Successive

Fig. 1. The simultaneous and successive discrimination paradigms. The "+" sign refers to the rewarded stimuli for each of the two settings of a problem.

the two stimulus configurations (BB or WW) is presented. Of course, the simultaneous paradigm could also be described as one in which the reward position depends upon which configuration is presented.

One of the earliest mathematical models for discrimination learning (Gulliksen & Wolfle, 1938a, 1938b) described this situation in terms of responses to configurations. Gulliksen and Wolfle argued that it was very natural to conceive of the rat as "going left" and "going right" and proposed that, as a result of discrimination training, these two responses come under the control of the appropriate stimulus configuration. Other mathematical learning models (Atkinson, 1959; Bush, 1965; Bush & Mosteller, 1951; Sternberg, 1963) have preferred a response selection characterization, perhaps because of its simplicity and perhaps also because of the strong tradition of psychologists to speak in terms of reinforcing responses. For either simultaneous or successive discriminations, there are two stimulus settings (BW and WB or BB and WW) and two responses, and learning can be described succinctly in terms of the probability of a left (or right) response given a particular stimulus setting.

While response selection theories seem logical, it may be equally plausible to describe a discrimination task in terms of stimulus selection. For example, the simultaneous discrimination of Fig. 1 could be conceived of in terms of learning to choose black and avoid white regardless of their position. An early theory based on such learning of approach and avoidance tendencies was that of Spence (1936). According to Spence, the cues of black, white, left, and right all acquire habit strength and the responses are determined by the stimulus complex of highest strength.

Stimulus selection versus response selection represents one controversy in psychology which was relatively short-lived. One possible explanation is that the experimental evidence failed to support response selection, although stimulus selection theories did not emerge from the foray untarnished. Let me briefly summarize the key experimental findings on stimulus and response selection, holding in abeyance for the moment discussion of difficulties with stimulus selection theories.

Nissen (1950) trained chimpanzees on a black–white simultaneous arrangement with the stimuli separated either in the usual horizontal orientation or in the vertical plane. A given animal was trained with a single orientation (e.g., left, right) and then given transfer tests with the stimuli appearing in the other orientation (e.g., up, down). The chimpanzees showed excellent but not perfect transfer of the discrimination across orientations. A response selection theory would have no basis for predicting above chance transfer, since during training the subject would either learn when to go left or right or when to go up or down and the new stimulus configurations were orthogonal to the old. A stimulus-selection view would directly predict the transfer, since if a chimpanzee learned to choose black during training, he should choose black during transfer regardless of its orientation. A tiny difficulty might be that a stimulus selection theory might predict that transfer should have been perfect, which it clearly was not.

Babb (1957) trained rats on a black–white simultaneous discrimination and then gave transfer tests involving two black (BB) or two white (WW) stimuli. He observed that his subjects responded quickly for two positive stimuli but slowly, if at all, for two negative stimuli. A stimulus selection theory would predict just this effect but a response selection theory would imply no differences in reaction to these two situations.

Referring again to Fig. 1, response selection and stimulus selection theories would tend to differ in terms of the relative rates of acquisition of simultaneous and successive discriminations. According to a response selection theory, since BW and WB (simultaneous) should be less distinctive situations than BB and WW (successive), simultaneous discriminations should be more difficult than successive discrimination problems. However, if we think in terms of stimulus selection, for the successive problem left, right, black and white are rewarded equally often and it is difficult to see how a successive discrimination could even be solved. There are ways around this prediction, but at the very least it seems that stimulus selection theories would predict that simultaneous discriminations should be easier than successive discriminations. Although there are a few exceptions which we shall presently consider, the weight of evidence (see Sutherland & Mackintosh, 1971) is strong in showing that simultaneous discriminations are mastered more easily than successive discriminations.

In summary, empirical evidence has tended almost uniformly to support stimulus selection over response selection models and recent discrimination learning models (e.g., Fisher & Zeaman, 1972; Lovejoy, 1968; Sutherland & Mackintosh, 1971; Zeaman & House, 1963) all fall under the framework of stimulus selection theories. Response selection theories, despite their attractive simplicity, do not seem adequate to account for discrimination learning phenomena.

B. STIMULUS DESCRIPTION

Questions about describing the stimulus situation are closely intertwined with the question of what is learned, one aspect of which was just discussed. Historically, quite a few different approaches have been taken to defining the major units of analysis. For both the simultaneous and successive discrimination paradigms shown in Fig. 1, one of two distinct settings appears on a given trial. Gulliksen and Wolfle (1938a, 1938b) proposed that each setting taken as a whole acted as the functional cue. At the other end of the continuum are component models (e.g., Burke & Estes, 1957; Bush & Mosteller, 1951; Spence, 1936) which assume that a stimulus array can be broken down into component aspects each of which may be associated with reward or nonreward. For example, Spence proposed that a rewarded response to the white triangle on the left would add habit strength independently to white, to triangle, and to left. A third point of view suggests that subjects may respond to compounds of component cues (e.g., white triangle). This proposition has been entertained as an auxiliary process by some theorists (e.g., Spence, 1952; Zeaman & House, 1963) but has also attained full status in other theories (e.g., the pattern and mixed models of Atkinson & Estes, 1963; Estes & Hopkins, 1961).

Configurational descriptions seem to lead to theories based on response selection and consequently embody their inadequacies. But component models have difficulties of their own. Because in successive problems all stimulus aspects are associated with reward equally often, component models predict that the successive problem is insoluble, which it clearly is not. To avoid this insolubility prediction, component-model advocates have been forced to add the assumption that under some circumstances subjects can respond to compounds of stimulus components such as white triangle (e.g., Spence, 1952). These circumstances have not been well specified, and compounds have generally been treated in an ad hoc manner. Consequently, there has been little analysis concerning transfer or generalization between compound and component cues. The mechanisms (e.g., compounding) evoked to explain successive discrimination learning have been given little or no role in accounts of simultaneous discrimination learning. The net effect of this practice is that the generality of many theories is severely limited.

An exception to this tendency to avoid formal treatment of compounding is the mixed model proposed by Estes and his co-workers, which assumes responses to both components and compounds. In the mixed model, component learning and generalization occur until the pattern (compound) associations are formed. The mixed model has been applied primarily to paired-associate learning and transfer and falls into the response selection framework with its attendant difficulties. However, it remains to be seen how well the model would do if the basic pattern-component interaction were developed from a stimulus selection orientation.

Overall then, while the consensus of effort has tended to shift toward component models with a stimulus-selection orientation, rather fundamental difficulties in accounting for discrimination learning remain. In the following paragraphs I shall suggest one reason for this state of affairs and then describe an alternative approach to discrimination learning which may avert some of the problems just discussed.

An attractive feature of component models is that stimulus similarity and associated generalization phenomena can be simply and directly represented by the number of components in common (the overlap) between pairs of stimuli. However, traditionally this orientation has carried with it the assumption that components acquire and maintain associative information in a completely independent manner, an assumption which is very strong (and I think incorrect). This tenet implies that if 10 units of strength are associated with white when it appears as part of a triangle on the left, then white will have 10 units of strength independent of the strengths of any other cues with which it appears, regardless of its position, no matter what form it appears on, and seemingly even independent of whether white is observed in or out of the experimental situation. To be sure, it is often acknowledged that some form of "stimulus change decrement" may lead to violations of the independence assumption, but this awareness has rarely been formally represented in any theory.

In the remainder of this chapter, a stimulus-selection theory is developed which does not assume that information associated with the component cues of a stimulus is stored and retrieved in an independent manner. The theory assumes no special compounding or configurational process but does give important weight to the role of context in the retrieval of associative information. To lay the groundwork for the theory, in the following section we consider the idea of context change or stimulus generalization decrement in some detail.

III. Basic Notions of the Context Theory

A. CONTEXT CHANGE

There seems to be increasing awareness that memory phenomena may have implications for theories of learning (e.g., Estes, 1973b). Forgetting was more or less ignored in early treatments of learning, perhaps because some early experiments seemed to show so little of it. Indeed, if animals are trained in a situation, receive little interfering training during the retention interval, and are tested in a situation identical to the training situation, they demonstrate remarkable retention up to at least two years (Liddell, 1927).

But what happens when the training and test situations are not identical? We know from countless stimulus generalization studies that performance varies directly with changes in the relevant cue or cues. Less plausible but also clear is the finding that changes in seemingly irrelevant or "background" features of a situation alter performance. For example, as early as 1917, Carr (1917) showed that performance on a spatial discrimination in a maze is lowered by (1) increases and decreases in illumination, (2) a change in the experimenter's position, (3) a change of position of the maze in the room, or (4) rotation of the maze. Using a classical conditioning paradigm, Girden (1938) found that forepaw flexion (the CR) to a buzzer (CS) depended upon the location of the buzzer in the experimental chamber. Zentall (1970) demonstrated that retroactive and proactive interference are strongly controlled by the similarity of the learning and interfering contexts. In the same theme, Robbins and Meyer (1970) and Glendenning and Meyer (1971) found that retrograde amnesia and retroactive interference were more strongly associated with similarity of motivational states rather than temporal relationships.

Nor are these effects unique to the animal world. For example, von Wright (1967) gave subjects paired-associate training where each stimulus-response pair was presented on a card of different shape and color and tested for recall with cards either of the same color or cards which were a uniform gray. A change to the gray cards led to a reliable decrement in recall.

Discrimination learning theorists have also acknowledged the importance of context. Sutherland and Mackintosh (1971) state, "When an animal learns to switch in a given analyzer, it learns to switch it in a given stiuation. The rat that has learned to respond in a jumping stand to a black-white difference will not show an increased tendency to control its responses by responding to brightness cues in totally different situations such as its home cage [p. 55]." And Estes, Hopkins, and Crothers (1960) propose, ". . . probability of a response reinforced on a training trial is reduced on subsequent test trials if components of the training stimulus pattern, including contextual, or 'background,' cues, have been replaced by novel ones in the test pattern [p. 338]."

In the theory to be proposed, context is promoted to a major status and the implications of this are explored.

B. A THEORY OF CONTEXT IN DISCRIMINATION LEARNING

In a typical discrimination learning situation the subject responds to a cue and receives some outcome or reward information. To illustrate this scheme, consider Fig. 2. A stimulus, in this case a red triangle, is responded to in some context, and the outcome may be associated with the stimulus situation. The basic idea to be advanced is that, in the course of learning, information concerning both cues *and* the context in which they occur are stored in memory. It is further assumed that to retrieve information about an event, *both* the stimulus and its associated context must be activated simultaneously. Changes in either cues or changes in the context will impair the accessibility of reinforcement information associated with the situation.

For the moment, cue and context will be only loosely defined. Roughly speaking, cues tend to be those aspects of a situation that vary and to which it is assumed subjects respond, while context refers to those relatively invariant aspects of a situation in which a response occurs. However, a particular stimulus may function both as a cue and as context for other cues.

To spell out the context model, two sets of assumptions will be introduced initially dealing with (1) retrieval and generalization of

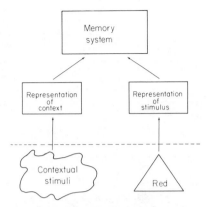

Fig. 2. Relationship between cue and context. When the red triangle appearing in a given context is selected, information concerning both the stimulus and its context are stored in memory.

information and (2) learning and choice behavior. The first set of assumptions conveys the essential aspects of the model, and the second set allows explicit predictions to be derived.

1. Retrieval and Generalization Assumptions

1. Information available from a stimulus in a context is reduced either by changes in the stimulus or by changes in the context. Cue differences along each stimulus dimension and context dimension can be represented by a similarity parameter ranging from 0 to 1, with 1 representing no change and 0 corresponding to a complete lack of generalization or transfer for that dimension.

2. The context or stimulus change decrements from the various dimensions are combined in a multiplicative manner to yield a single similarity measure governing transfer.

To illustrate these assumptions, we refer to Table I which represents the table of similarities for the stimuli from Fig. 1. The values in the table represent the similarities of the row and column stimuli, with $p(0 \leqslant p \leqslant 1)$ representing position similarity and $b(0 \leqslant b \leqslant 1)$ representing brightness similarity. The notation bp represents b times p.

The main diagonal represents the maximum similarity, identity. Looking across the first row, one may note that B_L (black on the left) differs from B_R in position (p), from W_L in brightness (b), and

TABLE I

SIMILARITY MATRIX FOR
THE STIMULI [a]

	B_L	B_R	W_L	W_R
B_L	1	p	b	bp
B_R	p	1	bp	b
W_L	b	bp	1	p
W_R	bp	b	p	1

[a]The letters p and b are parameters for
position and brightness similarity, respectively. B_L, B_R, W_L, and W_R stand for black
on the left, black on the right, white on the
left, and white on the right.

from W_R in both brightness and position (bp). This matrix of
similarities can be used to calculate the effect of a particular trial
event. Suppose, for example, that a subject responded to black on
the left and received a reward. The model assumes that to some
extent subjects will associate this reward with all four cues which
appear in the problem, with the extent of this generalization depending on the similarity of each of the stimuli to B_L.

These ideas concerning generalization will be made more precise
when consideration is given to the learning and choice assumptions.
Some general intuitions concerning predictions to be advanced may be
derived by examining Fig. 1 and Table I. Consider the transfer
between settings in the two problems after a rewarded response to
B_L. For simultaneous problems this associative information will
transfer to both stimuli in the second settting, being reduced by the
difference in position (p) for the B_R and reduced by the brightness
difference (b) for the W_L. Generally this would produce positive
transfer if p is greater than b $(p > b)$ and negative transfer if $p < b$,
since in the latter case the reward would generalize more to the W_L
than the B_R. One would also expect more positive transfer the less
distinctive the position cues (the greater p is) or the more distinctive
the brightness cues (the smaller b is). Comparable between-setting
comparisons for the successive paradigm indicate that a reduction in
transfer produced by changes in both position and brightness would
occur in the case of W_R and transfer would be reduced only by the
brightness difference for W_L. This means that negative transfer will

generally occur between settings for successive problems since $b \geqslant bp$. Within-setting generalization would also be greater for the successive than the simultaneous problem, so that one can anticipate that the model must predict that simultaneous discriminations would be easier than successive discriminations. These and other predictions will later be considered in detail. First, formal learning and choice assumptions will be presented and discussed, and then a more intuitive (but formally inaccurate) basis for predictions will be provided. Some readers may prefer to jump directly to the latter section.

2. Learning and Choice Assumptions

The following assumptions allow explicit predictions to be made for the context model:

1. Associated with each stimulus is a feedback value, F_i, which varies between 0 and 1, where F_i reflects the probability that (or degree to which) the expectation of reward is associated with stimulus i in a particular experimental context.

2. When a stimulus i is responded to on trial n and reward follows, then

$$F_{i,n+1} = F_{i,n} + (1 - F_{i,n})\theta, \tag{1}$$

where θ is a learning rate parameter ($0 < \theta < 1$).

When a response to stimulus i is associated with nonreward

$$F_{i,n+1} = F_{i,n} - \theta F_{i,n}. \tag{2}$$

3. Stimuli appearing within the learning context other than the one selected on a trial may also be associated with the trial event. For a stimulus S_j having similarity α to stimulus S_i,

$$F_{j,n+1} = (1 - \alpha)F_{j,n} + \alpha[F_{j,n} + (1 - F_{j,n})\theta] \tag{3}$$

after a rewarded response to S_i and

$$F_{j,n+1} = (1 - \alpha)F_{j,n} + \alpha[F_{j,n} - \theta F_{j,n}] \tag{4}$$

after a nonrewarded response to S_i.

4. Feedback from the problem stimuli generalizes to stimuli newly introduced into the learning situation as a function of their

similarity. Thus, if a new stimulus S_k is introduced after n trials of training have occurred to stimuli S_i and S_j, then

$$F_{k,n+1} = \frac{(\beta + \gamma - \beta\gamma)}{\beta + \gamma} \left[\beta F_{i,n+1} + \gamma F_{j,n+1} \right] + (1 - \beta)(1 - \gamma)F_{k,1} \quad (5)$$

where β and γ represent respective parameters for the similarity of S_i to S_k and S_j to S_k, and $F_{k,1}$ represents the initial feedback associated with S_k.

5. Choices are generated by scanning the stimuli and generating anticipated feedback according to the scanning model described by Estes (1962, 1966). In particular, the probability of choosing stimulus i (P_i) given a choice between S_i and S_j is as follows:

$$P(i/i,j) = \frac{F_i(1 - F_j)}{F_i(1 - F_j) + F_j(1 - F_i)}. \quad (6)$$

The first assumption betrays a bias toward recently advanced concepts of reinforcement (e.g., Estes, 1969a, 1969b, 1969c) in which learning is conceived of as a matter of acquiring associative information concerning stimuli and outcomes and the effect of reward is considered to be neither direct nor automatic. The second assumption employs linear operators to represent changes in expected reward, an idea common to many mathematical treatments of discrimination learning.

The third and fourth assumptions distinguish between stimuli appearing in an experimental situation and those outside the situation which may be introduced at some later time, such as for generalization tests. Generalization to stimuli within the learning situation and to new stimuli is affected by similarity but the underlying mechanisms are assumed to be somewhat different. Similarity affects the rate of generalization to stimuli within the situation and the total history of response and reward sequences in the situation is needed to ascertain current feedback values. A long series of rewarded responses to the correct stimulus on a problem will allow the feedback for the incorrect stimulus to increase toward 1 at a rate $\alpha\theta$, if α is the similarity of the correct and incorrect stimuli. In contrast, stimuli not appearing in a situation acquire and lose feedback strictly in accordance to their similarity to the situational stimuli, and only the similarity and current feedback value is needed to predict generalization from training stimuli to new stimuli.

This distinction may seem unnatural but there is some direct evidence favoring it. Behar (1962) gave monkeys a series of short problems where every few trials either the correct or incorrect stimulus was replaced by a new correct or incorrect stimulus object. On these shifts, monkeys preferred the old incorrect object to a new object if they had not responded to the incorrect object in the previous set of trials. The fact that the negative object had not been chosen previously indicates that it was not highly preferred. The present model, however, would predict just this effect by the process embodied in the fourth assumption. Brown and Carr (1958) have also shown that placing the objects which are to be correct on new problems 6 inches behind the currently correct object and pairing the future incorrect object with the currently incorrect object facilitates object discrimination performance of monkeys on these new problems. Other studies (e.g., Medin, 1974b) suggest that familiarity itself is not responsible for this facilitation of learning in monkeys.

The fifth assumption adopts Estes' scanning rule as the choice assumption. One of its basic properties, readily derived from Eq. (6), is that when F_i is equal to 1, then $P(i/i,j)$ will also be 1 for all F_j, provided that F_j is not 1. In other words, relevant stimuli will be actively selected rather than irrelevant stimuli being actively ignored. This represents a possible solution to the familiar overlap problem. The overlap problem refers to the fact that stimulus similarity can affect the rate of learning, yet problems involving very similar stimuli can ultimately be solved. Many theories can account for similarity effects (e.g., the component model of Burke & Estes, 1957), but these theories then predict that perfect discrimination performance would be impossible. With the scanning rule, stimulus similarity will affect the rate of learning, yet it will be possible to obtain perfect discrimination in the face of stimulus similarity.

The two sets of assumptions so far introduced allow one to make explicit predictions concerning problem solubility and speed of learning in a variety of problem formats. Since no explicit learning function could be developed, a computer program was written to assess the predictions of the context model. The flowchart in Fig. 3 illustrates the main steps in the program.

The program begins by reading in a set of stimulus descriptions (i.e., binary values on each of a set of dimensions), an assignment of stimuli to pairs (for two-choice problems), initial feedback values for each of the stimuli, and a code indicating which stimuli are to be associated with reward. The stimulus descriptions are then used to generate a matrix of stimulus similarities such as that shown in Table I.

The program next runs through a set of learning trials. A pair of

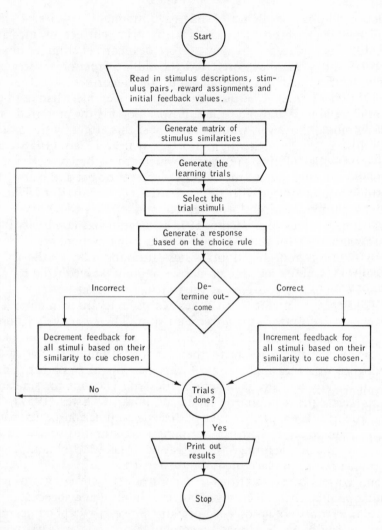

Fig. 3. Flow chart of the computer simulation of the context model.

stimuli is selected and the feedback values associated with the two stimuli are scanned according to the choice rule to generate a response. If the choice is a stimulus associated with reward, then feedback for all the stimuli is increased with a rate parameter governed by the similarity of each of the stimuli to the stimulus chosen (i.e., determined directly from the similarity matrix). Equation (1) applies to the stimulus chosen and Eq. (3) is used for the other stimuli. An analogous process operates after an error except that the feedback values for all the cues are decremented. The sequence is repeated for each of the learning trials. It is worth emphasizing that the simulation relies on no foreknowledge of the type of problem it is to be given (e.g., successive versus simultaneous) or even whether or not the problem is soluble. The presumed learning process is the same regardless of the type of problem involved.

The results from the actual simulations will be deferred to the appendix. In the next few paragraphs I would like to present a shorthand, more intuitive means of arriving at predictions of the context model. The reader is cautioned that, strictly speaking, the shorthand method is incorrect and does not have a one-to-one correspondence with the context model as presented. However, every prediction to be discussed using the shorthand method has been confirmed via computer simulation and the shorthand method will serve as a convenient, if rough, guide to bringing out the predictions of the context model.

3. An Algebraic Version of the Context Model

The algebraic version of the context model requires a more abstract treatment of information storage. Let the information acquired from a response to a stimulus be designated by I_R when followed by reward and by I_N when followed by nonreward. Potentially, all this information might be generalized to the other problem stimuli but will be reduced by differences in stimulus features. This is, in fact, necessary for learning because if the information were associated equally with both the incorrect and correct stimulus of a problem, there would be no basis for differential responding to these stimuli.

Referring again to Fig. 1 and Table I, consider now a problem where the two stimulus settings are randomly intermixed. For illustrative purposes we focus on B_L-W_R differences. On B_L-W_R trials, whichever outcome occurs will be associated with both stimuli but to different degrees. If B_L is chosen, the reward will be associated to B_L and to W_R but to a lesser degree to W_R because W_R differs from B_L in brightness and position. If an amount I_R is associated with B_L, then a reduced amount bpI_R will be associated with W_R and the net difference in information will be $I_R(1 - bp)$. Since this latter term is positive, reward will be associated more with B_L than with W_R. If

W_R is chosen, nonreward will be associated with W_R and to a lesser extent, because of the brightness and position differences, to B_L. The net difference in information concerning nonreward ($B_L - W_R$) would be $I_N(bp - 1)$, reflecting that nonreward would be more strongly associated with W_R than B_L. The total information (I) that would be favorable toward choosing a stimulus will be represented by $I_R - I_N$ and, with this notation, the net effect of one rewarded response to B_L and one nonrewarded response to W_R would produce I values of $I_R - bpI_N$ for B_L and $bpI_R - I_N$ for W_R. The net difference in information (ΔI) would then be $I_R(1 - bp) + I_N(1 - bp)$ or $(I_R + I_N)(1 - bp)$.

Now consider what happens to the $B_L - W_R$ difference on $W_L - B_R$ trials. When B_R is chosen, both B_L and W_R are associated with reward, the generalization to B_L being diminished by a position difference p and the generalization to W_R by a difference in brightness b. Likewise, nonreward is associated with B_L and W_R when W_L is chosen. Following one rewarded response to B_R and one nonrewarded response to W_L the I would be $pI_R - bI_N$ for B_L and $bI_R - pI_N$ for W_R. The net difference, ΔI, for B_L and W_R would be $I_R(p - b) + I_N(p - b)$. From this we can see that $W_L - B_R$ training will facilitate the $B_L - W_R$ discrimination when $p > b$.

For the present purposes it is convenient to let I_R and I_N be equal since the net gain in information will then not depend on the stimulus chosen. Further, we arbitrarily set I_R and I_N to unity. Now in the simultaneous discrimination paradigm just discussed, following a response to both the $B_L - W_R$ and the $W_L - B_R$ settings, the overall information gain for the $B_L - W_R$ differences (or the $W_L - B_R$ differences) will be $1 - bp + p - b$ which factors into:

$$\Delta_I = (1 + p)(1 - b). \tag{7}$$

From this we anticipate that simultaneous discriminations will be solved more rapidly the greater the distinctiveness of the relevant cue (the smaller b) and the greater the similarity of the positional cues (the larger p). Evidence on the first point is so common that I will cite only MacCaslin (1954) who showed that brightness discrimination in rats was related to brightness similarity.

There are almost no data on the effects of position similarity on a nonspatial discrimination. Spiker and Lubker (1965) found a 0-inch separation to be better than a 10-inch separation (edge to edge) of stimuli for a brightness discrimination with children in terms of trials to criterion (7.4 versus 4.8) but the trend was not statistically reliable. Using rats in a jumping stand, Elias and Stein (1968) obtained clear position similarity effects. The 4-choice discrimination used either a 6.67 cm or a 11.75 cm center-to-center stimulus separation. A triangle–circle discrimination was mastered much more rapidly for the large separation and a diamond–square discrimination produced evidence for learning only in the case of the larger stimulus separation.

The successive problem, shown in the right panel of Fig. 1, can also be examined in terms of Table I. The information difference between B_L and B_R on B_L-B_R trials is equal to $1-p$, and on W_L-W_R trials the information difference between B_L and B_R is $bp - b$. The latter term is negative and implies that W_L-W_R training would tend to interfere with the B_L-B_R performance, and more so the greater the brightness similarity. (If b were equal to 1, then this term would be $p - 1$ and the Δ_I would equal 0, implying an insoluble problem.) From the B_L-B_R and W_L-W_R settings we find that the total information gain will be $1 - p + bp - b$ which factors into:

$$\Delta_I = (1 - p)(1 - b). \tag{8}$$

From Eq. (8) one would expect that performance on successive discriminations will decrease with both position and brightness similarity. MacCaslin (1954) has shown that brightness similarity, and Medin (1974a) demonstrated that position similarity impairs successive brightness discriminations.

Using the logic of Eq. (7) and (8), one would expect that if one reward is associated exclusively with one position and a distinct reward is associated with another position, then simultaneous discriminations will be slowed and successive discriminations will be speeded up. Shepp (1962, 1964) has shown both these effects using retarded children as subjects.

It is important to make explicit a hidden assumption involved in the algebra of information differences. We are assuming that the greater the difference in information associated with the two stimulus alternatives on a trial, the faster the learning to discriminate between them.

One can use this assumption directly to compare the difficulty of various paradigms. The relative difficulty of simultaneous and successive discriminations may be assessed using Eq. (7) and (8). Since (7) will be larger than (8) except for the case when p is zero (or b is 1), we are led to predict that simultaneous discriminations should be easier than successive discriminations—which generally has been found (e.g., Bitterman, Tyler, & Elam, 1955; Lipsitt, 1961; Mac-Caslin, 1954; Price & Spiker, 1967; Spence, 1952; Spiker & Lubker, 1965; Warren & Barron, 1956).

There is an interesting exception to this general rule: when the choice responses are not to the relevant cues directly, successive discriminations are found to be easier than simultaneous discrimination problems (e.g., Bitterman & Wodinsky, 1953; Bitterman, *et al.*, 1955; Lipsitt, 1961; Wodinsky, Varley, & Bitterman, 1954). An example of this situation taken from Bitterman and Wodinsky (1953) is shown in Fig. 4.

Responses are to the gray stimuli rather than to the black and white cues. If we apply the logic for information differences between G_L and G_R on the top of either panel, we obtain $(1 - p)$ for trials on the top setting and $(p - 1)$ for trials on the bottom setting, for a net difference of zero. However, the center black and white stimuli differ between settings and, introducing c for the similarity of the center contexts, the G_L-G_R difference on the top remains $(1 - p)$ for responses to the top setting and becomes $c(p - 1)$ for responses to the bottom setting. The net difference then would be

$$\Delta_I = (1 - p)(1 - c). \tag{9}$$

From Eq. (9) we expect that the rate of learning will increase with position distinctiveness and will increase the greater the difference in center contexts between the top and bottom settings of the discrimination. It seems plausible that this difference would be greater for the successive discrimination than the simultaneous paradigm, from which would follow the result that in these circumstances, successive discriminations are solved more rapidly.

Before considering other detailed predictions from various para-

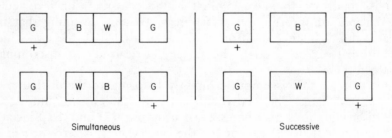

Fig. 4. Simultaneous and successive paradigms where responses are not directly to the relevant cues.

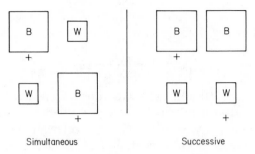

Fig. 5. Simultaneous and successive paradigms with redundant relevant cues of size and brightness.

digms, we note that the model as presented is not treating simultaneous and successive discriminations in any different manner. No new mechanisms are brought into play for one paradigm and not the other. Although this presentation may have built in some descriptive biases, it is even the case that is has not been necessary to distinguish between cue and context. Equation (7) results whether we assume that black and white are cues and all else is context, or left and right are cues and all else context, or black plus left is one cue, white plus left another, and so on. Thus, although we recognize the influence of many cue components, the subject can be viewed as choosing between but two stimuli rather than as selecting components. Within this framework we can generate a surprising number of predictions for which there is quite good support.

C. FURTHER PREDICTIONS OF THE CONTEXT MODEL

1. Effects of Relevant and Irrelevant Cues

We now consider procedures where either irrelevant or redundant relevant cues are added to simultaneous and successive discriminations. Figure 5 displays discriminations where both size and brightness are relevant cues. One can derive a measure of the net information gain using the method presented before. For the simultaneous problem in the left panel the difference between the top two stimuli from the top setting is $(1 - psb)$, where s represents the size similarity parameter, and the difference between the top two stimuli owing to generalization from a trial on the bottom setting is $(p - sb)$ so that

$$\Delta_I = (1 + p)(1 - sb). \tag{10}$$

By similar means we can find the value for the successive paradigm in the right panel of Fig. 5 to be

$$\Delta_I = (1 - p)(1 - sb). \tag{11}$$

Comparing Eqs. (10) and (11) with Eqs. (7) and (8), we conclude that the information gain will be greater and the discrimination will be solved more quickly when redundant relevant cues are present. This prediction has been repeatedly confirmed for simultaneous discriminations (for reviews, see Meyer, Treichler, & Meyer, 1965; Sutherland & Mackintosh, 1971; Trabasso & Bower, 1968) and has also been demonstrated for successive discriminations (Lubker, 1969; Warren, 1964).

Not surprisingly, there is an exception to this general picture. For very strong or salient cues, additional cues do not appear to facilitate the rate of learning. For example, in most monkey species color is a dominant cue and the addition of other cues such as form and size does not speed learning (cf. Meyer *et al.*, 1965). This does not necessarily mean that subjects do not attend to these redundant cues. Warren (1954) trained monkeys on redundant relevant cue problems and after a few trials, reduced the number of relevant cues from three to one or two. Although neither form nor size added to color produced better learning than color alone, eliminating form and size cues always led to a disruption of animals' performance, indicating that these cues had been observed. Medin and Davis (1967) also showed that additivity could be observed in the presence of dominant cues when a cue subtraction method was employed.

Looking again at Eqs. (10) and (11), we see that if either s or b is equal to zero (implying a total absence of generalization, which might occur for salient cues), then other relevant cues will not speed up the rate of learning even though subjects may learn something about all of the relevant cues. Thus the model is consistent with the pattern of results just discussed. An untested prediction of the model is that if a cue is so salient that the addition of less salient cues will not speed up the rate of learning, then the addition of more salient cues will also not speed learning. In other words, the main effect of salience of a cue on a dimension is presumed to be to reduce generalization to other cues on that dimension rather than to favor that cue in some competitive sense in comparison to cues on other dimensions, as other theorists have suggested.

Irrelevant dimensions may be added to simultaneous and successive discriminations in a number of ways. In Fig. 6, the irrelevant size cue

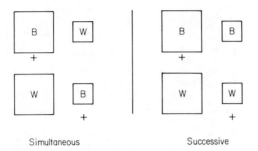

Fig. 6. Stimultaneous and successive paradigms with an irrelevant size cue confounded with position.

is confounded with spatial position. Deriving the value for net information gain from the two settings we find

$$\Delta_I = (1 + sp)(1 - b) \qquad (12)$$

for the simultaneous case, and

$$\Delta_I = (1 - sp)(1 - b) \qquad (13)$$

for the successive problem. Comparing Eqs. (12) and (13) with Eqs. (7) and (8), one can see that simultaneous discriminations should be impaired by the spatially confounded irrelevant cue but that successive problems should be facilitated by the irrelevant size cue. Both these predictions were confirmed in a single experiment with children by Price and Spiker (1967).

By adding two new settings to the basic paradigms, one can produce irrelevant cues not confounded with spatial position as is shown in Fig. 7. The procedure for deriving the net information difference is the same as before, with the difference being derived from all four settings. The result for the simultaneous paradigm is

$$\Delta_I = (1 + p)(1 - b)(1 + s), \qquad (14)$$

and for the successive paradigm it is

$$\Delta_I = (1 - p)(1 - b)(1 + s). \qquad (15)$$

Here the proper control comparison is a four-setting problem where $s = 1$, from which we can predict that the irrelevant dimension not

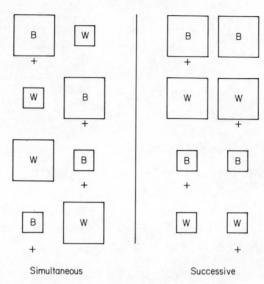

Fig. 7. Simultaneous and successive paradigms with an irrelevant size cue not confounded with position.

confounded with position will impair performance on both simultaneous and successive discriminations. For simultaneous problems, favorable evidence on this prediction has been obtained by Lawrence and Mason (1955), Lubker (1967), and Price and Spiker (1967), the last-mentioned study showing that the more distinctive the irrelevant cue, the greater the impairment. This prediction seems to have been assessed but once in the successive paradigm, and the result was that children's performance was worse in the presence of irrelevant cues (Tragakis, 1968).

It is perhaps worth noting another result which is not obvious in the algebraic simplification of the context model but which is strongly evident in the simulations. Effects appearing in simultaneous discrimination paradigms are magnified in size for the successive paradigm. Although the successive paradigm has not been extensively used, there is favorable experimental evidence on this point. Mac-Caslin (1954) found that similarity of cues along the relevant dimension slowed learning much more for successive problems than for simultaneous discriminations.

Another choice point in introducing irrelevant dimensions is deciding whether they shall vary within or between dimensions. In the left panel of Fig. 8, the irrelevant brightness dimension varies between settings, while it varies within settings in the right panel. The values for net information gain are

$$\Delta_I = 1 - sp + bp - sb \tag{16}$$

for the variable-between problem and

$$\Delta_I = 1 - sbp + bp - s \tag{17}$$

for the variable-within problem. Comparing Eqs. (16) and (17), we find that (16) exceeds (17) by $s(1 - p)(1 - b)$. Since this value is positive, variable-between problems should be easier than variable-within discriminations and this difference should increase with size similarity. At the extreme case of $s = 1$, the variable-between problem becomes a successive discrimination while the variable-within problem becomes insoluble. Spiker and Lubker (1964) found that size similarity did hurt performance, that variable-between was easier than variable-within, and that this difference increased as size similarity increased.

A more usual manner of comparing variable-within versus variable-between irrelevant cues uses four stimulus settings as in Fig. 9. The information analysis now yields the same equation for either manipulation,

$$\Delta_I = (1 - s)(1 + p)(1 + b), \tag{18}$$

and consequently, the model predicts no differences in these two paradigms. However, a word of caution should be added. Computer

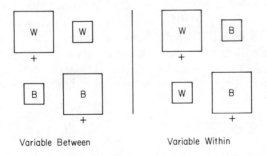

Variable Between   Variable Within

Fig. 8. A discrimination problem where the irrelevant brightness dimension varies either between settings or within settings for the two configurations.

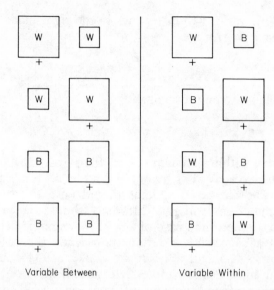

Variable Between   Variable Within

Fig. 9. A four-setting problem where the irrelevant brightness discrimination varies either between or within settings.

simulations of the model show that if subjects have stimulus preferences, an advantage for variable-between over variable-within irrelevant dimensions might be obtained. It is often assumed by discrimination learning theorists that subjects are less likely to attend to cue dimensions which are constant within a trial than to cue dimensions varying on a trial. Later on it will be seen that this assumption could be added to the context model, but the data are not especially clear. Lubker (1964) and Shepp and Gray (1971), obtained some data favoring variable-between over variable-within in acquisition but Caron (1970) found no differences for three-year-old children, and Evans and Beedle (1970) found no difference for retarded girls and variable-within bettern than variable-between for retarded boys. Regrettably, there are no direct comparisons of variable-within and variable-between irrelevant dimensions in animal learning.

2. Constant Irrelevant Cues

Because it is natural to consider now the effects of constant irrelevant cues, a slight detour from the main development of the context model will be taken. According to some theories (e.g., Fisher

& Zeaman, 1972; Restle, 1961; Shepp & Zeaman, 1966), constant irrelevant cues never enter into the choice process, but according to others (e.g., Bush & Mosteller, 1951; Restle, 1955) the influence of constant irrelevant cues diminshes in the course of learning a problem. In still other theories (e.g., Lovejoy, 1965; Sutherland & Mackintosh, 1971; Zeaman & House, 1963), constant irrelevant cues are not treated as distinct from other irrelevant cues but attention to all irrelevant cues diminishes with training. On the other hand, according to Spence (1936), all aspects of a stimulus situation are available to be associated with reward.

What all these theories have in common is the assumption that relevant and irrelevant features are independent. To test this prediction, Flagg and Medin (1973) trained monkeys on two concurrent discrimination problems, one having color relevant and form constant irrelevant, and the other having form relevant and color constant irrelevant. Transfer tests provided choices between the two previously rewarded objects, a new object formed by combining the relevant color and form cues, and a new object formed by combining the constant irrelevant color and form cues. Subjects consistently chose the previously rewarded objects during transfer, but of the new objects, almost always chose the object constructed of relevant features. Flagg and Medin demonstrated that the forementioned theories, which imply independence of features, cannot handle these data, since most such theories predict that modal choices should be of the stimulus comprised of both relevant features.

This pattern of results is consistent with the context theory and the stimulus interaction theory of Spiker to be discussed later. A recently completed followup study adds further support to the idea of nonindependence of features. Pig-tailed monkeys were trained on four concurrently presented object discriminations of the type shown in Fig. 10. For two of the problems color is relevant and form is constant and irrelevant, and for the other two problems form is relevant and color constant and irrelevant. One color and one form discrimination differ from the other two problems in both size and orientation. Transfer tests employ the previously rewarded objects and new objects consisting of combinations of previously relevant and irrelevant features. The comparison of greatest interest involves choices of stimuli comprised of previously relevant features in relation to between-problem similarity. For example, after training on the problem in Fig. 10, how will choices of a blue triangle combining relevant color and form features compare to choices of a yellow triangle combining the same relevant features? The context model

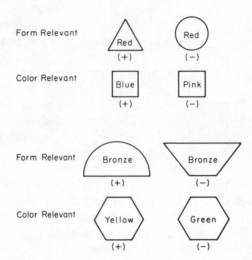

Fig. 10. A sample of the four pairs of concurrent discriminations used in the study. The large stimuli were presented in a vertical position while the small stimuli were presented horizontally (flat). Only one of the two settings for each simultaneous discrimination is shown.

predicts that the blue triangle will have greater strength because the strength of the blue feature will only be diminished by the form difference, while the strength associated with yellow will be diminished by the form difference *and* the size and orientation difference between the triangle and the yellow hexagon.

The transfer results showed that choices of new stimuli were related to the overall similarity of the objects from which they were constructed as predicted by the context model. Other experiments (e.g., House & Zeaman, 1963; R. J. Miles & Edenborough, 1968; Williams, 1967) using retarded children, rats, and pigeons, have demonstrated that constant irrelevant cues serve a major function in transfer and the evidence as a whole must be taken as favoring the idea that relevant and irrelevant features are not treated as completely independent.

3. Component versus Configurational Learning

Appreciable interest has centered around component versus configurational learning, which loosely corresponds to a stimulus versus response selection approach. Figure 11 shows the design of an experiment by Birch and Vandenberg (1955) which appeared to yield contradictory results. Subjects were trained on the discrimination G_L–W_R and B_L–G_R shown at the top of the figure which could be solved either by learning that black and white were correct or by learning to go right for a bright array and left for a dark array. The lower left problems (1 and 2) were tests to see if learning had been configurational. If subjects had learned to choose right for light stimuli and left for dark stimuli, then subjects given transfer condition 1 should perform better than subjects given transfer condition 2 at the start of transfer. This is what Birch and Vandenberg observed, and similar empirical results have been reported by B. Johnson (1962) and Lubker (1964). With the same reasoning one would expect that subjects would do better in transfer situation 4 than in 3 if they had learned "light-go right, dark-go left." Yet subjects performed better on task 3 than 4 as if they had learned to choose black and white rather than learning a configuration.

We can apply the present model to these data by measuring the similarity of the training and transfer situations. First, taking transfer situations 1 and 2, the W_R–W_L difference from the G_L–W_R training

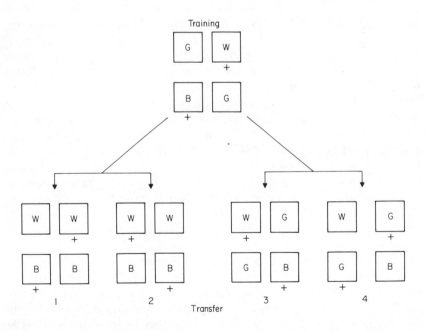

Fig. 11. The Birch and Vandenberg paradigm used to examine configural learning.

setting is $1 - p$ and from the B_L-G_R setting is $pb - b$, yielding a net difference of $(1 - p)(1 - b)$ which is positive, so that the model predicts that situation 1 will have an advantage over situation 2 at the start of transfer. (The gray training stimuli do not affect this prediction since they affect W_R and W_L equally.)

Transfer in situations 3 and 4 is slightly more complicated because there are both black–gray and white–gray differences (which we shall assume to be equal) and a black–white difference which would be expected to be larger than the other differences. We represent the black–white differences by b_1 and the black–gray and white–gray differences by b_2, where b_2 is between zero and 1. That is, gray and black are assumed to be more similar than white and black. Now one can obtain that the W_L-G_R difference is equal to

$$\Delta_I = 1 + 2p + b_1 - 2b_2(1 - p). \qquad (19)$$

Depending upon values of p, b_1, and b_2, we can predict either situations 3 or 4 to produce better transfer, although reasonable parameter values would tend to favor situation 3. For example, even if b_1 were zero, p would have to be less than .25 for situation 4 to produce better performance. The context model can predict the contradictory Birch and Vandenberg results, even if it does not predict them unequivocally.

A related, more frequently used paradigm is shown in Fig. 12. R, Y, B, and W stand for red, yellow, black, and white but there is no special significance to these particular colors. After training on the top problem, subjects are given transfer to both stimulus arrangements. Experimenters then measure whether subjects continue to select the same rewarded stimuli (red and white) or whether they select the same responses to the stimulus configurations. To obtain transfer predictions we use H for color similarity and use H_w and H_b to distinguish within- and between-setting color similarity since that has been an experimental variable. At the beginning of transfer, the difference in reward information between R_R and Y_L would be

$$\Delta_I = p - H_w + H_b - pH_b. \qquad (20)$$

From Eq. (20) we predict that a stimulus selection solution (choice of red) will (1) decrease with within-setting color similarity, (2) increase with between-pair similarity, and (3) increase with position similarity. I know of no evidence on the second and third predictions but favorable results on the first prediction have been reported by Turbeville, Calvin, and Bitterman (1952), White and Spiker (1960), Teas and Bitterman (1952), and Zeiler and Paul (1963).

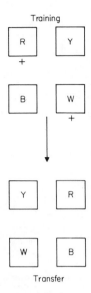

Fig. 12.   Paradigm design to evaluate configurational versus component learning.

Note that in terms of the model, compound and configurational solution modes are more properly thought of as properties of stimuli than of subjects as such. If the within-pair similarity varies in the two settings, then it is quite possible that one might obtain "configurational responding" for one pair and a "component solution" for the other setting pair. This outcome has been observed by Liu and Zeiler (1968), and by Campione, McGrath, and Rabinowitz (1971). Developmental shifts in patterns of responding (e.g., Zeiler, 1964) might simply reflect shifts in the salience of particular dimensions, such as a decrease in the salience of position cues, rather than distinct styles of learning.

4.   Conditional Simultaneous and Successive Discriminations

Quite complicated variations of simultaneous and successive discriminations have been shown to be soluble. Figures 13 and 14 show what might be called conditional simultaneous and conditional successive discriminations. The conditional simultaneous problem can be described as "large is correct for white stimuli, small is correct for black stimuli." The information value equation for this paradigm is

$$\Delta_I = (1 + p)(1 - s)(1 - b). \tag{21}$$

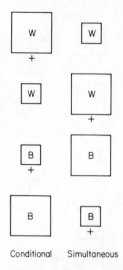

Conditional   Simultaneous

Fig. 13. The conditional simultaneous discrimination paradigm.

Thus there is a net gain of information on this problem which Lashley (1938) long ago showed was soluble. The computer simulations show that we can predict that this problem is soluble.[2] Hoyt (1960, 1962) found that brightness distinctiveness facilitates performance on this problem as Equation (21) implies.

The conditional successive problem in Fig. 14 can be solved as "for large stimuli, black-go left, white-go right; while for small stimuli, black-go right and white-go left." The appropriate equation is

$$\Delta_I = (1 - p)(1 - s)(1 - b). \tag{22}$$

Flagg (1974) ran monkeys on the paradigm shown in Fig. 14 and found that the problem was difficult but soluble. I know of no other relevant evidence on conditional successive discriminations.

5. Transverse Patterning

In the transverse patterning problem, stimulus A is correct in one pair and incorrect in another, B is correct in one and incorrect in another, and C is correct in one and incorrect in another (i.e., A^+B^-, B^+C^-, C^+A^-). These problems are soluble at least by chimpanzees

---

[2] Another problem with the algebraic simplification of the context model is that a difference in information implies above-chance performance but this in turn does not always imply that perfect performance is possible.

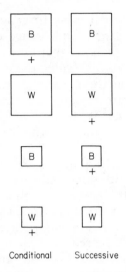

Conditional   Successive

Fig. 14.   The conditional successive discrimination paradigm.

(e.g., Nissen, 1942). The context model in its simplest form predicts such problems to be insoluble but could predict solubility if a distinction were made betweeen within-setting and between-setting transfer. Incorporating this assumption we can derive

$$\Delta_I = (1 - fp)(1 - B) \tag{23}$$

for the transverse patterning problem where f refers to object similarity and B represents between-setting similarities. Birch and Israel (1971) reported that increasing the distinctiveness of between-setting cues facilitated transverse pattern learning as Eq. (23) predicts.

Perhaps more significant for this analysis, the solution of the transverse patterning problem may depend much more on noticing between-setting differences rather than on abilities to perceive and abstract complex relationships. Consequently, it should not be surprising if some species to which we may not attribute such skills (e.g., cats) perform better on this type of problem than some species (e.g., monkeys) to which we would be much more likely to attribute such abilities (Joshi & Warren, 1959).

D. SUMMARY

We shall momentarily interrupt the main flow of development to offer some preliminary evaluations of the context model. As we have just seen, the context model leads to generally correct predictions concerning performance for a wide range of procedures and paradigms, and it is tempting to assert that they represent a broader range than any other discrimination learning theories have provided.

Most previous discrimination learning models have implied that different processes operate in simultaneous and successive problem learning and have been silent concerning predictions on still other paradigms. The single exception to this trend is Spiker's stimulus-interaction theory.

The stimulus-interaction hypothesis of Spiker (1963, 1970), formulated from a Hull-Spence orientation, comes closest to the present theory because it too does not assume that components are learned about in an independent manner. Spiker assumes that the habit strength occurring to a stimulus component from direct reinforcement of a compound will be reduced when that component appears in a different compound, and that the amount of reduction will increase with the average dissimilarity between the corresponding elements in the two compounds. This theory differs from the context model in that (1) information is stored separately concerning each of the component cues of a compound, and (2) the stimulus-interaction theory employs an average dissimilarity measure rather than a product rule for combining dissimilarities. The averaging rule leads to two incorrect predicitons: (1) that adding irrelevant nonspatial dimensions to successive discrimination will have no effect, and (2) that a conditional successive paradigm cannot be solved by inarticulate organisms. Of course, nothing about the stimulus-interaction hypothesis requires an averaging rule, so the theory could be improved with the addition of a multiplicative combination rule. The context theory seems to require a multiplicative rule to be consistent with the main ideas underlying the model.

The context theory suggests a different interpretation of learning paradigms designed to assess different "types" of learning. Component, compound, and configurational learning emerge as summary descriptions of performance in various situations but, according to the theory, represent neither styles nor distinct types of learning, since data from the various situations are predicted by the same process. At the least, this suggests a careful reevaluation of some implications which have been drawn from performance of different populations on various sets of paradigms.

The major shortcoming of the model as presented so far is that it contains no mechanism for predicting the various transfer effects such as faster intra- versus extra-dimensional shifts which have given rise to selective attention interpretations of discrimination learning. The next set of assumptions provides two alternative means of incorporating selective learning processes into the context model. This modification will leave the previously discussed predictions intact but will allow the model to account for many attentional phenomena, including some which have created difficulty for other attention theories.

IV. Extensions of the Context Model to Selective Learning

There is considerable sentiment that much of discrimination learning involves active processing on the part of the subject. One expression of this theme is the proposition that the salience, or degree to which an organism will attend to and learn about cues, changes during learning in such a way that irrelevant cues come to be ignored and relevant cues acquire increased salience or attention value. Lawrence's classic research on acquired distinctiveness and equivalence of cues (Lawrence, 1949, 1950) provided firm footing for such an idea and a recent careful and extensive review of research on selective learning presents a very strong case for the idea that the salience of cues can be altered by experience (Sutherland & Mackintosh, 1971).

While I believe there is little room for disagreement concerning the necessity of an attention construct in discrimination learning, it must be said that the particular forms attention theories have assumed are quite contentious. Most attention theories are characterized by two major assumptions: (1) that attention may be altered during learning in such a way that relevant cues become more likely to be observed, and (2) that attention is a fixed quantity allocated to the various dimensions so that an increase in the probability of attending to one cue must be accompanied by a compensatory decrease in the probability of attending to other cues. This latter assumption is often termed the "inverse hypothesis" or more loosely, the "pie hypothesis."

It is important to realize that these two assumptions are separable even though they seem to go together naturally. My personal impression is that research strongly favors the first hypothesis but that the inverse hypothesis is not at all well substantiated. Thomas and his associates (Thomas, 1969, 1970; Thomas, Freeman, Svinicki, Burr, & Lyons, 1970) have attacked the inverse hypothesis on empirical grounds, and theoretical alternatives to the inverse principle are beginning to appear (e.g., Kirk & Leonard, 1974; Mackintosh, 1973).

Since the solution to this issue of whether or not the inverse hypothesis ought to be embraced is outside the scope of the present chapter, I will offer two alternative forms of the model, one adopting the assumptions of a limited capacity attention model, assuming that only one dimension is observed on a single trial, and the other proposing an unlimited capacity attention model. The second form is intended to be illustrative of a general set of theories and was chosen simply because it is easy to add to a computer program and not because of its psychological content per se. None of the predictions to be considered will depend strongly on whether or not the inverse hypothesis is embraced.

A. ATTENTION ASSUMPTIONS

1. The similarity parameter for a particular dimension takes on one of two values depending upon whether or not attention is focused on that dimension. In particular, the similarity of stimulus i to stimulus j on dimension m ($G_{ij,m}$) is less when that dimension is attended to than when it is not (i.e., $G_{ij,m}$/attention $\leqslant G_{ij,m}$/no attention).

2a. (Limited capacity alternative.) Only one dimension is attended to on each trial. Reward following attention to a dimension increases the probability of attending to a dimension, while non-reward decreases the probability of attending to the dimension observed. The exact form of these changes is assumed to follow the Zeaman-House (1963) attention model.

2b. (Unlimited capacity alternative.) Every dimension is in one of two states: attended or not attended. On any nonrewarded trial, there is a probability C_i for each dimension i that a transition from its current state to the alternative state will occur. That is, after an error, subjects reevaluate their strategies and may start attending to dimensions which they did not attend to before, and they may stop attending to dimensions which were observed before.

Several comments are in order concerning these assumptions. Assumption 1 is much weaker than that of most attention theories, which generally assume no generalization along observed dimensions and complete generalization along dimensions not observed (i.e., $G_{ij,m}$/attention = 0 and $G_{ij,m}$/no attention = 1). The present assumption allows attention to control generalization but only proposes that generalization gradients generally are sharper along observed dimensions. That is, the subject can learn about all dimensions on a trial but learns relatively more about a dimension when it is observed than when it is not observed.

The second two assumptions alternatively adopt and discard the inverse hypothesis. The reader more interested in alternative forms and characteristics of attention theories is referred to Shepp, Kemler, and Anderson (1972) and Anderson, Kemler, and Shepp (1973) for further discussion.

One other important distinction, first formally considered by Lovejoy (1968), is between attention controlling choices and attention altering what is learned. The attention version of the context model assumes that attention does not directly influence choices but that it exerts its influence by controlling the amount of generalization and thereby learning. That is, since context controls retrieval of information, the feedback for *left* in a context where a triangle appears in that position is the same as the feedback value for *triangle* in the context of its appearing on the left. The advantage of this property is that the choice situation can still be viewed as involving just two choices when there are two stimuli, even though there may be many component cues present in the situation.

Consideration will now be given to the predictions arising from the context model which assumes that attention influences generalization. We shall focus on bringing out some predictions and findings which are not consonant with various other attention theories. Some data concerning such effects as relationships between pretraining and generalization are not considered because they may support the general construct of attention without necessarily differentiating the various attention models which have been proposed.

B. PREDICTIONS OF THE CONTEXT MODEL WITH ASSUMPTIONS CONCERNING ATTENTION

1. Form of the Learning Curve

Ogival forward learning curves and quite flat backward learning curves like those reported by Zeaman and House (1963) may be obtained. This will occur when the generalization between cues on the relevant dimension is high unless that dimension is observed (i.e., for weak cues). Such effects should not be evident for more salient cues since learning about the relevant dimension can occur even when the relevant dimension is not observed. This latter prediction also implies that as a result of a single trial, a subject may learn about more than just one cue, as was found by Eimas (1964, 1965) and House and Zeaman (1963), for example.

2. Shift Effects

a. Intra- and Extradimensional Shifts. Intradimensional shifts are predicted to be learned faster than extradimensional shifts. Attention to a dimension in the context model works by means of reducing the effective similarity of cues on that dimension. Since, in general, similarity of irrelevant cues facilitates and similarity of relevant cues impairs learning, intradimensional shifts should be easier because the relevant dimension is more likely to be observed, while irrelevant dimensions are less likely to be attended to at the time of transfer for intradimensional than for extradimensional shifts. Of course, if the change in context between learning and transfer is too great, one would expect little or no transfer (see, e.g., Blank, 1967; Campione, 1973; Campione & Beaton, 1972). This caution notwithstanding, intradimensional shifts have been shown to be learned faster than extradimensional shifts in rats, pigeons, monkeys, and children and adult human subjects (for a full review, consult Sutherland & Mackintosh, 1971).

Contrary to many other attention models, the context theory predicts that intra- and extradimensional shift differences may interact with salience of dimensions in such a way that an extradimensional shift to a salient dimension (i.e., one with large cue differences) may be learned faster than an intradimensional shift to a less salient dimension. This can occur if the similarity of cues along a salient dimension when it is not observed is less than the similarity of cues along a less salient dimension when it is observed. This predicted interaction has been obtained fairly frequently (e.g., Campione, 1969; Campione, Hyman, & Zeaman, 1965; Mackintosh & Little, 1969; Tighe, Brown, & Youngs, 1965).

The context model also predicts that optional intradimensional and reversal shifts are more likely to occur for salient dimensions, a result commonly reported (e.g., Caron, 1969; T. S. Kendler, Basden, & Bruckner, 1970; Schwartz, Schwartz, & Tees, 1971; Smiley, 1972; Tighe & Tighe, 1966). Again the prediction follows from the idea that the similarity of cues on a salient dimension is less than the similarity of cues for less salient dimensions. The training preceding the optional shift will proceed more rapidly for salient dimensions and subjects will be more likely to attend to these dimensions during the trials preceding and at the beginning of the optional shift.

b. Shifts between Simultaneous and Successive Discriminations. One finding often cited as supporting attention theories is the demonstration that subjects pretrained on a simultaneous discrimination subsequently learn a successive discrimination more rapidly when the same stimulus dimension is relevant in both tasks than when the relevant dimensions are shifted between the first and second problem (e.g., Lawrence, 1949; Mumma & Warren, 1968; Warren & McGonigle, 1969). The context model predicts such a result, but it is difficult to see the basis for this prediction in other theories. If a successive discrimination can be solved only by attending to compound dimensions (as these theories almost always assume), then the prediction of positive transfer must be based on the unstated assumption that attending to the relevant dimension on a simultaneous problem increases the probability of attending to a compound including the relevant dimension in the successive paradigm.

c. Reversal–Nonreversal Shift Comparisons. Previous investigators have shown that the relative rates of acquiring reversal and nonreversal shifts are not especially diagnostic for testing theories but that more detailed analyses of shift learning might be (see especially Tighe, 1973; Tighe, Glick, & Cole, 1971; Tighe & Tighe, 1972). One such analysis involves performance on the two subproblems of a nonreversal shift, one of which does not and one of which does change reward relationships between original learning and the shift. All attention models proposed to date have assumed that the two subproblems are treated as a single problem. When coupled with the assumption that the components are independent, these theories can be shown to fail to account for the relationships between performance on the changed and unchanged problems of a nonreversal shift (Medin, 1973). This failure extends to data obtained with rats, monkeys, pigeons, and turtles (e.g., Graf & Tighe, 1971; Medin, 1973; Tighe, 1973; Tighe & Frey, 1972). The context model is able to handle changed and unchanged subproblem relations because varying degrees of dependence and nonindependence may be observed at the level of subproblems because the components are not assumed to be independent. A more detailed account is beyond the scope of this chapter.

d. Objects-to-Position Shifts. The context model is capable of predicting transfer effects in situations in which the predictions of other attention theories are at best unclear. Consider the four para-

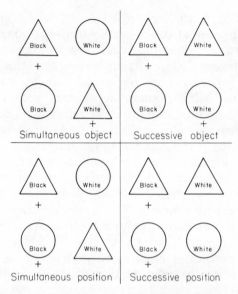

Fig. 15. Simultaneous object and position discriminations and successive object and position discriminations.

digms shown in Fig. 15. The comparison of interest centers on transfer from simultaneous or successive object discriminations to simultaneous or successive positional discriminations. Brightness has been added, correlated with position, so as to make the successive object problems easier and the simultaneous object problems a little more difficult. Expectations concerning transfer and relative rates of learning can be seen from prediction equations for the various problem formats. In the simultaneous object problem,

$$\Delta_I = (1 - f)(1 + bp); \tag{24}$$

for the successive object problem,

$$\Delta_I = (1 - f)(1 - bp); \tag{25}$$

and for both position discrimination problems,

$$\Delta_I = (1 + f)(1 - bp). \tag{26}$$

First, it can be seen that simultaneous object discriminations should be easier than successive object problems (unless bp is equal to zero). Secondly, in the simultaneous object problem it is advantageous to ignore brightness and position cues, but performance will improve when these cues are attended to for successive object problems. On the average, according to the context model, subjects will be more likely to attend to brightness and position after a simultaneous object discrimination. Consequently, there should be better transfer from successive object problems to position problems than from simultaneous object to position problems, since it is also beneficial to attend to brightness and position cues on the position discriminations. To test this implication, five test-experienced pigtailed monkeys were run on a series of four discrimination shifts representing the two kinds of object discriminations. Brightness differences were always present and perfectly correlated with position, but four distinct sets of forms were used for the four sets of learning and transfer problems.

As expected, successive object discriminations proved to be more difficult than simultaneous object discriminations (mean errors of 3.0 versus 10.7) and there was no difference observed between simultaneous position problems (average of 5.4 errors) and successive position problems (average of 6.0 errors). Performance on the position discriminations depended upon the type of problem preceding them. Following simultaneous object discriminations, subjects averaged 7.1 errors, and following successive object discriminations, they averaged 4.3 errors on position discriminations—a reliable difference.

Analysis of the two settings comprising the position discrimination problems brings out further relevant results. First, transfer between the two settings of a conditional position problem (involving a difference $f - fbp$) should be greater than transfer between the two settings of a simultaneous position problem (involving a difference $f - bp$). Although overall performance was comparable for the two position formats, errors in the simultaneous position problem were reliably more frequent when consecutive trials involved a switch in settings rather than the same two settings, in comparison with successive positional discriminations. In addition, subjects who had learned to ignore position and brightness (i.e., subjects pretrained on simultaneous object discriminations) should and did show these effects to a greater extent than subjects who had learned to attend to brightness and position.

One might attempt to account for these results by suggesting that successive object discriminations teach animals to attend to compound cues, but whether or not this would facilitate positional discriminations is most unclear. Nor is it obvious how attending to compounds would produce the observed differences in transfer between the two settings of the two formats for position discrimination learning.

   e. *Easy-to-Hard Transfer.* A discrimination between two similar cues may often be facilitated by pretraining on a problem with the same relevant dimension using larger cue differences (see Sutherland & Mackintosh, 1971, for a general review). The context model predicts easy-to-hard facilitation since attention will be directed to the relevant dimension. The only difficulty other attention models may have in accounting for this result is that many such theories contain no mechanism for cue similarity along the relevant dimension to alter the rate of learning.

   f. *Blocking, Overshadowing, and Incidental Learning.* What is learned about a cue on a problem depends upon what other cues are present and the previous history of reinforcement with respect to these cues. When a second relevant cue is added after training on a problem with a given relevant cue, sometimes nothing seems to be learned concerning the new relevant cue (i.e., blocking occurs), and sometimes something is learned about the new cue (incidental learning), but less than would have been learned had no pretraining been given on the other cue (e.g., D. F. Johnson, 1966, 1970; C. G. Miles, 1970; Vom Saal & Jenkins, 1970). By the same token, less may be learned about a cue when it is paired with other relevant cues than if it appears alone, again producing overshadowing effects (e.g., Lovejoy & Russell, 1967; Mackintosh, 1965; Williams, 1971). A general review of these data appears in the book by Sutherland and Mackintosh (1971).[3]

   The context model predicts that both blocking and overshadowing may occur but that results will interact with dimensional salience. That is, strong or salient cues may block and overshadow other cues, but weak cues will not block and overshadow salient cues. Weak cues may be overshadowed or blocked because generalization may be complete, unless their dimension is observed. Although this result appears to favor assumption 2(a), it may be obtained from assumption 2(b) because salient cues will produce learning with few errors

---

[3] It should be noted that the domain under consideration here is instrumental learning where subjects respond by approaching or avoiding cues. Very strong blocking is obtained in classical conditioning paradigms (see Kamin, 1969; Rescorla & Wagner, 1972; Wagner & Rescorla, 1972) but the scope of the present analysis does not permit consideration of these situations. Estes (1973a) has provided some initial applications of a model similar in spirit to the present model to these paradigms.

and it is less likely that learning will occur with the less salient dimension being attended to than in the case where weak cues are the only relevant cues. On the other hand, strong or salient dimensions cannot be overshadowed because the similarity of the cues will still be low even when the dimension is not observed. Mackintosh's (1973) recent review of the literature in this area seems consonant with these predictions.

By the same line of reasoning, the context model expects that subjects will generally learn about more than a single dimension in redundant relevant cue discriminations but that they may still show a negative correlation between the amount learned about one cue and the amount learned about the other cues. It is hard to make an unequivocal prediction (and the data are equally equivocal) because of a variety of reasons why one normally might expect positive correlations to be observed.

Overall, the modified context model seems consistent with the main sets of findings on selective attention and may even offer advantages over other attention theories. It does seem clear that it is possible to manage with only weak assumptions concerning attention. At the same time, it is equally clear that considerable effort is in order to sharpen up the assumptions concerning attention and to bring data and theory into more intimate contact.

V. Discussion and Summary

In perspective, what is this chapter about? Wondering whether irrelevant cues confounded with position helps or hurts learning in some particular paradigm seems a far cry from the "really significant questions" such as what the basis of transfer (or abstraction or schema development) might be or how perceptual processes are related to learning. It certainly seems appropriate to keep an eye on the broader goals, but at the same time the related task of adequately describing performance in a variety of species, situations, and paradigms may serve to allow the important variables to stand out in relief against a background provided by a range of experimental contrasts. The context model does succeed in predicting performance in many different problem formats without altering any basic assumptions and, with the addition of assumptions concerning attention, corresponds very well with data on selective learning.

I feel a note of apology or explanation is in order for the somewhat flippant manner in which studies on such groups as rats, turtles, cats, monkeys, and children have been thrown together. But in a real sense, it is not obvious what can be said. The strategy presented reflects the assumption that some processes such as those related to the influence of context may be widespread phylogenetically in their influence and that, when fundamentally different behavior appears ontogenetically or phylogenetically, our skill in interpreting this difference will vary directly with the breadth and accuracy of our current accounts of discrimination learning.

Having said this, I would like to offer one speculation concerning the ontogenetic development of discrimination performance. Since the early work of the Kendlers (T. S. Kendler & Kendler, 1962), it has been popular to assume that one of the major developmental changes in children's learning involves increased mediation or attentional processes common to selective learning theories. However, optional intradimensional shifts (one index of mediation) are preferred to optional extradimensional shifts even in rats (Schwartz *et al.*, 1971), and only modest changes in the predominance of these shifts occur developmentally in human subjects (Campione, 1970; H. H. Kendler, Kendler, & Ward, 1972). As either an alternative or a refinement to the idea that mediation develops, the present work may lead one to guess that the major developmental shifts could involve the ability to overcome the effects of particularized contexts on performance (i.e., abstraction skills). Not much research has been devoted to this topic. Rosenberg and Birch (1969) reported major age shifts in the influence of irrelevant stimulus changes on the maintenance of a learned size discrimination. On the other hand, Campione (1973) found little differences in carry-over between simultaneous and successive paradigms in second- and fifth-grade children. The idea that developmental changes in learning may involve a decrease in context-bound performance is not new (e.g., Tighe & Tighe, 1972), but the present context model may provide a useful beginning point for the development of a theory of contextual influences in transfer of training.

REFERENCES

Anderson, D. R., Kemler, D. G., & Shepp, B. E. Selective attention and dimensional learning: A logical analysis of two-stage attention theories. *Bulletin of the Psychonomic Society*, 1973, 2, 273–275.

Atkinson, R. C. A theory of stimulus discrimination learning. In L. J. Arrow, S. Karlin, & P. Suppes (Eds.), *Mathematical methods in the social sciences*. Stanford, Calif.: Stanford University Press, 1959. Pp. 221–241.

Atkinson, R. C., & Estes, W. K. Stimulus sampling theory. In R. D. Luce, R. R. Bush, & E. Galanter (Eds.), *Handbook of mathematical psychology*. New York: Wiley, 1963. Pp. 121–268.

Babb, H. Transfer from a stimulus complex to differentially discriminable components. *Journal of Comparative and Physiological Psychology*, 1957, **50**, 288–299.

Behar, I. Evaluation of the significance of positive and negative cue in discrimination learning. *Journal of Comparative and Physiological Psychology*, 1962, **55**, 502–504.

Birch, D. B., & Israel, M. Solution of the transverse patterning problem: Response to cue-cue relations. *Psychonomic Science*, 1971, **23**, 383–384.

Birch, D., & Vandenberg, V. The necessary conditions for cue-position patterning. *Journal of Experimental Psychology*, 1955, **50**, 391–396.

Bitterman, M. E., Tyler, D. W., & Elam, C. B. Simultaneous and successive discrimination under identical stimulating conditions. *American Journal of Psychology*, 1955, **68**, 237–248.

Bitterman, M. E., & Wodinsky, J. Simultaneous and successive discrimination. *Psychological Review*, 1953, **60**, 371–376.

Blank, M. Effect of stimulus characteristics on dimensional shifting in kindergarten children. *Journal of Comparative and Physiological Psychology*, 1967, **64**, 522–525.

Brown, W. L., & Carr, R. M. The learning of incidental cues by rhesus monkeys. *Journal of Comparative and Physiological Psychology*, 1958, **51**, 459–460.

Burke, C. J., & Estes, W. K. A component model for stimulus variables in discrimination learning. *Psychometrika*, 1957, **22**, 133–145.

Bush, R. R. Identification learning. In D. P. Luce, R. R. Bush, & E. Galanter (Eds.), *Handbook of mathematical psychology*. Vol. 3. New York: Wiley, 1965. Pp. 161–203.

Bush, R. R., & Mosteller, F. A model for stimulus generalization and discrimination. *Psychological Review*, 1951, **58**, 413–423.

Campione, J. E. Intra- and extradimensional shifts in retardates as a function of dimensional preference. *American Journal of Psychology*, 1969, **82**, 212–220.

Campione, J. C. Optional intradimensional and extradimensional shifts in children as a function of age. *Journal of Experimental Psychology*, 1970, **84**, 296–300.

Campione, J. C. The generality of transfer: Effects of age and similarity of training and transfer tasks. *Journal of Experimental Child Psychology*, 1973, **15**, 94–114.

Campione, J. C., & Beaton, V. L. Transfer of training: some boundary conditions and initial theory. *Journal of Experimental Child Psychology*, 1972, **13**, 94–114.

Campione, J. C., Hyman, L., & Zeaman, D. Dimensional shifts and reversal in retardate discrimination learning. *Journal of Experimental Child Psychology*, 1965, **2**, 255–263.

Campione, J. C., McGrath, M., & Rabinowitz, F. M. Component and configurational learning in children: Additional data. *Journal of Experimental Psychology*, 1971, **88**, 137–139.

Caron, A. J. Discrimination shifts in three-year-olds as a function of dimentional salience. *Developmental Psychology*, 1969, **1**, 333–339.

Caron, A. J. Discrimination shifts in three-year-olds as a function of shift procedure. *Developmental Psychology*, 1970, **3**, 236–241.

Carr, H. A. More studies with the white rat. I. Normal animals. *Journal of Animal Behavior*, 1917, **7**, 259–275.

Eimas, P. D. Components and compounds in discrimination learning of retarded children. *Journal of Experimental Child Psychology*, 1964, **1**, 301–310.

Eimas, P. D. Stimulus compounding in the discrimination learning of kindergarten children. *Journal of Experimental Child Psychology* 1965, **2**, 178–185.

Elias, M. F., & Stein, A. I. Relation of pattern spacing to pattern discrimination in the hooded rat. *Perceptual and Motor Skills*, 1968, 26(2), 447–454.

Estes, W. K. Theoretical treatments of differential reward in multiple-choice learning and two-person interactions. In J. Criswell, H. Solomon, & P. Suppes (Eds.), *Mathematical methods in small group processes*. Stanford, Calif.: Stanford University Press, 1962. Pp. 133–140.

Estes, W. K. Transfer of verbal discriminations based on differential reward magnitudes. *Journal of Experimental Psychology*, 1966, 72, 276–283.

Estes, W. K. New perspectives on some old issues in association theory. In N. J. Mackintosh & W. K. Honig (Eds.), *Fundamental issues in associative learning*. Halifax, Can.: Dalhousie University Press, 1969. Pp. 162–189. (a)

Estes, W. K. Outline of a theory of punishment. In B. A. Campbell & R. M. Church (Eds.), *Punishment and aversive behavior*. New York: Appleton, 1969. Pp. 57–82. (b)

Estes, W. K. Reinforcement in human learning. In J. Tapp (Ed.), *Reinforcement and behavior*. New York: Academic Press, 1969. Pp. 63–94. (c)

Estes, W. K. Context in conditioning. Paper presented at a conference on discrimination learning models, Rockefeller University, New York, April 1973. (a)

Estes, W. K. Memory and Conditioning. In F. J. McGuigan & D. B. Lumsden (Eds.), *Contemporary approaches to conditioning and learning*. Washington, D.C.: Winston, 1973. Pp. 265–286. (b)

Estes, W. K., & Hopkins, B. L. Acquisition and transfer in pattern vs. component discrimination learning. *Journal of Experimental Psychology*, 1961, 61, 322–328.

Estes, W. K., Hopkins, B. L., & Crothers, E. J. All-or-none and conservation effects in the learning and retention of paired associates. *Journal of Experimental Psychology*, 1960, 60, 329–339.

Evans, R. A., & Beedle, R. K. Discrimination learning in mentally retarded children as a function of irrelevant dimension variability. *American Journal of Mental Deficiency*, 1970, 74, 568–573.

Fisher, M. A., & Zeaman, D. An attention-retention theory of retardate discrimination learning. In N. R. Ellis (Ed.), *International review of research in mental retardation*. Vol. 6. New York: Academic Press, 1972. Pp. 169–256.

Flagg, S. F. Learning of the insoluble condsitional reaction problem by rhesus monkeys. *Animal Learning and Behavior*, 1974, 2, 181–184.

Flagg, S. F., & Medin, D. L. Constant irrelevant cues and stimulus generalization in monkeys. *Journal of Comparative and Physiological Psychology*, 1973, 85, 339–345.

Girden, E. Conditioning and problem-solving behavior. *American Journal of Psychology*, 1938, 51, 677–687.

Glendenning, R. A., & Meyer, D. R. Motivationally related retroactive interference in discrimination learning by rats. *Journal of Comparative and Physiological Psychology*, 1971, *i*5, 153–156.

Graf, V., & Tighe, T. J. Subproblem analysis of discrimination shift learning in the turtle (*Chrysemys picta*). *Psychonomic Science*, 1971, 25, 257–259.

Gulliksen, H., & Wolfe, H. L. A theory of learning and transfer: I. *Psychometrika*, 1938, 3, 127–149. (a)

Gulliksen, H., & Wolfe, H. L. A theory of learning and transfer: II. *Psychometrika*, 1938, 3, 225–251. (b)

House, B. J., & Zeaman, D. Minature experiments in retardate discrimination learning. In L. P. Lipsitt & C. C. Spiker (Eds.), *Advances in child development and behavior*. Vol. 1. New York: Academic Press, 1963. Pp. 313–373.

Hoyt, J. M. Effect of similarity of reversal cues on learning of successive stimulus reversals in children. Unpublished master's thesis, University of Iowa, 1960.

Hoyt, J. M. Serial reversal and conditional discrimination learning in children. Unpublished doctoral dissertation, University of Iowa, 1962.

Johnson, B. The effect of training on cue-position patterning in discrimination problems. Unpublished doctoral dissertation, State University of Iowa, 1962.

Johnson, D. F. Determiners of selective discrimination stimulus control. Unpublished doctoral dissertation, Columbia University, 1966.

Johnson, D. F. Determiners of selective stimulus control in the pigeon. *Journal of Comparative and Physiological Psychology*, 1970, **70**, 298–307.

Joshi, B. L., & Warren, J. M. Discrimination of ambivalent cue stimuli by cats. *Journal of Psychology*, 1959, **47**, 3–7.

Kamin, L. J. Predictability, surprise, attention and conditioning. In R. Church & B. Campbell (Eds.), *Punishment and aversive behavior*. New York: Appleton, 1969. Pp. 279–296.

Kendler, H. H., Kendler, T. S., & Ward, J. W. Ontogenetic analysis of optional intradimensional and extradimensional shifts. *Journal of Experimental Psychology*, 1972, **95**, 102–109.

Kendler, T. S., Basden, B. H., & Bruckner, J. B. Dimensional dominance and continuity theory. *Journal of Experimental Psychology*, 1970, **83**, 309–318.

Kendler, T. S., & Kendler, H. H. Vertical and horizontal processes in problem solving. *Psychological Review*, 1962, **69**, 1–16.

Kirk, R. J., & Leonard, D. W. Saliency modification of neocontinuity theory. Paper presented at the meeting of the Midwestern Psychological Association, Chicago, May 1974.

Lashley, K. S. Conditional reactions in the rat. *Journal of Psychology*, 1938, **6**, 311–324.

Lawrence, D. H. Acquired distinctiveness of cues. I. Transfer between discriminations on the basis of familiarity with the stimulus. *Journal of Experimental Psychology*, 1949, **39**, 770–784.

Lawrence, D. H. Acquired distinctiveness of cues. II. Selective association in a constant stimulus situation. *Journal of Experimental Psychology*, 1950, **40**, 175–188.

Lawrence, D. H., & Mason, W. H. Systematic behavior during discrimination reversal and change of dimension. *Journal of Comparative Physiological Psychology*, 1955, **48**, 1–7.

Liddell, H. S. Higher nervous activity in the thyroidectomised sheep and goat. *Quarterly Journal of Experimental Psychology*, 1927, **17**, 41–51.

Lipsitt, L. P. Simultaneous and successive discrimination learning in children. *Child Development*, 1961, **32**, 337–347.

Liu, S. W., & Zeiler, M. D. Independence of concurrent discriminations. *Journal of Comparative and Physiological Psychology*, 1968, **65**, 61–65.

Lovejoy, E. An attention theory of discrimination learning. *Journal of Mathematical Psychology*, 1965, **2**, 342–362.

Lovejoy, E. *Attention in discrimination learning*. San Francisco: Holden-Day, 1968.

Lovejoy, E., & Russell, D. G. Suppression of learning about a hard cue by the presence of an easy cue. *Psychonomic Science*, 1967, **8**, 365–366.

Lubker, B. J. The effect of training on cue-position patterning in discrimination learning by children. *Journal of Experimental Psychology*, 1964, **1**, 135–144.

Lubker, B. J. Irrelevant stimulus dimensions and children's performance on simultaneous discrimination problems. *Child Development*, 1967, **38**, 120–125.

Lubker, B. J. Setting similarity and successive discrimination learning by children. *Journal of Experimental Child Psychology*, 1969, **7**, 188–194.

MacCaslin, E. F. Successive and simultaneous discrimination as a function of stimulus similarity. *American Journal of Psychology*, 1954, 67, 308–314.

Mackintosh, N. J. Overtraining, extinction, and reversal in rats and chicks. *Journal of Comparative and Physiological Psychology*, 1965, 59, 31–36.

Mackintosh, N. J. A theory of attention: Variations in the associability of stimuli with reinforcement. Paper presented at a conference on discrimination learning models, Rockefeller University, New York, April 1973.

Mackintosh, N. J., & Little, L. Intradimensional and extradimensional shift learning by Pigeons. *Psychonomic Science*, 1969, 14, 5–6.

Medin, D. L. Subproblem analysis of discrimination shift learning. *Behavior Research Methods and Instrumentation*, 1973, 5, 332–336.

Medin, D. L. Position distinctiveness and successive discrimination learning. *Bulletin of the Psychonomic Society*, 1974, 4, 35–36. (a)

Medin, D. L. Reward pretraining and discrimination learning set. *Animal Learning and Behavior*, 1974, 2, 305–308.

Medin, D. L., & Davis, R. T. Color discrimination by rhesus monkeys. *Psychonomic Science*, 1967, 1, 33–34.

Meyer, D. R., Treichler, F. R., & Meyer, P. M. Discrete-trial training techniques and stimulus variables. In A. M. Schrier, H. F. Harlow, & F. Stollnitz (Eds.), *Behavior of nonhuman primates*. Vol. 1. New York: Academic Press, 1965. Pp. 1–49.

Miles, C. G. Blocking the acquisition of control by an auditory stimulus with pretraining on brightness. *Psychonomic Science*, 1970, 9, 133–134.

Miles, R. J., & Edenborough, R. A. The role of constant irrelevant cues in discrimination learning in the hodded rat. *Papers in Psychology*, 1968, 2, 20–24.

Mumma, R., & Warren, J. M. Two-cue discrimination learning by cats. *Journal of Comparative and Physiological Psychology*, 1968, 66, 116–122.

Nissen, H. W. Ambivalent cues in discriminative behavior of chimpanzees. *Journal of Psychology*, 1942, 14, 3–33.

Nissen, H. W. Description of the learned response in discrimination behavior. *Psychological Review*, 1950, 59, 121–137.

Price, L. E., & Spiker, C. C. Effect of similarity of irrelevant stimuli on performance in discrimination learning problems. *Journal of Experimental Child Psychology*, 1967, 5, 324–331.

Rescorla, R. A., & Wagner, A. R. A theory of Pavlovian conditioning: Variations in the effectiveness of reinforcement and nonreinforcement. In A. H. Black & W. F. Prokasy (Eds.), *Classical conditioning*. Vol. II. New York: Appleton, 1972. Pp. 64–99.

Restle, F. A theory of discrimination learning. *Psychological Review*, 1955, 62, 11–19.

Restle, F. *Psychology of Judgment and choice*. New York: Wiley, 1961.

Robbins, M. J., & Meyer, D. R. Motivational control of retrograde amnesia. *Journal of Experimental Psychology*, 1970, 84, 220–225.

Rosenberg, J. K., & Birch, H. G. Age effects of irrelevant stimulus changes on a discrimination by children. *Perceptual and Motor Skills*, 1969, 28, 467–475.

Schwartz, R. M., Schwartz, M., & Tees, R. C. Optional intradimensional and extradimensional shifts in the rat. *Journal of Comparative and Physiological Psychology*, 1971, 77, 470–475.

Shepp, B. E. Some cue properties of anticipated rewards in discrimination learning of retardates. *Journal of Comparative and Physiological Psychology*, 1962, 59, 856–859.

Shepp, B. E. Some cue properties of rewards in simultaneous object discriminations of retardates. *Child Development*, 1964, 35, 587–592.

Shepp, B. E., & Gray, V. D. Effects of variable-within and variable between irrelevant stimuli on dimensional learning and transfer. *Journal of Experimental Psychology*, 1971, 89, 32–39.

Shepp, B. E., Kemler, D. G., & Anderson, D. A. Selective attention and the breadth of learning: an extension of the one-look model. *Psychological Review*, 1972, 79, 317–328.

Shepp, B. E., & Zeaman, D. Discrimination learning of size and brightness by retardates. *Journal of Comparative and Physiological Psychology*, 1966, 62, 55–59.

Smiley, S. S. Optional shift behavior as a function of dimensional preference and relative cue similarity. *Journal of Experimental Child Psychology*, 1972, 14, 313–322.

Spence, K. W. The nature of discrimination learning in animals. *Psychological Review*, 1936, 43, 427–449.

Spence, K. W. The nature of the response in discrimination learning. *Psychological Review*, 1952, 59, 89–93.

Spiker, C. C. The hypothesis of stimulus interaction and an explanation of stimulus compounding. In L. P. Lipsitt & C. C. Spiker (Eds.), *Advances in child development and behavior*. Vol. 1. New York: Academic Press, 1963. Pp. 233–264.

Spiker, C. C. An extension of Hull-Spence discrimination learning theory. *Psychological Review*, 1970, 77, 496–515.

Spiker, C. C., & Lubker, B. J. Experimental tests of the hypothesis of stimulus interaction. *Journal of Experimental Child Psychology*, 1964, 1, 256–268.

Spiker, C. C., & Lubker, B. J. The relative difficulty for children of the successive and simultaneous discrimination problems. *Child Development*, 1965, 36, 1091–1101.

Sternberg, S. H. A path-dependent linear model. In R. R. Bush & W. K. Estes (Eds.), *Studies in mathematical learning theory*. Stanford, Calif.: Stanford University Press, 1959. Pp. 308–339.

Sutherland, N. S., & Mackintosh, N. J. *Mechanisms of animal discrimination learning*. New York: Academic Press, 1971.

Teas, R. C., & Bitterman, M. E. Perceptual organization in the rat. *Psychological Review*, 1952, 59, 130–140.

Thomas, D. R. The use of operant conditioning techniques to investigate perceptual processes in animals. In R. Gilbert & N. S. Sutherland (Eds.), *Animal discrimination learning*. New York: Academic Press, 1969. Pp. 1–33.

Thomas, D. R. Stimulus selection, attention, and related matters. In J. H. Reynierse (Ed.), *Current issues in animal learning*. Lincoln, Neb.: University of Nebraska Press, 1970. Pp. 311–356.

Thomas, D. R., Freeman, F., Svinicki, J. G., Burr, D. E. S., & Lyons, J. Effects of extradimensional training on stimulus generalization. *Journal of Experimental Psychology Monograph*, 1970, 83, 1–21.

Tighe, T. J. Subproblem analysis of discrimination learning. In G. H. Bower (Ed.), *The psychology of learning and motivation*. Vol. 7. New York: Academic Press, 1973. Pp. 183–226.

Tighe, T. J., Brown, P. L., & Youngs, E. A. The effect of overtraining on the shift behavior of albino rats. *Psychonomic Science*, 1965, 2, 141–142.

Tighe, T. J., & Frey, K. Subproblem analysis of discrimination shift learning in the rat. *Psychonomic Science*, 1972, 28, 129–133.

Tighe, T. J., Glick, J., & Cole, M. Subproblem analysis of discrimination-shift learning. *Psychonomic Science*, 1971, 24, 159–160.

Tighe, T. J., & Tighe, L. S. Overtraining and optional shift behavior in rats and children. *Journal of Comparative and Physiological Psychology*, 1966, 62, 49–54.

Tighe, T. J., & Tighe, L. S. Stimulus control in children's learning. In A. D. Pick (Ed.), *Minnesota symposia on child psychology*. Vol. 6. Minneapolis: University of Minnesota Press, 1972. Pp. 128–157.

Trabasso, T., & Bower, G. H. *Attention in learning: Theory and research*. New York: Wiley, 1968.

Tragakis, C. J. The effects of manipulating irrelevant dimensions in successive discrimination problems. Unpublished master's thesis, University of Iowa, 1968.

Turbeville, J. R., Calvin, A. D., & Bitterman, M. E. Relational and configurational learning in the rat. *American Journal of Psychology*, 1952, 65, 424–433.

Vom Saal, W., & Jenkins, H. M. Blocking the development of stimulus control. *Learning and Motivation*, 1970, 1, 52–64.

von Wright, J. M. The effect of systematic changes of context stimulation on repeated recall. *Acta Psychologica*, 1959, 16, 59–168.

Wagner, A. R., & Rescorla, R. A. Inhibition in Pavlovian conditionings: Application of a theory. In R. A. Boakes & M. S. Halliday (Eds.), *Inhibition and learning*. New York: Academic Press, 1972, Pp. 301–336.

Warren, J. M. Additivity of cues in visual pattern discrimination by monkeys. *Journal of Comparative and Physiological Psychology*, 1954, 46, 484–486.

Warren, J. M. Additivity of cues in conditional discrimination learning by rhesus monkeys. *Journal of Comparative and Physiological Psychology*, 1964, 58, 124–126.

Warren, J. M., & Baron, A. Acquisition of successive and simultaneous discrimination habits by cats. *Journal of Genetic Psychology*, 1956, 89, 61–64.

Warren, J. M., & McGonigle, B. Attention theory and discrimination learning. In R. M. Gilbert & N. S. Sutherland (Eds.), *Animal discrimination learning*. New York: Academic Press, 1969. Pp. 113–136.

White, B. N., & Spiker, C. C. The effect of stimulus similarity on amount of cue-position patterning in discrimination problems. *Journal of Experimental Psychology*, 1960, 59, 131–136.

Williams, D. I. Constant irrelevant cue learning in the pigeon. *Animal Behaviour*, 1967, 15, 229–230.

Williams, D. I. Discrimination learning in pigeon with two relevant cues, one hard and one easy. *British Journal of Psychology*, 1971, 63, 407–409.

Wodinsky, J., Varley, M. A., & Bitterman, M. E. Situational determinants of the relative difficulty of simultaneous and successive discrimination. *Journal of Comparative and Physiological Psychology*, 1954, 47, 337–340.

Zeaman, D., & House, B. J. The role of attention in retardate discrimination learning. In N. R. Ellis, (Ed.), *Handbook of mental deficiency: Psychological theory and research*. New York: McGraw-Hill, 1963. Pp. 159–223.

Zeiler, M. D. Component and configurational learning in children. *Journal of Experimental Psychology*, 1964, 68, 292–296.

Zeiler, M. D., & Paul, B. J. Intra-pair similarity as a determinant of component and configuration discrimination. *American Journal of Psychology*, 1963, 78, 476–480.

Zentall, T. R. Effects of context change on forgetting in rats. *Journal of Experimental Psychology*, 1970, 86, 440–448.

Appendix

To avoid unnecessary redundancy, the results from simulations will only be briefly presented. The format will be a summary statement, the parameters used (b, p, and s, plus a learning rate parameter, θ), the results, and a reference equation and figure. For some novel findings, a little more discussion will be provided. The initial feedback values for each of the choices was set at .50, and θ was set at .50 unless otherwise specified. In each case, 50 statistical subjects were run for 25 trials on each setting or until learning was complete.

Appendix

Statement	Parameters	Results [Mean Errors]	Equation	Figure
Simultaneous				
1. Position similarity helps	$b = .20$, $p = .30$ $b = .20$, $p = .70$	2.06 1.48	7	1(left)
2. Brightness similarity hurts	$b = .00$, $p = .30$ $b = .20$, $p = .30$ $b = .50$, $p = .30$	1.46 2.06 7.14	7	1(left)
3. Redundant relevant cues help	$b = .20$, $p = .30$, $s = 1.00$ $b = .20$, $p = .30$, $s = .30$	2.06 1.66	10	4(left)
Successive				
1. Position similarity hurts	$\theta = .50$ $b = .20$, $p = .30$ $b = .20$, $p = .50$	5.52 17.30	8	1(left)
2. Brightness similarity hurts	$b = .00$, $p = .30$ $b = .20$, $p = .30$ $b = .50$, $p = .30$	2.72 5.52 38.26	8	1(right)
3. Redundant relevant cues help	$b = .20$ $p = .30$, $s = 1.00$ $b = .20$ $p = .30$, $s = .30$	5.52 3.64	11	4(right)

(continued)

Appendix (continued)

Simultaneous versus Successive

Statement	Parameters	Results [Mean Errors]	Equation	Figure
1. Simultaneous easier than successive and more so as the distinctiveness of the relevant cue lessens:	$p = .30$	succ./sim.=1.86	7,8	1
	$b = .00$	succ./sim.=2.68		
	$b = .20$	succ./sim.=5.36		
	$b = .50$			
2. Irrelevant cues confounded with position hurts simultaneous and helps successive:				
Simultaneous	$b = .20, \quad p = .30, \quad s = 1.00$	2.06	12	6/(left)
	$b = .20, \quad p = .30, \quad s = 0.30$	2.90		
Successive	$b = .20, \quad p = .30, \quad s = 1.00$	5.52	13	6(right)
	$b = .20, \quad p = .30, \quad s = 0.30$	3.40		
3. Irrelevant cues not confounded with position hurts both simultaneous and successive:				
Simultaneous	$b = .20, \quad p = .30, \quad s = 1.00$	1.96	14	7(left)
	$b = .20, \quad p = .30, \quad s = 0.30$	3.66		
Successive	$b = .20, \quad p = .30, \quad s = 1.00$	4.74	15	7(right)
	$b = .20, \quad p = .30, \quad s = 0.30$	11.68		

Two-setting Variable-Between and Variable-Within Irrelevant Cues

	$\theta = .25$			
1. Similarity hurts				
Variable-Between	$b = .40,\ p = .10,\ s = .10$	4.12	16	8(left)
	$b = .40,\ p = .10,\ s = .40$	4.40		
Variable-Within	$b = .10,\ p = .40,\ s = .10$	4.58	17	8(right)
	$b = .10,\ p = .40,\ s = .40$	8.12		
2. Variable-Between easier and more so as similarity increases	Same as above			
	$s = .10$	With./Betw.=1.12	16	8
	$s = .40$	With./Betw.=1.85	17	

Four-setting Variable-Between versus Variable-Within Irrelevant Cues

1. No difference predicted if initial preferences (feedback values) are equal				
Variable-Between	$b = .20,\ p = .20,\ s = .20$	4.12	18	9(left)
Variable-Within	$b = .20,\ p = .20,\ s = .20$	4.10	18	9(right)
2. Initial preferences favor Variable-Between				
Variable-Between	$b = .20,\ p = .20,\ s = .20$	4.06	18	10(left)
Variable-Within	$b = .20,\ p = .20,\ s = .20$	4.54	18	10(right)

$F_i^*, 1 = .75$ for all black cues
$F_i^*, 1 = .25$ for all white cues

(continued)

Appendix (continued)

Statement	Parameters	Results [Mean Errors]	Equation	Figure
Conditional Simultaneous and Conditional Successive				
1. Conditional Simultaneous will be easier than Conditional Successive				
Simultaneous	$b = .20$, $p = .20$, $s = .20$	9.6	21	13
Successive	$b = .20$, $p = .20$, $s = .20$	25.36[a]	22	14
2. Both are soluble				
Simultaneous	See above $\theta = .80$			
Successive	$b = .00$, $p = .00$, $s = .00$	2.48	22	14

[a] In 80 trials and still not solved.

SUBJECT INDEX

A

Arousal, adjunct questions and, 109
Attention
  in context model, 296–303
  multidimensionality of, 42–43
Auto-shaping, 217–222

B

Bilingual coding, picture labeling and, 199–201

C

Choice, in context model, 273–277
Coding, see Encoding; Memory coding
Computer, tutorial dialogues and, see Tutorial dialogues
Conditioning, see Pavlovian conditioning
Content, in prose processing, 8
Context
  in discrimination learning, see Discrimination learning
  in selective learning, 295–303

D

Dialogues, see Tutorial dialogues
Directed movements, conditioning and, see Pavlovian conditioning
Discrimination learning, 263–264
  context change in, 269–270
  context model for, 270–295
  feature-positive effect in, 235–243, 250–252
  units of analysis in, 264–269

E

Encoding, in prose processing, 8–9
  sources of efficiency and inefficiency in, 12–42

Errors

Errors
  semantic, 173–175
  in speech, 137–143
    sound exchange, 143–148
    stranded morphemes, shifts, and exchanges, 154–173
    word and morpheme exchanges, 148–154
  tutor's response to, 72–74, 82–83
Exchange errors, 154–173
  sounds, 143–148
  words and morphemes, 148–154

F

Feature-positive effect, 235–243, 250–252
Feedback, adjunct questions and, 98–99
Fusion errors, 173–175

G

Generalization, in context model, 271–273

I

Imaginal encoding
  instructions for, 189–191
  repeated, 192–199
  semantic encoding and, 201–205
Instructions, memory coding and, 189–191
Integration, in prose processing, 9–11
Intersentence relations, as unit of processing control, 24–36

L

Learning, see also Discrimination learning; Selective learning
  stimulus-sequence, 253–258

315

M

Mathemagenic hypothesis, 105–108
Memory coding, 179–180, 208–211
  common-code theories, 183–184
  depth of processing in, 184–185
  distinctions in, 185–186
  dual-coding theory, 180–183
  repetition effects and independence in, 186–208
Morphemes
  exchanges of, 148–154
  stranded, 154–173
Motivation, adjunct questions and, 100
Movements, directed, conditioning and, *see* Pavlovian conditioning

O

Omission procedures, 245–253

P

Patterning, transverse, 292–293
Pavlovian conditioning, 216–217, 258–260
  auto-shaping and sign-tracking and, 217–222
  contingency between stimulus and reinforcer in, 222–225
  feature-positive effect in, 235–243, 250–252
  sign redundancy in, 225–229
  stimulus-stimulus versus response-stimulus relations in, 244–258
  type of CS in, 232–235
  type of reinforcer in, 229–232
Performance sets, in prose processing, 8
Pictures
  bilingual coding and, 199–201
  repeated coding of, 187–191, 195–199
Position, of test items, 94
Prose processing, 1–4, 42–45
  model for, 4–12
  sources of encoding efficiency and inefficiency in, 12–42

Q

Questioning
  as self-control, 36–42
  techniques for, 127–128

Questions

Questions, 90–91
  adjunct
    facilitative, 93–103
    indirect effects of, 103–109
  direct and indirect consequences of, 91–93, 109–127
  in tutorial dialogues, 67–71, 80–81

R

Reading, goal-directed, 43
Redundancy, of signs, 225–229
Rehearsal, in prose processing, 9–11
Reinforcer
  contingency between stimulus and, 222–225
  type of, 229–232
Relation, in prose processing, 11
Relevance
  of adjunct questions, 105
  in context model, 281–293
Repetition effects, 186–187
  experimental data for, 191–208
  picture-word, 187–191
Response mode, 96–98
  overt, 99
Response-stimulus relations, 244–258
Retrieval
  in context model, 271–273
  in prose processing, 11
Review
  indirect, 108–109
  in tutoring, 71–72, 81–82

S

Selective learning, context model for, 295–303
Self-control, questioning as, 36–42
Semantic coding, imagery and, 201–205
Semantic errors, 173–175
Sentence production, 133–137, 175–177
  semantic errors in, 173–175
  speech errors in, 137–173
Shift errors, 154–173
Sign redundancy, 225–229
Sign-tracking, 217–222
Sound exchange errors, 143–148
Speech errors, 137–143
  sound exchange, 143–148

stranded morphemes, shifts, and exchanges, 154–173
word and morpheme exchanges, 148–154
Stimulus
contingency between reinforcer and,
222–225
type of, 232–235
Stimulus-stimulus relations, 244–258
Substitution errors, 173–175

T

Test items, repeated versus new criterion, 93
Timing, of questions, 94–96
Topic
selection by tutors, 56–67, 75–80
as unit of processing control, 17–24
Transfer, adjunct questions and, 104

Tutorial dialogues, 49–50, 84–87
analysis of, 54–74, 84–85
computer and human compared, 74–83
SCHOLAR computer model for, 50–54
tutorial strategies in, 56–74

V

Verbal encoding
instructions for, 189–191
repeated, 192–199

W

Word exchanges, 148–154
Words
repeated coding of, 187–191, 192–195
as unit of processing control, 13–17